A Man of Salt and Trees

A MAN OF

SALT
and TREES

THE LIFE OF JOY MORTON

James Ballowe

To Cynthia Gong
for her love of botanical
drawing *Ballowe*

NORTHERN ILLINOIS UNIVERSITY PRESS

DeKalb

© 2009 by Northern Illinois University Press
Published by the Northern Illinois University Press, DeKalb, Illinois 60115
Manufactured in the United States using postconsumer-recycled, acid-free paper.
All Rights Reserved
Design by Julia Fauci

Library of Congress Cataloging-in-Publication Data
Ballowe, James.
A man of salt and trees : the life of Joy Morton / James Ballowe.
    p.   cm.
Includes bibliographical references and index.
ISBN 978-0-87580-398-2 (clothbound : acid-free paper)
1. Morton, Joy, 1855-1934. 2. Chicago (Ill.)—Biography. 3. Business people—
Illinois—Chicago—Biography. 4. Morton Salt Company. 5. Morton Arboretum.
6. Chicago (Ill.)—History—1875—Biography. I. Title. II. Title: Life of Joy Morton.
F548.5.M88B35 2009
977.3'11041092—dc22   [B]   2008047783

FRONTISPIECE—Joy Morton on the Joy Path at his Thornhill estate, Lisle, Illinois, 1925

PERMISSIONS

Most of the photographs that appear in *A Man of Salt and Trees* are used with permission of The Morton Arboretum, Sterling Morton Library. The following images are courtesy of other sources:

PAGE vi—One of a pair of acorns by sculptor Sylvia Shaw Judson. Once surmounting the Arboretum's gateposts, they are now in Arbor Court. Julia Fauci, photographer.

PAGE x—Morton Salt box, 1914. Used with permission of Morton International Inc., Sterling Morton Library.

PAGE 56—Nebraska City, c. 1860. Used with permission of Nebraska Game and Parks Commission, Arbor Lodge State Historical Park.

PAGE 62—Morton Salt box. Used with permission of Morton International Inc., Sterling Morton Library.

PAGE 262—Face of a mythical tree figure with oak leaves, sculpted above the west entrance to the Library wing at Thornhill. Julia Fauci, photographer.

PAGE 263—Chicago, 1880–1905. Used with permission of University of Chicago Library.

Contents

～ *For Ruth*

Acknowledgments

*W*hen I was introduced to The Morton Arboretum a quarter of a century ago by my wife, Ruth Ganchiff, I had no idea that I would eventually write a biography of Joy Morton. But when coming to know a great institution, one wonders, to paraphrase Emerson, in whose lengthened shadow it stands. Learning of the man who cast that shadow has coalesced Ruth's and my interest in both American natural and cultural history. This is her book as much it is mine.

As mentioned in the preface, I owe a debt to Gerard Donnelly, President and CEO of The Morton Arboretum, and Walter Becky, former president of Morton Salt International, Inc., who supported this work from the beginning. Both men also allowed me to call on their staffs, who have been an immense help.

Many arboretum staff members have an imprint on this book. No writer could be better served than I by the advice and encouragement of Craig Johnson, Director of Education and Public Programs at the Arboretum. And without the Sterling Morton Library staff of Michael Stieber, library administrator, and Rita Hassert and Nancy Faller, librarians, who diligently and with good humor ferreted out well-hidden facts and resolved ambiguities, this book could not have reached its conclusion. The librarians and resources at the Sterling Morton Library and archives make research a pleasure.

Of the many others at the Arboretum who have cheered for this biography for as long as it has taken to write it, I want to single out Susan Klatt, the Arboretum's executive secretary, whose calming advice and computer skills saved the manuscript from becoming a shambles in its earliest stages. I also depended upon the work and advice of Carol Doty, the Arboretum's former historian, who prepared the way for those who are determined to keep in the public mind that The Morton Arboretum as it stands today is the accomplishment of hundreds who have dedicated themselves to fulfilling Joy Morton's mission. And as a testament to the mutual benefits resulting from the Arboretum's educational mission, LeAnn Spencer, a student of mine in the Naturalist Certificate program, read the manuscript with the expertise of a longtime editor, a job that advanced this work in its final stages.

Morton Salt personnel have been no less helpful. Lynn Farm made my frequent visits to the salt offices on Wacker Drive in Chicago pleasurable and efficient by having at hand the materials I needed. (Those salt history materials have now been removed to the Sterling Morton Library archives.) I also appreciated the help of Chester Delp, manager of the Morton Salt warehouse on Elston and the North Branch of the Chicago River, who showed me around the warehouse (boasting a magnificent rooftop image of the little salt girl) that Joy built in 1927 and still serves as the Chicago regional distribution center since replacing the old warehouses at Illinois Central Railroad Pier I.

The state of Illinois and Chicago abound with sites on which Joy Morton had a lasting effect. I have benefited from the archival resources and personnel at the Chicago History Museum (which holds a significant Morton family collection), the Harold Washington Library, and smaller museums and archives – particularly those in Illinois along the Hennepin Canal as well as the Illinois and Michigan Canal, such as Lockport, Ottawa, and Sheffield. A resource of great personal value was Bill Hinchliff, one of Chicago's foremost guides to the art and architecture of the city. Bill spent a day with my wife and me visiting the near south side sites where Joy and his family lived from 1880 to 1905.

Further to the south in Illinois, between Lewiston and Havana, is The Nature Conservancy's Emiquon acquisition, a 7,000-acre wetland on land once farmed by Joy Morton. Here Mike Wiant, Director of the adjacent Dickson Mounds Museum (a division of the Illinois State Museum), and Alan Harn, Assistant Curator of Anthropology, helped me understand Joy Morton's crucial support of the early work done by University of Chicago anthropologists at the "Morton Village," a site still yielding valuable information nearly eighty years later.

I am especially indebted to the Nebraska State Historical Society at Lincoln, which willingly shared its J. Sterling Morton collection. But to understand Joy Morton's lifelong commitment and contributions to his hometown of Nebraska City requires that time be spent in that gracious and historical city, now known to the world as the birthplace of Arbor Day. I began my research there at the Morton-James Library, whose staff takes special pride in serving researchers. I also met Margaret Virgina Ott, the author of Sterling's Carrie, who shared notes and observations and gave a tour of the city and showed me the site of Talbot Hall, where Joy attended school. My visit with Joy Morton Porter in his home, where the septuagenarian Joy Morton also visited, was equally valuable. In the backyard stands the one-room school (now a storage shed) that Joy attended. These visits brought the past to life. I also walked Nebraska City with Larry Falk, a Nebraska City historian, who took me to historical sites Joy Morton would have visited while growing up and gave me copies of photographs that illuminated Joy's life there.

At Arbor Lodge, Randy Fox and Mark Kemper shared their knowledge gleaned from years of managing the estate and grounds and allowed me the opportunity to walk leisurely through the 52-room mansion. Laura Steinman, a volunteer, offered invaluable help accessing the Arbor Lodge archival photographs, and Angie Purdy kept me in communication with them all. At the Arbor Day Foundation in the Lied Conference Center across the road from Arbor Lodge, Suzie Wirth provided access to unpublished interviews and reminiscences of both Grove and Joy Morton Porter.

A book like this requires help from many unexpected sources. Among these I need to mention Kay Lant, the Warrick County, Indiana, historian with whom I spent a useful afternoon in Margaret Gray's hometown of Newburgh. And for solving some riddles about Michigan places and people, I am indebted to Frank Passic of Albion and Dan Muszynski of Erie, whose wife is a descendant of Ira Mayhew, Joy's great-uncle. Organizing Joy's family tree was a task well executed by my daughter-in-law Deborah Epstein Ganchiff, who, with the rest of my family, has dutifully listened to the story of Joy Morton as it unfolded over the years.

The people I have singled out here are by no means all to whom I am indebted. Others, particularly those I have interviewed or whose unpublished manuscripts I have used, are mentioned elsewhere. A biography that takes five years to research and write is a testament to the work of many. But how the book comes together and gains a life of its own depends on the coordinated work of the publisher. I am fortunate to have had this support from the people at Northern Illinois University Press. Alex Schwartz, the director, has been keenly interested in this project from the first. NIU Press staff—in particular Susan Bean, managing editor; Amy Farranto and Tracy Schoenle, editors; Julia Fauci, design and production manager; and Linda Manning, marketing director—have been immensely helpful in seeing this book come into existence. Joy Morton would have wanted no better attention.

In this project the growth of vegetation
has been promoted, not killed, by salt.

STERLING MORTON

Dedication of the Cudahy Auditorium,

The Morton Arboretum (9.17.1956)

Preface

$\mathscr{I}$ was completing a short history of The Morton Arboretum in 2002 when Gerard Donnelly, the president and CEO of that acclaimed museum of woody plants located twenty-five miles west of Chicago's Loop, suggested that there should be a biography of Joy Morton, its founder. After the publication of *A Great Outdoor Museum: The Story of The Morton Arboretum,* Donnelly again broached the subject, this time in a meeting that included Walter Becky, an arboretum trustee and then president of Morton Salt, which Joy also founded. We all knew that a biography of Joy Morton was long overdue.

Joy Morton's life's work is not just the sum of salt and trees. Those two notable but seemingly incongruous interests were bookends to a lifetime of achievement. Along the way, Joy left his entrepreneurial mark on banking, transportation, agriculture, communication, and architecture, while a personal interest in human and natural history led him to support significant studies in those areas. His public benefactions have continued to enrich the lives of generations far beyond the Chicago region.

Joy did not seek anonymity. He lent his surname—of which he was a careful guardian—to several enterprises, most notably, of course, the Morton Salt brand and The Morton Arboretum. He clearly wanted the Arboretum to be the monument by which future generations would remember him. His contributions to posterity remain; yet the life of the person behind them has been, until now, untold. History books refer to his father, Julius Sterling, the founder of Arbor Day in 1872 and Grover Cleveland's Secretary of Agriculture from 1892–1896. His younger brother Paul, Theodore Roosevelt's Secretary of the Navy in 1904 and, later, president of the Equitable Life Assurance Society of the United States, is also cited by historians. Joy is not mentioned.

Joy lived among Chicagoans who are recognized today by name and achievement—entrepreneurs, politicians, social thinkers, and architects credited with the city's remarkable emergence from the Great Fire of

1871. Among them are Potter Palmer and Marshall Field, merchants and real estate moguls; Carter Harrison, Sr., elected mayor five times and a catalyst for the 1893 Columbian Exposition; Philip and Herman Armour and Gustavus Franklin Swift, builders of the meatpacking industry; William LeBaron Jenney, the architect of the nation's first steel skeleton skyscraper in 1885; Jane Addams, the founder of Hull House and the social awareness and policies it spawned; and Daniel H. Burnham, the chief architect of the 1893 Exposition and the principal author of the *Plan of Chicago,* first published on July 4, 1909 and destined to become a touchstone for urban planners yet today. Their contributions evoke the essence of the visionary ethos of Chicago. Ironically, the historical spotlight that illuminates these iconic citizens casts a shadow over the identities of many who also were instrumental in making Chicago the international city it is today. Joy Morton is one of these.

*L*ike most successful Chicagoans of the latter half of the nineteenth century, Joy was not a native. But unlike them, he spent his early years in the pioneer west, not the settled east. Born in 1855 and reared in Nebraska City, a bustling village in the Nebraska Territory, he grew to manhood on the western bank of the Missouri River as the unruly territory was maturing into statehood. His formal schooling lasted only until he was fifteen, but by the time he left school, he had gained practical experience managing the family farm, hauling goods by wagon train between Nebraska City and Lincoln, and working on a railway survey crew. At fifteen he became a bank clerk and later worked his own farm. In his early twenties, he took railroad jobs first in Omaha and later in Aurora, Illinois. By age twenty-five, Joy had saved enough money to become engaged to be married and to invest in a junior partnership in a sales and distribution salt firm located in Chicago. Five years later, he owned the firm, named it Joy Morton & Co., and set about extending the scope of its operations. Financial success soon allowed him to invest in related businesses in Chicago and Nebraska City.

In 1905, Joy moved the offices of Joy Morton & Co. from the bustling Illinois Central Pier I at Lake Michigan to the newly constructed Railway Exchange Building at Michigan Avenue and Jackson Boulevard overlooking the Illinois Central Railroad tracks, a sliver of land known as Grant Park, and the lake beyond. His move from cramped quarters in a wooden replica of the first Boston public building (designed by his ancestor Thomas Joy in 1657) into the Railway Exchange Building (designed by Daniel Burnham and financed by the Standard Office Company over which Joy presided) marked a pivotal point in his relationship with his adopted city. Joy Morton & Co. occupied the seventh floor; Daniel Burnham's architectural firm was on the fourteenth. In the building's penthouse, built for the purpose of conceiving a plan for Chicago's future, Joy, as chairman of the Commercial Club's railway terminals committee, was among the dozen or so men who met regularly with Burnham on the *Plan of Chicago*, the book that for over a century has affected how planners think about the development of the city, particularly in regard to the lakefront.

$\mathcal{H}$ow Joy managed the complex changes that occurred within the nearly eight decades of his personal and professional life provides the narrative of this biography. His life (1855–1934) spans the period between the Civil War and the Great Depression, during which the country evolved from agriculture to industry, from pioneer restiveness to settled community, and from unthinking exploitation of the environment to an emerging consciousness that preservation of the natural world contributed to the health of humankind. Historians and novelists commonly describe industrial entrepreneurs of Joy's generation as insensitive men who, to ease their guilt, gave a modicum of their wealth to benefit the public. To be sure, the prevailing culture of competition in late nineteenth- and early twentieth-century America bred both an offensive and a defensive ruthlessness, or at least the appearance of it. Darwin's phrase "the survival of the fittest" had already become a rationalization if not a prescription for the way business was and is often conducted. While Joy was a strong competitor in the marketplace, he was, from the first, in a position to be the businessman others would have to challenge. The salt business was an industry for which he was well suited and was necessary to the very life of the nation. The production and distribution of salt was generally shielded from radical economic and social changes. Joy prospered from the start and was able to invest profitably in related enterprises.

When he thought it necessary, Joy could put on a coldly impenetrable business persona, made more formidable by a six-foot frame and piercing eyes. What kept him from carrying this over into the rich and productive private life he lived were an ability to separate business from personal and family relationships and an unerring self-awareness mixed with a quiet sense of humor. If his family life was filled with generous periods of contentment, it was also marked by a cruelly extended period of personal sorrow. Throughout, he displayed a commitment to family, friends, and community that equaled his focus on business. To subordinate his personal life to his business life would distort who Joy Morton was and what he valued.

Joy's ultimate goal, like that of many other businessmen who strove for financial success in the cultural zeitgeist of the late nineteenth and early twentieth-centuries, was to gain sufficient wealth to give advantages to his family and ultimately to become philanthropic on his own terms. Even as a young man, he had in mind the sort of environment he thought best suited the human condition. Having grown to adulthood within a family where caring for trees was an essential part of life, it is natural that Joy left as his principal legacy an arboretum dedicated to the enjoyment and education of the public and to preservation of woody plants through cultivation and research. For some people, it is no doubt ironic that the means to this end was the manufacture and distribution of salt, generally considered inimical to woody plants. Joy's son Sterling was mindful of this when he said, "In this project the growth of vegetation has been promoted, not killed, by salt."[1]

$\mathscr{P}$revious attempts to chronicle Joy's life and accomplishments have been made. The two most comprehensive are composed from personal interviews with Joy at Thornhill, his estate at the fledgling Morton Arboretum. In 1931, at age 75, Joy, wanting to tell his own story, hired Frank Dalton O'Sullivan, a professional biographer from Chicago, to help him write it. Later, Joy told Stephen Ira Gilchrist of the Henry B. Joy Research in Detroit, "I have been writing a book myself—or, rather I have a man who has been at work on it for several months. It is a sketch of my life, written in person, the aim being to show the course of a western farm boy over a period of three-quarters of a century."[2] When that biography was found unacceptable by Joy and his children, Sterling, Joy's son, began a rewrite of the manuscript. Joy's business responsibilities kept him from completing it, and within a year after his father's death in 1934, Sterling abandoned the project.

$\mathscr{I}$ approached my own research into the life of Joy Morton cautiously, grateful at first to find that I had the opportunity to conduct interviews with a few people who knew "Mr." Morton when they were children, remembering fondly his kindnesses to them, although it had been over seventy years since their encounters. But soon I was confronted by an avalanche of letters, diaries, and other documents in the archives of the Chicago History Museum, the Sterling Morton Library at The Morton Arboretum, and the Nebraska Historical Society. Other resources turned up in Nebraska City at the Morton-James Library; Arbor Lodge (the Morton family home eventually deeded to the State of Nebraska); and the Lied Conference Center, the location of the Arbor Day Foundation.

Like many of their contemporaries, Joy's family wrote prolifically to one another as well as to others. Their letters were handwritten, and after the invention of the typewriter, some were typed. The sheer bulk of the letters is daunting. How, an e-mail-specific correspondent might ask, did they have the time? That, of course, is a question borne out of not knowing the importance of written communication even two generations ago. Absent the invention of the telephone or means of communication other than the laconic telegraph, most individuals related by letter; they took the composition of these seriously.

For over sixty years, scarcely a day went by without Joy posting a personal letter to one or another recipient and receiving one or more in return. Letters generated letters. Within the Morton family, a tardy respondent was sternly rebuked. Younger letter writers learned grammar, spelling, and syntax from recipients who would not let their indiscretions go by without comment. The letters were conversational in tone and style. They read as if the correspondents were in a drawing room talking with one another. And that is the way I present them in this book. In Joy's lifetime, letter writing was not just a casual means of communication. Joy's family and friends revealed what they thought and felt, knowing that their correspondence might well be kept for a long period of time and read by others, or might even become part of the historical record. While the hand- or typewritten letter has been replaced by e-mail and text messaging, for readers, biographers, and historians it remains the clearest way into the past for those who want to journey there. There is no little irony in the fact that Joy, who besides his many other accomplishments became a pioneer in telecommunications, is revealed to us today primarily through his handwritten correspondence.

A Man of Salt and Trees

Part

ONE

1854 ~ 1879

Prologue—1854–1859

Caroline Morton knew that if she and Joy, her newborn son, were to get from Detroit to the freshly minted territory of Nebraska before winter set in, she must leave as soon as they were able to travel. On November 6, 1855, six weeks after his birth on September 27, Caroline, Joy, and a nurse began the arduous trip west. The three rode the Michigan Southern Railway to Chicago where they were joined by Hiram Joy, Caroline's father. The party then traveled southwest through Illinois to LaSalle on the Rock Island, to Bloomington on the Illinois Central, and to Alton on the Alton and Sangamon. Their jarring trip along the still emerging railway system that bisected the newly plowed Illinois prairie was exhausting. At Alton they boarded a packet boat for St. Louis, looking forward to a more restful journey up the meandering Missouri to the pioneer village of Nebraska City, nearly 700 miles distant.

It was not to be. Amid the confusion of milling settlers, adventurers, and traders waiting for the arrival of the steamboat *Herald* to take them north, the nurse mislaid Joy on the levee at St. Louis. Later in life, Joy would refer to this incident with good humor, offering it as evidence that he had been favored by fate: "When I was missed and the party returned, they found me lying close to the water's edge, where I might easily have dropped into the river—and there would be no Joy Morton!"[1] He might well have added that there would have been no Morton Salt, no Morton Arboretum, and none of the impact Joy Morton had on Nebraska and Illinois over the nearly eight decades of his life.

The first leg of the trip upriver produced no further excitement, and J. Sterling, Joy's father, duly met the party at St. Joseph, Missouri, ninety miles from Nebraska City. He and Hiram went on with the baggage in their wagon as Caroline, Joy, and the nurse resumed the journey up the Missouri, an option believed to be safer in rapidly deteriorating weather. But halfway to Nebraska City, the captain of the steamer *The Star of the West* was forced to dock when the river filled with mush ice.

Undeterred, Caroline hired a local farmer to drive them to the ferry landing on the Iowa side of the Missouri, where they could cross over to Nebraska City. After a day of constant jostling over deeply rutted roads, cushioned only by a layer of prairie hay and warmed by buffalo robes, they were met with another obstacle. The threat of ice floes and darkness prompted the ferryman to try to dissuade Caroline from crossing that evening. In the end, however, she prevailed, and he delivered them by skiff safely to the other side.

That night, November 28, 1855, J. Sterling and Hiram were in the Downs Tavern near the landing dock. Certain that they would not see Caroline and Joy until the next day, they were astonished when Caroline walked in with Joy in her arms. Joy was two months old. For three weeks, he had traveled well over a thousand miles by train, packet boat, steamer, wagon, and skiff to arrive in the place where he would grow into manhood. Thirty-two years later, in telling the story of the journey, his father said to Joy, then the owner of Joy Morton & Co. in Chicago, "I remember that you were . . . a 'Kicker' of such constitutional vigor that you had in the journey from the river, up over the bluff, to the hotel 'Kicked' off and lost one of your little socks and your short, fat dumpling of a foot was quite blue with the cold of that November night."[2] Joy came to think that the most remarkable part of the journey had been his mother's decision to start out at all from the comfortable Victorian home of her foster parents, Deacon David and Cynthia French, where she had been lying in. "One can imagine," Joy mused to his son, Sterling, almost eighty years later, "that it took a great deal of fortitude on mother's part to start back from the comforts of the home in Detroit to that prairie cabin."[3]

$\mathcal{J}$oy's parents, J. Sterling and Caroline Morton, came to the Nebraska Territory in October of 1854, five months after the Kansas-Nebraska Act — which guaranteed popular sovereignty to settlers in the newly formed territory—was signed. When they arrived, there were fewer than 2,000 sodbusters, trappers, traders, and adventurers clustered along the Missouri and Platte Rivers on the eastern cusp of the vast grassland that was then referred to as the Great American Desert, the home of the Pawnee. Both were unlikely emigrants to this unsettled territory. Neither was escaping a shady past; nor was J. Sterling randomly seeking his fortune. He had powerful political connections and an understanding of the role he might play in the evolution of the new territory. Both he and Caroline had received the best educations available to them in the first half of the nineteenth century.

J. Sterling and Caroline were repeating the sagas of their successful colonial ancestors. They traced their progenitors to tradesmen and artisans who had lived in Massachusetts, Connecticut, Vermont, and New York City. The earliest Morton to settle in the Colonies had been George, a Puritan who had helped negotiate with the English for the *Mayflower*, which brought the first Pilgrims to Plymouth. Before immigrating to Plymouth himself, George published *Mourt's Relation of the Beginning and Proceeding of the English Plantation settled at Plymouth in New England*, 1622, likely written by Edward Winslow and William Bradford and thought to be the first book on New England published in Great Britain.

J. Sterling's paternal grandfather, Abner, moved to Adams, New York, from Vermont in 1817 and distinguished himself as a vigilant conservative publisher and editor. His newspaper, aptly named *The Censor*, was located at the time of J. Sterling's birth in nearby Watertown. Abner held a bachelor's degree from Dartmouth, but because he had to work his way through, he attended no more than thirteen weeks of lectures over four years. J. Sterling would later find Grandfather Abner's stubborn conservatism and literary talent to be admirable models.[4]

The oldest of three children, Julius Sterling—he used the single initial "J" to distinguish him from his father, Julius Dewey ("J.D.") Morton—was born in the western New York river valley village of Adams on April 22, 1832, where his father had become the proprietor of the general store. J. Sterling's mother, Emeline Sterling, was the daughter of a local businessman whose family settled in Adams soon after its founding in 1800.

One of Caroline Morton's American ancestors also played a notable role in the Colonies. Thomas Joy was a master builder and architect who came to America from England in 1635. In 1657, Thomas constructed a building in the Boston marketplace that became Boston's first seat of government, serving the city as an armory, courthouse, and town hall.[5] Over two centuries later, Joy replicated Thomas's structure for the first office building he erected in Chicago. In the eighteenth century, members of the Joy family moved to New Hampshire and Maine, becoming farmers, ship caulkers, and traders.

Hiram Joy was born in 1810 in Winthrop, Maine, where, after little education, he apprenticed to the trade of saddler and harness maker and then went into business for himself. At age twenty-three, he married Caroline Hayden, who gave birth to Caroline Ann on August 9, 1833, in Hallowell, Maine. A year later, following a move to Detroit, Caroline Hayden Joy became terminally ill. Knowing that Hiram would find it difficult to bring up their daughter alone while tending his business interests, she requested that their friends and neighbors Deacon David and Cynthia Eldredge French, a childless couple in their late forties, be allowed to raise their daughter. Reluctantly Hiram agreed, but he never consented to a legalized adoption, even though later he approved his daughter's use of the French name.[6]

When Hiram moved to Chicago in 1850, his contact with Caroline remained cordially parental. She always referred to him affectionately as "Pa Joy." But her development and education were overseen by the more cultured Frenches. Cynthia French saw to it that Caroline understood how to manage a domestic residence with servants and value the finer things of life.[7] And Deacon David helped give her an education available only to a few American women in the early nineteenth century.

J. Sterling began his education in the town of Monroe, a thriving community south of Detroit to which Julius Dewey and Abner moved in 1834; at that time, Monroe exceeded the new village of Chicago in promise and population. J.D., as Julius preferred being called, entered a shipping and commission business that eventually became prosperous and bore the name of Morton and Walbridge.

Abner went forthrightly into printing and journalism in Monroe, and soon, with his other son Edward G., became owner and editor of *The Monroe Advocate*. Under the tutelage of his uncle Edward, who held even stronger conservative views than did his Grandfather Abner, J. Sterling began an apprenticeship that helped nurture in him an uncompromising independence of mind, a lively writing style, and a zest for political contests. Edward, a states rights Northern Democrat, was several times mayor of Monroe and served five terms in the state legislature. James Olson, J. Sterling's biographer observed, "There was a more truly marked resemblance between uncle and nephew than between father and son."[8]

When J. Sterling was fourteen, J.D., a Methodist leader and outspoken pro-union Republican, enrolled his son in Albion, Michigan's Wesleyan Seminary (later Albion College of which J.D. became board president in 1864). The seminary was far removed from the politically contentious environment of J.D.'s brother's newspaper. J. Sterling soon proved that he could meet the intellectual challenges with a keen mind and counter the dour Methodist discipline with irreverent high jinks.

A year later J. Sterling was a cynosure on campus when the attractive and talented Caroline Joy French arrived at the Albion Female Collegiate Institute, an affiliate of Wesleyan Seminary. At fourteen, Caroline had already shown talent as an artist and pianist at an Episcopal girls' school in Canada. J. Sterling and Caroline were immediately drawn to one another and vowed they would marry as soon as they finished their education. They would wait another seven years. After graduating from Albion in 1850, J. Sterling began four years of study at the University of Michigan, and Caroline completed her education at a highly regarded finishing school in Utica, New York, operated by the Misses Kelly. Years later, J. Sterling offered a philosophical reason to Joy for his immediate and lasting interest in his mother, saying that when he was only fifteen he had come upon a work by Dr. George Combe in the seminary's library that convinced him that he "should marry a brunette of energy and force of character, just such as your mother proved to be in every particular."[9]

J. Sterling arrived at the University of Michigan with a propensity to learn from those he respected and to reject authority when he disagreed with it. Literature and debate were his strengths, and he was active in a debating fraternity, a literary periodical, and a secret society. One professor with whom J. Sterling boarded in his sophomore year wrote to his father, ". . . his ambition was rather literary than scholastic."[10] In the end, J. Sterling's choleric defense of his beliefs cost him his degree but cemented the view held by many that he was principled. The occasion was the arrival in his junior year of Dr. Henry Philip Tappan as president. Tappan immediately set about imposing a Prussian-style curriculum and campus behavior that threatened J. Sterling's outspoken literary and social inclinations. After publicly criticizing Tappan for summarily firing a popular professor, J. Sterling was dismissed by the faculty six weeks before he was to graduate. Immediately, several newspapers and political figures in Michigan took interest in the matter, for Dr. Tappan had disappointed many powerful men with the direction in which he was taking the university. J. Sterling was urged by Michigan's lieutenant governor to meet with Tappan. He did so and was conditionally reinstated. But the next day Tappan issued a statement which J. Sterling believed to be contrary to the agreement they had made—that only *if* the charges against him could be proved would he apologize.

J. Sterling then directed a letter to Wilbur F. Storey, the publisher of the *Detroit Free Press*. Storey—who in 1861 became editor of the *Chicago Times*, a paper with which J. Sterling would have a lengthy relationship later in life and which would figure in Joy's early education—was a Tappan opponent who believed in the efficacy of invective in journalism. He published J. Sterling's letter, which refuted that he had relinquished his right of free speech and had asked the faculty for mercy. J. Sterling proclaimed that he would not *"six weeks longer sojourn at the feet of Gamaliel, and the Latin-scratched integument of a dead sheep,"* adding, "I am not the *crawling* kind, and I have recalled from the faculty the paper I signed and informed them that I will remain a 'removed student' rather than have it understood that I had skulked back into the fold."[11]

J. Sterling's letter to the editor assured his permanent dismissal.[12] Storey—who in his statement of the aims of the *Chicago Times*, said in June 1861, "It is a newspaper's duty to print the news, and raise hell"[13]— liked J. Sterling's fearlessly flammable prose, his political conservatism, and his courage to make his views known to the public. J. Sterling was hired on as a reporter for the *Detroit Free Press*, where he would work for the next four months while he and Caroline planned their wedding and their future. J. Sterling's father had also moved to Detroit to become General Agent of the New York Central Railroad and President of the Farmers and Mechanics' Bank.

During the summer of 1854, J. Sterling decided that political and journalistic opportunities lay westward. The issues addressed by the Kansas-Nebraska Act affirmed his belief in states rights. Introduced into legislation by Illinois Democratic Senator Stephen A. Douglas and signed into law on May 31, 1854, the bill effectively nullified the Missouri Compromise of 1820, which restricted slavery to Missouri. The people of the new territories, the act said, could settle "all questions pertaining to slavery in the Territories, and in the new States to be formed therefrom . . . through their appropriate representatives." The right of new territories to take control of their own affairs and to make Native American land available for those willing to settle it appealed to J. Sterling as it had to his college friend Andrew J. Poppleton who had gone there a few months earlier. Others, such as family friend Lewis Cass, a United States senator from Michigan and chair of the Military Affairs Committee, and Storey, whose paper had championed the Kansas-Nebraska Act, encouraged J. Sterling to think seriously about finding out for himself what the Nebraska Territory might hold for him. They would provide him with contacts.

J. Sterling, then twenty-two, and Caroline, twenty-one, decided to leave Detroit on their wedding day, October 30, 1854, even though the free state issue was a cause for concern. The Kansas-Nebraska Act had extended to a vast geography the raging debate on states rights, slavery, and the appropriation of lands long claimed by American Indians. Although the Nebraska Territory was much the larger of the two—it stretched north to Canada, west to the Continental Divide, south to the Kansas border at the 40th parallel, and east to the Missouri River—Kansas became the battleground. Advocates of slavery believed Kansas offered the best opportunity to extend the practice westward across the river from neighboring Missouri. Resistance to their efforts was strong, and few believed reconciliation would be attained without violence.

The abolitionist John Brown had entered Kansas with his five sons only a month prior to the trip made by Caroline and Joy. In May 1856, retaliating against a proslavery raid on Lawrence, Kansas, Brown's forces massacred five men at Pottawatomie Creek. For this and other acts of violence, the territory became known as "Bleeding Kansas." Pitting citizen against citizen, the conflicts foreshadowed the Civil War. J. Sterling and Caroline believed that Nebraska was far enough north to avoid slavery, the most contentious of all the states rights issues. They were largely right. But the issues remained front and center in the household in which Joy and his three brothers were raised.

*C*aroline completed her first journey into the interior with her genteel innocence intact. What she observed on the trip up the Missouri delighted her. Soon after arriving in Bellevue, Nebraska, she wrote to J. Sterling's sister Emma back in Detroit that on the steamer she had found it difficult to distinguish the dirty-faced children of white passengers from those of "colored" slaves. From the vantage of the stagecoach they took north from St. Joseph, she thought the slaves they passed "to be perfectly happy, laughing and joking" and appearing to be "a great deal more independent and at home than our white servants." She was content, she told Emma, to think that Nebraska would never "hold many slaves."[14]

Bellevue was a safe destination. The settlement had been organized into a town company as recently as February 9, 1854, in anticipation of the Kansas-Nebraska Act. It had served principally as an Indian trading post for decades before 1854 and traced its pioneer history to 1804, when Lewis and Clark passed through. In spite of there being fewer than a dozen houses, J. Sterling thought that this community and the surrounding region already served by a newspaper might have a good chance to become the territorial capital and would be a propitious place to launch a career in politics. While he set about becoming known as a spokesman for Bellevue and the region—particularly in the pressing matter of the location of the territorial capital—Caroline became friends with Mrs. Fenner Ferguson, a former resident of Albion, Michigan, and wife of the territory's first chief justice. She was the only woman settler who shared Caroline's education and background.

The couple did not need to be concerned, as most settlers were, with preparations for their first winter on the Nebraska plain. They moved into a two-story, four-room log cabin on a bluff overlooking Iowa. The lower part of the house consisted of a kitchen, parlor, and a bedroom decorated and insulated with buffalo robes. Travelers to Bellevue often used a single room upstairs because public accommodation was in short supply. Their nearest neighbors were Omaha Indians who lived in tepees below the bluff. On occasion, Caroline offered them food—with the stipulation that they learn to use the knife and fork she provided.[15]

Caroline, like her neighbors, had to learn quickly to master a household that was comparatively primitive in its furnishings and supplies. To Emma she described the provisions available: "beef, venison, and wild game, vegetables of all kinds, and two or three stores where they keep all kinds of eatables, drinkables and wearables—even oysters put up in cans, pickles and preserves can be procured."[16] Colonel Peter Sarpy, an Indian trader, had been at Bellevue for some time and was experienced in stocking what the emigrants might need. An advertisement for his store listed "Crushed, clarified, loaf and brown sugar, molasses, syrup ginger, nutmegs, snuffs, tobacco, cigars, vinegar, pickles, pepper sauce . . . medicines for fevers, fever and ague, and the common complaints of the country."[17] J. Sterling was less sanguine about the fare they had to eat, writing to his sister, "Our diet is rather plain at present being made up of bread & pork & pork & bread."[18] But like many of his male neighbors, he contributed to the table with game that he killed.

On Thanksgiving Day 1886, J. Sterling recalled for his four sons the first Thanksgiving dinner that he and Caroline had hosted at their home in the new territory thirty years earlier. Their guests were Colonel Sarpy and Judge Ferguson and his wife. J. Sterling remembered the "spread" as being "a delicious saddle of venison, skillfully cooked, and with such condiments as the times and circumstances would permit." Even though she had left the "society of Detroit" and was now but one of three white women in the settlement with only "the Omaha village of a thousand aborigines for her neighbors," their mother, J. Sterling told them, remained "full of energy and courage."[19]

Nevertheless, J. Sterling admitted to his sons that their optimism had not kept them from being constantly mindful of their great distance from the civilized comforts they had known. J. Sterling looked back from 1886 to 1854 and found the change to be "a miracle of modern magic." When he and Caroline first came to the territory, the nearest railroad was over two hundred and fifty miles away. The population of two thousand "bonafide inhabitants" occupied a territory that included what would eventually become four states: Wyoming, the Dakotas, and Colorado. By 1886, J. Sterling estimated, the population was in the hundreds of thousands, "—nearly a million and the railroad is all through all of those territories and states."[20]

The excitement of celebrating the 1854 holidays in the territory ended abruptly with the reality of political wrangling into which J. Sterling entered with relish. He had been elected representative to the first territorial legislature, to which his friend A.J. Poppleton had also been elected from Omaha, and he had become clerk of the territorial supreme court presided over by Judge Ferguson. But the efforts of J. Sterling and others to bring the territorial capital to Bellevue were soon thwarted. President Franklin Pierce, a states rights Democrat, had appointed as the first territorial governor a South Carolinian by the name of Francis Burt. The citizens of Bellevue expected Burt to be favorable to their cause, but Burt died within days of his arrival, and the thirty-year-old territorial secretary Thomas B. Cuming became acting governor. For personal reasons Cuming named Omaha the capital, even though it was a newly fledged town.

J. Sterling's championship of Bellevue, a dozen miles south of the upstart new capital, was to be but the first of his political causes for which he fought and usually lost. The defeat concentrated his interest on that portion of the territory south of the Platte River. While he continued to clerk for Judge Ferguson, he began to seek a community that would support him in his fight for the South Platte region. He would soon find it in the leading citizens of Nebraska City, who wanted him to edit their newspaper. In the spring of 1855, Nebraska City, forty miles south of Bellevue, was still a miscellany of settlements, following the removal to the west of Fort Kearny, the government installation that had briefly occupied the site from 1846 to about 1848.

When J.D. Morton learned that his son, who had lived in the territory for only a little over three months, was on the losing side of the capital question and was now spokesman for disgruntled citizens south of the Platte River, he seized the moment to give him advice. J.D.'s tone and method of argument must have impressed J. Sterling, for he was to use both in the many letters of remonstrance he would later write to Joy. J.D. spoke not only of his own but of J. Sterling's mother's anguish (a favorite device J. Sterling used on Joy) in reading of his son being reviled by his enemies in the papers "as going into college at one door & being kicked out at the other &c &c. . . ." In J.D.'s opinion, J. Sterling had become the tool of speculators in land and politics who were out to use him badly. It would be better, J.D. wrote, if J. Sterling were to return home, "settle down, study law, establish a character & then begin the world understandingly." With advice that J. Sterling would use when writing to Joy years later, J.D. urged his son to concentrate on one thing at a time, whether it be farming, milling, or law: "In a word, fix on something & *do it, don't fail*. . . ." Above all, J.D. intoned, "shun the papers and politics as you would the 'Devil and Dr. Tappan'. . . ."[21] Caroline wrote to Emma that her father-in-law's words had been met by her husband with a characteristic assertion of independence. J. Sterling "would not leave Nebraska in five years, not until he had achieved some great undertaking," she said.[22] He had already decided to become editor of *The Nebraska City News* in the more politically hospitable South Platte settlement.

Nebraska City, incorporated in March 1855 by the Nebraska territorial legislature,[23] welcomed the young editor, whose reputation as a fearless political figure and writer promised that he would be an assertive political force for their prominence within the state. *The Nebraska City News* gave him a ready-made forum and a $1,000 annual salary to provide for his coming family. J. Sterling was ten days shy of his twenty-third birthday when he took over the paper in this town of some fifty new cabins and a bustling business district that included a thriving market in which stock in new territorial towns was being bought and sold. He hired Thomas Morton (no relation), the printer for Bellevue's failed paper, The *Palladium*. Thomas later purchased the paper. He and J. Sterling considered *The Nebraska City News* to be a continuation of *The Palladium*, thus making it the oldest paper in Nebraska today. The pressman was Shack Grayson, a slave loaned to the paper by Stephen F. Nuckolls, a recent proprietor of the town company that had persuaded J. Sterling to come to Nebraska City.[24] These men and a printer's devil by the name of Johnny Freeman put out the paper.

Like other frontier papers closely allied with a town company, *The Nebraska City News* had the job of luring easterners to the opportunities awaiting them in the Nebraska Territory. Even in Nebraska City, one of the more promising settlements, this was a difficult task, for opportunity brought risk, the community was continually begrimed by dust or mud, the senses were pummeled by the noise of building and commerce, and the location was virtually undistinguished but for the fact that it was an embarkation point to the west for a steady stream of goods and travelers deposited by Missouri River boats.

J. Sterling journeyed alone to Nebraska City while Caroline, who was three months pregnant, waited in Omaha until he could find appropriate quarters for her lying-in. Soon, however, they decided that it would be best if she returned to Detroit, where she could receive better medical care and give birth in the comfort of the Frenches' home. In July, less than a year after their departure from Detroit, they retraced the trip to St. Louis, where J. Sterling left her in the care of Pa Joy for the remainder of the journey to the Frenches' home.

J. Sterling returned to Nebraska City with a load of trees to plant on his recently acquired grassland acres. Determined to build a suitable home for his wife and child, he had found a quarter of a section of high land sufficiently removed from the noisy activity of the town. On the bank of a creek that ran through the property, a squatter had built a two-room cabin in which J. Sterling lived while he supervised the construction of the house. The original house, built in 1855, is a tiny portion of what is today a fifty-two room mansion known as Arbor Lodge; the original structure was thought then to be the only frame house between the Missouri River and California. Built in the shape of an L, the home had western windows that faced the uninhabited plain, and its eastern porch looked out upon the bustling village of Nebraska City.[25]

While in Detroit, Caroline was intrigued by J. Sterling's account of the construction of their house and his initial efforts to make the grounds attractive. "I have no talent as a carpenter," he wrote, "but I keep busy working on the lawn area and caring for the trees I brought back from St. Louis and set out. I have engaged a local man to begin breaking the prairie south of the house. We will plant corn there next year. A well has been dug and lined. The water is clear and sweet."[26] In the letter he also created great concern for both Caroline and his family in Detroit. He described how he and some friends, wanting to see whether the "the Great American Desert" might be tillable, had ventured out about four miles from Nebraska City where they were engaged by a roving band of over one hundred Pawnees who appeared menacing. J. Sterling's account of both his home and his unnerving encounter spurred Caroline to consider returning home as soon as possible after Joy's birth.[27]

After hearing of Joy's birth from J.D., J. Sterling, with typical finality, made his own parental authority known from afar. When his father telegraphed J. Sterling that he had dubbed his grandson with the patriarchal name, saying, "You have a son; his name is Abner," J. Sterling telegraphed back, "Glad I have a son; his name is not Abner."[28] J. Sterling and Caroline had agreed in advance that their son's given name should be Joy, honoring her family name while at the same time describing the emotion they expected their firstborn would give them.

$\mathscr{A}$lthough the prairie home to which the twenty-two-year-old Caroline returned with Joy was not that of the sodbusting family striving to wrest a living from the land, it was far removed from ready transportation and lacked the stability and amenities to which Caroline had long been accustomed. Moreover, while J. Sterling's family and farm were his personal consolation and pride throughout his life, he spent most of his time pursuing political and business interests to garner the influence, respect, and financial well-being that he had come to Nebraska to find. His various professional interests often required long-term absences from his family. From the start, he relied on a farm manager and laborers, a nurse for Joy, and a cook for the family. Caroline managed the household and oversaw the farm accounts during J. Sterling's frequent absences.

In the fall of 1855, J. Sterling was seated in the second territorial legislature. To the delight of his South Platte constituents, the twenty-three-year old immediately began to question the integrity of Secretary Cuming who, when acting governor, had become his political enemy. During the forty-day legislative session in Omaha, J. Sterling hounded Cuming with questions about documents related to his advocacy of Omaha and to his handling of federal funds to pay territorial employees. When his efforts had little but an annoying effect, J. Sterling petitioned ·Congress to allow the section of the territory south of the Platte to be annexed to Kansas, arguing that the Platte River was a natural boundary and that annexation could "prevent the establishment of slavery in either of the territories, and . . . guarantee the freedom of the Territory of Kansas."[29] These issues, designed primarily to antagonize Cuming, were neither well conceived nor effective. Yet, having launched them, J. Sterling defended them with his customary rhetorical vigor.

On an economic matter J. Sterling rose above political machination. At the center of land speculation, many of his Nebraska City constituents welcomed legislation that created banks with power to issue money before they were vested. J. Sterling came out strongly against the majority of his fellow citizens in condemning easy money that would, he felt, endanger "the prosperity of our Commonwealth at home and [be] ruinous to our credit abroad." In spite of their appreciation for his sectional advocacy, the voters turned him out in his run for the third territorial legislature. But when the winter of 1856 brought terrible suffering from bank failures compounded by unbearably frigid weather, the youthful legislator and newspaperman was heeded once again and reelected to the fourth territorial legislature.[30]

Prior to the opening of this session, J. Sterling had returned with Caroline and Joy to Detroit, where she once again stayed with the Frenches until she gave birth to their second son, Paul, on May 22, 1857. By the time she and her two babies returned to Nebraska City, J. Sterling's political prominence was assured. At first, however, his involvement in the fourth territorial legislature was inauspicious, though characteristically tempestuous. The session itself appeared doomed from the start because of the question about the placement of the capital. J. Sterling disappointed many of his Nebraska City constituents when he decided that more important issues faced the territory than this controversy that quite literally divided the legislative body. The majority adjourned to Florence, leaving J. Sterling among the minority who remained in Omaha. Though vilified by his adversaries, he stood his ground and, in the bargain, risked further damage to his political career.

J. Sterling did not represent his restless constituents for long. After John Buchanan succeeded his fellow Democrat Franklin Pierce as President of the United States in 1857, he appointed William Richardson of Quincy, Illinois, to be governor of the Nebraska Territory. In that year, just north of the Morton property, the government signed a peace treaty with the Pawnee Indians under a stately elm tree. J. Sterling was among the dignitaries representing the Nebraska Territory, and Caroline was the only woman in attendance. Then, in the spring of 1858, Cuming died, leaving open the position of secretary of the territory.[31]

On April 30, 1858, a few days after turning twenty-six, J. Sterling received that appointment, which required him to live for longer periods of time in Omaha. Soon Caroline, Joy, and Paul moved with him to the Herndon House, a new hotel frequented by the most prominent families in the territory. There on November 22, 1858, Caroline gave birth to Mark, their third son in just over three years. When Governor Richardson resigned on December 5, 1858, J. Sterling became acting governor and served in that capacity until May 2, 1859. Caroline, with two toddlers and a baby, temporarily assumed the role of the first lady of the territory.

J. Sterling remained secretary of the territory until, at age twenty-nine, he was replaced by the Republican administration of Abraham Lincoln in May 1861, a month after the Civil War erupted at Fort Sumpter. Although at the outset his job had been merely functional—one of his first tasks was to approve the construction of a privy for the new government office building in Omaha—he eventually gained a reputation as a fiscal conservative who could balance the budget, an efficient liaison between the federal government, and a forceful administrator during a time of frontier rowdiness and unrest.[32]

Before he was thirty, Joy's father had established himself as the dominant Democratic voice in the Nebraska Territory, and demands on his time away from Nebraska City and his family increased. In the summer of 1860, the year Stephen Douglas and Abraham Lincoln were contesting the presidency, he made the decision to run for a territorial legislative seat in the United States Congress. J. Sterling emerged the apparent winner of a disputed election and went to Washington, D.C., where he remained unseated throughout the first session of a Congress confronted by the Civil War. Eventually, the majority Union Republican Party seated his opponent in May 1862, and J. Sterling returned to Nebraska.[33]

As an unabashed Northern Democrat, J. Sterling was out of sync with the momentum of the nation. The issues of union or states rights, abolition or slavery were creating schisms within families as well as the nation in 1858. The day after the first senatorial debate between Lincoln and Douglas in Ottawa, Illinois, J. Sterling's father-in-law wrote from Chicago in remarkably illiterate prose and contorted logic that J. Sterling was "misinformed" about Lincoln: "You seam [sic] to be aprehensive [sic] he, Lincoln, is a goin [sic] to amalgamate with the blacks that is not so, he does not want any thing to do with [them], he wants to keep them where they now are & not premit [sic] them to come any further north he thinks there will never be know [sic] chance to mix if we keep them away from us. . . . Lincoln and Douglas met at Ottaway [sic] yesterday in debate there was about 20,000 people there."[34] Following the debates, the rift between J. Sterling and his own father over the question of states rights led him to accuse J.D. of "Black Republicanism."[35] Four years into the Civil War and Lincoln's presidency, J. Sterling despaired of what the effect on future generations might be, writing in his annual birthday letter to his mother, "I am 32 today—thirty two under the imbecile and malignant administration of A. Lincoln. The transition from A. Jackson to A. Lincoln is very great—from hard money and hard sense, to no money and no sense at all, from incipient prosperity to full-born misery is very afflicting. . . ." Like many other northerners of his persuasion, J. Sterling believed that democracy would not survive the Civil War. He ended his letter with this question about the future: "Under what sort of despotism will your grand children grow up; amidst what degradation of all that is American will your posterity be reared?"[36]

As J. Sterling's eldest son, Joy grew up during the time his father was a virulent Northern Democrat antagonist of Lincoln Republicans in a territorial culture embroiled in deadly serious and passionate debate over such issues as how best to subsist on and settle the land, how to reconcile states rights and federalism, and how to resolve the most volatile national controversy of all: slavery. Just before Joy's tenth year, the Civil War came to an end and Lincoln was martyred. The day after Lincoln died, J. Sterling wrote that his assassination was a "sad and portentous crime which greatly imperiled life, liberty and the Union."[37] He and other anti-war, anti-Lincoln northern activists at first thought President Andrew Johnson might invoke a wholesale punishment of dissenters. But this did not happen. J. Sterling returned to private life and once again became an active editor of *The Nebraska City News*. Though J. Sterling held tenaciously to the idea that choosing peace over abolition would have preserved the Union and assured a stronger future,[38] his hatred of the Lincoln administration and the Civil War slowly dissipated and he remained active in the nation's political process. Perhaps as a reaction to his father's single-minded ideology, Joy would, in later life, eschew political controversy, supporting those candidates he believed could serve the country in a utilitarian manner.

*W*hile J. Sterling was engaged in his turbulent political career, Caroline took on the complex task of managing an expanding farm and household. In 1858, J. Sterling purchased contiguous land and planted an apple orchard and, in a typical attempt to set his endeavors apart from those of his neighbors, began to call the place the "Morton Ranche." In the summer of 1859, Nebraska City hosted the first territorial fair, sponsored by the Territorial Board of Agriculture, whose founding members were J. Sterling and Robert Furnas, the latter of which became governor of the State of Nebraska. On September 21, 1859, a week before Joy's fourth birthday, the fair opened at the southern edge of Nebraska City, by then a booming frontier town of 2,000 people. In his opening address, J. Sterling declared, "We stand today upon the very verge of civilization—riding upon the head wave of American enterprise, but our descendants, living here a century hence, will be in the center of American commerce—the mid-ocean of our national greatness."[39] The Morton Ranche won prizes for a stallion and a Suffolk boar.

Caroline relished being the mistress of the Morton Ranche. She managed the servants and farm workers, kept the accounts, gardened, designed walks and an entrance drive, played the piano, painted, did needlepoint, visited with friends in town, attended to the development of her sons, and entertained when J. Sterling was at home. She also was active in St. Mary's Episcopal Church, which, in the spring of 1860, was given the designation of cathedral, coming under the leadership of Joseph Cruickshank Talbot, Missionary Bishop of the Northwest.

Caroline and J. Sterling handled lengthy absences from one another with relative equanimity. Although Caroline's role as mother and manager was forthright and decisive while J. Sterling seemed to grow more authoritative, intransigent, and at times mercurial in his political views and pursuits, each aspired to what would seem an idealistic dedication to one another, to their sons, and to the place they had chosen for their home. Caroline approached this ideal as a matter of course. But J. Sterling, who could become as passionate about his intent to create an exemplary Morton dynasty as he was about his belief in the virtue of a conservative state and union, often adopted techniques of sentimentality, nostalgia, or even lugubriousness to make his case.

Yoked by a fierce love of family but marked by the irony of constant separation, these two contrasting personalities made indelible impressions on their sons. Their influence was no doubt intensified by the fact that they nurtured their children within a closed if not charmed family circle on the edge of the Nebraska frontier that just before the Civil War had become the temporal and geographical stage for what the nation had achieved and what it might yet become.

CHAPTER 1

A Prairie Education—1860–1870

Not surprisingly, Joy's earliest memories were of the farm where he spent most of his time with his mother. In his seventies, writing a brief memoir of his childhood for *The Nebraska City News-Press*, he recalled the sight of the freighters heading west on the Overland Trail that bordered on the north of the Morton Ranche. The wagons were of "uniform size" and "hauled by six yoke of cattle, each with a bull whacker to drive them—all supervised by the wagon boss, a man on horseback, who seemed to us boys, to have about as good a job as any reasonable boy could ask for, his only superior being the overland stage driver."

Selling apples to these freighters from the orchard planted in 1858 was Joy's first merchandizing experience. They "sold like hotcakes" because it was the freighters' "very last chance to buy any kind of fruit on their slow route to the Rocky Mountains." Joy, who in his seventies owned a productive apple orchard in Nebraska City, made a lesson of this memory: "We got far better prices than we can get now and we did not have nearly so many to sell, nor such good varieties as we have now, as the early pioneers had nothing to go by and each early planter seemed to think the more varieties he put in, the better his orchard—which was not at all in accord with modern practice."[1]

During the infrequent occasions when the young brothers were allowed to go into Nebraska City, they sometimes were given a dollar to spend. Joy remembered that they were "commended" not for what they bought but for the amount of money with which they returned. Once, having gone to town with the usual dollar in their pockets, Joy returned with seventy cents, Mark with a few pennies, and Paul, "who always believed in getting the good things of life whenever he had an opportunity," with nothing. From then on, Joy thought, he was always considered the thriftiest son.[2]

Household chores occupied much of Joy's childhood. One of these, making candles, he linked to his fondness for reading. Though his wicks often emerged from the side of the candle, he was proud of their practicality: "My candles served the purpose of illumination, but they were not comparable to the kerosene lamps which came afterward." He was better at making soap from lye, tallow, and grease, getting the lye from wood ashes soaked in water. "It made a crude soft soap," he said, "used principally in the kitchen sink and for washing dishes, woodwork, etc."[3]

Early on, Joy informed himself of what was happening in the nation. At seven, entranced by Civil War battles, he read to his younger brothers Wilbur Storey's notoriously anti-Lincoln, anti-war paper, the *Chicago Times*, to which his father contributed articles. Later he would say that reading had gratified his lifelong interest "in current affairs as well as the commercial and social progress of mankind."[4]

At seven, Joy began what proved to be a foreshortened period of formal public schooling. Each term was about three months long with lengthy intermissions, a result, Joy surmised later, of the difficulty of paying teachers for extended periods. Salaries of the elementary teachers—mostly young women with little more than a high school education—were paid for by subscription, primarily from students' parents, who sometimes provided room and board instead. School terms were also curtailed by the seasonal work of farming. Nebraska City did not differ from other frontier towns in its educational expectations, and at first there was only an elementary, one-room education available. "There were few educated men on the frontier in those days," Joy said, "and little culture of any kind."[5] Joy's elementary curriculum matched those expectations, not extending beyond the rudiments of reading, writing, and arithmetic, although his parents, far better educated than most Nebraska settlers, expected Joy and his brothers to excel among all their classmates.

In 1862, Joy began attending Belmont, a small brick schoolhouse constructed close by the Morton homestead.[6] It was presided over by Esther Closer, the first teacher in Nebraska City. In later years, Joy thought he had "learned something" during that time, "perhaps more than I might have if there had not been a hazel brush patch adjoining the school (now part of Morton Park)." Teachers used the switches effectively to preserve discipline, "particularly for the boys; the girls I then thought, were not switched as much as they ought to have been."[7]

Joy was in the second reader when he was sent to a single-room school that was over Whittinger's drug store on Main Street in Nebraska City. In the center of a busy frontier town filled with transient freighters, river men, and migrants attempting to escape the perils of the Civil War, the location of this school brought Joy directly into contact with a life he had not previously witnessed.

Joy particularly admired Ben and Green Majors, the sons of Alexander Majors, whose overland wagon depot was located in the heart of Nebraska City. He remembered that Ben, big and strong for his age, wrested a gun away from a drunk on the playground "and sent him about his business." Ben, he said, was "used to that sort of thing from being around with his father's men, who operated the big freighting wagons on the western trail."[8] Few of Joy's early school experiences had more impact than this.

Trips Joy took with his parents during the Civil War were as instructive as his intermittent schooling. Travel in the 1860s was difficult enough without the hazards of war, but in 1864, he accompanied his delegate father to the Democratic National Convention in Chicago. That convention nominated General George McClelland, who disappointed J. Sterling by adhering to a platform that took a stand against making peace. Joy later recalled being impressed by the crowds outside Chicago's Coliseum while inside the conventioneers were decrying the war and Lincoln. But within a year, he observed, the war was won and Lincoln was martyred. "I made up my mind," Joy said, "that the condensed wisdom of the Convention wasn't worth much."[9] After that year, Joy was to attend one presidential convention each year for the rest of his life, except for 1884 and 1932 when he took in the conventions of both parties.

Travel across the state of Missouri during the Civil War was particularly dangerous, and Joy and his family barely escaped one near disaster. A "famous guerilla leader, Bill Anderson," he recalled, led a band that burned the Hannibal and St. Joseph Railroad bridge at Stewartsville, Missouri, just east of St. Joseph, as a prelude to wrecking the train and robbing the passengers. Fortunately the plan was discovered and soldiers transferred the passengers safely to the other side of the burned bridge where a train from Quincy, Illinois, took them on east.[10]

The meandering connections from Nebraska City to Chicago that prevailed before the Union Pacific Transcontinental Railroad linked the coasts on May 10, 1869, did not deter the Mortons. Joy made at least nine trips to Chicago and Detroit before he was ten. In the summer after the birth of his youngest brother, Carl, on February 18, 1965, and the end of the Civil War in the spring, Joy traveled east with his mother. The return trip included a leg on the Kansas City, St. Joseph & Council Bluffs Railroad. The rails for this train were left unfinished at Amazonia, Missouri. There they boarded a stagecoach that brought them a day and a half later to Eastport, Iowa, the site for the ferry they took across the Missouri River to Nebraska City.[11]

From both his travel and farming experiences, Joy learned early on the critical importance of timeliness and packaging in shipping perishable goods. When the Morton Ranche became a producer of cattle and swine, he helped butcher, salt, smoke, and freeze hogs. After the family's needs were met, the meat would be shipped to Chicago. Its market value depended on whether the weather en route remained cold enough to keep the meat in good condition. He remembered one of the pork packers telling him some years later that those who believed they could beat the market by taking shortcuts might find their hogs slicing their own throats with their hooves in heavily drifted snow.[12]

In the fall of 1866, shortly before Nebraska was admitted to the union, Joy's formal schooling became a more serious matter. J. Sterling and Caroline enrolled him and Paul in Talbot Hall, an Episcopal boarding school founded by the first Episcopal bishop in Nebraska and inaugurated by his successor, Bishop Robert Clarkson, who had come to Nebraska from St. James Cathedral in Chicago. Located some five miles from the Morton Ranche, the school offered a more literary education than the boys had heretofore received. The headmaster, Rev. John Gassman, made a strong impression on Joy. He remembered him as "a man under thirty . . . ; six feet tall, and with a hand the size of a small ham." Joy "liked and respected" Gassman. Sixty years after being his student, Joy visited Rev. Gassman in Alameda, California, and found him to be "as full of life as ever, and had just learned to drive an automobile."[13] Joy had no difficulty in admiring Gassman, who was vigorous and prepared to master new technology even at an advanced age.

During their two and a half years at Talbot, Joy and Paul competed well among the twenty-five or thirty male students. Although most of the boys were from Omaha, several were children of "army officers, Indian traders, or sutlers" and two "were Indian half breeds." Referring to those students from frontier posts, Joy said, "As I remember these pupils, they were all very crude and much in need of book learning but never got very much, for they didn't seem to want it." In 1867, Joy won a prize for oratory and Paul for sacred studies, two of the core programs within the Talbot curriculum. "Now I wasn't an orator and Paul was not particularly addicted to sacred studies," Joy declared years later. "I thought afterward that these awards were probably intended as tributes to my father, who was a public speaker, and to my mother, who was a devout church member. Probably I am wrong in this, but at the time we did not feel that we were justly entitled to the distinctions."[14]

Joy's fondest memory of Talbot Hall was of baseball, which in 1867 was in its infancy, particularly on the frontier. He and his schoolmates learned the game from an older boy. Although Joy did not make the team, which he thought to be the first club in Nebraska, he was a loyal fan. When Talbot Hall was defeated in a match game by a team from Nebraska City called the Otoes, Joy believed "life was no longer worth living."[15]

At Talbot Joy also witnessed the annual return of the Indians in June from their reservation some sixty miles away. While waiting for their government annuities, several hundred native Otoe families would camp along a creek not far from Talbot Hall. Joy recalled, "We boys had lots of fun playing with Indian boys, and we would almost always defeat the little redmen at games, except in shooting the bow and arrow." He assumed that the reason the "little Indian boys were not at all equal to the whites in physique" was "principally because they were undernourished." Joy believed this was caused by the elders not allowing them to eat until after they were filled up, and, he added wryly, "they were hard to fill."[16]

*A*s Joy reached his teenage years, school could not match the experiences open to him on the plains. Nourished by farm produce, game hunted on the plains, and staples shipped from Chicago, Joy, Paul, and Mark quickly developed into robust young men of a stature surpassing that of many of their peers. Throughout their childhood they had done strenuous work on the farm and were encouraged to be self-reliant. By the age of thirteen, Joy was already approaching six feet, and he relished hard physical labor. In May 1869, J. Sterling, who was negotiating with the Burlington & Missouri for a direct link from Nebraska City to the east, got Joy a job on a crew of about thirty men surveying near Creston, Iowa, more than eighty miles to the east of Nebraska City. It was a heady time for railroad building, for communities throughout the region were wooing railway access, and Joy was excited about playing a part.[17]

Joy was the only boy in the group. Most of the surveying party had served in the Union Army under General Dodge, and after the Civil War they worked for him—work that sometimes required them to fight Indians—on the construction of the Union Pacific. Just a few years earlier, Joy and his brothers had read of the battles these men had fought. Now they were Joy's "excellent companions" whom he described as being "mostly of high character, competent, painstaking. . . ." When he remembered those five months away from home, he couched the experience in the words of a veteran who had in his youth reveled in the camaraderie and the accomplishment. The food, though plentiful, was "rough and rudely prepared; but the appetite of a growing boy made light of that, and the conversation and stories of those around the campfire, especially the veterans of the War, were calculated to thrill the very soul of a youngster." But not all was idyllic. There were also "many battles with rattlesnakes," and he would never forget the stench of grass smudges made to ward off swarms of mosquitoes.

He was most impressed by the high level of productivity and devotion of the men. He remembered them as being forty to fifty years of age. They were experienced at surveying and, having had military experience, were accustomed to making repairs in the field. He marveled at the efficiency with which they quickly met and overcame difficulties. For Joy, these men came to embody the discipline and energy that should characterize a workforce.

Joy's own tasks were light at first. He had time to look around the countryside and determine that its agricultural future would be "fertile and promising." Later he was occupied in helping bring the survey into line with earlier surveys done by the government. This required that he count the revolutions of a large wheel attached to a cart or wagon, thus measuring the distance from the former survey markers to the new line. "It was a primitive but sufficiently accurate method of measurement," he explained, "provided the human factor did his work as well as the red rag; and when I realized the responsibility of the job, it was a somewhat thrilling experience for one so young."

By the summer's end, the party had surveyed a line from Red Oak, Iowa, to Nebraska City and was then sent to survey a thirty-five mile line from Red Oak to Sidney, Iowa. The survey party had to walk the thirty-five miles in the heat of summer. Joy had on a new pair of boots that he soon removed because of the pain. He walked the rest of the way barefoot. When they arrived at Sidney, they slept in an unfinished schoolhouse. "I used my boots for a pillow, and had no mattress or blankets," Joy said, "but those pine boards seemed soft and I have seldom had a better night's sleep."[18]

*T*he summer of 1870, Joy's fourteenth, was almost as satisfying. It had been preceded by a rather uninspiring winter in which Joy and Paul returned to "the little red brick schoolhouse" because their father deemed Talbot Hall to be too expensive. There Joy completed his final year of education in Nebraska City. But in the spring of 1870, after Joy and his eleven-year old brother Mark had helped with planting, J. Sterling supplied them with a wagon and mules they could use to experience the rough and tumble business of freighting. Their job was to haul freight from the Nebraska City landing fifty miles to Lincoln—the capital recently established in 1867—then attempt to get a load in Lincoln to make the return trip profitable. This opportunity offered a welcome challenge to the mind, body, and imagination of both brothers.

In 1870, the freighting business that had been so important to Nebraska City since 1855 was undergoing rapid change. Rail transportation was diminishing the profitability of wagon trains, and oxen were being replaced by mules and horses capable of pulling heavy loads over upgraded trails. Joy and Mark used mules, finding it, as Joy said, "a comparatively easy matter to crack the whip over the backs of the team and urge them, with language of varying intensity, to splash through the mud and over the plains." Along the way, the boys were regaled by stories and instructed in the harsher language and methods the old timers used to persuade teams of six yoke of oxen to move 4,000 to 8,000 pounds of freight over difficult terrain.

Alexander Majors, the father of Joy's schoolmate Ben, had written a code of conduct for his freighters to which they were asked to pledge themselves. As Joy talked of this code while being interviewed by his son, he took a book from his library shelves that contained a quotation from Sir Richard Burton, the English adventurer. It contained, Joy thought, a proper perspective on the impracticability of Majors' code. After meeting with Majors during a tour of the American plains, Burton remarked that

Majors' workers, in spite of being required to practice abstinence from alcohol, gambling, and cursing and being urged to read the Bibles he supplied them with, were seldom sober and swore with language that "would make a flush of shame crimson the cheek of the old Isis bargee."

Joy thought well of Majors and reasoned that he created the code in order to "make some slight impression on the frontier's younger element." More than that, the pledge exacted three promises from employees that Joy, at the end of his lifetime, found to be central to the conduct of a successful business: "I will conduct myself honestly, be faithful to my duties, and so direct all my acts as to win the confidence of my employers." In actuality, Majors was generally tolerant of everything but abuse of the livestock, which, Joy declared, was the most "effective way of being dropped from a Majors outfit. . . ."

Driving in a wagon train from Nebraska City to Lincoln may not have then been as difficult as in the preceding fifteen years, but a successful trip still required diligence and clear judgment. Joy described their summer's "freighting enterprise" as being "successful while it lasted." They received "about sixty cents a hundred pounds" for hauling from the Missouri River "a varied assortment of freight, sometimes including whisky, of which a great deal was transported by the freighters in those days." At Lincoln they had to compete for return cargo and "were unusually lucky" in getting loads of flour to take back to Nebraska City.

After unloading and loading for the return, they started back immediately. The round-trip took up to four days, with "three and four outfits moving in one train and camping together," assuring that there would be help should a wagon become stuck in the mire or other difficulties arise. One minor incident stuck in Joy's mind. After leaving Lincoln on one trip, Mark fell ill from the combination of too much custard pie, a hot sun, and a jolting wagon. "We had to stop and administer first aid," Joy said, "whereupon [Mark] apologized, saying that it wasn't the custard pie that had made him sick—but he was sure there had been a fly in it!"[19]

*A*fter the excitement of freighting, it was difficult for Joy to contemplate a return to school in the fall of 1870, even though that, too, promised an adventure. J. Sterling had decided to send Joy to London, Ontario, where he would enroll in Hellmuth College, an Episcopal institution advertising itself as "based . . . upon the model of the great public schools of England and Germany" and bestowing "the utmost care and attention . . . on the Moral and Religious training of the Pupils, under the direct charge of the Rev. the Head Master." Students of Joy's age would be instructed in mathematics, modern languages, English literature, history, geography, composition, and bookkeeping. Many of the 125 young men who attended Hellmuth were from Canadian and American families of some means and distinction. Joy remembered his classmates as "a fine class of boys, interested in good clean sports. Many of the boys afterward distinguished themselves in public and commercial life." But Joy gave faint praise to the headmaster, the Rev. Mr. Sweatman, whom he deemed "a very efficient" English educator but added without conviction, "I am sure he merited a high place in his denomination."[20]

Through his only term at Hellmuth, Joy suffered from homesickness, from a lack of interest in his studies and teachers, and from his father's constant condemnation of his failure to excel. J. Sterling was anxious that Joy not squander this opportunity for an education, particularly since it was being given to him during a time of financial distress in the family. But within a few days of his enrollment at Hellmuth, Joy's mother sensed that all was not well and asked him to write and let the family know how he liked the school. "I judge you are homesick," she said. "I expect though by this time you have got over it and feel quite contented. I am sure it is a good school. Every boy and girl has to go through the same torture when they go away to school."[21]

A month later J. Sterling felt it necessary to urge Joy not to disappoint his family, telling him, "No school however good can make a stupid boy smart nor a lazy boy a good scholar. The individual himself decides to be satisfied with a reputation for mediocrity or resolves to stand at the head—in the front rank." He ended his letter plaintively, asking, "Will you try?"[22] But when J. Sterling's letter was crossed by one from Joy saying that he did not like Hellmuth, J. Sterling became derisive, telling him, "I am surprised at your superior knowledge of the Character of Hellmuth College." He reminded Joy that young men but a little older than he were freshmen at Michigan University and, "They study wherever they are." J. Sterling had little patience with Joy's complaints about his teachers. "You are too fastidious to your instructors to ever find one who will please your exceedingly refined taste." Fed up, J. Sterling told Joy that he would no longer send him money. At the end of the term at Christmas, Joy was to return home and select a trade. The clothes he already had would be good enough for that. "I have sent you to good schools and you have liked none of them," he wrote, "and after fifteen years have passed over your head you write me that (in speaking of horses), 'The two *would way* as much as Tom and the two bays.' . . . I presume such an infamous bit of spelling came entirely from drunken teachers."[23]

Joy's mother slipped a note into the envelope hoping to ease the sting of J. Sterling's invective. Apparently that encouragement and a visit to Joy she made with J. Sterling's sister Emma gave Joy a better outlook on Hellmuth. Sensing a change of attitude in his son, J. Sterling tried to uplift rather than upbraid him. Once more he tried platitudes, asking Joy to, "Cultivate a high ambition. Aim at the sun and you will hit higher than if you aim at a fence." J. Sterling was asking Joy to succeed for him and Caroline. "Let me be proud that you are my son and rejoice in the fact that you are distinguished among your schoolmates as *the best* student, *best* writer and *best* speaker in the school! If you will let me have this pleasure I will do anything and everything in my power to promote your happiness and to advance your interests in life." He wanted Joy to promise him that he would stand at the head of the school as a way of saying, "I shall make my father and mother proud that I am their son."[24]

J. Sterling pleaded with Joy with all the rhetorical clichés he could muster. A day after he asked Joy to make him and his mother proud, he asked Joy to read Longfellow's "Psalm of Life" and tell him whether he quoted it correctly: "Lives of great men all remind us/We can make our lives sublime,/And, departing, leave behind us/Footprints on the Sands of time. . . ." J. Sterling wasn't completely accurate in copying the quotation, perhaps as a way of testing whether Joy would read the poem.[25] Within a few days, he declared, "*Truth* at all times and *honor*, always, should be your leading characteristics. Never lie! Never deceive!"[26] But as far as Hellmuth was concerned, Joy had had enough. At the conclusion of the term, Caroline wrote to Joy in Detroit where he was visiting his grandparents, "I expect when you receive this letter you will be happily out of the clutches of Johnny Bull."[27]

J. Sterling was still interested in Joy pursuing his education. When Joy mentioned tentatively that he might like to go to the University of Michigan, J. Sterling was pleased but again began to lay down conditions. Joy would have to "promise faithfully" to stand at the head of his class. "It must be understood . . . that a son of mine can not remain at Ann Arbor except to distinguish himself as a young man of ability—and promise. What do you say?"[28] While Joy was in Detroit in December, J. Sterling told him that he might allow him to attend Ann Arbor for a trial period of three months, following which, if he found himself behind, he "must quit and return home." J. Sterling was specific about what Joy had to do: ". . . if you evince an earnest desire to please me, and benefit yourself, by excelling in Declamation, Writing, Compositions and in all of your studies I shall take great pleasure in keeping you there and, if you wish it, sending you through College."[29]

In spite of J. Sterling's exhortations, Joy did not commit to Michigan, and his correspondence with his family became less frequent, perhaps because of J. Sterling's exacting standards for perfect English. But Joy was also busy over the holidays working for the banking house owned by his uncle, William D. Morton. J. Sterling could not have been pleased to read the letter Joy wrote to his youngest brother Carl on the stationery of the banking house: "I am sorry I could not write to you sooner. Aunt Sarah told me you was expecting a letter from me and so I thought I would write to you right off. . . .When I come home next summer I am going to bring Mother a nice plant from the university Greenhouse there are some nice ones there."[30] "Captain Jinks," as Carl was called by his older brothers, was six years old.

Joy's fourteen-year-old brother Paul, understanding Joy's desire to return home as soon as possible, kept him abreast of what was happening on the farm and also couched a plea to Joy to be more considerate of their father's concerns about his education. Obviously, the family was tiring of J. Sterling's lectures on Joy's ingratitude. Paul revealed his devotion to his brother and his interest in helping settle family disputes in the following narrative, the style of which J. Sterling would most certainly have disapproved: "Your sow has Eight Pigs. [Thieves] tried to get Tom and Gypse again they Bursted the door of the shed down and shot at our dogs twice we had fun shooting at geese I suppose there are geese there as they called them Canadian geese we have been unsuccessful yet Ed Moore is up here now he has got a gun Single Barrel & broke your gun. But I will have it fixed. Please don't write such to father anymore for it makes him awful mad to think that he had sent you away and that you don't appreciate it at all there is an awful Big Owl in our woods & will shoot him yet Tome Jerry Brick Billy & David [farm animals] are all right."[31]

Both Joy and Paul realized that they needed to improve their style and grammar, and they began to correct one another's writing as thoroughly and with as much derision as their father had ever done. When Paul was feeling "a little spunky" about one of Joy's criticisms, their mother told Joy, "He was always correcting you and needed a reproof."[32] Later, Joy penciled at the bottom of one of Paul's letters that he used the word "now" too often, later softening his objection by writing, "I have just received your letter which was a vary [sic] good one with the exception of having the word now in too often."[33]

By February 1871, Joy's independence of spirit prevailed. He enrolled in a three-month program of study at his great-uncle Ira Mayhew's Business College in Detroit.[34] J. Sterling sent him $150 dollars, telling him that he had "cheerfully and almost gladly given up" hope that he would ever attend a post-secondary school and offered to help him go into business.[35] Joy pursued his studies in the practical curriculum at Mayhew's with pleasure and industry, writing to his father, "I am very busy and do not have much time to write, I am in school 7½ hours every day except Saturday, I study very hard. The harder I study the sooner I shall be home. I have finished Single Entry, and have almost finished Business Correspondence." He added, "I wish you would write to Uncle Ira. I think he is one of the best men that ever lived, certainly the best school Teacher."[36]

$\mathcal{W}$hile Joy was studying, J. Sterling made a business trip to Salt Lake City where he speculated in a mining operation and paid a visit to Mormon cousins, including Brigham Young. He described a dinner party to Caroline: "I was introduced to 11 Mrs. Youngs, and thirty young Youngs. . . . About seventy persons young and old gathered at the family board. The scene was ante-deluvian [sic]."[37] Upon returning home, he became bedridden for a month. But in early April he assured Joy that he was well. Caroline, too, he said, "is well and very happy with her plants and flowers which are all flourishing finely." And the prospects for fruit in the orchards "were never better than now. Plumbs [sic], peaches, pears, apples, & cherries are all full of fruit bloom."[38]

Such news helped Joy anticipate completing the final stage of his education in good fashion and return home directly. He and Mark, whom Joy affectionately called "Farmer," increasingly exchanged letters on what was happening on the farm, particularly with the animals, and all four brothers began to exchange photographs of one another. Joy was anxious to return to Nebraska City: "Uncle Ira says I have done very well and got through in good season, since night-school had closed I have brought my books home and studied in my room as I want to get through and improve my times," he wrote to Paul. "I hope and expect to be home by the 1st of next month."[39]

Joy's formal education was ending six month's shy of his sixteenth birthday. For over nine years, he had had a mixture of reading, writing, and arithmetic, a dose of "literary" instruction, and a three-month immersion in business methods. For all its brevity, it was a great deal more than most young men received in Nebraska in the 1860s. Paul, Mark, and Carl were soon to follow Joy's lead, chafing under the time spent in school while yearning to get started in business. But in their education, Joy and his brothers also benefited from having parents who were better educated than many of their instructors. The boys grew up in a home where ideas, books, and art abounded. If Joy's parents were disappointed that Joy's education ended short of university, they were aware that he at least was prepared for life.

A Prolonged Apprenticeship—1871–1879

Throughout his life Joy credited his three months at Mayhew's Business College with giving him "an idea of business methods and of the value of system in recording business transactions." He also thought that his full eight months away from Nebraska City had made him "far better equipped for the business of life" than he had been. In both London, Ontario, and Detroit, he had had an opportunity to observe human behavior on a large scale. In his seventies, he "remembered perfectly" the vastly different reactions of the large German and French immigrant populations in Detroit to the cessation of hostilities in the Franco-Prussian War in the spring of 1871. The celebration "was the biggest thing of the kind that I had ever seen up to that time," he said. "I was greatly interested in the enthusiasm of the Germans and the grief and hostility of the French, who were numerous in the population of Detroit. Never had I seen so much bock-beer consumed . . . but though feelings ran high, I do not recall that there was any bloodshed."[1] The German victory led to the unification and strengthening of Germany and a weakening of Napoleonic France's unequaled power in Europe, setting the stage for

Germany's prominence in the twentieth century. On October 10, 1871, only five months after Joy witnessed reactions from the Germans and French, the Morton family heard of a devastating fire in Chicago that marked a historical turning point for the people and the city that Joy was destined to inhabit within a decade.

Returning to the small town life he knew well, Joy happily assumed tasks usually reserved for older men. On May 1, 1871, at the age of fifteen, he went to work for James Sweet & Company, Bankers, at $200 a year. Within eighteen months, he proved himself an accurate bookkeeper and a quick study of the basics of banking. His salary rose to $500 a year, and, at sixteen, he appeared to be on his way to a career in banking.

As the eldest son, Joy also assumed the duties included in overseeing the farm during his parents' long absences. Caroline, who was weary of being tied to the farm while J. Sterling was away on business, was especially relieved. During Christmas 1871, she wrote to Joy from Detroit of her impatience with the lack of social life in Nebraska City. In Detroit she had attended a party in which "the military were out in gorgeous array and their elegant uniforms added brilliantly to the scene. It will be twenty years . . . before Nebraska City could get up anything so fine as that party. . . ." She was convinced, she complained to her sixteen-year-old son, that she and her friends were wasting their lives "in that old fogy town" and wished that the people she liked "would come up here."[2]

Joy did not share his mother's attitude. He was comfortable in his role as a banker, occasional head of the household, supervisor of Captain Jinks and Mark, and chief correspondent with Paul, who had followed him to Mayhew's. His was a regimen that would have taxed the mind and energy of most men. Still he took time to indulge his passion for hunting and to engage in the social pursuits of a frontier teenager. Nebraska City suited him.

*S*oon after Joy's return home, an event took place that was to link the name Morton with tree planting in the minds of generations to come. In 1858, as Secretary of the Territory, Joy's father helped organize a board of agriculture and planted his first apple orchard. At the third annual state fair in 1869, he and twenty-two other men established the Nebraska State Horticultural Society, whose members included Robert Furnas and Dr. George Miller. Fellow editors of influential Nebraska papers, both had disagreed publicly with J. Sterling's extreme stance against Lincoln and the Civil War. Still, Furnas, a Republican, and Miller owned orchards and understood the importance of agriculture and arboriculture to Nebraska.

Their mutual championing of the planting of trees in Nebraska made the three a powerful combined voice for arboriculture within the state. All three competed for recognition as the best apple growers in Nebraska. By 1871, they and other Nebraskans were gathering American Pomological Society prizes for apples and pears.

Wanting to make the most of any venture he undertook, J. Sterling wrote a "Fruit Address" for delivery on January 4, 1872, at the annual meeting of the Horticultural Society in Lincoln and then presented a resolution to the State Board of Agriculture, also meeting on that day, calling for Wednesday, April, 10, 1872, to be named Arbor Day and "consecrated for tree planting in the State of Nebraska." The board urged "upon the people of the State the vital importance of tree planting. . . ." When the first Arbor Day was duly celebrated, the 800 trees that the Mortons ordered for planting at their home did not arrive on time. Nevertheless, the first Arbor Day was deemed a great success with over a million trees planted in the state.[3] From the first, the Morton farm was considered the birthplace of Arbor Day, and it fell to Joy in his role of manager to assure that the orchards and surrounding trees remained worthy of the honor.

Representatives of the Mutual Life Insurance Company of New York asked Joy, on the strength of his reputation as a reliable bank employee, to become an insurance agent for their firm in Nebraska City. After finding that Nebraska City citizens were carrying "more than a million and a quarter of dollars of Life Insurance," he promised nothing "more than to try."[4] By the end of 1872, he was earning insurance commissions in addition to his bank salary.

Near Christmas 1872, Paul, age sixteen and recently graduated from Mayhew's, left for Burlington, Iowa, to work at the land office of the Burlington and Missouri River Railroad. Caroline, Carl, and J. Sterling were once again celebrating the holiday in Detroit, and Joy and Mark were on their own at the Morton Ranche where Joy now had the job of filing the family's voluminous correspondence as well as keeping track of documents related to his father's complex business dealings in land and bonds, which J. Sterling insisted should be "under lock & key all the time."[5] Joy relished being in charge. He was particularly proud of a barter agreement he had negotiated that resulted in an estimated profit of one hundred dollars. Just after Christmas, he wrote to J. Sterling, "I have today disposed of Jinks, Dick, Charley, the old work Harness and Lumber wagon for fifty cords of good straight Sycamore wood to be delivered in town next week, which at Six dollars per cord would come to three hundred dollars and the same kind of wood is selling for from seven to ten dollars per cord on the streets."[6]

But Joy assured his parents that the year-end had not been spent entirely on work: "I enclose to mother a program of the party at the city hall last Friday night at which I had the best time I ever had at a party. We had the Omaha String Band."[7] Joy had begun dancing lessons the summer before. He followed another business letter to his father with the comment, "Do not be in any hurry to get home as we are very comfortable here and if you do not get home until '74 it will make no difference," adding, "The sleighing is very good here, there being about nine inches of snow upon the ground, which is very good for the Fruit and Fall wheat. Every thing on the Farm is doing well. Mark included."[8]

From New York City at the start of 1873, J. Sterling responded to Joy's letters with salvos of paternal admonitions softened by occasional humor: "Be careful of yourself; stand straight up and avoid 'stooped shoulders.' Am glad you attended the dance. Hope you will not fall in love before I get home."[9] Of Joy's writing style, he averred that it had improved somewhat: "The one recd today bears date 9th and is very interesting to me and gratifying too because it is the best and most correctly written letter I have ever recd from you."[10] A few days later, J. Sterling told Joy to write "good and encouraging letters to Paul" and not to "fail to keep some good apples nicely for Mother until spring."[11] A month later, J. Sterling gave Joy this advice: "N.B. Learn to remember the names and faces and residences of men. Aptness in memory of this peculiar kind will make money for its possessor. Never forget a name, a face or place of residence."[12]

Joy had already developed a good deal of confidence in his own judgments. Having learned that one of J. Sterling's debtors was in Chicago betting on wheat margins, Joy was exasperated, saying, "I suppose he expects to get rich, as men sometimes do at 'Poker.'" The debtor had also sold a cord of the Morton's "Horse" wood for $5.50, but had kept the money. Joy was unforgiving of such behavior, even though he admitted, "Perhaps I am a little hard on H. but I think he has treated you shamefully this winter."[13] For the most part, however, Joy was satisfied with how the winter had gone. He had been talking with a prospective renter of one of the fields, and he was waiting for J. Sterling's decision about what to do. He had also decided to send Paul $10 to help pay his board, because he thought Paul should be getting better pay for the work he was doing.

In contrast to J. Sterling's more serious letters, Caroline's were filled with lighthearted banter. Writing from the Frenches' where she was recuperating from a lingering illness, she used the occasion of a boast Joy had made on the health of his chickens to chide him about his churchgoing: "I am afraid those chickens won't be the best raised chickens in Nebraska if you build their house on Sunday. . . . Don't grow up a heathen entirely. I should be glad to have you write to me that you had been to church once."[14] Joy responded with mock surprise: "You say you would like to have me say I had 'been to church once,' that is rather queer as you know I used to go to church quite often with you. . . ."[15]

Knowing what his mother wanted to hear, Joy sent all the stored up news of the farm and town: he planned to measure Mark for tailored clothes and had killed and butchered a penned deer that had broken its forelegs. He also told her of the adventures of Charley Woolworth, the son of a family friend—"every paper in the state has had more or less about him in, it seems he played a game of billiards for $1,000 got beat and stole the money and 'lit out.'" Joy mentioned the progress on the chicken house; wrote of "Tom (the horse)," his horse Gypsey, his new colt and "Tom (the cat)," who "sends his regards to Jinks"; and finished by saying, "I escorted to the party you spoke of Misses Fowler, Bacon, Bennet, Coe, and the old lady Coe, and could have taken one or two more if it had been necessary."

Typically, J. Sterling used Charley Woolworth's difficulties to tell Joy how to conduct himself. As he often did when he felt Joy needed caution against temptation, he issued commands: "Do never *learn* to play billiards. Avoid saloons & saloon society. Do not allow passion to assume superiority over Reason nor permit your animal parts to run away with your head. *Women* made a thief of young Woolworth. Watch the habits of Mark & look well after your own."

J. Sterling's concern was ultimately that of a Victorian patriarch who did not want his family name blemished. "In you Boys center all my pride and hope and disgrace or dishonor to either of you would kill both Mother & Father at once, absolutely." Protesting that he did not often lecture Joy, J. Sterling impressed upon Joy the depth of his feeling by saying, "In a word then: **Die** rather than betray a trust or do a dishonorable act. I could look calmly upon your early grave and cherish sweet memories of your promise and your success but your dishonor would leave me no pleasure and nothing of happiness save the hope of Death speedy and sure."[16] J. Sterling could not have known that in but a few months his morbid imprecation would come close to fulfillment.

Joy thought little of Charley Woolworth's plight. He was busy with his work at the bank and was planning for the summer on the farm. He wrote to his father, "I think it would be a good plan not to put any crop in the field by the house and summer fallow it this summer and sow it with Timothy in the fall as I think we could make more by selling hay than corn."[17]

The summer passed with a flurry of letters. By June Paul's job with the B&MRR had taken him thirty miles north of Nebraska City to Plattsmouth, a distance sufficient to make trips home inconvenient. Caroline was back in Monroe, Michigan, with Carl, visiting the Frenches. And J. Sterling, consulting for the B&MRR in Chicago, was more dependent than ever on Joy's help. In July he wrote asking Joy to make certain that a new phaeton would not cost more than its contracted price, that Joy needed to sell an old harness and a load of cordwood, and that the hired man and Mark should hoe walnuts and willows from a new orchard without damaging newly planted honey locusts. J. Sterling did not know when he would be home. He was negotiating a contract that he expected would pay him $5,000 a year to write public relations articles and to lobby for the B&MRR.[18]

In late summer, at the outset of the economic Panic of 1873 that occurred in the first year of President Ulysses S. Grant's second term, Joy accompanied his father and Furnas, who had been elected Nebraska's governor, to the American Pomological Society's exhibition in Boston, intending to promote the quality of fruit grown in Nebraska orchards.[19] The B&MRR sponsored the trip and furnished a railcar containing displays of Nebraska fruit. Well prepared, J. Sterling, after recovering from an illness for which Joy administered brandy on the trip out, placed articles in East Coast newspapers extolling Nebraska orchards. At the exhibition, Nebraska won the society's first premium, the second such award it had received in three years.

Conference attendees visited neighboring arboretums including the Hunnewell at Wellesley and Harvard University's Arnold at Jamaica Plains, established only a year earlier. The Arnold's founder and director was Charles Sprague Sargent. In his early thirties, Sargent had already earned a reputation as a botantist specializing in dendrology, the study of trees. Of course, neither the seventeen-year-old Joy nor Sargent could have known that fifty years later they would become friends when Joy would call upon the then-octogenarian, who had brought the Arnold to international prominence, to advise him in planning his own arboretum.[20]

The Massachusetts visit was complemented by perhaps an even more seminal visit to New York, where Joy—a teenager comfortable in Nebraska City and acquainted with Detroit and Chicago—found in New York City a dramatization of what might be called the bookends of his life's work.

Joy accompanied his father on a ride through Central Park, which had been completed in the early 1860s according to the plans of Frederick Law Olmsted, who was quickly becoming the foremost urban landscape designer and city planner in the United States. In fewer than ten years, Joy would come to know firsthand the work of Olmsted and his partner Calvert Vaux for the city of Riverside, Illinois; and in Chicago Joy would live near the lakefront along the greenway leading to Chicago's south parks, which Olmsted and Vaux began laying out in the year that Joy and his father made their brief visit to Central Park. Chicago's south parks (Jackson and Washington), joined by the Midway Plaisance, would, with Olmsted's consultation in cooperation with Daniel H. Burnham, become the site of the World's Columbian Exposition of 1893, within an easy carriage ride of Joy's south side residence. Olmsted's designs had a long lasting influence on Joy. Twenty years after the New York trip, Joy saw Olmsted's work again at George Vanderbilt's Biltmore estate in North Carolina, which he visited with his father—a visit that helped inspire and coalesce his own ideas about the arboretum that he would create some twenty-five years after his visit to Biltmore.

Joy and his father completed their tour of New York with a visit to Wall Street and the Stock Exchange, which was reeling from the panic that was precipitated by the bankruptcy of the investment banker Jay Cooke's banking empire located primarily in Philadelphia, Washington, and New York. Cooke, who helped finance the Union during the Civil War, had overextended his investments in the Northern Pacific Railway and, because of monetary policies instituted by Grant's administration, was unable to recoup. The resulting effect on the economy was overwhelming, with the stock market in deep retreat. It was Joy's initial introduction to the institution that from its beginnings in the early eighteenth century has dominated American corporate activity and been a bellweather to the nation's economic health and direction. Thus, just days before his eighteenth birthday on September 27, Joy was introduced to the nation's most impressive urban landscape and its titular economic center at a time when one was fresh and promising and the other was in chaotic distress. Both events were deeply imbedded in his consciousness.

Joy returned to the tranquility of home from his trip east to take up work in the bank, farm, and family. The national depression caused by the Panic of 1873 sobered the country that had reveled in what Mark Twain and Charles Dudley Warner branded as the Gilded Age in their collaborative 1873 novel by that name. Reconstruction of the South and the frantic pace of railroad development following the Civil War had created a culture of political corruption and economic opportunism that finally crashed of its own weight. But the Mortons, with their farm in Nebraska City, which remained an active depot and transportation center on the Missouri River, remained relatively secure financially.

The family was dispersed, however, and continually complained of not hearing often enough from one another. In the fall of 1873, eighteen-year-old Joy was the keeper of Arbor Lodge and had watch over Carl who was in elementary school and Mark who was at Nebraska College, formerly Talbot Hall; Paul was working at Plattsmouth; Caroline was in Detroit visiting J. Sterling's family; and J. Sterling was traveling on behalf of the B&MRR. Thanksgiving and Christmas loomed as Joy carried out his duties. For entertainment he attended the Crystal Palace in Nebraska City, where he saw performances of Donizetti's "Lucretia Borgia," a show of "Poultry, Pigeons, & Rabbits," and an organ performance.

In the midst of this relative calm, Joy's parents became embroiled in two complex legal affairs that occupied them for the next several years. In December, J. Sterling sent news from Chicago that Pa Joy, who had died in 1868, had left his property in Chicago to "two little girls—Bell & Kate or whatever their coy names may have been . . ." declaring that "the deeds were secured by the vilest fraud."[21] This was the sort of sarcasm to which J. Sterling resorted when he was faced with a conundrum that he could not easily solve. The situation was compounded by the fact that in the past few years Caroline's father had been less than communicative with her, and little was known about the relationships he had formed in his later years. As the will was being contested, J. Sterling learned that the Nebraska Supreme Court had ruled that he did not have legal ownership of salt lands he and others had speculated on in the sixties because they had been "set aside by an act of Congress as mineral lands." Caroline's suit dealing with Hiram's estate did not reach a final decision until January 1878. She had to testify in Chicago, answering charges that she had taken large sums of money from her father without paying them back. In both cases, J. Sterling remained hopeful, urging Caroline to pursue a court battle for Pa Joy's Chicago property and taking the salt lands case all the way to the United States Supreme Court.[22]

As his parents' court cases proceeded, Joy took on greater responsibility for family affairs. On one occasion when J. Sterling chastised Caroline for overspending, Joy responded, beginning disarmingly enough: "Mother received a letter from you yesterday. Last week we had a very gay time . . . went to Home Circle Tuesday, Theatre Thursday . . . , to a party Friday, and Theatre again Saturday and yesterday Joe & Henry were out to dinner." Then without transition, he asked his father not to "say anything more about economy when you write to Mother. It makes her feel bad. I will run the house on the cheapest possible basis." In closing, he added not too subtly, "Hoping you are well, enjoying yourself and making money and friends and that hereafter all our correspondence will be satisfactory."[23]

*A*fter turning eighteen, Joy took over the task of keeping the journal entitled "Morton Farm," a daily observation and record of weather, farm procedures, and land acquisitions that he often embellished with humorous marginalia intended for his father's eyes. Following an epigraph that his father had likely entered—"He who by the plow would thrive/ Himself must either hold or drive"—Joy wrote, "Death to monopolists" and "Down with the railroads."[24] The Grangers, whose slogans Joy was using in jest, were even then enough of a force in Nebraska agriculture to be an annoyance to his father. The farm organization founded in 1867 to bring a concerted voice to agriculture in the Midwest decried their perceived enemies, middlemen wholesalers, and railroads.

During the winter of 1874, Joy worked at the bank, tended to errant hogs, medicated or disposed of injured horses, supervised the building of an icehouse, butchered livestock, dealt with his mother's frequent firings of cooks and maids, and, in the extreme cold, kept water open in the creek for livestock to drink and a fire in the cellar, where temperatures dipped below freezing. Even so, he managed to keep up his spirits. His entry on January 19 included an echo and ongoing mantra of his father: "'Economy the road to wealth' but as the above is a very hard road for the Morton Family to travel I think it will be some time before they are very wealthy."[25]

Joy celebrated Arbor Day 1874 by building a hotbed for his mother's seedlings, and on the first day of spring, he planted a white birch in front of the house. Two days later, J. Sterling took Caroline, who had suffered from the effects of the Nebraska winter chill, to Chicago for a change of scenery. Joy plowed, planted trees, looked after his two rambunctious younger brothers, and oversaw the hired men as they set out a new orchard. His May 1 entry into the journal ended apruptly: "Pd. Mark for a window broken by him at school. .25 cents."[26]

J. Sterling, on his return with Caroline from Chicago, took up the journal a week later: "Yesterday Joy Morton the regular writer of this Journal was taken quite seriously ill with an attack of bilious fever. . . ." The next day he recorded, "Joy very sick and indications of the spine disease with which Fred Fusting died are very strong. The head's thrown back, eyes glassy and mind delirious." A physician from town spent the night with Joy, whom J. Sterling described as "dangerously ill."[27]

Joy had spinal meningitis. For a week he was attended by as many as three doctors who prescribed a purgative, ice packs to the head, as well as a body poultice of heated corncobs, a treatment Joy later remembered as being exceptionally uncomfortable during the hot spring.[28] By the middle of June, after being bedridden for five weeks, Joy recovered sufficiently to put on his clothes. J. Sterling was relieved to write in the farm journal, "Joy rode out in the Phaeton to the gate and returned with his Mother. He has in his life done many things very gratifying to me, and few things to cause me or his Mother regret, but his little ride to the gate tonight was the grandest cause for gratitude I have ever experienced. Thank God!"[29]

For the rest of the year, the lingering effects of his disease made it impossible for Joy to seek a position away from home. In July, when Joy was able to resume the journal, J. Sterling traveled on business once more. At home with Carl, Mark, and his mother, Joy had little to do but recuperate, although a local drama served as distraction. Peter, a hired man, stole Joy's double-barreled shotgun and his silver, mounted shot pouch and powder flask. Joy put the venture in perspective when he entered these words in the journal: "Peter's latest exploit was capturing the dresses in which the sheriff and assistant were disguised. . . . Last night three men came out to watch for Pete and about 10 o'clock one of them named Adle fired off his pistol and made a fool of himself. . . . On examining their firearms we found that Adle's pistol was not in condition to hurt anybody, and another had a musket that had been loaded a year and the caps had come off the other man's shot gun. We sent them all home."[30] But that was the end of that drama.

Late summer, the temperature 100 degrees in the shade, brought monotony. The usual invasion of grasshoppers damaged the crops. Joy and a friend killed twenty-two prairie chickens. Although Joy still had symptoms of his illness, he accompanied his father to Chicago in September simply to get away. His mother wrote in the journal, "Corn stopped growing until Joy returned home."[31] Back home, he packed apples for the state fair. Among the twenty-seven varieties the orchard had produced were, he recorded, "four unknown varieties." He also included "some Duchess of Oldenberg and Sickely pears."[32]

Throughout the late summer and fall, Joy pursued healthful but desultory outdoor activities. He went to the state fair in Omaha to see Randall "trot a mile in 2 minutes twenty-four and one-half seconds."

On the banks of the Missouri hunting with Mark, he "killed five quails at once, shot on the wing." He trained a hunting dog Paul had given him and that fall gained the respect of his brothers and peers in local hunting competitions. In Nebraska City, he saw Robert McWade play in *Rip Van Winkle* and accompanied his mother to a lecture. And, as had become customary, he sought a new cook and maid because of his mother's impatience with the household help. [33]

When Joy compared his prospects with Paul's, he realized how far he was falling behind. By 1875 Paul had had four years of management experience and in December had moved from Plattsmouth to Chicago to work for the Chicago Burlington and Quincy Railroad at $50.00 a month. When J. Sterling prevailed on his acquaintances at the Michigan Central office in Chicago to give Joy a job, Joy agreed, even though he was still feeling the effects of his illness. In late December, he carried with him to Chicago a letter of recommendation from James Sweet, J.T. Thompson, and Henry N. Shewell, for whom he had worked in the bank until his illness, attesting to his "good character, honesty, faithfulness and mature judgment, for his years. . . ."[34]

J. Sterling was buoyed by Joy's prospects, writing in the farm journal on the evening of his departure, "A truthful, honest and efficient young man, he steps into the paths of commerce with a brave heart, a clear head, and good habits. Ten years hence, if his life and health are preserved, he will have earned a name and place of which his family will be gratefully proud. God Bless him!!"[35] Before starting work, Joy went with Paul to the theatre for a performance starring Edwin Booth. All Joy knew about his new job was that he would be working in the office of the president. He did not know his salary.

In the winter of 1874–1875 Chicago was in the third year of robust rebuilding after the catastrophic fire of 1871 that destroyed the heart of the city, leveling 18,000 buildings, killing 300 citizens, and displacing thousands more. Joy could not have helped but been impressed by the activity. But he had to settle into work in the office of the president of the Michigan Central, learn what was expected of him, and observe closely how the office was conducted. Paul wrote to their mother, "Joy seems to like it in the Front Office first rate. Says they think he writes well and is a good accountant."[36] In his meager spare time, Joy took in the sights of the city, going with Paul to minstrels and out to dinner and making at least one visit to the stockyards.

Within days, Joy's mother wrote from Detroit asking for Joy's help in finding a good boarding school in Chicago for both Carl and Mark.

Like Joy and Paul, Mark had gone to Mayhew's Business College and was studying German and accounting. But Caroline told Joy, "He has got to a point in bookkeeping that is too hard for him—and he cannot get along."[37] Joy looked into a school at Lake Forest, but in the end he argued that both Carl and Mark should return to Nebraska College.

Joy was wondering whether he, too, should return to Nebraska City. A few weeks into his work, he had begun to experience increased symptoms of his illness. When, in February, Henry Shewell wrote to say that his successor at the bank had proved incompetent and that he wanted Joy to rejoin the bank, Joy needed no urging.[38] He was happy to return to Nebraska City and fresh air.

$\mathcal{J}$oy took up his old duties on the farm and at the bank, where he was now being paid $60 month. He wrote to his parents who had gone to Chicago, where J. Sterling was consulting for railroads, "I take a run in the woods with the boys after bank hours and think it does me a great deal of good, as I feel stronger than when in Chicago." He was prepared to weather the winds off the plains of his native Nebraska but urged them, with tongue in cheek, to remain where they were: "People here all ask when you and Mother are coming home, but I tell them not until warm weather, and I would not advise you to come before April 15 as now the country looks exceedingly bleak to a person from Chicago."[39]

Joy's letter found J. Sterling depressed. His railroad career did not give him the money or leisure he wished, the depression caused by the Panic of 1873 lingered on, and, as he often did when anxiety about money overtook him, he told Joy to put no more money into the farm and to sell the buggies and horses. Overwhelmed by the harsh Chicago winter, the lingering economic downturn, and the court fight over Hiram Joy's will, J. Sterling built his letter into crisis proportions, urging Joy to sell the house, too: "It don't suit us. We only need a home in a boarding house, a hotel, a hash hospital." It was a familiar story. J. Sterling was flailing out. The farm, too, should go, he concluded: "We shall never settle down and be happy there again and I hope you will find a customer for it soon."[40] J. Sterling's gloom had deepened even more when he heard from one acquaintance that Nebraska orchards had been decimated by a freeze and from another that Joy had been offered his position back in Nebraska City "out of pity," that Paul "had no ambition," and that Mark "was a fool."

As usual, the task of helping his father out of his funk fell to Joy, who reassured him on the matter of the orchards, telling J. Sterling that after he and an expert horticulturist had examined the fruit buds, they found the apples in a good state, the peaches expected to yield two-thirds of a crop, and the pears, though badly damaged, to produce some fruit. Of himself and his brothers, Joy was adamant. He could take care of himself; Paul was "entitled to more credit for the way he has been doing for the last two years than any other member of the Morton or Sterling families, without any exception, for the last few generations"; and Mark, was "about as well abused by certain people as anyone I know of, and I don't think he is a fool by any means. . . ."[41] Mollified, J. Sterling replied, "Your long letter came this morning just as Mark was leaving for home. It was good medicine for me and I thank you for it, very sincerely."[42]

But during the first few months of 1875, both parents remained depressed. After a winter in Detroit and Chicago, being ill off and on, and involved in the court battle over her father's estate, Caroline returned to Nebraska City only to find it unbearable. She penned a long letter of complaint to Paul: "I think you ought to feel happy that your lot was cast on different shores from the rest of the family. Of all desolate, forlorn God forsaken places I ever knew or read about, this is the worst. I never was so lonesome anywhere in my life as I am here. I feel like crying all the time."

Caroline's "blue"—a word the family used for any family member who felt melancholic—was not helped by J. Sterling's recurring concern about expenditures. She told Paul that his father had criticized her "foolishness" in buying seeds for her garden, an important part of her life at the farm: "I am tired [of] hearing about my expenses again and I have made up my mind I will not buy a cent's worth of anything for myself and see if we are any better off." She was especially irked because J. Sterling lived in hotels in Chicago rather than saving money by rooming with Paul.[43]

Through the winter and early spring, Joy continued to bolster the spirits of his parents while showing signs of increasing boredom. He wrote to his father, "Business very dull and time hard but prospects for a good crop of fruit are flattering."[44] By April his mother, her spirits improved, was in her garden, using hotbeds Joy had made for her. She rejected an invitation to visit Paul, saying, "The weather is delightful here and I am out doors all the time."[45] But in May, Joy himself was deeply affected by the blues, exacerbated by a grasshopper invasion and recurring symptoms of his illness. He told his father that the grasshoppers "are going to clean us out again" in spite of his having "rolled them & burned them."[46] Caroline wrote to Paul, "Joy is blue enough about [the grasshoppers] and wished last night he was well enough to leave this country and go back to Chicago."[47]

Increasingly concerned that Joy, approaching his twentieth birthday, was falling behind Paul in opportunities (Paul was now being paid $75.00 a month by the CB&Q), J. Sterling wrote to Caroline, "Just as soon as Joy is 21 we must move over to Chicago and give him and Mark a chance like Paul's, if we can possibly get our affairs in shape to do so."[48] Agreeing, Caroline said, "I am so sick of this town and being so separated all the time and Joy would be so glad to get away."[49] But only Mark went to Chicago, enrolling in the Mount Vernon Military Academy in Blue Island at Morgan Park.[50] He remained there for only a few months, writing to the family comical accounts of the drunken exploits of the headmaster. J. Sterling soon returned him to Nebraska College to complete his schooling.

Joy's health problems required that he remain on the farm. On New Year's Day 1876, he duly recorded in the journal the farm inventory that included riding and workhorses, family dogs, two milk cows, twenty-six "fat hogs that will average 300," forty-two head of stock hogs, and another fifty fat hogs that Joy himself owned. He described the land as "160 acres of the best land in Otoe County with at least twenty hundred apple trees in it, 400 of which will have fruit this year," then added that "we think we can get through with the year comfortably as Fathers income for the last six months has been about $25 per day and Joy gets $60 per month from James Sweet & Co. and Paul $75 per month from the CB&QRR in Chicago. Mark and Carl will go to school at the Nebraska College and Mother will raise plants at home."[51]

But by February, on his doctor's advice that he have more fresh air, Joy left the employ of James Sweet & Co. for good and rented a 160-acre farm, working it with a single hired man. He also continued to manage the affairs of the family farm, now called Arbor Lodge, a name J. Sterling had started using following the 1874 Arbor Day celebration.[52]

J. Sterling was once more in Chicago pursuing the family's fortune. His old friend and mentor Wilbur F. Storey had invited him to invest in the *Chicago Times*. J. Sterling thought that doing so might guarantee an income of $5,000 a year, though as Storey's co-publisher he would have to live in Chicago for most of each year. Initially he was euphoric and wrote to Caroline that his "orcharding days" were over, although he thought that Joy and Caroline would need to remain in Nebraska City while he became settled. A couple of years on the farm, J. Sterling said, would do Joy good and give him a chance to make some money. Shortly, however, J. Sterling backed out of Storey's offer, finding that he would have to encumber the family's funds. He redoubled his efforts to sell

Otoe County bonds, planned a business trip to Europe, and represented the railroads by lobbying and writing articles on their behalf.[53]

In the summer of 1876, Joy looked after Carl, while Caroline, J. Sterling, Paul, and Mark (who had just completed his schooling at age seventeen, having spent two years more at school than either Joy or Paul) attended the Exposition and Centennial Celebration in Philadelphia. Upon their return home, a week after Joy's twenty-first birthday, Mark took a job in the general offices of the CB&Q with Paul. Joy hated to see Mark leave, for they were the closest of companions. In the margin of the journal he wrote, "Mark starts into the world to make his living,"[54] and in a few days, entered despondently, "Mother and Joy attend a small and stupid gathering at Sweets."[55]

After the harvest, Joy traveled alone to Philadelphia, where the exposition failed to enliven his spirits. He was there only "long enough to find out how tiresome it was wandering around."[56] He came home just in time to cast his first presidential vote for the Democratic candidate, William Tilden. The results of the election mirrored his mood. It ended with the country deeply divided. Rutherford B. Hayes lost the vote to Tilden but was declared the winner by the electoral college. J. Sterling and his fellow Democrats who had hoped for their first presidential victory since 1856 were outraged.

More convinced than ever that he had no future in Nebraska City, Joy briefly adopted his father's speculative impulses. In late October, a letter from Paul to J. Sterling revealed that Joy thought of starting a starch factory believing that with the family's railroad connections he could undersell eastern producers. Paul offered to go to Ottawa, Illinois, with Joy to visit a starch factory there, but Joy could not muster enthusiasm for the trip.[57]

Later Joy mulled over a scheme of moving to the Black Hills, possibly to raise a herd of long-eared mules, a venture that both troubled and intrigued his father. "The Black Hills may be a good field for you to search for fortune in and possibly I will consent to your going, and *go with you*, in April or May, just to look the ground over," J. Sterling wrote to Joy. But he offered a rationale for Joy remaining at Arbor Lodge: "You must not permit yourself to fret over doing nothing, as you express it, but during odd hours apply yourself to the accumulation of knowledge. That is as good as money, better than money, and the library is open to you at all times."[58]

Joy was not encouraged by such advice, but he had little time to dwell on his discontent. Throughout the late spring and summer of 1877, Nebraska was again beset by a grasshopper invasion that Joy did not suffer passively. He experimented with ways of killing them in large numbers by destroying their eggs, while at the same time he recorded with fascination the waxing and waning of their invasion. In May, Mark wrote to his father, "I see by the Press some time ago, that Joy had invented a machine for killing them, which it pronounced a good invention."[59] While the onslaught of the grasshoppers challenged Joy, he was also kept busy overseeing renovations on the family home, including the installation of its first modern bathing facilities.

Even though he was fully occupied, Joy was convinced that Nebraska City held no future for him. Paul was now making $1,020 a year. J. Sterling thought of a compromise for Joy. An office of the Union Pacific and CB&Q proposed for Nebraska City would allow Joy to work at home, he believed. But when that did not materialize, J. Sterling resigned himself to the fact that Joy must move elsewhere if he were to become successful and make him as proud as Paul and Mark were doing. He had written to Caroline that in Chicago, Paul and Mark were regarded as "trumps, everybody . . . praises them to me. And I am quite fond of being their paternal progenitor."[60]

But when Paul and Mark, working in Chicago, took temporary decreases in pay during the final throes of the depression that followed the Panic of 1873, J. Sterling asked Joy to remain for a while at Arbor Lodge, writing, "Kill rats persistently. Sow turnips. . . . Castrate young swine: count the big ones. Look after water gates. We are a fortunate family in that we have a Home and good health."[61] Doggedly, Joy prepared for harvest and burned two dozen pigs that had died of an unknown disorder.

Joy's spirits had reached a nadir, and J. Sterling knew that he must finally act. Through his efforts, Joy was offered a position in the assistant treasurer's B&MRR office in Omaha. The job promised advancement and travel throughout northeastern Nebraska. In Joy's absence J. Sterling would have to give more of his attention to Arbor Lodge, although Carl, now thirteen, boasted to Joy, "I am the man of the house."[62]

Joy was in his job for only a few weeks before he learned that his beginning salary of $50.00 a month was but two-thirds that of a predecessor deemed incompetent by his employers. This was unacceptable, he explained to his mother: "The road is making more money than ever before and I don't see why they want to be so mean. . . . I am as disgusted as I can be."[63] As usual Joy thought of Nebraska City. He and Paul had recently been deeded 160 acre farms by J. Sterling, who, with the prospect of railroad links for Nebraska City to the east and the west, had begun purchasing land in Otoe County. Soon, with money he had carefully saved while farming, Joy initiated construction of a small hunting shack he would call Cedar Lodge. J. Sterling sympathized with Joy's disappointment in his salary, suggesting that he might want to return to farming. "If you are not worth to the Company more than $50.00 a month you are not worth anything at all," he told him.[64]

Though he remained upset about his pay, Joy persisted at Omaha. His job took him throughout the eastern portion of Nebraska, where he paid railroad taxes in counties that could be reached only by stagecoach. As he traveled, he made some extra income from selling Otoe County bonds. By November he told his father that he was also making friends and liked railroading the more he became accustomed to it. He thought of applying for the job of paymaster in the office of the president of the CB&Q.[65]

By the end of the year, Joy had received a 20 percent raise, and on New Year's Day, 1878, J. Sterling proudly entered in his diary the growing annual salaries of each of his three working sons: Paul, now being paid $1,200, Mark, $600, and Joy, "who only left home in August 1877, $720." Then he mused philosophically on the relationship of work, character, and wealth, writing that the three eldest "sons of Arbor Lodge" had exhibited an "education and character" that could provide the world a service, and that they should be able to demand a price that would enable them "to live in comfortable style." J. Sterling noted that Joy (twenty-two), Paul (twenty), and Mark (nineteen), were "mentally and morally developed."[66]

To enhance his social life, Joy became a member of Entre Nous, a dancing and social club whose members were from established families in Omaha. Not surprisingly, this move was an opportunity for J. Sterling to lavish paternal advice, reminding Joy that he had been married when he was twenty-two, Joy's age. The success of his own marriage and popularization of the Darwinian notion of survival of the fittest emboldened him to caution Joy to marry well to assure that his offspring "—in part, a perpetuation of your Mother and Father—may not make my own and your own existence a mistake. . . ." As usual, once begun, J. Sterling felt compelled to press his point: "Select with a view to improving your race," he urged. "Use judgment, taste, common sense of a skilled breeder of domestic animals, who never selects from those afflicted with a diseased ancestry."[67]

Joy responded pointedly: "I have not become enamored of any female of either blonde or brunette complexion and do not propose to until I am making money enough to keep her from starving." He had not received a promised promotion. But he hastened to add that he was not "tired of the business." Joy even petitioned his father—who had recently written that he was expecting to make $10,000 in 1878 with combined income from lobbying for the Atchison, Topeka, and Santa Fe and the CB&Q and from farm proceeds—to put in a word on Joy's behalf with J. Sterling's new employers at the AT&SF.[68]

In June 1878, after being transferred to the freight department of the B&MRR, Joy learned that Paul had been made Assistant General Freight Agent of the CB&Q and would make $150 a month. Even the carefree Mark, who, in Paul's opinion was smart enough but had no temperament for office work and took too much pleasure in smoking cigars he could not afford, had been promoted and his salary raised to the same level that Joy, three years his senior, was making.

For a while longer, Joy tolerated his meager railroad income. He was not only learning a good deal, but he was also having some success selling Otoe County railroad bonds and crops from the farm. There was another reason he was content to remain in Omaha. In spite of his protestation to his father, he had become interested in a young woman by the name of Carrie Lake, the daughter of George B. Lake, a Nebraska Supreme Court judge and his second wife, Zada Poppleton, who died when Carrie was a baby. Both Judge Lake and Zada's brother, A.J. Poppleton, had been long-time political colleagues of J. Sterling. Joy's and Carrie's interest in one another promised to unite three of the most powerful political families in the state.

Joy's social life increased with his courtship of Carrie, once more giving J. Sterling an opportunity to deliver admonitions. While his own preference for fine cigars and expensive brandy gave him an upset stomach, J. Sterling cautioned Joy, who had complained of dyspepsia, to "Eat less and walk more. You have no dyspepsia except by your own imprudence. You inherit none; you invent it for yourself, by over-feeding and over-smoking."[69] Before they were out of their teens, all four of J. Sterling's sons adopted their father's habit of smoking fine cigars. One week before Joy's twenty-third birthday, J. Sterling offered this caveat: "Too much 'society' makes an ass of a man, who otherwise might amount to something in the world; and I have observed many men utterly ruined by too much polite and soft-headed society."[70]

Except for Carrie's presence, Omaha held little interest for Joy. When Carrie was in Chicago during the holidays and left again in February to be with friends in Fremont, Nebraska, Joy spent his free time writing letters. Although he had been the most laconic writer among the Mortons and was often berated for not writing at all, he responded to Carrie's twelve-page gossipy letters immediately and in kind. When his physician found that he was bilious, a problem exacerbated by his discontent with his job more than by smoking or lack of exercise, Joy made light of it, telling Carrie that he was "billiouser than a defeated candidate for alderman. . . . I have now so far recovered that I hope to get down to the office by tomorrow and be as mean as usual by the end of the week. Meanness in our family being indicative of health."[71]

The late winter and early spring offered little to interrupt the attentions Carrie and Joy paid to each other nor to improve his humdrum business life. But in May, one bit of troubling news began to emerge from Arbor Lodge, which was in the process of being enlarged and renovated. J. Sterling wrote to Emma that all were well but Caroline, "who fell down those diabolical stairs—where you lamed yourself—night before last and is quite banged and bruised and crippled. Those stairs are doomed."[72] While any injury to Caroline would be of deep concern to the men of the family, the significance of her fall was not immediately understood. Joy continued on in Omaha, becoming more attached to Carrie, but longing to move ahead in his career.

*T*hen, rather suddenly, Joy's earning power increased and his spirits lifted when he accepted a position with the CB&Q. At the end of May, Paul told Joy of a promising job in Aurora, Illinois, as storekeeper for the CB&Q. It would pay $110. Within days, Joy was the successful applicant and on June 27, 1878, he arrived in Aurora where he found a letter from Carrie waiting for him at the Fitch House, where he was to live. He replied in a lighthearted tone, saying that during a short walk by himself after supper he found that Aurora was a nice place. He was particularly pleased that the Fox River that ran through town was supposed to be a "a good stream for small fish," adding, "The CB&Q runs through the town also and is a good road for small boys to work for."[73]

On the day Joy arrived in Aurora, the Omaha National Bank informed J. Sterling, "You have credit $1,500.00 deposited in Chicago by Joy Morton for your use." Over the years, Joy had saved carefully from his relatively meager farm and bank income. He was now in a position to make a loan to his father, who was in Silver City, New Mexico, looking into a silver mining investment in which he and friends had formed a syndicate. In Aurora Joy quickly made commissions from another Otoe County bond sale of $20,000. He made a loan of $800 to Paul to pay off the mortgage on his farm, and he offered his father an additional loan.[74]

For Joy the loans were a sound investment. He charged interest at the going rate of 10 to 12 percent and clearly stated that the loans could be called in at any time.

Although Joy settled comfortably into the "storekeeping business" and Paul and Mark visited frequently, often staying overnight, his separation from Carrie soon became a matter of concern. Jessie Raddis, a friend of Carrie's and an energetic matchmaker, wrote to him of a complication in his and Carrie's separation. Two other suitors were courting Çarrie. She urged Joy to propose, saying, "If you are as fond of her as I begin to think you are, that is if she will do for the *victim,* why don't you tell her so? Carrie has talked lots to me of late and I tell you Joy it will be all right."[75]

Still, Joy held off. He attended a party at Riverside, Illinois, and sent Carrie the program, along with a detailed account of the hotel and grounds at which the party took place. Situated on the Des Plaines River, Riverside had been laid out by Frederick Law Olmsted and Calvert Vaux only a few years before. Joy was impressed with the surroundings: "The Hotel where these parties are given is composed of two large buildings, of rustic style of architecture, about one hundred feet apart. Between them is a well kept lawn laid out with crooked walks, bordered with flowers in the most approved fashion. Broad porches girt the buildings and from the second story a walk connects the two. In the center of this is a large music stand where on this occasion a band of twenty-five pieces discoursed the music on the programme hereinbefore mentioned."[76] Paul and Mark were there with Joy, as were some other young male friends and a few young women whom Carrie knew. Joy named all the girls with whom he danced in an effort to assure Carrie of his fidelity.

In late summer, Joy had to turn his attention once again to Nebraska City when J. Sterling asked him to help with the development of a co-partnership between himself, T.W. Harvey, the owner of a large Chicago lumber company, and D.P. Rolfe, J. Sterling's friend. Paul, however, told Joy that the venture might jeopardize an account the CB& Q had with a major lumber dealer in Chicago. After talking with Paul, Joy designed a plan for joining the co-partnership himself and making his father a silent partner. In this way, Paul, an employee of the CB&Q, and his father, a consultant for the railroad, had no interest in the venture. When told of the plan, J. Sterling, acting petulantly against Joy's intervention, accused Joy of wanting to make money from his investment. On the eve of his twenty-fourth birthday, Joy replied with an indignant letter to his father, denying that he was trying to compromise his investment. He was also upset that J. Sterling had criticized him for failing to get enough for a recent sale of Otoe bonds. Joy offered to give up his portion of the coupons on the bond sale and protested that he had no intention of making money from his father's investment. "I will go to bed now," he said, "to begin my 25th year feeling like a convicted horse-thief."[77]

J. Sterling replied to Joy's letter with what was for him a profuse apology: "I cheerfully recall every harsh word ever spoken or written to you." He assured Joy that the lumber venture would "be fixed up satisfactorily" and that the bond sale would "be closed amicably," adding, "Do not fret. Do not get sick. Smoke less and you will be less subject to headaches. We are well."[78] A day later, Caroline, a practiced mediator between her husband and sons, attempted to explain J. Sterling's behavior by saying that an unsatisfactory business matter unrelated to the lumber deal had bothered him.

The lumber business opened without further incident, with a notice from D.P. Rolfe that read, "We are now opening out in the Lumber business corner of 6th and Otoe Streets in this city. . . .We have come to stay and mean business, and have NO CONNECTION WHATEVER with any other yard here. . . . D. P. ROLFE & CO." J. Sterling and Joy were silent partners.

In October, Joy joined the family at Arbor Lodge to celebrate his parents' twenty-fifth wedding anniversary. Only Paul missed the event because of work, an absence that J. Sterling found difficult to forgive. On his way back to Aurora, Joy stopped in Omaha and asked George Lake for Carrie's hand, later writing Carrie from Aurora, "How my courage oozed out when I came to ask your father for my wife: how she came in and helped me as she will in life's trials yet to come. All this has been passing through my mind as I sit here gazing into the fire and seems almost a dream. It would be nice if dreams were always so satisfactory and pleasant."[79]

Joy's brothers were delighted with the news of his engagement. Paul bombarded Carrie with puns on Joy's name, saying, "I have heard the news and wish you Joy. . . . Joy has always been my pet brother and I have always greatly admired him and his taste. This last action of his still further excites my imagination."[80] Paul was hinting at his own impending engagement.

Throughout December, Joy exchanged letters almost daily with Carrie while settling contentedly into his life in Aurora. He was happy to tell her that Paul had, indeed, made public his engagement to Charlotte (Lottie) Goodrich of Chicago. For the most part, Joy's letters continued in a tone of repartee that he and Carrie had established with one another. But in response to a question about religion, Joy made clear his position, though delivering it with usual dry humor: "Am glad you don't lay any claims to being a missionary as I do not admire that kind of an animal nor want anything to do with them. Don't think I am hard to talk to you about this thing my dear girl for I think we ought to understand each other thoroughly as I think we do on this."[81]

*A*s usual, Joy continued to look after J. Sterling's affairs at Arbor Lodge, acting as his absentee father's accountant. J. Sterling had gone once again to Silver City, New Mexico, looking into investments in mining for his syndicate. In early December he wrote to Joy, "Try and get my books and figures up by Jan 1st when I hope to arrive at Arbor Lodge."[82] Alone, as she often was, over the holidays with Carl at Arbor Lodge, Caroline wrote plaintively to Joy, who had to work in Aurora, "Christmas has been a sad one."[83] As 1880 began, she continued to be blue, telling Joy, "I think the monotony of life in the suburbs of Nebraska City is enough to wear out the patience of Job," adding that she would like to live "in a real live place just to see how it would seem."[84]

Joy spent the year-end holidays of 1879 apart from Carrie. They contended themselves by describing in detail holiday parties that each attended. The day after Christmas, Joy told Carrie about going to dances in the towns of Sandwich and Joliet, both over twenty miles from Aurora. When Carrie wrote that she attended an Entre Nous Christmas dance three miles outside of Omaha, Joy, displaying a touch of jealousy, told her that she and her friends showed little "common sense" in doing that.

But on the heels of this letter, Joy wrote an unusually lyrical letter that began, "This is a lonesome kind of a night and I have been sitting here in my room looking into the fire and thinking of you for two hours. Do you know that you always appear to me first as you looked after we got home from Minnie Hall's that night always clothed in that maroon dress and sitting and kneeling as you were in that interview," and ended, "I thought then and long after that you were to bless someone else my darling girl and now to be writing to you as I do in this gives me more solid satisfaction than I can possibly express on paper. It is after eleven now and I must get up early so will bid you good night again and retire to sleep, perchance to dream of that maroon dress and its wearer's first kiss."[85] Joy was committed to the woman he would have for his wife, and in expressing that fact to her, he revealed that he knew the language of romance as well as that of business.

Both their sons' engagements delighted J. Sterling and Caroline. From New Mexico where he stayed until spring, J. Sterling wrote a holiday letter to his mother and sister of his and Caroline's pleasure. Their two oldest sons were without debt and, besides their salaries, owned productive farms. He thought Carrie to be "decidedly superior in mind and character but . . . not handsome as to nose." Lottie he pronounced "exceedingly loveable, industrious, accomplished and helpful."[86] J. Sterling was satisfied that his sons were marrying women of good breeding.

Joy, too, was delighted with his marriage prospects. Yet he was now at a time in his life when men of his talent and background were expected to have made their mark, if they were ever going to do so. He had proved capable and diligent at banking, farming, and railroading since leaving school at the age of fifteen, and he had been the mainstay of the family at Arbor Lodge during the prolonged absences of his mother and father. But his illness at eighteen and obligations to the family had kept him from having the freedom to unleash his talents as Paul had done years before. Aurora was a start. But it did not offer the opportunity for running his own business that Joy knew he had prepared himself to do. Before his marriage, however, he would have his chance.

(above) Morton "Ranche" with
Carl Morton, c. 1870.

(left) Joy's parents: J. Sterling
and Caroline Morton, c. 1855.

Nebraska City, c. 1860.

Left to right: Mark, Carl, J. Sterling, Joy, and Paul, c. 1885.

Joy and Carrie, with children Jean and Sterling, c. 1897.

Illinois Central Pier I (end of Randolph), "Boston Town House" office building and warehouse, c. 1897.

Morton Salt Co., replica of Boston Town House and ware–house, Illinois Central Pier I, Chicago, c. 1897.

Pouring salt through roof into Morton Salt Co. warehouse at Illinois Central Pier I, c. 1897.

(*above*) Joy Morton in "Boston Town House" office, Illinois Central Pier I, c. 1900.

(*right*) Morton Salt box.

(above) Originally the Railway Exchange Building. Now known as the Santa Fe Building, designed by D.H. Burnham and Co., 1903–1904, and financed by Standard Office Company, Joy Morton, Chairman. New offices of Joy Morton and Company and D.H. Burnham and Co. Penthouse dedicated to development of the *Plan of Chicago*, 1909. Jim Natchel, photographer.

(right) Joy and salt merchant in the Egyptian Sudan, 1905.

Arbor Lodge, Nebraska City, Nebraska, 1905, after Joy
Morton's final additions.

Dedication of monument to J. Sterling Morton,
Arbor Lodge, 1905.

Top row, left, fourth and fifth from left— **Daniel Peterkin**,
Secretary-Treasurer of Morton Salt, and E.P. Ripley,
president of the Atchison, Topeka, and Santa Fe Railroad.
Top row, middle, left to right—Cleveland's Secretary of
the Interior, **David R. Francis**; **Mrs. Grover Cleveland**;
former president **Grover Cleveland**; Cleveland's Secretary
of the Navy, **Hilary A. Herbert**; and former vice president
Adlai Stevenson. *Bottom row, left side, second and thirdfrom
left*—**E.A. Potter**, president of Chicago's American Trust
and Savings Bank, and **Joy Morton**. *Bottom row, right side,
second, third, fourth, and fifth from left*—**John C. Black**,
president of Chicago's Continental Bank; **Paul Morton**,
president of Equitable Life Assurance Society and former
Secretary of the Navy under Theodore Roosevelt; **Charles
Deere**, president of John Deere & Co.; and **Emma Morton**
(over Deere's left shoulder).

Looking from north side of Lake Marmo to bridge and dam, c. 1925.

Ossian Cole Simonds, landscape advisor for The Morton Arboretum, c. 1922. TMA

Excavating Lake Marmo at Thornhill, 1921.

Thornhill Library, 1925.

Joy and Margaret Gray Morton, at dedication of Arbor Lodge to State of Nebraska, 1923.

Thornhill estate, 1925.

Celebrating Joy's seventieth birthday, Thornhill, September 25, 1925.

(left, standing) Sterling, Margaret Gray, Joy, Mrs. Jeanette Peterkin, Jean Morton Cudahy, and Daniel Peterkin at the same celebration.

72

(right) Telephotograph of Joy, sent in 7½ minutes from New York City to Chicago, November 15, 1925.

(below) Joy's granddaughter Suzette in the May T. Watts Reading Garden, dedication of The Sterling Morton Library, October 22, 1963.

A Place in Chicago—1880–1881

Early in 1880 Paul told Joy that Ezra Wheeler, the owner of the Chicago distribution agency for the Michigan Salt Association, was looking for a junior partner. Paul had been tempted to join with Wheeler, but his pay and prospects with the CB&Q were too promising. Paul knew that Joy could bring to Wheeler's firm experience in banking, transportation, and agriculture along with an understanding of the relationship between marketing and sales. He also thought that the position would give Joy the opportunity he had been seeking to have a say in management. Both Wheeler and Joy were interested.

By Chicago standards, the company known as E.I. Wheeler Co. had enjoyed a long history of success, both planned and serendipitous. The demand for salt by migrants settling west of the Mississippi had been expected. They and their livestock required sodium chloride in their diet, and salt was the principal means of food preservation. Wanting to reach the expanding market to the west, Onondaga Salt of Syracuse, New York, had helped Alonzo Richmond start the sales agency in Chicago in 1848, the year the Illinois and Michigan Canal opened. The waterway provided an economical and efficient means of transporting heavy loads of salt from Chicago to the Illinois River at La Salle and on to Mississippi and Missouri river ports. By the 1860s, emerging railway transportation promised to augment the company's ability to distribute its salt. The Civil War brought an increased demand for salt from producers and suppliers in the North when transportation of salt to northern and western markets from the South was stopped and southern salt producers were targeted by Union forces wanting to cut off the supply of this essential product to the Confederate Army. The development of the Chicago meatpacking industry following the war kept the demand high.

Wheeler entered the company as a partner in 1867 and became its sole owner only a few months before talking with Joy. A decade earlier, the company had ceased handling Onondaga Salt and become the exclusive dealer for salt provided by the Michigan Salt Association, formed by a group of lumbermen in 1870. Both their production method and location gave their salt the edge in the western market. They profited by sinking wells in easily accessed salt springs, extracting the salt brine, and evaporating it with heat fueled by refuse from their mills. They used wood slabs for barrel staves. Soon they improved the quality of their salt by extracting it from deep underground deposits. The finished salt was shipped by steam ship from Ludington, Saginaw, Bay City, St. Clair, and Manistee across Lake Michigan to Chicago.[1]

Joy's accounting experience at James Sweet & Co. and at Arbor Lodge led him to examine Wheeler's books meticulously. Once he was convinced of the stability of the agency, he purchased a one-fifth interest for about $5,000, a sum that five years earlier he had begun to save for just such an opportunity. By his reckoning, his investment and pay—"based on business done for the past five years"—would yield $4,000 to $6,000 a year. Such a job, Joy wrote to Carrie, "is better than railroading by a large majority besides being a perfectly independent position. . . ." Joy could not wait to begin, exclaiming, "I feel as happy as a new sunflower this morning. . . ." He tied up his affairs in Aurora and moved to Chicago the first of May.[2]

Nothing Joy had done in his first ten years of work came close to the promise the salt company held for him. Its facilities stood at the very center of shipping and railway activity that by 1880 linked the country's commercial east and west. The time twenty years earlier when Joy was fascinated by oxen-drawn freight wagons driven by gee-hawing bull whackers was no more. Even his first venture in Chicago five years before must have seemed far distant. The remnants of devastation caused by the Chicago Fire of 1871 had largely disappeared from the inner city, and the Panic of 1873 was yielding to a robust economy. Potter Palmer, one of the city's leading merchants and real estate holders, had rebuilt his small hotel, The Palmer, which had been destroyed by the fire only two weeks after it opened in 1871. Completed in grand style in 1875 and named The Palmer House, it was lighted in 1880 by the city's first incandescent bulbs. Chicago was already established as the nation's railway metropolis, and in the nine years since the fire, it had grown in population from 300,000 to over half a million. Such was the commercial environment that Joy had dreamed of entering on his own terms. He knew he had arrived; to survive he knew he would have to be more diligent than ever before.

A few weeks after becoming a junior partner in the company, Joy informed his father—on letterhead stationery that read "Dealers in Salt, Agents of the Michigan Salt Association, 41 Lake Street: E. I. Wheeler/ Joy Morton"—that the salt business was all that he had hoped for. He was reveling in the long but productive hours and spending his brief moments of leisure with Paul and Mark, with whom he boarded. By June, he was so busy that he informed his mother that he could not visit Arbor Lodge until at least September, the month in which he was to be married in Omaha. "The salt business," he explained, "demands and must have pretty much all of my attention, but as it paid me over $500 last month I can well afford to stay with it."[3]

*C*aroline understood Joy's excuse for not coming to Arbor Lodge. Her experience had led her to believe that if her eldest son were to get ahead, concentrating all of his time on business was his prerogative. Her father had left her in the care of foster parents to pursue business, and during their quarter century together, J. Sterling had spent months away from Arbor Lodge in pursuit of political and entrepreneurial schemes. On the other hand, Joy had made another commitment that placed extra demands on his mother. His absence from Arbor Lodge meant that Caroline had to do all the Morton family preparation for his September wedding to Carrie in Omaha and for Paul's October wedding to Lottie in Chicago.

Although Caroline had not altogether recovered from the injury to her right knee she had suffered in a fall at Arbor Lodge two years before, she eagerly took on the tasks of managing Arbor Lodge and the coming weddings. In July, she entertained her prospective daughters-in-law at Arbor Lodge and later paid her respects to Judge and Mrs. Lake in Omaha. But in Omaha, she aggravated her knee once again when exiting her carriage. At first, the injury did not appear to interfere with her wedding preparations. She kept Joy informed of what she was doing, complaining only that J.

Sterling had absented himself from the "confusion and bustle."[4]

In August, in spite of her severely swollen and aching knee, Caroline accompanied Carrie to Chicago to visit Joy, Paul, Mark, and Lottie and to make final purchases for the wedding. Later, back at Arbor Lodge, she helped Carrie make up the Morton side of the invitation list, stating decisively to Joy on August 24, "You must send to everyone or to no one. And we concluded it would be best to send to no one in *Nebraska City*. There are so many and there someone might be overlooked that would be grievously offended."[5] Joy was pleased not to have the bother. His mother relieved him of details that seemed insignificant compared to his work.

One decision, however, he believed should be his alone. A couple of weeks before the wedding Joy told Carrie that he had chosen a place for them to live in Chicago and expected that she would be pleased. Joy was unused to seeking advice on domestic matters. But Carrie, who lived with a doting father and stepmother, was used to having her desires seriously considered. Joy had rented a house at No. 40 Aldine Square, between 37th and 38th streets, just west of Vincennes Avenue, a place recommended by Paul, who knew the departing tenant. From Chicago he proclaimed proudly to Carrie that he had "gone and done it sure enough." The house was "completely furnished from cellar to garret," he said, "kitchen utensils, furnace, cracking bed clothes, furniture, carpets, and all that goes to make up a well arranged house." As an extra benefit, they could keep the departing tenant's servant until her own could be broken in. Joy was confident: "The family that have been living in it are first class in every respect and you will find no vermin or dirt in the house. . . . I feel as though we had begun to get settled and am sure you will like the house, the locality is good and the square in front is beautiful."[6]

Joy was stunned when he received an angry response from Carrie, scolding him for having made a decision independent of her. Where and how they would live in the city had been of great interest to her, she reminded him. She especially wanted to live in a home where she could place her own household things. But of even greater importance, she also had expected that they could live near Joy's work so that he could join her for lunch at home.

On the defensive Joy explained to Carrie that he had done everything for her benefit. The move, he reminded her, was temporary: "I took this house," he said, "because I thought it would let us get settled at once and by spring we would know how we like housekeeping and . . . would know just what we wanted. . . . " Then, he abruptly shifted to the offensive, saying, "Your letter has sort of put a damper on my ardor," and added sharply, "you must try and make up your mind to like it." They could not at that time afford a house of the sort she wanted, he said, and ended peremptorily: "My time is valuable in the day time. . . ."[7]

Though unsettling in that it defined for the first time their mutual independence if not differences, the dispute did nothing to affect the wedding plans. Their wedding at Trinity Cathedral, Omaha, on September 23, was presided over by the diocesan bishop Robert H. Clarkson, J. Sterling's old friend and the former rector of St. James Cathedral in Chicago from 1848–1863. Carrie and Joy honeymooned at the Grand Pacific Hotel in Chicago; while they were there, Joy let his parents know that Carrie had seen and liked the house and felt that she could manage with but a single servant. He was also happy to report that business "had been exceedingly good" in spite of his few days' absence, with monthly sales larger than ever. "I shall always have to consider Sept 1880 a star month for me," he said with satisfaction.[8] Joy turned twenty-five on September 27th.

$\mathcal{A}$s fall began, there was no reason for Joy to think that his good fortune would not continue. On October 13, the Morton family gathered in Chicago to celebrate Paul and Lottie's marriage at the Universalist Church located between 18th and 20th Streets. The couples began setting up their respective households near one another on the south side, and when business demands allowed, they participated in the city's cultural life. Carrie's transition from Omaha to Chicago was smoothed somewhat by the fact that railway transportation between the two cities gave her the opportunity to return home for a few days when she felt lonely.

Joy, too, kept close ties to Nebraska, but for a different reason. Claims on his time by both the salt company and married life did not keep him from having to look after his father's financial affairs for, as usual, J. Sterling was otherwise occupied. He had been outraged by the victory of the Republican Rutherford B. Hayes over the Democrat Samuel J. Tilden when the popular vote went to Tilden but Hayes won by a single vote in what was widely considered to be a manipulation of the Electoral College. In the wake of what J. Sterling believed to have been a fraudulent election and hopeful gains by Democrats that followed in the midterm, J. Sterling broke his vow to avoid politics. During the 1880 election year, he accepted the chairmanship of the Nebraska State Democratic Central Committee and membership on the national committee, thus adding greatly to his time absent from Arbor Lodge.

With J. Sterling tending to the upcoming election, which would yield yet another defeat of the Democratic slate by the Republican ticket of

James A. Garfield and Chester A. Arthur, Joy inquired of the son of P.W. Hitchcock, J. Sterling's old friend, whether he and his father would sell their interest in mica mines to his father's syndicate. Even during the heat of the campaign, J. Sterling was planning another prospecting trip with friends to Silver City, New Mexico, where in 1870 silver had been discovered just forty miles north in the Black Range. By early November 1880, J. Sterling was ready to leave for New Mexico, from which he did not expect to return until the following January.

J. Sterling asked Caroline to accompany him, but she declined, reminding him that someone had to stay behind to manage Arbor Lodge. When he departed, she communicated to Joy with unusual candor about what she thought of his father's passions. She expected him to succeed in making "lots of money," having known him to be successful in most of what he did, "*except in politics.*" Politics, she said, "always did *pull* him down and make him lose money and almost his identity." J. Sterling's predictable defeats for office had convinced her that politics were "a curse to a respectable man, as nobody succeeds in them except the most unprincipled." Certain that Joy agreed with her, she said, "We want no more."[9]

Caroline concluded with a despondent plea to Joy. She did not want to face the coming holidays at Arbor Lodge with only two young children present. Carl would, she said, be joined by Della Chandler. As Mrs. French had done for her, Caroline had taken Della into her care in 1879 as a favor to a widowed male friend of the family. She hoped that her three sons in Chicago could join them, if only for Christmas dinner.[10]

The unusual moodiness of her letter resulted from more than the prospect of facing the holidays without her family. The pain in her knee had worsened. When her sons and daughters-in-law were able to visit Nebraska City during the holidays, they became seriously concerned. Paul sent word to his father that Caroline felt "very little better" as far as her stiff leg was concerned.[11]

On New Year's Day 1881, Caroline received word from J. Sterling that symptoms of rheumatism in his arm had kept him from corresponding over the holidays with his usual regularity. She replied with an irony that seemed to have little effect: "I . . . hope your rheumatism is not preventing you from writing. It is very painful anywhere but I think I had rather have it in my left arm than right leg."[12] In a plaintive letter to Joy, J. Sterling compounded the irony of his seeking sympathy for his own health while Caroline's painful condition persisted. He told Joy that he would make some money from his investment in mines and land grants in New Mexico but that there was a good chance he would not live to see the results. In the event of his "sudden death," he wanted Joy to know everything about his affairs so that they could be arranged for Caroline's "protection." His rheumatism, he said, troubled him, and he complained of the abominable weather, "snow or slush."[13]

As usual, Caroline was determined to keep busy in spite of her pain. In early January, she and Della journeyed over forty miles to Omaha in her carriage so that Della could visit her father. While there, Caroline stopped to see Carrie, who had remained in Nebraska with her parents after the holidays. But following a harrowing trip back to Nebraska City in a snowstorm, Caroline took to her bed. She told Joy that she would be unable to come to Chicago to see Sarah Bernhardt, the most famous actress of the Gilded Age, perform in Alexandre Dumas's *La Dames aux Camélias*, something she had been determined to do.[14]

Although they were concerned about Caroline's persistent pain, Joy and Paul remained optimistic about her recovery. At Arbor Lodge to see about his mother, Paul was more interested in telling Joy about names he had thought of for new hunting dogs they each had purchased: "The dogs I spoke about . . . are not slim ones so I do not think that Bernhardt would be a very good name for one of them." Then, punning on Joy's new occupation, he quipped, "'Salty'—I think that that is a good name for queer kinds of animals."[15] That nickname would stick with Joy, though only intimates would ever dare to use it.

When he returned to Arbor Lodge in mid-January, J. Sterling was surprised to find Caroline much worse than he had thought. He complained to Joy that her trip to Omaha had been "a terrible mistake and set back the convalescence two or three weeks. She is suffering much pain and, this morning, is quite despondent and blue."[16] Less than a month later, however, J. Sterling, thinking Caroline had improved, left Arbor Lodge for New Mexico again. This time he bore an inventory of his holdings prepared by Joy and a written agreement that he could, in the name of the syndicate, "purchase, lease, bond, and otherwise secure title to an interest in and control" of mining property in the Black Range. In late February from Santa Fe, he wrote Joy, "Things are so promising here I do not wish to leave for some time except upon the most urgent business."[17] His excitement over the prospects of making a fortune in the Black Range was so great that he overlooked the fact that Caroline was not able to travel. He asked her, "Would it not be well to take Carl and come to Las Vegas?"[18]

J. Sterling did not anticipate going home before April, although he urged Caroline to wire him if she needed him. Caroline continued to downplay the seriousness of her illness. When J. Sterling complained of a cold, she sent descriptions of various potions he might take to ease its symptoms. But when he learned in March that Caroline was unable to dress herself and was eating nothing but broth, Sterling returned home. Bedridden, Caroline was attended to night and day by servants and by her good friend Mrs. D.P. Rolfe. A shocking deterioration in Caroline's condition had occurred during his six weeks' absence, J. Sterling discovered. He would not leave her side again.

For the next three months, Caroline's illness occupied the minds and emotions of the family. On the day after Joy left on a weeklong business trip to the west coast at the end of March, Carrie reassured him of his mother's health in a telegram, saying simply, "Dear Old Saltie. All well."[19] But in April, J. Sterling brought in a doctor from Chicago and one from Omaha to advise the Nebraska City doctors on Caroline's condition. They could find no permanent treatment for her constant pain, now complicated by bedsores and bouts of delirium.

Emma Morton, J. Sterling's sister, arrived from Detroit in late March to take care of both Caroline and her brother. Sensing the end was near, J. Sterling said in his customary birthday letter to his mother, "This is a sad birthday letter, written so near, I am shuddering to think—the Death Day of my loved and petted Carrie the wife of my youth, the consolation of my life, and the mother of my four noble sons. There is no hope in my soul. . . ."[20]

While J. Sterling remained at Caroline's bedside, Joy and his brothers did all they could to keep both him and their mother interested in life away from Arbor Lodge. In one of many letters to her, Joy told his mother that Ezra Wheeler, who was in New York, had no reason to hurry home to Chicago, because the business was running smoothly under his direction. He also told her of his and Carrie's new apartment at 3653 Vincennes, near where they had first lived in Aldine Square. Joy continued to try to bolster his mother's spirits, telling her that he had talked with one of her doctors who had been positive about her recovery. In Chicago, he assured her, all was well. Mark's and Paul's business prospects were steadily improving, and Carrie was healthy and "busily engaged" in getting their new residence prepared for their move. Carl, who was staying in Chicago with his brothers during Caroline's illness, was enjoying himself and had been a good boy who stayed out of mischief.[21] To his father, Joy wrote of business, saying that he and Wheeler might be interested in joining him in his speculation by "taking hold of the thing ourselves if the mica is as good as any, and handling it as a sort of side show."[22]

These letters were but diversions from the inevitable. By the end of May, J. Sterling told Paul that the circumference of Caroline's knee was 21¾ inches "and very obstinate."[23] Desperate, J. Sterling set his sons about the task of making inquiries in Chicago of people who had used homeopathic approaches to cure symptoms similar to Caroline's. On one of Caroline's increasingly rare good days, J. Sterling asked Joy to find a trained nurse in Chicago, "one who will obey instructions implicitly and give no medicine except 'on time' as directed by the Doctor."[24] Sensing that the end was near, Joy hurried to Arbor Lodge. He was the only son at his mother's bedside when she died on June 29, 1881, at the age of forty-seven. J. Sterling was emotionally unable to function. It was up to Joy to make the funeral arrangements.

J. Sterling's inability to cope with Caroline's death held immediate consequences for all the Mortons, but most of all for Joy. Joy and Carrie returned to Chicago the first week in July, leaving J. Sterling in the care of his mother and sister Emma. J. Sterling wrote to Joy, berating himself for not having attended St. Mary's Episcopal Church when Caroline wanted him to. Then, providing his usual object lesson to Joy, he warned him, "And when your Carrie—your wife—indicates that your attendance with her at Church will gratify her, fail not, with alacrity, to accompany her. Then you will be better than I have been and will have, if she goes first, one less regret. . . ."[25] Though secular by choice, Joy was patient with his father's gratuitous advice, for he knew it came out of J. Sterling's deep despondency and guilt.

Joy set about helping his father regain an interest in life, beginning by finding a sculptor in Chicago who could fashion a stone image of a blighted tree for the grave site in Nebraska City's Wyuka Cemetery, where Caroline was buried near her foster mother, Cynthia French. The tree would signify not only the emptiness that Caroline's death held for J. Sterling but also her centrality as the matriarch of the family. J. Sterling had the idea that the burial plot would one day contain the remains of all of his and Caroline's extended family, and he had his sons' names carved into the stone, with the stipulation that if any of his sons dishonored Caroline in any way, the name would be removed. As a distraction for his father, Joy informed him of the details of his work and life in Chicago, as he had done with his mother in the weeks before she died. Of the salt business he wrote, "Last week sales were over 40,000 barrels—550 cars—how is that?"[26]

But J. Sterling was inconsolable and failed to react even when Joy urged him to become interested once again in a New Mexico mining venture. He insisted on staying at Arbor Lodge, where Caroline's agonizing death had played out, thinking that he, too, might soon follow her to the grave. He revised his will, naming Joy as his executor and the guardian of Carl, who was sixteen. Joy would also become the sole owner of Arbor Lodge, which would be under a deed of entail, assuring that it could not be sold and would, J. Sterling, believed, "be always the home of a Morton descended from my marriage with your dear and perfect Mother."[27]

Joy's response was sympathetic but firm. Addressing his father as an equal, he assured him that he would never allow "strangers" to occupy Arbor Lodge, thinking it to be a more appropriate monument to his mother than the stone tree that would stand over Caroline's grave. Arbor Lodge is, Joy said, "a living monument to her taste, industry, and indomitable pluck, made as it was out of the desert, so to speak, and outside of her love and tender care of us all, seems to represent, and does, a large part of her life and work." But while promising J. Sterling that he would fulfill the trust "squarely to the letter," Joy urged him not to become "discouraged and blue." He reminded him that J. Sterling was still young and "a very strong man physically and intellectually. . . ." It was, Joy said, time for J. Sterling to return to the person he had been before "this terrible affliction." Then, using an argument his father had often used with him over the years, he urged his father, "Do it for her sake."[28]

Joy did not just implore his father to renew his interest in life: he had practical suggestions that he thought might help him do so. He asked J. Sterling to come to Chicago, suggesting that he might "connect himself with the *Times* or do something of that kind which would occupy your mind and relieve you somewhat of the melancholy, which, given full sway might be too hard to bear."[29] He even offered to purchase a house in Chicago in a location J. Sterling might pick or to have his father live with Carrie and him, saying that they would all return each summer to Arbor Lodge.

J. Sterling resisted going to Chicago. But at one point in the summer, he had thought that if he had to leave Arbor Lodge, even for a short time, he would have to "lock up." He asked Joy to have "a lot of door key tags, metallic, stamped" to all the rooms in the house. When Joy did not send them immediately, J. Sterling became petulant: "I need tags for door keys . . . and I want them *now*."[30] Concerned by his behavior, Paul sent him an expensive box of Havana cigars and, as Joy had done, urged him once again to write for the *Times*. Mark, who was unattached and loved farming, offered to give up his railroad job in Chicago and return to manage Arbor Lodge, since Carl would soon be going to work and J. Sterling would then be alone.

$\mathscr{B}$y August, Joy had a great deal more than his father to think about. Unable to adjust to Chicago's humidity and pollution, Carrie fell ill and had gone to Omaha to convalesce at her father's home. Soon Judge Lake wrote to Joy saying that Carrie had dysentery and that the doctor thought it was "superinduced by malarial influences, perhaps of long standing."[31] Joy was unable to visit either Carrie or his father, because, as he explained to J. Sterling, his partner also was ailing and was taking a trip to the Eastern seacoast with his wife. Aware that he might have to be absent more frequently because of his health, Wheeler had encouraged Joy to become a member of the Board of Trade so that the firm would have constant representation. Through Wheeler's connections, Joy was able to buy a seat from an estate at about half the $2,500 cost, leading him to rationalize the purchase to his father: "Prospect is that it will be a good investment even if I should not use it. Besides this it gives me standing among businessmen and is, altogether, a good thing to do. I had the money and have paid for it myself."[32]

On the day that he wrote to his father, Carrie, who was recovering her health, penned a stern rebuke to Joy almost a year after the first angry letter she had written before their marriage. The topic was similar, but this time she was more decisive. Without consulting her, Joy had begun to discuss with Paul and Lottie where they would live when they were able to build their own places, which they were thinking of doing in the near future. Joy and Paul decided that it would be a good idea to set up housekeeping together or in houses next door to one another. Carrie was adamantly opposed, telling Joy that she thought it was a topic that "would not have to be discussed again in our family." She was clear on the subject: "If ever such a mode of living as you write of is adopted by yourself and Paul, it will be directly against my wishes." Her reasons, she said, could wait until she returned to Chicago. She would then "speak plainly on the subject" to Joy—and Paul and Lottie, should they wish to listen. "To you dearie," she added scornfully, "I would say that I am a little surprised that you should agree with them so perfectly in all these new arrangements before saying anything to me in the matter and thus put me to all the blame of a refusal etc." Still, she ended the letter by admitting how "very *very* harsh" it had been "to be ill and away" from Joy.[33]

The duty fell to Lottie to tell J. Sterling that plans for Joy, Paul, and their wives living in proximity were not going forward, saying, "All things considered, I presume it is best that we should not go to housekeeping together, but it is more or less disappointing as we looked forward to having you visit us all with so much pleasure." She and Paul, she said, were "nicely fixed," and she hoped that Joy and Carrie could soon find "a house or flat to suit them."[34]

The day before his twenty-sixth birthday, Joy informed his father that he and Carrie might move and be "quite near 'St. James,' Bishop Clarkson's old church, when we get into our flat . . ." adding—to please his father—that they would "take a pew and try and be regular in attendance on Sunday mornings."[35] But by October, Joy wrote that they had failed to get the flat on the near north side and that they would likely stay where they were through the winter. He persisted in thinking, in spite of Carrie's opposition, that it might be a good idea if he and Paul built two small houses next door to one another. He still could not comprehend Carrie's reluctance to set up housekeeping with Paul and Lottie. Finally, anxious to have a place of their own, they settled on a row house already being constructed on Oakwood Boulevard. Carrie took personal control of the details.

$\mathcal{B}$y October 1881, J. Sterling felt that he could travel to Omaha to preside over the Democratic state convention, which, in a nonelection year, had only perfunctory duties. The event helped him recover his interest in public and business affairs. The next month Joy and J. Sterling's friends from the syndicate were successful in interesting him once again in the "Surprise" mine in which they had invested in the Black Range. Joy and Wheeler, as promised, put a small amount in the syndicate, and Joy tried to convince his father to give the venture more of his personal attention on-site. Joy was concerned that the investors were not being told everything they needed to know about the progress of the mine.

At first, during a lengthy visit with other investors, J. Sterling exhibited his usual optimism about how much the New Mexico mine would return on their investment. Writing to Joy from New Mexico in late November, he mused about using his share to build a chapel at the Wyuka Cemetery for the use "of all the people," describing in detail the way he would design the building, if only he lived until the following year. Although he was in good health, he implored Joy, "Should I die away from Arbor Lodge you must have my poor remnant taken home to Wyuka and placed beside the grave of your Mother."[36] Soon, however, J. Sterling learned that the mine manager had lied to him and his fellow investors and that they would be lucky to come out even. Joy considered this a learning experience for his father, one that would help make him more acutely aware of the necessity of investigating entrepreneurial investment opportunities as thoroughly as possible before engaging in them. It was a lesson his father had always been slow to learn or at least to remember.

J. Sterling returned to Arbor Lodge by Christmastime, but Joy was unable to visit him as he had to close Wheeler & Co.'s 1881 books, a task he considered of crucial importance and one on which he focused assiduously. Joy explained to his father that his brothers would also have to attend to business. Paul had gone to St. Louis with E.P. Ripley and Mark to Akron, Ohio. Carrie was keeping a close watch on the construction of the Oakwood Boulevard house that was to be finished the following week, and Carl was with her. Joy hoped his father could visit them there by the end of January.[37] Ironically, J. Sterling, who often had been away from his family on business during holidays, was alone at Arbor Lodge, although he visited friends in town and attended church. Predictably, he fell into a deeper melancholy. Shortly before the end of the year, he recorded in his farm journal, "These six months have been like a long nightmare, a hideous dream, an aberration, indescribable." On New Year's Eve, just before retiring, he entered into the journal, "What a year! And it is going out in gloom here at Arbor Lodge where I alone muse mournfully tonight . . ."[38] While the year had been difficult for Joy, too, he was ready to meet the challenge of being depended upon more than ever before. He would need to work within the confines of his father's depression, Carrie's adjustment to Chicago, and Wheeler's uncertain health. Still, he remained confident that his marriage and his move to Chicago had been the right decisions.

*W*ith the beginning of 1882, J. Sterling seemed once again to take an interest in life. He did not visit Joy and Carrie in their new lodgings on Oakwood Boulevard, but with the encouragement of Joy and Paul, he briefly considered the *Chicago Times* position again. Finally, he arranged for his mother and sister Emma to come live with him at Arbor Lodge.

On Arbor Day, April 22, 1882, J. Sterling's fiftieth birthday, Joy took the opportunity to encourage his father to view the past and future with a fresh perspective. In an eight-page letter that revealed Joy had not forgotten his classical education nor his father's insistence on good writing, he gave a bucolic account of his childhood in Nebraska City, knowing that the lyrical and intimate litany of events would raise his father's spirits.

Boyhood with its many little trials and lots of fun, of which our dear good Grandma has so enjoyed telling us of the next generations; youth, with its happy days at Albion where the love began which made us all; the Bridal Trip to the new Territory and the winter at the Trading Post, this ostracism from civilization and society showing the pure, brave devotion of our dear dead Mamma, must make bright the morning of the past. . . .

I remember as far back I believe as 1860, when Wm Pray was with us, how Paul and I went with him to the Major's farm once for a load of corn and I drove the horses part of the way and made little Paul awfully envious—then a little later how quickly Joe Burton was permitted to become a raw recruit in the service of our Uncle Samuel because we asked at dinner one day, 'What sort of stuff' some minute pudding was. I remember perfectly well when a man named Mullen plowed the now old orchard with a yoke of oxen because he could plow all of the ground by letting the trees pass under the yoke and between the cattle. . . .

Then Paul's speeches, the yoke of calves we used to have, old Brutus our companion in many a juvenile expedition 'way over in the woods,' the time Paul got stuck in the creek and the time you and Lyman Richardson cut off our curls, when their protector was in town—how frightened I was once when Mark, who was stealing a ride on the tongue of an empty 'Pikes Peak' wagon, hitched behind another and on its way into town to load west, in trying to jump off 'like a bull whacker' missed his footing and was run over by the front wheel of the wagon—I remember though I was speedily relieved by seeing him do some lively crawling soon as the front wheel had passed over his shoulder, to prevent the rear wheel taking the same course. After he got out and found he was unhurt he bawled loud and long.

Once we all went 'swimming' in the little frog pool we called 'Golden's Pond' (over on the Gilman place) and after each had gotten as much mud on himself as was possible and got his clothes on over it we thought we would, just for fun, see how the baby (Carl) would like the pond, so we took him to the top of the hill in his carriage and then let it take a back shoot into the water. One trial led us to think the baby did not enjoy his bath that way and an administration of 'hickory oil' and 'elbow grease' upon our arrival home convinced us all that the baby was correct in his views.

To any one but our selves all these little things would no doubt seem very trivial but by us they will always be remembered, and often these young 'old times' are talked over. They don't amount to much in themselves but they all happened on the old farm and now it begins to seem as though everything that ever occurred to us then, when we were little shavers, was replete with happiness, even to a thrashing. The most satisfactory of the latter, to the other boys, was one you gave me once, you being in a hurry and not stopping to get particulars of a disturbance, when <u>they</u> deserved it. This is often related by our fair-haired brother as one of the pleasantest little incidents of our boyhood.[39]

The letter accomplished its purpose. J. Sterling sent it to his old friend and fellow journalist, Dr. George B. Miller, asking that it be returned "to the proud father of this writer," and he later told Joy that it was the best letter that he had ever written.[40] Joy took pleasure in remembering his early life in Nebraska City and Arbor Lodge, and he did so often when he felt that audiences needed to be reminded of his agrarian past. Like the letters he wrote to Carrie, its tone was far different from the language of business in which he had become accustomed to conversing daily. What is remarkable is that at a time when he was so thoroughly surrounded by the cacophony of the marketplace, he could close the door and write reflectively on topics that he expected would bring comfort to his father.

CHAPTER 4

Joy Morton & Co.—1882–1887

By 1882, Joy had been at Wheeler & Co. for two years, during which time his intention to make the business his absolute center of attention had been challenged by commitment to family and his investments in Nebraska City; yet, during Wheeler's increasing absences, those who dealt with the company came to regard Joy as the person in charge. He was now occupied not only by the day-to-day supervision of the office, storage, and shipping, but also by traveling to secure new markets. From Kansas City in May 1882, he gave his father an account of having spent six of ten nights in sleeping cars while on a profitable business trip.[1] But there was a cost to his success.

Carrie was not sanguine about Joy's increased involvement in the business. Mark told his father that Carrie had been especially put out when Joy left abruptly on the westward trip at a time that an Omaha relative was coming to visit. Since his own domestic life had been defined by coming and going in the name of business and politics, J. Sterling proceeded to counsel Joy in his old familiar manner about how he saw the situation: "I am glad your business improves and that you are happy in your domestic and other social relations. There is nothing in this world to equal the comfort and solace of a quiet and pleasant home where one's going makes regrets and coming causes smiles and gladness."[2]

What mattered most to J. Sterling was that his sons continue to succeed and be close to one another and him. Paul and Mark were flourishing with the railroad. When Paul and Lottie's first child was born on June 29, 1882, J. Sterling was thrilled that they named her Caroline. Encouraged by J. Sterling, Carl, still at Arbor Lodge, asked Joy for a job in his office. Joy's fortunes were rapidly advancing, and given the pattern of the Morton commitment to help each other, he was poised to respond favorably to Carl's query.

But Joy's willingness to help his family was limited by his growing monetary investment in the salt company. Since the purchase in 1855 of the property on which Arbor Lodge was located, real estate had long been a focus of investment for J. Sterling and his sons. By 1880, Joy, Paul, and J. Sterling together owned over 1,200 acres whose value with improvements amounted to more than $50,000. Joy's 160 acres were worth approximately $2,000; Paul's, unimproved, a little less. When J. Sterling asked Joy for a loan in August 1882 to purchase a nearby piece of farmland, Joy had the cash to lend and was disposed to do so—but with a strict stipulation. He wanted the money returned in sixty days because at the end of the year, he said, "I propose to put all the money I have into the salt business and I shall therefore call on you for the balance, besides advance now to be made."[3]

As usual, intra-family loans were strictly negotiated at the going market rate. In this case it was 8 percent, and Joy cautioned his father: "In regard to our corn trade I want to notify you that I cannot stand any deductions, when corn is shelled, for rottage, rotten corn or loss of any kind, in consequence of its being held six months in the crib after I sold it."[4] Joy was all business, but J. Sterling was not to be outdone. Accepting the loan as "entirely satisfactory," he noted, "I have some taxes and charges against you which will be duly deducted; and I bought of you one thousand bushels of corn or as much over or under as you had at 50 cents a bushel. I shall charge you nothing, nor make any deduction for rats or heated corn."[5]

*O*ne of the clearest indications that J. Sterling had returned to his old self was that in September 1882 he accepted a draft to become the Democratic candidate for governor of Nebraska. Neither he nor his sons thought he had a chance of winning, but it was a sure way of distracting him from mourning Caroline, and it gave him a platform to talk about issues that were dear to him, such as free trade and sound money—both, he believed, requiring the absence of government intervention in the economy. Joy hoped that his father would "show that there is still some life in the party," asking him not to "follow the course of most of the Nebraska nominees of late years and accept about as a man would his death sentence and then sit down and wait for the inquest." He was prepared to help his father go all the way and offered to pay the salary of a full-time stenographer who could not only take shorthand but who also was able to perform on a new technology, the typewriter.[6] J. Sterling accepted.

For the next two months, J. Sterling used the typewriter and its operator to deluge newspapers and politicians with his ideas. Still the effort was not enough to propel him to victory. J. Sterling's message of free trade, Joy consoled him after the election, would eventually "fetch the Nebraska Grangers sooner or later sure."[7] If the typewriter did not serve for a political win, it nevertheless had emboldened Carl to learn to type enough to send Joy a gentle reminder of his availability, saying, "If you would like to hire a good type writer I am your man."[8]

In November, Joy announced to his father that he and Carrie would "increase cares and responsibilities of Grand-papa by at least one half—possibly, Carrie thinks, two thirds."[9] Carrie was four months pregnant, lending urgency to Joy's desire for cash, not just to invest in the salt business but also to build a home for his family. He even went in with his father once more on another mining venture in New Mexico, this time on the basis of a favorable on-site report of a member of the mining syndicate. Both were hoping for a bonanza. But Joy never counted on luck. His father now owed him $5,000 at a fixed interest rate of 8 percent, and Joy and Paul, who was now First Assistant General Freight Agent for the CB&Q, were hoping to sell their farms in Nebraska and build larger houses in Chicago for their families. By the end of 1882, Joy had invested a total of $15,000 in the firm.[10]

Joy was also considering expanding into other businesses. He, Wheeler, Paul, and Mark (who had left the CB&Q to sell lumber for T.W. Harvey of Chicago) were looking into raising a herd of cattle in New Mexico, an enterprise that some Chicagoans, including Gustavus Swift, the head of the meatpacking company, then known as Swift Brothers, later Swift and Company, were already engaged in. This time it was J. Sterling, in a letter to Joy, who offered his sons cautious advice, attempting to dissuade them from the cattle venture: ". . . the Salt business is good enough for you, and Railroad for Paul is also healthy while Lumber for Mark will give a good return. One vocation until you are forty will occupy each of you and after that age—if you have spare money—you can branch out. Make haste slowly in your endeavor to secure comforts and a fortune for your family."[11]

The cattle venture did not materialize. But J. Sterling's advice to focus on but one enterprise at time—similar to that his own father had given him thirty years before when he was in both politics and journalism—was heeded by Joy as much as all of J. Sterling's sons heeded their father's continuing warnings about smoking. Their love of fine cigars sold by G.W. Faber of New York rivaled that of their father's.

*O*n April 27, 1883, Carrie gave birth to their daughter, Jean. Joy welcomed the child enthusiastically, but at the time of her birth, he found himself more deeply involved in work than ever as Wheeler became less and less able to attend to business. Complicating matters, Joy, who had hired Carl, had hoped to rely on him to keep the books. Carl, then eighteen, was older than the other brothers had been when they had gone to work, but he was also much less robust. Carl had, in fact, grown up in a far different way from his older brothers, who had been companions and competitors at sports and on the farm. They were gone from home by the time he reached his teens. A few weeks before Carl took the job at Wheeler & Co., his father had accused him of being interested in nothing but baseball. Carl responded wittily from Detroit, where he was studying at Mayhew's Business College, that he was in fact busy reading Lesbian poets (among them Sappho) and Shakespeare, as well as doing algebraic formulas.[12]

At Wheeler & Co., Carl was in a far different world than he had known as a child and student. Chastised by his father for not writing regularly to him, Carl informed J. Sterling that it was impossible for him to write every day. "I am too busy," he complained. "I have to be at the office at 7.20 every morning and stay until 6 o'clock at night, and I am busy from the time I get here until I leave for home. Our 'Bill Clerk' is sick with typhoid fever, and will not be at the office for a month probably."[13] J. Sterling concluded that Carl was being mistreated at Wheeler & Co., and, unwisely, he decided to intercede. Carl had appealed to his father to do just that.

Joy was prepared. Early in 1884, J. Sterling told Joy that he was paying Carl too little and working him too hard. Joy's response left no doubt that in the matter of his business, he would tolerate no outside interference, even from his father. After carefully explaining to his father that he would not be forced into a position of having to give Carl automatic raises, he reminded him that the $45.00 Carl was getting per month (including salary and board) was within $5.00 of what he had been paid at the age of twenty-three and with seven years' more experience at the Burlington and Missouri Railroad. Joy let J. Sterling know that if he continued his complaint on behalf of Carl, he would "prefer that he was with some other house." Joy ended his letter to his father definitively: "Whatever conclusion you arrive at please advise me promptly for if there is to be any change we want it made now and not when the season's business gets fairly started. If he stays we want it understood that it is to be during the year."[14] The letter, signed by both Joy and Wheeler, was strictly business.

Flabbergasted, J. Sterling, in Washington, D.C., on railroad business, made notes in the margins of Joy's letter, that read, "And I paid Joy $500 a year & board for farm labor when he was 14 to 20 years of age." Then on the back of Joy's letter he wrote to Paul, "I have answered the within and send it to you to keep and read. When I get to Chicago I will take it home to keep, and meantime I ask you to help Carl get away from Joy, where he will, I am afraid—never do well, as he may elsewhere."[15]

Paul immediately sided with Joy, explaining to his father that Joy and Carl cared for one another but that "business between relatives and friends is much more satisfactory when conducted on business principles than when transacted on other grounds." Paul then launched into a strident defense of Joy and a criticism of his father. If there were a "row in the family," he said, J. Sterling was the "prime mover." In his remarks to Paul, J. Sterling had hinted at retaliation against Joy for his treatment of Carl. Paul angrily concluded, "For myself, I can't help but think that you keep on treating Carl as the baby of the family while you want Joy to treat him as a man and that in doing it you are spoiling Carl & worrying Joy."[16] Mark, too, had entered the fray by convincing Carl to stay with Joy. The brothers stood united, as they had been from childhood. Over the years Joy would have ample occasion to return their support.

The uneasiness that lingered between Joy and his father was somewhat abated by their having to deal together with the dissolution of the lumber partnership among D.P. Rolfe, J. Sterling, and T.W. Harvey, for whom Mark was selling lumber. In early March, Joy, who had himself invested in the partnership, stepped in to handle the sale to Harvey of one of the D.P. Rolfe lumber holdings, writing to J. Sterling that "I am surprised and disgusted at the showing the yards made for last year."[17] Sensing that J. Sterling was still not reconciled with Joy, however, Paul once again felt it necessary to come to Joy's defense. He told his father that Joy was doing everything he could and that "the Carl difficulty" had eased. Carl was now, Paul seemed to think, content with both his job and his boardinghouse. Once again, Paul told his father, "the Morton family appears happy." He closed by asking his father to abandon any idea that Joy might have ill-treated him or that he should have handled Carl in any way other than he had.[18]

J. Sterling apparently heeded Paul's admonishment. After all, Paul, who was only twenty-seven, had gained national recognition for a startlingly successful railroad career. As First Assistant General Freight Agent for the Chicago Burlington & Quincy Railroad Company, he was making $4,800 a year and had thousands of miles of track under his personal supervision. (He had just turned down a higher-paying passenger position because passenger traffic held "no charms" for him.) And Joy, too, after only four years at Wheeler & Co., was becoming recognized as one of the country's savviest salt men and was making his investment in the company pay handsomely. Both of his elder sons, still in their twenties, could reason as equals with their father as men who had made the most of the considerable responsibilities that they had willingly accepted.

*T*he spring of 1884 found Joy once more balancing the demands of business and family. Carrie, "gaining rapidly with help of Hoff's Malt Extract," was recovering from a miscarriage. Joy was happy to spend time with their daughter, writing to his father, "Jean is as well as it is possible for mortal mites to be and is almost ready to walk. She is developing into a good fighter and has a set to with her cousin every day or two." He also was overseeing the move of the Wheeler & Co. office to 13 Lake Street, which, he said, in contrast to the dank office at 41 Lake Street where he had started four years earlier, would give "plenty of light and lots of air."[19] Not finding the time on April 22 to pen a long letter of the sort he had written J. Sterling two years earlier on his milestone birthday, Joy greeted his father on his fifty-second with a congratulatory telegram.

In other correspondence, however, Joy discussed their common interest in the coming presidential election. Joy was convinced that business and politics were closely intertwined, explaining to his father, "In trade an axiom is that competition is life. Likewise politics, so long as the prospect of your party's success is but dim at best, a little 'opposition' it would seem to me would act about the same way—make the game more interesting."[20] In 1884, Joy attended both the Republican and Democratic national conventions held in Chicago, the latter nominating Grover Cleveland, the eventual winner of the election and the first

Democrat to be elected to that office since the Civil War. In spite of its being a Democratic victory, Cleveland had not at first appealed to J. Sterling or to Joy, mainly because he was not as strong on free trade as Senator Thomas Bayard, J. Sterling's preferred candidate, seemed to be.

Joy turned easily from thoughts of politics to his pleasure in his daughter, Jean, writing, "She walked up to the end of the block and back without my having hold of her—don't you think this is pretty good work for a little tot not thirteen months old until tomorrow." Showing that he had his father's fondness for children, Joy proudly added that Jean was "as cute as it is possible for such a mite of humanity to be and is growing splendidly, has never been sick except a little while cutting teeth." Carrie, too, was doing well, Joy reported.[21]

Upon his return to Arbor Lodge from Chicago, J. Sterling, emboldened by the apparent Democratic strength on the national level, decided to try politics once again, this time to run as a "fusion" candidate for governor of Nebraska where he would represent a coalition of Democrats and anti-monopolists against the Republicans. In doing so, he might have appeared to be following Joy's view that running for office, even though his success was doubtful, would give the opposition competition and would allow him once again a statewide forum for his political views. Yet in this instance, the probability of J. Sterling's success was so low and his expedient relationship with the anti-monopolists—who argued for regulation of big business—so politically unsavory that neither Joy nor Paul found the prospect of his candidacy a good thing.

Both Joy and Paul sent letters advising J. Sterling against standing for election, and they specifically urged him against becoming associated with the "anti-monop." Instead, they thought it would be best if he were to run for Congress while lending his support to another gubernatorial candidate. As usual, however, J. Sterling was determined, thinking that his candidacy could possibly upset the Republicans and that he could speak selectively, airing only those views of the fusion platform that he endorsed. He and the anti-monopolists were anti-tariff and anti-Republican, but the anti-monopolists were for government regulation and he for laissez-faire. The combination failed miserably. J. Sterling, as everyone had predicted, lost this second attempt at the governorship to James W. Dawes, who had also defeated him in 1882.

Joy knew that his father's political involvement—no matter that he seemed forever destined to be an unsuccessful candidate in a Republican state—continued to be a useful distraction from his recurring depression over the death of Caroline four years earlier. But J. Sterling's campaigns and his other interests that took him away from Arbor Lodge also meant that Joy had to continue looking after family business in Nebraska and to act as his father's banking adviser. Having performed this filial duty for a number of years, he had become familiar with his father's idiosyncrasies in handling money. During the fall and winter months of 1884 and 1885, he was still attempting to settle the matter of the sale of the D.P. Rolfe lumber property in which his father had a large stake, but he was frustrated by his inability to receive timely inventories and accounts that were for him the cornerstones of good business.

Joy's intimate knowledge of the banking business in Nebraska City led him to make his first major capital investment there. He purchased a sufficient block of shares in the bank of James Sweet & Company to be named a director. Having worked at the bank as a young man, Joy knew it to be committed to sound money, the economic principle he shared with his father. In 1934, Joy's son would say that Joy took "great pride in the fact that the bank . . . successfully weathered all the financial upheavals which have occurred since its organization."[22] In his last years as a director, the bank became the Merchants National Bank of Nebraska City.

*D*uring the next few months, Joy had much less time to spend on his father's affairs in Nebraska. Another addition to his family was imminent, and he would soon come to an unexpected crossroad in his career. By May 1885, Carrie was five months' pregnant and staying with her parents in Omaha. When Joy told her that he would have to cancel a planned visit with her and Jean, she replied angrily, "Your letter telling me of Mr. Wheeler's illness and his departure from Chicago came yesterday, and *I am terribly disappointed and perfectly disgusted.*"[23] Wheeler, then only 41, had been in failing health since Joy's entry into the business five years before. In late May, thinking that his death was imminent, Wheeler and his wife left the country for Switzerland to try one more time for a cure. "Wheeler's absence and an irregular Salt market," Joy told his father in June, kept him "unusually busy."[24] On August 25, Carrie gave birth to a son, whom, in honor of Joy's father, they named Sterling.

Nearing his thirtieth birthday, Joy was without doubt an authority figure in business and family. He was looked up to by Carl and Mark, while Paul, Joy's equal in age and position, valued his opinion and thought highly of his character. At twenty years old, Carl was still trying to adapt to Joy's standards, even taking on a tone of managerial authority himself. In early September, he typed a letter to his father, pleased to report that Wheeler & Co. had both a typewriter and "a young lady who performs upon the machine very rapidly indeed." The shorthand man had disappeared but was not missed by Carl, who said, "His habits were not the best."[25]

After his stints at the CB&Q and selling lumber on the road, Mark was entering a new job with the Nebraska and Iowa Packing Co. in Nebraska City. But when Joy heard rumors of Mark's social life in Nebraska City, he sent him big brotherly advice straightaway. He had learned that Mark had gone hunting at a time when he should have been at work.. "You are no longer a boy," Joy reminded him.[26] Paul, too, was concerned by how Mark conducted himself in his hometown. Nebraska City, Paul knew, would not allow Mark to be as happy-go-lucky as he had been in Chicago. On the heels of Joy's admonition, Paul told Mark to quit playing poker because it might reflect badly on J. Sterling and could be used against him politically. Joy and Paul had discussed what they should say to Mark, but Paul was more direct than Joy, who was always more tolerant of his sometimes wayward brother. Paul, acutely conscious of his own appearance, advised Mark, "When you left Chicago and our company you were a stylish, refined-appearing fellow and because the average yahoo in Neb City does not care how he appears does not justify you in looking like a pig sticker."[27] Mark heeded his brothers' concerns and settled into the meatpacking business, intent on distinguishing himself at last as his older brothers had done.

During the summer, Wheeler had written encouraging letters to Joy, filled with the usual confidence in Joy's handling of the business and including observations of the spa scene. So when news of Wheeler's death came on November 3, Joy was stunned. He immediately asked Paul and Mark, who were in town on business, and Carl to join him that evening at his home to talk over how he should proceed. Paul remained with him late into the night. Writing to J. Sterling that same evening, Carrie described Joy's state of mind. She thought he looked "very much worried," if not ill. Carrie believed that he needed advice from J. Sterling. It was a letter written in unusual confidence to her father-in-law. "Of course it is a critical time in his business life, and now, if ever, he needs you."[28] Joy did not know of her letter.

Taking a day to weigh the crucial decisions he must make, Joy sent his own letter to J. Sterling, with full details of his intentions and asking for his advice and help. The question was not so much about what to do but about how to raise the capital that would allow him "to assume the responsibility of this business." He was thinking of deeding his 320-acre farm to Paul for a portion of the funds he needed. He and Paul believed they could muster up to $30,000, and Joy needed another $10,000. He hoped his father would come in for $7,000, a tenth of which his father already owed him. He asked that J. Sterling borrow the rest for ninety days. "I will see that you don't lose it," Joy promised. And he ended by urging his father not to tell why he wanted the money. *"Credit is a delicate thing,"* he said. *"I must be careful."* Then he invited his father to come to Chicago to *"arrange for a co-partnership,"* adding, *"It is a paying business."*[29]

Joy knew how important it was to move quickly. The recent growth of the business, for which he had been largely responsible, had made it attractive to other investors, in particular to the Michigan Salt Association, which supplied the salt. But Joy had earned the confidence of the Michigan Salt Association president, W.R. Burt. On November 7, D.G. Holland, the association's secretary, wrote, "We see no necessity for making any change in our business at Chicago and have no intention of doing so. We think you are capable of running the business and are perfectly willing for you to keep on."[30] After Wheeler's funeral, Joy told his father that the Michigan Salt Association had offered $25,000 for his share of the business, with Joy to remain in charge in a salaried position. He had refused. Wheeler's wife, Belle, also wanted to retain her part of the business for the time being.[31]

J. Sterling replied to Joy's letter, advising patience, a trait he himself had often regretted not exercising in his own business dealings. He noted that the contract Joy and Wheeler had signed did not run out until May 1886 and said, "Do not try to hurry matters. Make no propositions. Ask questions."[32] Later, J. Sterling sent another piece of advice, urging Joy to "Endeavor, by all means, to amicably adjust matters with Mrs. Wheeler & to go on with the business in a smooth style as Joy Morton & Co. Should she remain in, you must live up to the agreement *precisely*."[33] Joy was ahead of his father. He wrote that he had completed a deal with Mrs. Wheeler in which he would buy her assets and give her 50 percent of the profits for a year, at the end of which she would leave "without any bonus whatsoever." Joy considered the contract "liberal" for Mrs. Wheeler but the "best thing to do under the circumstances."[34] He was, he said, relieved.

On New Year's Eve 1885, Joy was putting the finishing touches on the company's year-end inventory. Firmly convinced that an accurate tallying of the year's accounts and inventory was basic to sound business practice, he approached the task this time with the knowledge that he would have a much larger role in the future of the company. His final letter of the year to his father read, "We are all very busy closing up the old concern which starts out tomorrow on a career which I sincerely hope may be successful."[35] On New Year's Day 1886, the salt company's letterhead read, "Joy Morton & Co. / successor to E. I. Wheeler & Co. / Dealers in Salt / Agents for the / Salt Association of Michigan." Wheeler's name continued to be included on the letterhead, since under the articles of agreement, Belle Wheeler would remain Joy's partner. They each pledged to keep $25,000 in capital stock in the company until the co-partnership's scheduled conclusion of December 31, 1886, at which time the business would "become the sole property of, and be continued by, the said Joy Morton, his heirs or assigns." One stipulation was that Joy "should devote his whole time during reasonable business hours to the business of the firm, and shall have full charge of said business . . . in all its details, he agreeing to at all times use his best efforts to promote the interest of the firm." Joy was now in both deed and fact in complete charge of the firm's operations.

One of Joy's first actions was to ask his father to lobby in Washington for the Butterine Bill, enabling the production of oleomargarine. The bill was supported strongly by, among others, Armour, the Chicago meatpacking house. If the bill were passed, Joy Morton & Co. would benefit through gaining larger orders from Armour & Co. Two months later, Joy wrote to J. Sterling that Armour was pleased with his work, and reported, "Business has been unusually brisk lately, and I have been tied down to the office or should have written oftener."[36] Joy's reliance on his father's good will in Washington was a natural consequence of the close family loyalty that prevailed between the father and his sons. The practice would continue.

Joy's management of the company was tested by unusual labor unrest throughout Chicago in the spring of 1886. On the evening of May 4, the city was plunged into chaos when a bomb exploded during an anarchist gathering in Haymarket Square. One policeman was killed, and in the subsequent melee between laborers and police, ten more people, including six policemen, died. The leaders of the gathering were jailed. In the ensuing weeks workers throughout the country staged strikes, both for support of those awaiting trial and for what they believed to be just work issues. On June 18, Joy wrote to his father that close to one hundred men were striking at the company's south warehouse and that he thought they would have to be replaced with "new men under police protection." In addition, there were threats at the Pier I docks, and Joy had two "propellers," steamships, coming in soon. He would, he said, "have to postpone my trip home another week."

Within a day, however, Joy again wrote to his father, who was heading for a European vacation, that he had settled the south Chicago strike with a 2½ cent per hour increase and was "paying for actual time." The strikers had wanted guaranteed eight-hour workdays. With the settlement, workers who earned $1.75 for a ten-hour day would now get $1.60 for an eight-hour day. Joy concluded, "'What fools these mortals be,' especially strikers." Joy may not have respected the strikers for their negotiating prowess, but his company was among the first in the nation to guarantee an eight-hour day.

By early September, Joy was confident enough of the health of the firm to take an unusual week off to hunt prairie chickens near Nebraska City. Upon his return, Carrie, who had been quite ill throughout the late spring and summer with her third pregnancy, miscarried. He wrote to his father that he might try to take her on a trip in October. He even had reason to believe that his work might be eased a bit. Not only was Carl working more efficiently, but Joy had also persuaded Mark to come back to work in Chicago for the salt company. On October 17, Mark wrote to his father, "Friday last at once commenced work with the Salt Dealer. Think I shall like it very much and make Joy a good helper."

Clearly Joy was envisioning an agency of which he would be the sole head but that would also be beneficial to those brothers he employed and to those in the family who would invest. On November 29, as the end of the year approached, Joy wrote to his father of how he planned to purchase Mrs. Wheeler's half of the business. He himself could put together $35,000 "without borrowing a dollar." Paul would help him with another $10,000, and $5,000 more could be raised on their two farms. Joy wanted the total capital to be $55,000 and asked his father to put in the balance, "becoming a partner in fact, although so far as outsiders are concerned it will be understood that your interest and capital is same as Mrs. Wheeler's has been. It is not policy for me to have it otherwise."[37]

Joy also included Mark in his plans, telling his father that Mark was "doing nicely." Though the genial Mark was in Joy's estimation "slow" at his work, he thought him "reliable and level headed" and thought he would make a "good man" for him. Joy expected to make Mark a partner in the near future and give him an interest that would pay "considerably more" than he was making. Joy felt that Carl, too, was performing well enough to put him in "full charge of the City business." Joy was pleased to tell his father that Carl had "begun to climb the financial ladder quite rapidly."

Joy had carefully laid the groundwork for his sole ownership. On January 1, 1887, Joy Morton & Co. issued a notice that Belle F. Wheeler had retired from the firm at the end of the past year and that the firm would be reorganized. The total cost to Joy for the Wheeler interest was $42,736.91.[38] In an exuberant mood, Joy wrote to his father on the 8th, "We are busy settling 1886 business and the showing will be quite satisfactory. My earnings will be better than $15,000 which will go a long ways toward clothing the babies."[39] On the 10th, Joy paid $10.00 for a year's membership on the Chicago Board of Trade Stock Exchange. Carl proudly sent the firm's new stationery to his father, with an expanded letterhead reading, "Joy Morton & Co. successors to E. I. Wheeler & Co., Dealers in Salt, Agents, Michigan Salt Association, Michigan Dairy Salt Co., 13 Lake Street." The letterhead included a picture of the 250,000 barrel capacity south docks.

*E*ven as the process of consolidating Joy Morton & Co. went steadily forward, Joy found he was once more being distracted by family affairs. Mark had been engaged to Martha Parkhurst Weare of Cedar Rapids, Iowa, and Joy, Paul, and their families attended the wedding celebration. The only Morton not present was J. Sterling, who had to attend to business in Washington, D.C. Following the death of his old friend Wilbur F. Storey, J. Sterling was once again being courted to take over the *Chicago Times*.[40] Joy hoped that his father would get the appointment and settle down. But J. Sterling's inclinations were elsewhere. Joy, as usual, had to oversee much of his father's activities, occasionally becoming directly involved himself.

J. Sterling had decided to create a lake at Arbor Lodge by damming up the creek that ran to the south of the estate. He called it Lake Jopamaca, using the first two letters of his sons' names. On August 4, even as Joy reported from Chicago that business was "remarkably good notwithstanding higher prices and the drought," he was anxious to know whether Jopamaca had filled and whether it would soon be stocked with buffalo and channel cat. The idea of a well-stocked pond on the property intrigued Joy, who was an avid fisherman.

Even J. Sterling's interest in mineral mining in the west continued to attract Joy's attention, and he had invested as well. J. Sterling was in a mining syndicate in Idaho; Joy was in one in Colorado. But Joy, as usual, was much more circumspect than his father. When his father tried to interest him in silver mining near El Paso, Texas, Joy, knowing that the mine production there had begun to wane in 1879, told his father that he had "all the mining schemes on hand that [I] have the money, or time to indulge in. . . ." He cautioned his father against paying for a report on a prospective mine in Idaho and on an analysis of mineral specimens because of a conflict of interest on the part of the engineer who issued it, saying, "They probably want to make a stake for their winter's grub."[41]

September 1887 had been unusually hectic for Joy, and, uncharacteristi-cally, he decided to take some time away from his business and oversight of his father's affairs. He and Paul set out for Idaho to hunt big game, leaving Mark, who had earned Joy's confidence, in charge for several days. Mark was pleased to tell his father how well things were going during Joy's absence. He was at the office while Carrie and Martha, Mark's wife, attended the theatre, seeing Edwin Booth in *Julius Caesar*. The bear hunters arrived home the next day, but Joy would find, Mark boasted, that business had been getting along as well as if Joy had been there.[42]

*O*n September 27, 1887, Joy turned thirty-two. He had been a co-partner of the salt firm for over six years and had been its sole owner for nine months. During that time, he had solidified his reputation as one of the leading young businessmen in Chicago; as head of the fledgling Joy Morton & Co., he was becoming nationally known by producers and traders. J. Sterling, however, took Joy's birthday as one more opportunity to advise him on how he should manage his life and career. While congratulating him on his domestic life, he hoped that the coming years would "intensify its desirable qualities and obliterate its follies." He went on to caution him about his growing prosperity, which, he felt, was "so great that it may be dangerous." Joy should also "keep a cool head" and "deliberate before speaking or acting," he added. J. Sterling, having managed but a few farm employees and political appointees, told Joy to treat his clerical, sales, and labor force "with candor and always with the courtesy in language and manners existing among gentlemen." At the top of the stationery was a new motto for Arbor Lodge, chosen by J. Sterling: "*Virtutis Praemium*" (Reward of Virtue). It was accompanied by the customary tree and photograph of Arbor Lodge.[43]

As the first anniversary of Joy Morton & Co. approached, life for the Morton family seemed to have reached a level of moderate stability, in spite of continued labor unrest throughout the country. On November 10, the eve of the hanging of four of the anarchists convicted for fomenting the Haymarket riot, he and Carrie attended a lecture on Lord Byron. The house was not full, Joy thought, because people were worried about the possibility of trouble over the hangings. But Joy did not believe there would be another riot. And there was not. The next day he wrote to his father, "The anarchists are hung. Chicago still here."[44]

Joy's focus was on making the company that now bore his name a robust concern of which he would remain sole head but in which members of his family would share. At the beginning of every year since entering into the business with Ezra Wheeler in 1880, he had helped prepare and had signed a document that described the exact investment and commitment expected of each of the co-partners. In keeping with this practice, as 1888 approached, Joy sat down to write out the details of an agreement that spelled out the commitments he expected from himself, his father, and his brothers Mark and Carl. Without legal counsel, he penned—without corrections on two sides of legal-sized paper—an agreement of approximately 650 words. It was signed by Joy, Mark, J. Sterling, and Carl.

The document was straightforward, declaring that the four Mortons were co-partners in a company known as Joy Morton & Co. "for the purpose of dealing in salt in the City of Chicago." The capital stock was $55,000: $50,000 contributed by Joy and $5,000 by J. Sterling, from which the two stockholders were entitled to a return on the principal of 7 percent per annum. Joy, Mark, and Carl were required by the agreement "to devote their whole time during reasonable business hours . . . and at all times use their best efforts to promote the interest of the firm. . . ." J. Sterling was not required to work for the firm. Joy would receive 70 percent and Mark 16 percent of the profits.

The agreement limited Joy, J. Sterling, and Mark from drawing money from the company if the amount exceeded the accrued profits. They also were responsible to the firm in the amount of their percentages to pay losses that might accrue to the firm. Carl would receive 9 percent of the profits but would not be able to draw on this for more than $90 per month, the rest to be credited at the end of the year if he owed the company "nothing on account." Joy included a clause that said, should he fail to comply with the agreement, the other co-partners (but for Carl, who, at twenty-three was still being tested) would divide the remainder of his interest by a ratio that mirrored their own interests. The document concluded with a clear statement that at the end of 1888, failing a renewal of the co-partnership, Joy would have sole authority for closing the business and paying the partners the money that might be due them. Joy Morton & Co. was in fact as well as in name the absolute property of Joy Morton.[45]

After coming to Chicago at the age of twenty-five, Joy, at thirty-two, was the caring head of a family of four and the owner of a thriving business that seemed tailored to his talents and interests. His lengthy and often frustrating apprenticeship, prolonged by illness and beset by frustratingly low pay, was in the past. Joy thrived in Chicago but remained bonded to Nebraska through family and devotion to the agricultural and arboreal surroundings in which he had been raised. The question now was how he would be able to satisfy the longing he felt for Arbor Lodge and Nebraska City while living and working in Chicago.

CHAPTER 5

Two Cities—1887–1893

During their first six years in Chicago the Mortons had lived in three places near the southern-most city limits, which were then at 39th Street. In 1887, finding their Oakwood Boulevard residence too cramped for their growing family, Joy leased a house adjoining an identical one at 32 Groveland Park,[1] prompting J. Sterling to comment, "I am pleased to learn that you will soon be located with your dear wife and Jean & the House destroyer."[2]

Groveland Park, located at 33rd and Cottage Grove, is but a small parcel of the 53-acre Oakenwald estate on Lake Michigan once owned by Senator Stephen A. Douglas. During the Civil War, the area then known as Camp Douglas held 26,000 Confederate prisoners, of whom some 6,000 died of yellow fever and other diseases. The creation of Groveland Park in the 1870s helped obscure memories of that gruesome saga. It was designed for two rows of residences to the north and south, separated by a 500-foot wide park. Just south is the smaller Woodland Park, and to the south of it the Douglas Memorial Park, on which the 60-foot monument and tomb honoring Stephen Douglas was erected in 1871. Atop the column stands Leonard Volk's ten-foot sculpture of the "Little Giant," surveying the lake and the tracks of the Illinois

Central Railroad, which Douglas helped bring to Illinois. Both Joy and J. Sterling were, no doubt, pleased by the family's proximity to the memorial of a hero of northern Democrats.

Groveland Park had a number of advantages. Joy could travel to his office by horseback, the Illinois Central, or horse-drawn cars. Within a year, however, he would be able to take the newly constructed cable car that ran from 39th Street (then the southern-most street in the city) downtown. A major consideration for the move was that as a private and gated residential area Groveland Park was relatively free from noise and intrusion. To the west, just across Cottage Grove, rose the towers of the "old" University of Chicago. To the east, beyond the Illinois Central tracks, lay Lake Michigan.

In the summer, residents could sit outside, cooled by lake breezes and shade provided by a magnificent grove of elms. Like Joy and Carrie's first residences on the south side, Groveland Park did not suffer as much from the soft coal grit that settled over the city to the north. Adding to the attractiveness of the area was the fact that the "old" University of Chicago, built on ten acres of land provided by Stephen Douglas, had been across Cottage Grove from 1858 to 1886.[3] Its last buildings were torn down at the time J.D. Rockefeller made possible the "new" University of Chicago, founded in 1892 and situated along the Olmsted-designed Midway Plaisance linking Jackson and Washington parks twenty blocks south. The swath of unoccupied space provided additional quiet for the residents of Groveland Park.

Joy was interested in Groveland Park's botanical setting, which included the elm grove and an extensive planting of lilacs. In 1869, Frederick Law Olmsted, having designed New York City's Central Park, had drawn up plans for an interconnected park system along Chicago's southeast side, but the development of the concept was halted by the fire of 1871. The plan also included the extensive boulevard system intersecting where Joy and Carrie had lived in Chicago. Two years before Olmsted received the commission to complete his ideas for the lakefront's Jackson Park to the far south for the 1893 World's Columbian Exposition, Joy wrote enthusiastically to his father that he was going to have an interview with a landscape gardener who was with the park system. "[He] tells me the South Parks were laid out exactly as we proposed, the plan having been made by a Mr. Olmsted many years ago. Nothing whatever has been done since by a landscape gardener, but all work is toward carrying out the Olmsted plans." In referring to "a" Mr. Olmsted, Joy appeared to have forgotten that Olmsted had been responsible for New York's Central Park that he and his father had toured when he was seventeen. But J. Sterling could not have helped being pleased that the eldest son of Arbor Lodge valued design in natural surroundings.[4]

As 1889 approached, Joy purchased a lot on the north side of the park where he had decided to build a permanent residence. Getting their new house completed before 1890 was a priority, for Carrie was expecting again. The construction of the new house at 15 Groveland Park was well under way by May 1890 when Carrie, who had been seriously ill during her pregnancy, lost her baby.

Still, the family remained determined to move into the house that would be one of the most distinctive in a neighborhood of homes built by a successful group of Chicagoans. Among them were J.A. Moffett, a trustee of Standard Oil; Herbert Jones, a founder of Inland Steel Company; J.K. Robinson of the Diamond Match Co.; Elias Porter, a historian of the Chicago fire and journalist who worked for the *Chicago Times* and later was science editor of the *Tribune*; and Robert A. Warren, whose sons Robert K. and A.G. were later hired by Joy and would eventually become vice president and treasurer, respectively, of Morton Salt Co.[5]

The architecture of the house was influenced by H.H. Richardson's popular Romanesque style. Its conical-roofed towers, complete with windows, rose from both corners of the front of the house, with second-story windows set parallel between them. From between the towers emerged a pyramid roof with a triangular dormer. Although Richardson had favored stone exteriors, Joy decided to use brick instead. The residence reflected Joy's achievement as a successful Chicago businessman.

Decades after the Mortons no longer lived in Groveland Park, Jake Solenski, their coachman, recalled the Morton family. He taught Jean and Sterling how to ride ponies in the park, and once or twice a week he took them in the carriage to dancing lessons at a dancing school called Bornique's on Prairie Avenue. Often he would drive Joy to the salt works near what was then the mouth of the Chicago River. Solenski's most vivid memory of Joy was the "keen interest he took in the trees and the flowers of Groveland Park."[6]

From the perspective of the 1930s, Sterling, too, remembered living a simple but fulfilling childhood in Groveland Park. He had had a "complete home life," spending evenings on the porch looking out upon the park or reading in the "cozy library." His father, not much given to "dinners, tea and receptions," preferred instead to sit on a neighbor's porch or enjoy a poker game with a few friends. The Mortons had the first telephone in the neighborhood, and Jean and Sterling ran to get neighbors who were called on the Morton's telephone, until eventually those neighbors obtained their own. Joy had a horse for pleasure riding, but he preferred to walk the three blocks to the Illinois Central station at Cottage Grove and 31st to get to work quickly and conveniently.[7]

For the first time in Chicago, Joy had found a place in which he and his family could settle down. At Groveland Park, Carrie, Jean, and Sterling might live in healthful and interesting surroundings. As the house moved toward completion, Joy urged his father to visit them in a letter dated September 23, 1889, his tenth wedding anniversary. "How 'tempus' does 'fugit,'" Joy exclaimed.[8] He would be thirty-four in three days and had been in the salt business only a little longer than he had been married.

*W*ith the approach of 1890, changes abounded in the city of Chicago as well as in the Morton family. The city's population exceeded 1,000,000—nearly twice what it had been when Joy came to the city a decade earlier. Intent on showing the world that it had recovered from the Great Fire of 1871, Chicago was busily planning the World's Columbian Exposition, an opportunity for the city to become the stage for the most modern aspects of culture and technology four hundred years following the explorations of Christopher Columbus. In 1889, confident in the future of the city he had now made his home, Joy invested in the newly organized American Trust & Savings Bank of Chicago, which had as one of its chief officers Edwin A. Potter, who became a trusted business friend.[9] On a more personal level, Paul, who had become Joy's confidant during the eighties, was about to leave the city to take a job in Denver with the Colorado Coal and Fuel Company. Paul's leaving Chicago meant that Joy's only confidante nearby would be Mark.

Joy was also gaining a reputation as one of the city's more advanced business owners in terms of cultivating employee relationships. In February 1890, Paul left his job as a general freight agent of the CB&Q to become the chief executive of the Whitebreast Coal Company and the Colorado Coal and Fuel Company in Denver. On that occasion, the *Chicago Daily Tribune* featured Joy and Paul in an article noting the respect in which they were held for their business acumen. The reporter chose to emphasize how well liked Joy was by the large workforce he employed and to recount acts of Joy's generosity which "many less liberal" employers would not have engaged in, citing two notable instances of how Joy treated his employees: he kept a young female stenographer on the payroll and sent her flowers "almost daily" even though she was unable to work for three months, and when Joy learned of the illness of a teamster who had been unable to work for a week, he sent a note of sympathy and a twenty dollar bill to his home. Apparently less impressed with Paul, the reporter told a story of how Paul, though Joy's junior at Arbor Lodge, had ruled it over his brothers, displaying his power by locking himself and a younger brother in a room and playing circus, a sport that entailed chasing the brother around the room with a whip.[10] The reporter's curious recounting of this story seems to be his less than subtle way of informing his readers that Paul and Joy displayed quite different ways of exercising their authority as business leaders. Joy had gained a reputation in Chicago as a demanding but understanding employer, a management practice that was worthy of note before labor laws began to mandate the behavior of employers.

Joy's leadership in the salt industry had become unquestioned, and Joy Morton & Company was a visible as well as an economic presence in the city of Chicago. In 1888, Joy leased Illinois Central Pier No. 1, an extension of Randolph Street jutting into Lake Michigan just south of the mouth of the Chicago River. There he built large storage and packaging warehouses covering seventeen acres. From this strategic site, bulk and barrel salt delivered from Great Lakes ports was readied for delivery throughout the west by rail and barge. Joy's plant contained its own cooper shop and a mill for refining table and dairy salt that was packaged into cartons or cloth bags, the latter stitched by hand by an assembly line of women. The facility was designed for ultimate efficiency, a necessity if the cost of transporting this unwieldy staple were to remain affordable to consumers.[11] To be closer to the heart of the salt business, Joy moved his offices from Lake Street to one of the new warehouses. From there, he maintained oversight of his Nebraska investments as well, keeping in touch daily by telephone and telegraph.

The warehouse was but the first step in assuring that Joy Morton & Company's salt business would remain competitive. Joy was also seeking ways to expand beyond distribution. A trip to Hutchinson, Kansas, in 1888 had whetted his appetite for diversification. He found his first opportunity in 1890 when the Michigan Salt Association seemed on the verge of collapse, because it had, Joy said, "too many concerns outside."[12] For one thing, the supply of sawmill waste that fueled the fires for brine was diminishing as the Michigan forests were thinned. While the Michigan Salt Association soon righted itself, Joy built a coal-fired evaporation plant in Wyandotte, Michigan, the first such plant in the nation.[13]

But as much as the salt company and his family made Chicago the center of his attention, Joy remained emotionally and financially linked to Nebraska City and divided his allegiance to the two cities for many years. He owned farmland there, and he was a director of the Nebraska City National Bank (which would later become the Merchants National Bank), the successor to James Sweet & Company, the bank where he had begun working at the age of fifteen. In late 1887, Joy also bought a one-third share in the Union Stock Yards of Nebraska City for which he was now purchasing property next to the Nebraska City packing plant.

Little did Joy think that this latter investment would provide him a way to resolve the troubling question of how to help Carl, who seemed to Joy to be reverting to his lackadaisical work habits at a time when Joy needed even more from him. Joy's mandate of full devotion to the salt company, while agreeable to Mark, was a burden for Carl, who thought it necessary to tell his father that Joy himself was working so hard that he would, like Wheeler (who died at forty-two after accumulating $500,000), not live long enough to enjoy his wealth.

Carl sensed the irony of his words. He blamed his own ill health over some six months for making him unable to complete an important ledger he had been assigned. He expected, he said, to be the first of his brothers to die. Still, he was reluctant to complain. From past experience, he knew that his more robust brothers would find it difficult to pity him.[14] It was difficult for Joy to fathom why Carl could not keep up with the work, and in the early spring of 1888 he made plans to release him. He asked J. Sterling to send Carl on a European vacation with J. Sterling's brother, William, then wrote to his uncle saying, "It is agreed that he will not come back with us, as I have made up my mind that a few years with some one else will do him more good than to remain with me." Joy added that Carl had "been a sort of hypochondriac for six months, but has promised to brace up and see all there is to be seen while on the trip, to go clear to the top of all the ruins you tackle, and climb all the mountains you visit, and I want you to insist that he does this." He concluded that Carl lacked "courage, and staying qualities, especially when he tackles a ledger" and he hoped he would "be in better fighting trim" upon his return and "have his mind made up to fight the battle of life cheerfully hereafter. Heretofore he has made it altogether too melancholy."[15]

On the same day Joy sent his letter, Carl derailed the scheme by telling his father that he would stay to finish the ledger because he owed it to the kindness of Joy and Mark. Joy's next solution was to ask his father if Carl could go to Arbor Lodge for a few weeks of rest. When Carl balked at that idea, Joy, exasperated, wrote to his father that Carl lacked the "courage, and pluck, and persistency to make a success as a book-keeper, or anything else. . . ." He still doubted Carl's illness, saying to J. Sterling that "there is a good deal of humbug in it."[16] Joy could not understand how Carl, after five years of working for him, had failed to achieve when his older brothers, now in their early thirties, had exceeded expectations at his age. Paul had just been promoted by E.P. Ripley (Traffic Manager of the CB&Q and later president of the Atchison, Topeka, and Santa Fe) to General Freight Agent, the youngest person ever to hold that responsibility for thousands of miles of rail shipping. Even the carefree but dependable Mark could be counted on by Joy to manage the salt company when he was away.

Finally accepting that Carl's health might be an issue, Joy created a place for him in Nebraska City. The solution proved salutary. In July, he arranged for Carl to go into a stockyards commission business with A.P. Stafford, a Nebraska City businessman. He carefully explained to J. Sterling, "I am not particularly anxious to dispose of Carl's services, but I think that there is a fine chance at Neb City for him to make *more money* for awhile anyway than he is now making and at the same time be benefited in health and also perhaps by becoming more self reliant, the natural result of working for one's self."[17] Carl echoed Joy's thoughts, saying, "I think by being in business out there by myself with Joy to advise and have an interest with me as he will it would be a good thing for me."[18] By the end of the year, Carl was finding that his move from Chicago had indeed been a good thing. He had proposed to Boatie Payne, a local girl, and they were married before the end of the year.

Joy expected, too, that the Union Stock Yards, located in the center of the hog producing farms of northern Missouri, western Iowa, and southeastern Nebraska, would flourish in concert with the nearby packing company. Typically, though, he was cautious, believing that the business culture of Nebraska City, for whom his father had been a spokesman for as long as it existed, would have to change. "The problem with Neb City proper," he told his father, who had questioned his judgment, "is they are not accustomed to large transactions. You don't appreciate the magnitude of this deal and because I understand it, after thorough investigation, you think I am losing my head. Time will show that you are mistaken."[19] The Union Stock Yards Company listed J. Sterling as president, a convenience of his nearby residence in Nebraska City and also a means of keeping him occupied. Henry Botsford, president of the Chicago Packing Company, was vice president. Joy, who served as the secretary and treasurer, lost no time in joining forces with the packing company next door to investigate the idea of rail access to Nebraska City for more convenient shipping.[20]

$\mathcal{A}$s Carl settled into the commission company of Stafford and Morton and the stockyards started up, Joy's interest in Nebraska City took a new turn. The year 1888 was a presidential election year in which J. Sterling could not help but be involved. During his first term, President Cleveland had disappointed all of the Mortons with his ambivalent approach to tariff laws, which threatened free trade. They were certain he would be defeated if nominated for a second term.

So when J. Sterling decided to accept the draft of the Nebraska Democrats to run for Congress, both Joy and Paul were pessimistic about his candidacy, although it again would help distract him from his lingering grief over Caroline's death. Paul expressed their view to their father in November 1888, saying that even in the unlikely event that he could win, J. Sterling would have little patronage to hand out in Nebraska under a Republican president. Paul added wryly, "Some men are born great and others live in pivotal states." When, as predicted, J. Sterling lost, he wrote to a friend that he could not accompany him to Russia because he was trying "to repair the damages of a recent political extravagance. I always punish myself for acting the fool and I am consequently perpetually under sentence, 'doing time,' for having let politics 'do me.'"[21]

Joy hired a private railcar to take the directors of the Michigan Salt Association to the national Democratic Convention in St. Louis where, in spite of doubts as to his electability, Cleveland again received his party's nomination. Joy's primary purpose, however, was to travel on to Hutchinson, Kansas, so that the directors could get a firsthand look at a recent boom in salt production that was occurring in that region. As usual, Joy wanted to study the probabilities for making a profit were he to invest there. W.R. Burt, the president of the Michigan Salt Association, concluded that the Kansas salt field was being overbuilt to the extent that excessive production and competition would "demoralize" prices. Joy came to the same conclusion. The time was not right for Joy to go into the production of salt. It was several years before he determined the time propitious for investing in Hutchinson.

But even as he concluded that it was not time to expand his business to Kansas, Joy turned his attention once more to Nebraska City. When he learned from J. Sterling that he might invest in a new opera house in

Nebraska City, Joy agreed that it would be a good idea if he could get a $10,000 bonus. He seemed more interested, though, in the architectural features of the enterprise and told his father he would consult the architect who was building his house in Chicago. Joy already envisioned how the opera house in Nebraska City should be built: it should be at least three stories and include five stores fronting on the principal streets of Otoe and 6th. Including the stores, Joy calculated, would cost about the same as a stand-alone house and would provide rental income.[22]

For the time being, however, the situation at the Union Stock Yards was more pressing than a new opera house. The venture was not playing out as Joy had hoped. The best part of the investment at that point was that it had given Carl a chance to succeed in his own business and regain his health in the Nebraska City environment. That it was not making a profit led Joy to take personal charge. "We must get expenses down to bedrock and then bye and bye we may make some money," he wrote to his father from his Chicago office in late March. He thought the superintendent who had built the yards should be let go because he did not have the ability to attract hog shippers and keep them. He also agreed with the Chicago stockyards magnate Henry Botsford that cattle should be added to the yards. A nearby hotel that the Mortons owned had also become unprofitable as the stockyards developed close by. Joy advised his father to sell it.[23]

When things did not pick up in his businesses as quickly as Joy would have liked over the summer, his enthusiasm for investing in Nebraska City began to ebb. He told J. Sterling that he would not lend more money in Nebraska and had decided to put surplus funds into Chicago real estate. But in October, deciding that he needed to make a bold move in order to protect his investment, he arranged for the purchase of the Nebraska City Packing Company by the Union Stock Yards Company of Nebraska City for the sum of $80,000 and initiated a restructuring of the entire company.[24]

In spite of impatience with what he believed to be a lack of imagination on the part of Nebraska City citizens toward industry, Joy continued to seek ways to urge them on. In January 1890, he explained to his father his successful arrangement with investors for a Nebraska City cereal plant, promising, "We will have a manufacturing city there before we get through."[25] Joy had bought stock in the Nebraska City Corn Milling Company. At the same time, he backed the development of a starch-making operation that he thought Carl could oversee, and he convinced a number of Nebraska City citizens to purchase stock in the company.

When it failed to produce to expectations within a short time, Joy stepped in to underwrite the capital, allowing investors to keep their stock up to the point of their initial investment. He later would reorganize the business under the name Argo Manufacturing Company.

Joy's investments in Nebraska City made him increasingly desirous of developing a transportation bridge across the Missouri River from Nebraska City to Fremont County, Iowa. By 1890, rails ran north, south, and west, but a convenient way to connect with a rail system directly to the east had not yet been developed. Joy urged his father to renew interest around Nebraska City in a wagon bridge that would carry traffic across the Missouri River to nearby rail lines, predicting that "the Missouri River Bottom will soon be thickly populated." When his father expressed concern that the stockyards and the packinghouse would be heavily taxed for such a venture, Joy admonished him, saying, "Don't be so much afraid of taxation. Go in more for progress." Days later he told his father that the bridge would be of great benefit to the town and that he didn't want to do anything to prevent its erection.[26]

The roles of son and father during this time were reversed. J. Sterling still openly mourned the loss of his wife, and he seemed at a loss as to what to do. He repeatedly indulged in quixotic projects such as a plan to raise silkworms for silk production in Nebraska. But his most futile project was Lake Jopamaca. For Joy it had become a virtual metaphor for his father's poorly conceived and executed projects. In the spring of 1890, Joy commented on yet another failure of the dam, saying he had been a "little skeptical . . . on account of the way the timbers looked. . . ." Fortunately, J. Sterling had had it tested before the guarantee expired.[27] In the summer, Paul urged his father to stop wasting his talent on dams in Nebraska City.[28] Even so, Joy and Paul sent a boat to J. Sterling to use to fish for carp and channel catfish in the newly stocked pond.

In the summer of 1890, J. Sterling could find little in his world that was going right. Carl had been quite ill, even as Boatie was giving birth to their son, Wirt. When Carl recovered, he told his father, "I am the first Morton boy to be the proud father of a boy. (I mean first child.) The other Morton boys are large in stature, but it takes a man to get a boy." It was a plaintive pronouncement, not one that could have reassured J. Sterling of the strength of his youngest son. Joy, too, had been bedridden by a liver ailment. By August, however, he was back at work, brimming with practical ideas for his father, such as putting in an evaporator for the orchards to keep the apples from rotting.

Finally, with the death of his mother in September, J. Sterling suddenly seemed to take a fresh, if not eclectic, interest in life. In the fall he bought back the park and the one-room brick schoolhouse that he had given to Nebraska City two years before.[29] He returned to Chicago to lobby for the railroad. To his sister, Emma, he declared once more that he had given up politics, and he contemplated a trip around the world, though he dared not voice such an outlandish thought to acquaintances in Nebraska City.[30] When his work for the railroad helped assure the funding of the bridge to Nebraska City, Joy sent his congratulations.[31] But Joy still oversaw his father's interests. At the end of 1890, he admonished his father for not having a farmer operate Arbor Lodge farm, saying, "If I were running Arbor Lodge, I would have a man who would work and do as I bid him."[32]

Joy also remained skeptical when it came to investment schemes proposed by his father, such as when, in January 1891, he wrote to J. Sterling, "I am not inclined to join you in a private scheme to prospect for coal at Nebraska City."[33] As an object lesson, he could point to the success he had made in but a short time in Nebraska City. His holdings in Nebraska City were such that he was promoting the idea of a railroad link that would appreciably shorten the time required to transport goods to Denver. In February 1891, Joy gave a detailed account to his father of his Nebraska City holdings, beginning with his one-third interest in his newest acquisition, the Nebraska City Cereal Mills. He planned to erect an elevator that would hold 100,000 bushels of grain, a warehouse, and a feed mill. The stockyards were doing well, and the Morton Produce Co. had been reorganized with A.P. Stafford, president; Carl, treasurer; and Duncan Manning, secretary and manager. Joy and Paul owned 25 percent of the stock. "Seems to me I am becoming quite a gleaner in S. E. Nebraska," Joy said. "Hogs to the C. P. & P.—corn & oats to Cereal mill—eggs to Morton Produce Co—milk to the Creamery—in all of which I am interested. Each concern handles food for humanity. . . . My total investments in the old town now aggregate over fifty thousand dollars." Joy knew from the salt business that his success depended upon putting the right people in place to manage things for him when he was not there. In Chicago, the salt company was running so smoothly that Joy finished his summary of Nebraska City activity, by saying, "Salt business is quiet, in fact dull."[34]

Joy, however, was not immune from a few investment failures. In Chicago he secured patents on cold process gas lighting and organized the Sterling Fuel & Light Company, of which the principal customer was

George Pullman, the Chicago sleeping car magnate. In July, Joy told his father, "We are going to light a big knitting factory at Pullman and also the Richelieu Hotel—the latter because it will be a good place to show the light."[35] Prospects for the company seemed good, because the Richelieu, located between Jackson and Van Buren on Michigan Boulevard, catered to a well-heeled clientele. But just a few months later, Joy informed his father that the gas burners, after being turned on for just fifteen minutes, self-destructed. It was a speculative failure of the type that Joy had heretofore largely managed to avoid. But it was one he could absorb.

 *A*s the presidential election year of 1892 dawned, J. Sterling, in spite of his usual vows never to reenter politics, once again was contemplating becoming a candidate for governor of Nebraska as his own party was being wooed by a message that he could not abide. William Jennings Bryan, the young democrat who had come to Nebraska from Illinois in 1887 and was at first taken under J. Sterling's wing, had quickly become an oratorical champion of the Grange and the populism that it injected into the Democratic Party. He lured voters with ideas of tariffs, silver, public ownership of communications and transportation, and a union of agricultural labor. J. Sterling, adhering to the principles of free trade and the gold standard, quickly distanced himself from what he considered to be threats to the more conservative ideas on which the Northern Democrats had based their platforms. Although Joy remained relatively indifferent to the prospects of the coming elections, he attended the Democratic Convention in Chicago's Wigwam, the convention center in which Abraham Lincoln was nominated in 1860 and where Grover Cleveland and Adlai A. Stevenson of Illinois were given the Democratic nominations in 1891. The year end would see Cleveland elected to his second term as president, giving more conservative Democrats a temporary edge over the Bryan-led populists, who maintained that economic and social elitism was responsible for such occurrences as the Panic of 1873.

In early March, Joy headed south with his family to escape the end of the long Chicago winter, stopping in Washington, D.C., to visit the agricultural museum. Two weeks later, he was busy organizing an event to showcase Nebraska City products in the way his father had done years before. It was to be held at the Nebraska City Commercial Club, which he helped establish. To George B. Harris, the son of an early booster of Nebraska products, Joy sent a special invitation written in phrases reminiscent of J. Sterling's prose: "Today the lands are sold, and have for years produced bountiful crops, but it is only recently that any attempt has been made, within the State, to manufacture these cereal food products into articles of commerce." The event on May 21 would be, Joy said, one "at which only the refined products of Nebraska, manufactured in Nebraska, will be served. There will be no speeches; it will be simply a practical, palpable verification of the fact that what your father then claimed for Nebraska is now a reality."[36]

In late July and early August, Joy took another vacation, this time with Carrie, Paul, and Lottie, leaving the children with grandparents. The trip was a prelude to Paul's return to the railroad industry in Chicago as a supplier of steel rails. Both men hoped to do some big game hunting on their way to Spokane Falls, Washington, but the plan was nixed by their wives at Yellowstone, as Joy wrote: "We have changed our plan and won't go hunting big game as this place doesn't suit the ladies as a permanent residence," adding, "Carrie is very well and has enjoyed the trip immensely."[37]

Shortly after their return to Chicago, Joy learned that J. Sterling had accepted his party's nomination for governor. Joy congratulated him on the nomination and offered whatever help he could, including paying for the printing and mailing of a circular that stated J. Sterling's strong advocacy of free trade and the gold standard. But when J. Sterling once more suffered an inevitable defeat by his Republican opponent, Joy displayed his exasperation about the political savvy of Nebraskans: "I am not going to be interested in anything whatever of a political nature. I have got enough of it and don't propose to neglect this business any more, not in the slightest design. Salt will 'energize my activity' from now on. I have lost my interest in Nebraska's welfare politically or otherwise and the sooner I can get out of the things I am in out there the better it will suit me."[38]

J. Sterling soon learned that he was being considered for Secretary of Agriculture in Cleveland's cabinet. Joy, however, still resolved to concentrate on the salt business and ignore politics, voiced his half-hearted support, saying, "Your Forestry & Entomological friends and perhaps some of the Nebraska damphool [sic] democrats may do some good."[39] For his part, J. Sterling, who, because of Cleveland's position on tariffs in his first term, had initially been lukewarm to his candidacy, believed his chances for the appointment were slim. But Cleveland appreciated J. Sterling's advocacy of both agriculture and sound money policies. J. Sterling received the appointment on January 18, 1893. Both Joy and Paul, pleased by the honor accorded their father, were aware that

J. Sterling was now in a position to execute administration policies in the nation's agricultural sector in which both were deeply involved.

It was necessary, of course, for J. Sterling to live in Washington, D.C., where his sister, Emma, accompanied him as his hostess. Arbor Lodge would be unoccupied. It seemed natural that Carl move in with his family to keep a Morton presence there. But at that moment, Carl's job was in jeopardy. Joy's efforts to reorganize and subsidize the starch works were not going well, and he laid a good deal of the blame on Carl's inability to find directors who would invest in the company. Joy told J. Sterling, "Am sorry for Carl, if he can't induce Directors to run he must not expect me to risk a lot more money to keep him a job. I had better make him a present of a few months salary."[40]

But the possibility of marketing Argo Starch at the Columbian Exposition encouraged Joy to stay with it for a while longer. In March 1893, he wrote to his father that he had arranged to exhibit starch and cereal products in the World's Fair Agricultural Building and that he expected to make a "creditable show." Joy became involved in every aspect of the display that emphasized that starch was a production "of the Great American Desert of 40 years ago." He arranged to have "old geogaphics and guide books" that would show the public how the area was regarded by various authors. Joy vowed he would hold his own "with the older concerns in the Starch business."[41]

The display contributed to the starch company's abrupt return to solvency, and J. Sterling proposed that Carl, whose management of the company was no longer in jeopardy, should move into Arbor Lodge. Joy agreed even though he remained doubtful of Carl's stamina and abilities. Demanding that it be a business deal that he would monitor, Joy required Carl to sign a contract in which he would be allowed to make decisions on purchasing hogs, cattle, and seed but would have to consult with Joy and his father on other matters. Carl and his family were also required to leave Arbor Lodge within two months of J. Sterling's return.

The letterhead of Joy Morton & Co. in 1893 described the extent of some of Joy's principal investments in both Chicago and Nebraska City: "Joy Morton & Co. Dealers in Starch SALT Sal Soda Rolled Oats: Agents Michigan Salt Company / Lehigh Salt Mining Co. / Agents Argo Starch/ Quail.Brand. Oats." Appealing to the domestic market, and particularly focused on the technologically advanced Chicago exposition, the company's advertising message was comprehensive: "We make for Table use and Pack in Packages Corn Grits, Meal and a self-rising Pancake Flour containing 25% Wheat and balance Corn, also Rolled Oats. . . . We take great interest in your

Cooking Oven, as we realize that cheap fuel is to go with cheap food."

Carl once again was the proud general manager of the Nebraska City Starch Company, Manufacturers of the Argo brand gloss starch. But Joy was less than satisfied with his brother's work at Arbor Lodge. He and his father agreed that Carl's future as a farmer was "not brilliant," and Joy thought that "the attempt to help Carl out [was] a failure," expecting that he would cost him and J. Sterling $1,000.[42] Carl was oblivious to Joy's criticism, writing to J. Sterling the day before Joy sent his letter that his father's directive to put salt around the apple trees resulted in many of them dying from an overdose. "The trees in this orchard are too close," he added and asked his father, who had had them planted that way, "Don't you think we had better cut every other one out?"[43] Carl's letter could not have pleased the new secretary of agriculture, whose horticultural practices were being questioned.

Joy's renewed impatience with Carl might have been heightened by the Panic of 1893 that descended on the country at the outset of the second Cleveland administration. Like the Panic of 1873, overbuilding of railroads and a tightening of credit as banks began to fail on bad loans created a depression that would last for at least three years. Some considered the event an extension of the economic downturn of twenty years before, when a similar pattern of railroad bankruptcies and bank failures occurred. Though its effects in Chicago were at first somewhat muted by the opening of the World's Columbian Exposition, Joy did not relish distractions that would interfere with his preparations for meeting the looming economic challenges. Because of reduced prices, the salt business, which had generally remained stable during periods of economic recession, was "exceedingly lively," he told his father. "We sold more salt in two days last week than have ever sold in some time."[44]

But a month later he was lamenting the need of having to "trim . . . sales very close. . . ." Underwriting of the starch works and cereal mills in Nebraska City had caused Joy to be "stuck" with a loss of hundreds of dollars.[45] By late June, the nation's economy had gotten so bad that President Cleveland called a special session of Congress, and Joy informed J. Sterling that he was shutting down "all the expenditures that we possibly can." Even so, he was determined to go ahead with building another salt storage shed on the Illinois Central Pier I for $8,000. "If the strain continues," he explained, "we are going to have lots of trouble, but we (JM&CO) are not going to be affected by it to any extent."[46] He had anticipated the downturn, and the salt industry supplied an essential commodity increasingly in demand by an expanding country.

In spite of the depressed economy, the 1893 Exposition brought to Chicago's lakefront the world's latest offerings in technology, culture, and pleasure. Living nearby, the Mortons took full advantage of its many attractions. Carrie was the most frequent visitor, often accompanied by Jean and Sterling, who were ten and eight. On full day visits, the family rendezvoused at the "Porto Rico" building for lunch and convened there for the return home. The Groveland Park house was a convenient place to entertain friends, relatives, business acquaintances, and, of course, political dignitaries who visited the fair, including President Cleveland. Joy was prompted to purchase a pair of horses and "suitable carriages" to transport the guests.[47]

$\mathscr{J}$oy was busy restoring his own enterprises to profitability as the panic waned in late summer. He completed moving his offices to his warehouse at the Illinois Central Railroad Pier 1, telling his father that he owed nothing on his new buildings. In Nebraska City, the mill and the starch company were thriving. Joy arranged for Mark, under a lease to a new business entity, Mark Morton & Co., to assume oversight of the starch company while Carl retained the title of general manager. Joy resigned as president but maintained his financial interest.[48]

Joy was in fairly good spirits, but the excitement of the hectic summer had taken a toll on Carrie, who had suffered a second miscarriage and whose stamina continued to be tested by what her Omaha doctor had diagnosed in 1881 as malarial influences of long standing. On his thirty-eighth birthday, Joy told his father that Carrie was recovering, Jean was home from school with stigmatism, and Sterling, who was in third grade, having skipped second, was "afflicted only by an apparently uncontrollable desire to talk continuously." Joy's businesses were "more than usually profitable," and he was distributing salt in Tennessee, Mississippi, Texas, and other southern states with excellent results.[49] But Joy's reports on Arbor Lodge, on which he kept a close eye while Carl lived there, were less sanguine. The dam at Lake Jopamaca had failed once again. When Joy and Carrie visited Arbor Lodge in October, Joy concluded that he was not in favor of doing anything more about the dam, having found that things at the home place were otherwise "o.k." but for a "water famine."[50]

The end of the world's fair was marred by the assassination on October 28 of Mayor Carter Henry Harrison, who had been central to the event's immense success.[51] And Carrie, who experienced a relapse and stayed on in Omaha to rest, had returned so ill that she had to be placed under the care of a doctor and nurse, and the family could not visit J. Sterling over Christmas. The economy had also not improved as quickly as Joy and his fellow Chicagoans had expected. As 1893 came to a close, Joy invoked the old family description of depression: "I don't like the looks of the business world. We are having lots of failures and it seems as though everybody here is bluer than indigo. It may be the natural result of too much boom during the fair but it isn't at all comfortable."[52]

Even with the dire economic news and Carrie's uncertain health, Joy could look back with some satisfaction over the past seven years. The salt industry remained stable; his family was settled in a pleasant home in Chicago; J. Sterling had attained a post in President Cleveland's cabinet; and Carl was developing into a responsible businessman. Joy, while certain that becoming a part of the salt industry was the best decision he had ever made, had invested profitably in Nebraska City, where he thought he might retire. For now, there was no doubt that Chicago suited him.

Business and Politics—1894–1896

Joy was regaining his optimism as 1894 began, saying proudly to his father, "It may be pleasant for you to know that your eldest son was this afternoon elected First Vice President of the American Trust & Savings Bank, which now has $1,250,000 of Capital and surplus and over four millions of deposits."[1] The bank in which he had invested in 1889 and that had weathered the Panic of 1893 had offered him a directorship a year earlier, but he waited until the vote of the directors was unanimous. Soon, on the retirement of Gilbert B. Shaw, his friend Edwin A. Potter became president and Joy vice president, a role to which he brought a strong habit of fiscal conservatism.

By February, Joy had more positive news for his father. He had returned from Saginaw, Michigan, where the salt association had been reorganized. He wrote to J. Sterling, "Shall have the most solid Association for the next two years that we have had for many years. It will be a good thing for both the Manufacturers and the Agents."[2] And in March, he reported on generally positive developments in his Nebraska City businesses, which were now under the management of both Mark and Carl. Mark Morton & Company were listed as the lessees of the Nebraska City Starch Co., manufacturers of Argo Brand Corn and Gloss Starch. Joy wrote, "The Mill & Starch Co, both going on steadily and making a little money, ditto stock yards, but the Produce Co has made a loss on the last year's business."[3] The faltering Morton Produce Company was described on its letterhead as "Wholesale Dealers and Brokers in Butter, Poultry, Apples, Small Fruits and Vegetables, no. 414 Central Ave., Neb. City, P. Stafford, President, Joy Morton, Vice President, Carl Morton, Treasurer, D. A. MacQuaig, Secy Manager."

*W*hen Joy visited his Nebraska holdings and Arbor Lodge with Paul, Lottie, and Carrie in March 1894, he made a decision that would be significant for both his childhood home and for the extended Morton family for years to come. The families had agreed "after a full discussion" to make Arbor Lodge their "country home."[4] The Chicago-based families would fix up the grounds and supply horses and carriages, a pony cart for the children, and extra domestics so that Carl and Boatie would not be burdened during visits. Joy was particularly interested in giving his own children an opportunity to experience the country life in which he had been brought up. J. Sterling, too, was thinking of Arbor Lodge, to which he would return after leaving his post in President Cleveland's cabinet. In Washington, D.C., he redid the logo of Arbor Lodge, using the directive "Plant Trees" under the image of a tree, emphasizing that Arbor Lodge was the site of Arbor Day.

While at Arbor Lodge, Joy and Paul made plans to join their father on a fall trip to Europe. Typically, Joy looked into arrangements. His preference, he wrote on the first day of spring, was to go on the best steamer possible, because "We don't go often enough to warrant us in taking a slow boat to save a few dollars in passage money." Joy's father might have talked about economizing because he had not built up the fortune that Joy and Paul already enjoyed. But his sons insisted on traveling well.

Although Joy was not particularly concerned with saving a few dollars, he was in the process of liquidating a salt manufacturing plant he had purchased from the Diamond Salt Co. near Hutchinson, Kansas. As the Michigan Salt Association representatives predicted, sixteen competing salt makers had finally driven their companies into insolvency, helped along by the Panic of 1893. Within months, a major flood of nearby Cow Creek shut down Joy's plant, and by May 1894, he was completing the final details of the disposition of the plant.[5] Even this business did not keep Joy from taking time to relax on a brief fishing trip, leaving Mark in charge.

New problems awaited him, however. In June the 150,000 members of the American Railway Union headed by Eugene Debs went out on strike. Although the strike was general throughout the country, Chicago was its center. When Governor John P. Altgeld called out the state militia, his attempt to quell the violence was trumped by President Cleveland, who, in the interest of intrastate commerce, brought in federal troops. The strike and its aftermath extended the Panic of 1893 and was a significant factor in the ensuing decades-long split between labor and management. Joy Morton & Co. weathered the strike. As a large employer of hourly workers, however, Joy Morton & Co. had entered into an era in which working conditions, pay, and benefits would be constantly on the agenda between labor and management. By paying close attention to their laborers' welfare throughout the prolonged struggle of the labor movement, Joy and Mark allayed work-stopping unrest at the salt firm.

Joy's new focus on Arbor Lodge, where electric lights were part of the planned improvements, motivated him to become more active in investing in Nebraska City. In June he told J. Sterling that the starch company had once again been reorganized with capital of $100,000. With a majority interest, Joy was confident that since the Argo brand had been "fairly well introduced," the company would be profitable. He reported that business at the cereal mill was also "excellent." Joy Morton & Co. was now a major producer of grain products and was seeking national recognition. Mark wrote to ask his father to speak at a dinner in Chicago hosted by Joy Morton & Co. The dinner would show off only Nebraska products. Referring to the new starch company, Mark told his father, "Our company is now called Argo Manufacturing Company."[6] The Morton Produce Co. investment in which Joy, Mark, and Carl were involved dealt in much of the Nebraska produce that would be featured at the meeting.

By late August, Joy was still trying to get J. Sterling to make a decision on the steamer he, his brother Paul, and J. Sterling would take to Europe. They planned to leave by the second week in September. Joy urged the fastest line possible and suggested the Cunard line, saying, "If I do go am going by the best & fastest steamers. Five days and a fraction on shipboard with nothing to do will be more 'restfulness' than I have ever yet had and is as much as I want to contract for. . . ." Finally, they decided on the steamer *Lahn* of the North German Lloyd line. The fare, Joy wrote, was "the enormous price of $50 each for the best kind of a stateroom and grub. The latter may not cost the steamboat company much if [it] is very rough."[7]

The three Mortons spent two weeks in Europe, where J. Sterling stayed in France attending to official business, while Joy and Paul toured Italy, Germany, Denmark, and the Netherlands before returning to London and home with their father. They found the nation alive with the clamor of the mid-term national elections, the results of which boosted Republican membership in Congress, giving a sound defeat to William Jennings Bryan's "free-silver" Democrats, who had wanted to place silver on an equal footing with gold, thereby allowing for a wider availability of currency, particularly in the south and west. Joy was especially buoyed by both the election and the trip. Mark wrote to his father, "Think Joy received the most good from the visit. He has settled down to business nicely. I am pleased to say that he is very well pleased at the way the business of this firm was conducted during his absence."[8] But Joy was not so optimistic about the future. Realizing that the economy had not fully recovered from the Panic of 1893 and labor unrest, he told J. Sterling that the coming year was not promising.[9]

At Groveland Park, major remodeling had been completed by Thanksgiving. But Carrie's recurring health problems interfered with plans for the holidays. Just before Christmas, Joy wrote to his father that Carrie could not visit him, saying, "She has been far from well for a month and this week is quite miserable; so much so that I feel quite alarmed about her. She needs absolute rest and quiet and I am trying hard to induce her to go to a sanitarium near Riverside where some ladies of our acquaintance, similarly affected, have been much benefited."[10] Carrie's fragile health was becoming a major concern for the family. She seemed never to have recovered from her miscarriages or from what her father had called "malarial symptoms of long standing."[11] With the approach of the new year, the "blues" had set in once more in Joy's household.

*W*hen the economic slowdown lingered into the opening months of 1895, Joy intensified his disposition of holdings that were chronically unproductive. Among these was a belt line of streetcars, which included the Joliet & Eastern, serving Matteson, Chicago Heights, and Joliet; the Joliet, Plainfield & Aurora, serving those three towns; and the Aurora & DeKalb, connecting with the Northwestern Railway in DeKalb. The first two components were electrified and delivered passengers and freight effectively, but the Aurora & DeKalb began badly, experimenting with an unreliable gas-propelled engine being developed in the earliest days of the automobile. Joy managed to divest himself of the DeKalb streetcar and soon withdrew from the Aurora to Joliet venture, which was a money-losing proposition. He stayed with the more profitable Joliet & Eastern until the motorcar forced it out of business, at which time, during World War I, he sold what could be salvaged for scrap metal.[12]

Joy had also purchased stock in 1891 in the Macon, Dublin, & Savannah Railroad. In 1895, he joined other investors on a trip to Georgia to take a hard look at the business. What they saw was not promising. Joy decided to sell immediately, but he was not anxious to travel to woo potential buyers, among them representatives of the Atlantic Coast Line. This proved to be a useful strategy, his son observed in the 1930s: "Apparently his aloof attitude had some weight with the prospective purchaser, for an arrangement was soon closed by which the large system became the owner of the Macon, Dublin & Savannah."[13] In July, Joy wrote to his father, "We were successful in having disposed of our Georgia R. R. at a satisfactory price."[14]

Joy's investments in railroads were not all losing propositions, however. He backed Paul and Theodore P. Shauntz in the purchase of the Indiana, Illinois & Iowa Railroad, running from South Bend, Indiana, to Streator, Illinois, via Kankakee. This railway was far enough south of Chicago that it avoided the often severe congestion of other lines. When the three decided to sell, the line was purchased by the New York Central Lines, and the line became known as the Chicago, Indiana, & Southern.[15]

One other failing investment was in Nebraska City. In February 1895, Joy decided to close the Morton Produce Co., because the secretary and manager had mismanaged the books. Joy had to cover a loss of $4,000 from the year before and some $18,000 since the company's inception in 1891, but he took the loss with equanimity. He was certain that as the country continued to recover from the Panic of 1893, his other business ventures would regain their profitability, telling his father, "Most of the bubbles have already 'busted.'"[16]

Following two years of weak economic growth, the nation's industry was again expanding and marketing to new customers. In late July 1895 Joy sent Paul a sample of a 3 x 5 card that succinctly summarized the comprehensive work of Joy Morton & Co. Stating that the company was the agent for the Michigan Salt Co., Retsof Mining, and Argo Starch and a dealer in salt, starch, and sal soda (a salt product used as a cleaning agent), the advertisement announced, "Improved methods of manufacture, combined with cheap *Lake Freights*, enable us to offer you MICHIGAN SALT at lower prices than have ever before been made in the history of the Salt trade. Our facilities for receiving and forwarding Salt are unequalled. We can load assorted car lots, including COMMON No. 1,

DAIRY, TABLE and ROCK SALT."[17] Prospective customers could write for prices for salt delivered to the closest railroad depot.

Over the years, Joy had learned to read national trends as harbingers of what he should do in his own businesses. Confident in his ability to analyze economic conditions, Joy advised his father freely as the nation moved out of its economic downturn. He argued that the high cost of meat to the consumer was due not simply to the cattle raisers producing less. The journey of the product from hoof to the retail store, he calculated, was ten times the amount that the cattleman received. He singled out private refrigerator car owners as culprits of high costs for western beef in the east because they were, in the age of monopolies, becoming a monopoly in themselves and were not beholden to the railroads. Finally, he reminded his father, "You are working for 3 classes (assuming 3rd class can't afford to not eat meat) as follows: Class 1, The Beef Producer; 2 Beef eater; 3 Railroad people."[18] Joy was also concerned that his father's habit of forthrightly voicing his political opinions, particularly to newspapers, could jeopardize his effectiveness in carrying out the duties of the office of Secretary of Agriculture for President Cleveland, saying, "You can't hunt this sort of duck with a band."[19] William Jennings Bryan was already laying the groundwork for obtaining the presidential nomination in the next election, and J. Sterling found it difficult to remain silent on the prospect of his antagonist becoming the party's standard-bearer.

*B*usiness and political strategy were not the only topics of correspondence between Joy and J. Sterling in the closing months of J. Sterling's term as secretary of agriculture. J. Sterling had always been acutely interested in how he would be remembered by posterity. Joy, too, was beginning to contemplate ways he could use his wealth to the best advantage in order to be remembered by future generations. While his fortune paled beside that of tycoons of the latter part of the nineteenth century, he believed that he would eventually have an amount that could do some good in both Nebraska City and Chicago. Joy wrote to ask his father if he could send him pictures and plans of public buildings; he was thinking of a building that could be used "for a library, picture gallery and museum, and more room to be devoted to the gallery and museum than to the books." This was the first step in what would prove to be a thoroughgoing investigation into the sort of public building that he could give to the citizens of Nebraska City.[20]

Joy's interest in giving a library building to Nebraska City was furthered by a Nebraska law that emphasized the obligations of the citizenry to become partners in the care and maintenance of donated buildings. The mandate corresponded with Joy's own idea of how benefactors and recipients should share responsibility. In a letter in which he told his father that he was furthering his industrial investment in Nebraska City by expanding the Argo starch plant, he thanked J. Sterling for sending a report on Massachusetts libraries. "The more I think of the Library scheme the better it seems," he wrote. "My idea is that a nice lot in town, with trees around it, would be the proper place but I will go slow about deciding."[21]

Joy had by now given much thought to the library, and he knew what he wanted. After hearing from his father that he believed the library should be located nearer Arbor Lodge, Joy responded, "I think the Library should be built in the most central part of town. . . . The Library would be much more of a success so located and more convenient to you personally than if it were planted in the suburbs as you suggest." J. Sterling had also questioned Joy's decision to enlarge the starch plant, to which Joy replied forcefully, "The enlargement of the Starch Works was absolutely necessary."[22]

That the presidential election year of 1896 would mark J. Sterling's final year in a powerful political office was not lost on either Joy or Paul. From the beginning of his tenure in Cleveland's cabinet in 1893, J. Sterling had established a reputation as a fiscal conservative who brought order and honesty to the office and policies of the Department of Agriculture. Nevertheless, both Joy and Paul were driven by their respective business interests to test his principals throughout his service. They seemed to confuse the role that J. Sterling had played as a lobbyist in Washington, D.C., in the 1880s with his official appointment. As early as March 1893, at the behest of Armour and Co., Paul tried to convince J. Sterling to retain some "good and efficient people" in the Department of Agriculture. Later in 1893, he asked that he be informed if J. Sterling knew anything about the Union Pacific Railroad going into receivership. "I know a young man," he said none too subtly, "who would like very much indeed to be one of the Receivers, if it could be so arranged without embarrassment to his paternal ancestor. . . ."[23] There is no evidence that J. Sterling complied with either request.

Compared to Paul's supplications, Joy's first request of his father was completely benign. He asked that one of his office employees who was seventy-three be shown around Washington, D.C., in good fashion. "He has had only one short vacation in 15 years," Joy told his father, "and I would like to have him have a good time and if you can have him shown around in a carriage it would please him immensely. . . . He has been very loyal to me always and if you will pay him some attention I shall be very much pleased. . . ." J. Sterling readily obliged, prompting Joy to say, "Ed Haynes is home and is about the best satisfied man from Washington I have ever met. He said it would likely be his last pleasure trip before he left home, and now he thinks he can die happy."[24]

But as it became clear that J. Sterling had the opportunity to have a major impact on policies that would affect railroads and the food industry, both Paul and Joy decided that they should make the most of what they considered to be their opportunity for advantage. In his father's second year at his post, Joy broached the matter of what he considered an "unfair report" being made by agricultural investigative agents of the meat industry. Joy thought that if such a report condemned the industry wholesale, it "would be a great calamity," and he believed bad practices could be stopped without the sort of publicity that general charges against the Chicago meat industry would generate.[25]

In J. Sterling's final year of office, the requests became more urgent as the presidential conventions loomed and the courts were enforcing the 1890 Sherman Anti-Trust Act, which called for the prosecution of companies that joined together to form monopolies for the purpose of eliminating competition. Paul, who had been appointed third vice president of the Atchison, Topeka, and Santa Fe, petitioned his father to "do anything" he could to have the Democratic convention in Chicago, saying, "I think that the Santa Fe road can make more money out of the convention here than they can anywhere else. . . ."[26]

Writing on behalf of Armour and Swift, Joy lobbied J. Sterling to use his influence to squelch the government's subpoenas of the beef trusts, saying that he had "just got things into splendid shape . . . with these people" who, of course, were major users of salt. The prosecution, he said, "isn't necessary and will only react on the interests of those you care most for and I wish you would take an active interest in squelching the thing."[27] In his response, J. Sterling wisely distanced himself from the issue by simply explaining that he could do nothing, since prosecution was the domain of the Department of Justice.

Joy's attempts to use his father's influence were based on his belief that if government did not support successful business, the country's extraordinary progress would be halted. One area he wanted the government to participate in more than it already had was the improvement of both natural and man-made waterways in the Midwest. For example, he was convinced that the relatively undeveloped Calumet

River could become a more efficient commercial shipping waterway than the Chicago River, which had been overbuilt by bridges and could not be deepened for the passage of larger Lake Michigan ships. He minced no words in admitting his personal stake in the matter, saying, "We can get the cheapest freights only by chartering the biggest boats. Hence you can readily see why I take so much interest in this. There isn't any patriotism about it." Thinking that his last remarks had weakened his case, he followed this letter with another on the same day, arguing beyond self interest: "The trouble has always been that the Calumet River appropriation was coupled with appropriations made to improve the Chicago River, and the result has been that the Calumet has practically got nothing. It is now, in my judgment, the most important harbor on Lake Michigan. Certainly it is growing faster than any of the others."[28]

The letters on the Calumet are early indications of Joy's passion for proving the efficiency and economy of waterways over other transportation routes for carrying bulk goods like salt. It was a subject he would not only talk and write about throughout his life, but would also single-handedly put into practice as man-made waterways in Illinois were being largely abandoned. Joy's businesses in Nebraska City caused him to think, too, of water transportation there. Within a few days of writing the letter on the Calumet, Joy asked his father for information on what the government plans might be to increase barge use along the Missouri River. "It is my judgment barges, like those used on the Rhine," he said, "will some day take most of the Missouri Valley products to market. Coal and Iron are now transported in barges from Pittsburgh to Memphis for $.60 cents per gross ton. There is more water in the Missouri than in the Ohio."[29]

*J*oy had a more immediate problem to deal with in Nebraska City. The former operator of the mill had left debts against the corporation. As principal stockholder, Joy felt that he should try to make good on those debts himself. He explained to his father, "It is a long and pitiful story. I don't want to expose [the operator's family] as it will do no good since nothing can be recovered from the estates. I will try and make up my loss. If I don't it won't embarrass me particularly."[30] Carrie's father, Judge George Lake, helped him with the settlement.

In the same letter, Joy warned his father against speculating in grain—a conflict of interest with his role as secretary of agriculture. "If your salary isn't enough to cover proper expenses," Joy advised him, "why not write for the Magazines." Knowing that writing would not produce the income that his father wanted, Joy offered an incentive: "If you will do this I will cheerfully duplicate the amounts you may receive if you need the money as we all are proud of your magazine articles and would like to encourage them now while you are in official position as it seems to us all it should be your business after you retire to Arbor Lodge and now is the time to get started." Joy reminded his father of a pledge he had taken two years earlier. "See your letter of April 25th 1894 and my reply dated 27th regarding your having taken 'God cure' to overcome habit of speculating. I have it posted in my Ledger. Have you had any deals since you wrote that letter?" A few days later Joy urged his father "to devote a little less time to the service of our Uncle Samuel and put in a couple of hours daily on Magazine work."

Joy's concern about his father did not keep him from giving attention to the cereal mill, which he was busy reorganizing, or to Nebraska City. He was ambivalent about lending the Morton name to the cereal business and finally decided against it, "because some day we might want to sell out, then we would not want to sell our own name, and yet, if we are successful, the good will and name of the corporation might be worth considerable."[31]

In March 1896, Joy accompanied his father, who was recuperating from an illness, to Biltmore, George W. Vanderbilt's new estate in Buncombe County, North Carolina. Vanderbilt, the youngest son of William and grandson of Cornelius, the nineteenth-century railroad magnates, had inherited sufficient money to pursue his love of horticulture on a grand scale. Joy and his father saw firsthand how private wealth could be employed to create a natural surrounding that had both practical and aesthetic purposes. Biltmore had already become the stage for one of the most significant confluences of talent in American architectural and horticultural history. Begun in 1890, the 250-room French chateaux had been designed by the noted architect Richard Morris Hunt, who was a friend of the young Vanderbilt. Among Hunt's accomplishments had been Harvard University's Fogg Art Museum, the Tribune Building in New York City, and the prize-winning administration building at the World's Columbian Exposition in Chicago. Vanderbilt had also hired the seventy-year-old Frederick Law Olmsted, by then the nation's most celebrated landscape architect, to design the surrounding grounds and Gifford Pinchot to plan the reforestation of some 95,000 acres that had been cut and farmed by previous owners of the land. A graduate of France's L'Ecole Nationale Forestiere, Pinchot was the first United States citizen to be professionally trained in forestry. Biltmore was Olmsted's final major work, and in 1897, Pinchot became the chief of the forestry division of the United States Department of Agriculture under William McKinley. Carl Alwen Schenck, the German forester chosen by Pinchot to be his successor at Biltmore, had been working on the grounds for a year. In 1898, he became the founding director of the Biltmore Forest School, the first such institution in the United States. Its development was of great interest to J. Sterling.[32] Pinchot, Olmsted, and Hunt had completed their work at Biltmore by the time the Mortons arrived. Schenck was busy with reforestation and with the early stages of planning the forestry school.

The visit to Biltmore inspired J. Sterling to write a prophetic letter to Joy, one that encapsulated a mission and a blueprint for action that were coincident with Joy's own long-range thoughts. J. Sterling lingered at Biltmore when Joy departed, and he had been, as he said, "quite at a loss for a confidential, closely-related friend." After wandering the estate, he returned to "that magnificent library" from whose windows, he "fixed in [his] mind the image of Mt. Pisgah and the Rat," mountainous formations looming in the distance. Then he philosophized at length on what George Vanderbilt had begun to create with his wealth. Biltmore was a "lasting monument" composed of "forestry, floriculture, horticulture and other embellishments." The monument, J. Sterling pointed out, was the result of the frugality of George's grandfather, Commodore Cornelius Vanderbilt, when he began his business career ferrying passengers across the Hudson for ten cents each. "Unlike other ferrymen of his day," J. Sterling pointed out, "he was economical, accumulated money, bought more rowboats, and lastly steamboats, and when steamboats were going out of use he purchased railroads. From such a beginning accrued all the millions of the Vanderbilt family, and if this vast aggregation of money had never accomplished anything more for humanity than the erection of the chateau at Biltmore and reforesting the hills thereabouts, it would at least have made a better return to the race than do most accumulations."

Biltmore was an object lesson in J. Sterling's deep-seated belief that the accumulation of wealth in the Gilded Age was a necessary goal in life but not an end in itself. Wealth meant security and respect for family, but it also brought an opportunity—if not an obligation—to leave a meaningful legacy, a monument to one's achievements. Arbor Day was J. Sterling's. And Arbor Lodge, the home that stood proudly on a hill amidst its acreage of trees, was still becoming, in incremental stages, a mansion that would signify the achievements of the entire Morton family.

In J. Sterling's mind, George W. Vanderbilt, seven years Joy's junior, was erecting an unparalleled living monument at Biltmore. It was both aesthetic and utilitarian, a combination, J. Sterling thought, that was necessary for a successful environmental project. Charles McNamee, the manager of the estate, oversaw 762 men on the grounds. "The profits on the capital invested in wages paid these men will not begin to materialize for some years to come, but they are as certain as the trees are to grow," J. Sterling noted. Dr. Schenck had told J. Sterling that the 95,000 acre forest would have yielded $500,000 in lumber but would have been denuded and infertile within ten years. But the management practices being put in place would guarantee renewal and a $5,000 net profit each year "in perpetuity."

J. Sterling's discourse on wealth and its uses had a special purpose for a final directive to Joy—delivered albeit obliquely—urging him to begin to think seriously of the sort of legacy that he himself would leave either around Nebraska City or Chicago:

> In view of the foregoing, I do wish that some enterprising man of wealth who loves his kind and who desires to be remembered in generations to come, would undertake somewhere in Nebraska the establishment of an estate something like the Vanderbilt, only, of course, it need not be one-tenth as large. Some Chicago citizen of means might purchase the Van Wyck farms and run down and take in Walnut Creek as far as the mill, including the Hawke farm, Mark Morton and Buchanan farms, and there make a wonderfully instructive object-lesson in forestry and horticulture. But I do not presume there is anyone disposed at this time to undertake such an enterprise, notwithstanding its beneficence to this and coming generations must be obvious to all who think or study at all as to the incalculable value of forests to human life as well as to the fertility of the soil.
>
> The more I think about the Vanderbilt place, the more I am impressed with its importance as a great lesson to the American people, and especially am I convinced that it will be an incentive to others to do, in proportion to their means, like things for the embellishment of their homes.

J. Sterling's letter set forth a grand idea and a blueprint upon which it would be left to his oldest son to act. It would be a quarter of a century before Joy did so.

For Joy, the future of his businesses, particularly in Chicago, was uppermost in his mind. In 1896, Joy Morton & Co. was building a salt plant at Hutchinson, Kansas, near the site he and the Michigan salt producers had visited several years before. In Chicago, an independent investment in the Western Cold Storage Company that he and Mark had made in 1894 was also showing promise. The plant had a value of $600,000. Its annual report noted that the company's "present prosperous condition could not have been obtained" without Joy's counsel, service as treasurer, and "strong and ready financial aid."

As a new century was nearing, Joy was particularly careful in the appointments he made at the salt company, finding young men whose work ethic matched his and who could be counted on to assure continuity in management. As Mark became more involved in the Western Cold Storage Co., eventually becoming president, Joy had to look for others whom he could trust. In March 1896, Joy acquired the Standard Salt Company of Chicago and with it a young Scottish immigrant by the name of Daniel Peterkin. In 1893, at the age of eighteen, Peterkin, the son of a well-to-do family, had come to America to work for an Indianapolis meatpacker and later the Standard Salt Company. Impressed by Peterkin's initiative and energy, Joy hired him as a private secretary, even though he had no skill in typewriting and shorthand. Peterkin immediately enrolled in night school and within a short time was efficient at both. His propensity to plan carefully and to give attention to detail led Joy to move him into management. For several years Peterkin continued taking courses in business and management and made himself indispensable.[33]

While Peterkin seemed a natural, no one could have predicted that three young men who grew up in the Groveland Park neighborhood might one day be hired by Joy. Coming to the firm around the time Peterkin was hired were B.W. Carrington and the brothers A.G. and R.K. Warren, known as "The Groveland Park Boys." Joy hired these young men to work in his office, even though not many years earlier they had vandalized the construction at 15 Groveland Park. In 1934, Robert K. Warren began a letter to Sterling by recalling the damage he, his brother, and Carrington had wrought on the site, leading the contractor to remark that although he had done work in Chicago's notorious "back of the yards," he had never had as much trouble with vandalism as in the upscale neighborhood of Groveland Park. "The happy crowd," wrote Warren, "would run along the top of the freshly laid brick walls, dump nails and mortar down the vent pipes and as a crowning job, pushed the large capping stones (which were on top of brick columns supporting the porch roof) into the basement."[34] Warren told Sterling that they were "forcibly reminded" of Joy's irritation with the delay. But Joy's subsequent experience with them, Sterling later said, convinced Joy that they were worthy and that their imagination and energy could be channeled effectively into his business. After all, Joy and his brothers, particularly Mark, had exhibited some of the same rambunctious behavior in their youth in Nebraska. The Groveland Park boys spent most of their working lives in the salt industry in key management roles, and, like Peterkin, contributed to a remarkable tradition of longevity with the firm.[35]

The offices of Joy Morton & Co. that Peterkin, the Warrens, and Carrington came to as young men were Dickensian. In his 1934 letter, R.K. Warren described what his clerk's life was like. "I found at the pier a long wooden stair case running up the west side of one of the large frame warehouses to a small vestibule which opened into a good sized room with imitation blue and white tile paper on the walls," he remembered. The clerks of Joy Morton & Co. occupied the room. In the center sat a single large drum heater that provided too much heat for those next to it and not enough for those near the outer walls. For light, each clerk had a kerosene lamp "of doubtful lineage," and arguments broke out as to who would get the ones that worked best. The toilet facilities were "crude." Drinking water had to be drayed from a fire hydrant located at South Water Street and Michigan Avenue, "for which privilege we paid the City five dollars per year." Joy had his own small office, a working kerosene lamp, wash basin, and heating stove, which Warren, as a new clerk, fed with coal.

According to Warren, Joy also did not look favorably upon scheduled vacations for his office workers. He recalled being told by Joy that vacations "were a detriment to employer and employee" for the reason that "the clerk spent more money than he could afford and came back all tired out and was not much good for a week or so after his return." Joy did let the clerks who had done their work go home at 1:00 p.m. during the unbearably hot days of July and August. But he believed in setting an example for his office workers. Warren remembered that Joy was "one of the first ones down in the morning and last ones to leave at night. He personally kept and figured what costs they had and the results he entered in a small bound book kept in his safe."

Streetlights in Chicago in the late 1890s stretched east only as far as Michigan Avenue, and Warren recalled that "it was a long dark walk in the winter time from the office south to Randolph Street" to Michigan Avenue. Nevertheless, Warren remembered the city as having been relatively safe, and he had no difficulty taking the cash payroll from the pier office to the South Chicago dock on the Calumet River. This required walking over the Randolph Street viaduct to the Illinois Central suburban station, traveling to 95th Street, boarding a trolley car to 102nd, and then walking through a freight yard.[36] The working conditions that Warren described, though customary at the time, were a concern for Joy. A simple task of delivery often consumed hours, and office workers as well as administrators were at the mercy of Chicago's erratic weather. Joy understood the advantage to business of new technologies that would make employees' working lives less arduous and thus more productive. As the twentieth century loomed, Joy's faith in technology led him to embrace the opportunities it offered for himself and his workers. Inspired by the World's Columbian Exposition, Chicago's business culture had become a crucible for new ideas and methods in business. Now in his prime, Joy was poised to become an integral part of Chicago's future, even as he was continuing to invest in the town of his boyhood and was perhaps thinking of one day returning there.

Joy and Carrie were also thinking of the near future for their family. While they maintained their love of the places in Nebraska where they had grown into adulthood, they had raised their children in Groveland Park for the past ten years and had reason to regard Chicago as their permanent home. Although Carrie's health sometimes took her back to Omaha to rest, she was resilient and was able to recover from exhausting bouts of illness. When she was well, both she and Joy were intent on giving their children all that a major city could offer as well as providing them with the chance to know the life they had lived back in Nebraska. They both took pleasure in their children, now growing into adolescence at Groveland Park, and they planned that Jean and Sterling would have the best education and experiences they could provide.

Toward a New Century—1896–1902

At forty, Joy had achieved the security of wealth that had eluded his father. Joy was in a position to contemplate how best to use his time and talents in the future, not just for business but also for his family and the public good. In 1896, as he thought about his father's impending return to Arbor Lodge, Joy focused on what J. Sterling had proposed a year earlier when he wrote from Biltmore about building a "grand estate" near Nebraska City or Chicago. Where Joy would build an estate and how the grounds would be developed depended upon where it might best satisfy his desire for a meaningful legacy, much in the way that Arbor Lodge would do for his father.

First on Joy's agenda in the summer of 1896, however, was preparation for a lengthy tour of Europe. For the first time since forming Joy Morton & Co., Joy felt he could rely totally on Mark and others whom he had personally hired for key management positions. The occasion for the visit to Europe was Joy and Carrie's intent to school Jean, thirteen, and Sterling, eleven, in either Paris or Geneva for a year. Paul and Lottie's daughters, Caroline, fourteen, and Pauline Joy, nine, would join their cousins in the year abroad, a custom many well-to-do Chicago families followed in the 1890s. Carrie and Lottie would chaperone the children and get them settled, and Joy and Paul would follow at the end of the year for an extended visit.

After investigating Parisian schools, Carrie and Lottie found in Geneva exactly the sort of situation they wanted. While the children attended boarding schools, they could live nearby in comfortable quarters. Paul explained the decision to J. Sterling, saying that Geneva was "a much better place for them than Paris, morally and physically."[1] Not deigning to criticize Paris, Joy wrote, "All we want is for them to learn French and they can now hardly help doing that."[2]

Their wives and children had been gone for but a few weeks when Paul said half jokingly to his father, "I never could stand it without Joy and I guess he could not without me. We are constantly together and even the spiciest gossip pertaining to railroads, starch, salt and business generally, fails to keep us up after half past nine or ten o'clock."[3] But the brothers occupied themselves with more than work. In November, they spent a few days hunting in Missouri.

*A*rriving in Geneva without Paul, who had to stay behind to tend to business, Joy was delighted to find Carrie in apparent good health and spirits and the schools to be to the children's liking. Sterling had received a report of *tres satisfaits* for his first trimester. "The discipline of [Chateau de Lancy, the boys' school]," Joy told his father, "is like that of the German Army, but the boys seem to like it."[4] Joy had planned to take everyone to Nice and on to Cairo during the children's holiday vacation, but Carrie, exhausted from attending Geneva's holiday festival, needed rest. Knowing that Mark would enjoy hearing of the New Year's celebrations, Joy described the scene in detail: "The town is full of all kinds of cheap side shows merry go rounds and shooting galleries, in tents, chiefly." The "plain people" were having "a hell of a time" and didn't go home until morning. "The noise is terrific," he continued, "but there don't appear to be much fighting nor many people with too much booze to navigate, after a fashion."[5]

When Carrie felt strong enough, the group set off for Nice and Monte Carlo, and again Joy was anxious to give Mark his impressions of both: "[Nice] is a great town, the swellest folks you ever saw, and most of them have money to burn, and they can burn it very rapidly over at Monte Carlo, only 14 miles from here. We were there all day yesterday, greatly entertained. It is a most beautiful place, palm trees and tropical foliage of all kinds, with all kinds of flowers in full bloom; the day was fine."

Joy observed the gamblers at Monte Carlo closely, knowing their habits would interest his brother, of whose gambling he disapproved. "They sling one hundred franc gold pieces about like we do 1½ chips in a 25 cent game, and don't seem to think any more of them. At the tables the women are in the majority, and all look like professionals. There were probably over 1000 people in the salon, all the afternoon. The games are roulette and '*trente et quarante*,' and you have no idea how easy the game moves along."[6]

Joy indulged in the card game *trente et quarante* (thirty and forty) only long enough to make the experience an object lesson for Mark in the foolishness of risk taking. He purchased a book on the game, read it, and then made a single twenty-franc bet that he immediately lost, telling Mark, "you never saw $4 get away from a fellow quicker." The women had better luck, but Joy put their success in perspective: "Lottie bet 5 francs at Roulette and won 5 francs. So now the girls think they know it all about Monte Carlo, since they have beaten the bank. But they refused to play again for fear of a different result."[7]

By February, the party was in Paris, where Joy made certain that they include botanical gardens in their itinerary. Intent on learning from the agricultural and horticultural practices of the country, Joy had in mind incipient plans of an estate of his own. He was fascinated by how French landscape gardeners managed large-scale projects at the Bois de Boulogne, the Jardin des Plantes, and Fountainebleau. "The French folks" he told his father, "are good at landscape gardening and seem to have learned how to move trees better than we do in America." On one occasion, Joy saw what he believed to be a fifty-year-old elm moved "up the Champs Elysses on a wagon drawn by six horses. . . . The mass of earth and roots was apparently solid although not frozen. The roots looked as though the cutting had been done two or three years ago. There were many small roots but no large ones which had been recently cut."[8]

Joy was equally impressed by the planting of large trees around lakeshores. He thought that if J. Sterling would do this sort of planting at Lake Jopamaca, he could enhance the bank aesthetically as well as structurally. Observing that "the prettiest banks are those thickly covered with Pines," Joy made specific recommendations. The Mortons should, he thought, thin a white pine orchard near Arbor Lodge and transfer the trees to the lake's bank, about ten feet up from the waterline. He promised his father that once they took root, he would try to "renew the dam with masonry and earth embankments with a good wide waste way next time."[9]

During his European trip, Joy became convinced that building an estate near Arbor Lodge was what he wanted to do. About the time that his father left Cleveland's cabinet to resume his life in Nebraska City, Joy returned to Chicago, thoroughly pleased with his trip and, after receiving a letter from Carrie that Sterling had "licked" the class bully, more certain than ever that he and Paul had done the right thing.[10] Back in Nebraska, however, J. Sterling had time on his hands to assume the patriarchal condescension he had long perfected. Appearances meant everything to him, and he made the mistake of questioning Paul's and Joy's wisdom regarding schooling their children in Europe. He had the feeling that people might find fault with the Morton children being educated in a foreign country. In the tone he had learned to use when his father overstepped his boundaries, Joy was quick to put his and Paul's decision into perspective: "We are doing what we think is best. . . . I care little for what folks think or say. Would much prefer to have you approve and encourage at least the good motive which has prompted Paul and I to do what we have done for our children."[11]

This discordant exchange was temporary, as usual, and did not deter Joy from wanting to build next to Arbor Lodge, where he already owned improved acreage. In the spring of 1897, he told his father that he wanted it to be "a place which would be worth having as next door neighbor to Arbor Lodge."[12] He already had fixed in his mind how the estate would be designed once he was able to purchase some contiguous land. He drew up a detailed map for his father, including trees that had already been planted and roadways yet to be built, one of which would run directly into the grounds of Arbor Lodge. The entire estate, Joy wrote in September, would also be an attractive vacation place for his family and "extensive enough to produce enough to sustain itself aside from improvements."[13]

More than that, Joy was thinking that such a place could provide Carrie with a much-needed place of rest. In the spring she had "quietly fainted away" during a social evening in Geneva. Unusually dispirited, she complained, "Oh, it does seem some times as tho I must see you and when I am not feeling well, I am in great terror of being homesick."[14] Carrie's illnesses had become more frequent than at any time since their marriage. Besides lingering respiratory problems, she had miscarriages in 1886 and 1889 and had a difficult birth with Jean. As her sojourn in Europe continued, her physical and emotional health took an even more ominous turn. From Montreaux, she wrote, "The trials come too often—you know the sort I mean,—but I am learning all the time better how to keep quiet. But the nervousness of it all scares me dreadfully, and since we have been here I have fainted again."[15]

After Carrie and the children returned to Groveland Park in late July 1897, her health deteriorated rapidly. She needed to have an operation – most likely to address problems having arisen from her two miscarriages in the 1880s—that both she and Joy realized should have been performed before she left for Europe a year before. By October Joy told his father that he would be "satisfied if she gains enough strength to feel like herself again."[16] She required a place where she could rest and be taken care of. An estate near Arbor Lodge would provide that with the added value of placing Carrie nearer to her father and stepmother.

*E*ven before he committed to building an estate in Nebraska City, Joy complemented his financial interests with a major philanthropic investment. Work on the library had begun in 1896 and was now nearing completion. Schoolchildren and other residents had raised $1,450 toward the project, efforts that fulfilled Joy's principle that a community should commit resources of its own to a benefactor's gift. Joy was also contributing more than money. Before he left for Europe, he established a board of trustees, including Carl Morton and J.W. Steinhart, an original settler of Nebraska City. He hired the Omaha firm of Fisher and Lawrie to develop a design in the H.H. Richardson style that he had used for his Groveland Park house. "It will be a nice looking building," Joy had told his father, "40 feet wide, 84 feet long, slate roof—rockfaced brick—brown stone trimmings." While his father was still in Washington, D.C., Joy had appealed to him to do whatever he could for the library. Remembering J. Sterling's desire to have the library located on Arbor Lodge property, he said, "I think when you see it and become accustomed to using it, you will like it better than to have an isolated building on Arbor Lodge and located in town it will do the community more good."[17]

As the library was being built, Joy had initiated another project to welcome the return of his father to Arbor Lodge. He had commissioned the young illustrator Haskell Coffin to do a painting of the 1857 Table Creek Treaty ceremony at which the Pawnee had ceded the rights to their land around Nebraska City. J. Sterling had been a participant in the ceremony, and Caroline had been the only woman in attendance. Joy was adamant that Coffin should "get the painting right" and asked J. Sterling to help with details. Although Joy believed Coffin was "enthusiastic on art," he said, he thought he was "not very long on practical common sense." The painter, Joy thought, needed to "study up on the Pawnee. . . ." Joy described the context in detail: ". . . the Indian dancers the most prominent place in the picture. The white men making treaty next and a lot of frontiersmen, squaws, bucks, etc. as spectators around the edges. The landscape must be correct and the point of view should be looking south east, toward where the town is now." Just before sailing for Europe in December, Joy supplied Coffin with sketches and photos of the site.[18] As the Pawnee treaty painting neared completion—Coffin had enlarged it from 7 to 10 feet in width—Joy decided that it should first be loaned to the library. His idea was to have copyrighted photographs *"sold only"* for the Morton Library's benefit.[19]

Joy was also preparing to begin construction of another cultural addition to the town: the opera house that he and his father had long discussed. Once again Joy was intent on encouraging citizen participation. But unlike the library, this building costing $15,000 was intended to turn a profit for its principal investor. Joy told his father, "If the people of Nebraska City succeed in raising not less than $5,000 for the first two night's entertainment I think it would be a good investment for us to build them a theatre. . . . We could build the theatre in four months, and it will be as handsome inside and as well adapted for the purpose as any theatre in the country in a town of the size of Nebraska City."[20]

In Chicago, Joy resumed the day-to-day operation of Joy Morton & Co. as the country was emerging from an economic and political adjustment. While in Europe, he had followed in the *Paris Herald* news of the banking crisis caused by the failure of the National Bank just at the time when Republican William McKinley was replacing Grover Cleveland as President. Although Mark assured him that salt sales remained strong, Joy responded, "Had I an idea of what was going to happen I should not have come over here. McKinley prosperity, as Chicago is getting it, is of a very peculiar sort surely. . . ."[21]

The Mortons, however, were content with the election of McKinley's Republican administration because he had soundly defeated William Jennings Bryan. To a man, the Cleveland cabinet repudiated the Democratic standard-bearer before they left office. Bryan's populist agenda of free silver and government ownership of corporations for the Democratic Party was a principal reason that many Northern Democrats began to turn to the Republican Party as the twentieth century approached. The Morton men were among them.

The salt company offices and other holdings under the name of Joy Morton & Co., including the Western Cold Storage Company, were still located in the old extension of the ICRR Pier 1 warehouse. The addition of telephones, lighting, typing equipment, and a growing staff required that Joy construct a new building apart from the Pier 1 warehouse. He set about the task in his usual singular manner. He traced his maternal lineage to the colonial architect Thomas Joy who had designed the Boston Town House built in 1657. Joy decided that he would house his modernized offices in a replica of the seventeenth-century building.

Although he was looking forward to having greater leisure for family and travel, Joy's pursuit of new projects and his insistence upon making plans for the future seemed to grow rather than wane. He approached the library, opera house, painting, land development, and business enterprises with increased passion, intense personal oversight, and fiscal responsibility. When, in September 1897, J. Sterling warned Joy against getting in over his head monetarily, Joy responded, "Your caution as to getting too many irons in the fire will be carefully considered. I have enough as you say and am not likely to spread out too thin. All I have now is fully paid for."[22]

Joy's confidence in the future remained firm even though within a day of writing to his father about his solvency he looked on as his South Chicago warehouse shed, located on the Calumet River, burned with 43,000 bushel barrels of salt. The fire would have been a total disaster but for the fact that Joy knew that fire in the dry wooden salt sheds was common: he had purchased insurance to cover his losses. In the same week, he received news that it was unlikely that all the pieces of land he wanted for his proposed estate in Nebraska would be available. He immediately wrote to his father that he would likely "give up the idea of making a fine place near Nebraska City." Instead, he would repair an existing farmhouse for a tenant farmer. He added with a logic akin to Thoreau's, "The idea of creating a nice estate was very attractive in itself, and perhaps I am fortunate in having felt like a landed proprietor for a few months at so small a cost."[23]

In spite of these setbacks, Joy kept up his activity in Nebraska City, purchasing a few more available acres in the vicinity of Arbor Lodge and shipping the painting to the Nebraska City Public Library, where it would remain on loan until Arbor Lodge was made ready for its hanging. In late December, the Overland Opera House was ready for its grand opening. But Carrie, who was still convalescing from her operation and had come downstairs at Groveland Park for the first time in nine weeks on December 22, was still too ill to accompany Joy to the grand event.

*A*s Carrie's health slowly stabilized, Joy heeded her doctor's suggestion that they escape the remainder of the Chicago winter by staying in Florida in February and March of 1898. Joy wrote to J. Sterling from the Hotel Royal Poinciana in Palm Beach, "Carrie is still improving and I am delighted over the progress made and the fact that she is taking no medicine except Florida air and sunshine." Joy hoped that she could spend a few weeks at Arbor Lodge after they arrived home in April, saying, "She will be interested in our farm work and by that time the weather will be favorable. I want to avoid 15 Groveland Park for awhile."[24] By mid-March, Carrie's progress restored Joy's own spirits. He wrote enthusiastically to J. Sterling that she had landed an eight-and-one-half-foot shark: "I asked her to hold the line while I lighted a cigar. She took it and in a minute or two was the most excited invalid you can imagine. All ailments were forgotten."[25]

But Carrie's progress did not last through the spring. Throughout May, she was in and out of bed at Groveland Park and was becoming increasingly nervous around others. In June Joy informed his father that he was taking her to Alma Sanitarium in Michigan, believing it to be "the best place in the west for nervous troubles. The hotel and baths are very fine and I sincerely hope she will derive some benefit. . . . She has been failing for a month and am afraid to let her stay here any longer. The children will remain at home until schools are out . . . and then may send Sterling out to you and Jean to Omaha." Carrie's treatment for a general nervous disorder was standard: "Dr. Pettyjohn has been very successful," Joy reported to his father shortly after he and Carrie arrived at Alma. "He depends more on Electricity, massage and good food than on medicine. The place is very quiet and Carrie has agreed to give it a good fair trial." Carrie's treatment lasted a month. Upon their return to Chicago, she needed the constant care of a personal nurse. At first, Joy believed she was improving, but by mid-July he admitted to J. Sterling, "I do not believe she has made any progress whatever. . . ."[26] Joy sent Sterling and Jean to Arbor Lodge and Omaha, respectively, to spend the summer with their grandparents while their mother convalesced.

Although he was unable to acquire contiguous land for an estate, Joy renewed his interest in Nebraska City once his father returned there. He put plane trees in cold storage, preparing to send them to Nebraska City for planting on his farm, telling his father, "Hope the plane trees will do as well in Nebraska as in Academus and Epicurus and that a twentieth century Plato may teach and preach in the shade of some of the trees we have planted this year."[27]

A year later, when Sterling was approaching fourteen, Joy gave him some of the acreage near Arbor Lodge to manage during his summer vacations from school. He wanted Sterling to prove his mettle at hard work and management as he himself had done when he was a teenager. Joy explained to his father the precise business arrangements he had with Sterling. Joy would furnish the capital, but Sterling would operate the farm "according to his best judgment." Sterling would keep the income less taxes and 4 percent interest on the investment Joy had made. "I have realized from my own experience," he said to his father, "that it is a good thing for a boy to have responsibility. It not only makes him appreciate the value of money but it is beneficial in other ways. . . ."[28] J. Sterling must have been satisfied to hear his own sentiments echoed by Joy.

Nebraska City also recaptured Joy's imagination as the location for his father's newspaper. Knowing the paper would keep J. Sterling from the depression into which he often fell when he had little to do, Joy approached the project with more than his usual precise planning. He knew that J. Sterling's recent tenure as secretary of agriculture and his sound money policies would appeal to a large audience of new sound money enthusiasts. J. Sterling's arguments against William Jennings Bryan's presidential candidacy had brought him an appointment as vice president of the anti-silver National Sound Money League, which had its main offices in the Monadnock Building in Chicago. It was an honor that assured him a central role in lobbying Congress for the creation of a Department of Commerce and Industries, even though his primary residence and newspaper office would be in Nebraska City.

Joy decided to underwrite the paper, tentatively named *The Dynamo*, as an advertising and opinion vehicle for his own enterprises and for those of conservative businessmen throughout the Midwest. To ensure that his father would have the services of the best printing facilities, Joy built a new print shop in Nebraska City. Even before the paper's publication, he ordered a year's subscription for one hundred Argo customers.

Relishing the role of being his father's publisher, Joy freely offered his views on the influence that the paper might have and the topics it should cover, bringing his expertise in marketing and agricultural business to bear. He believed the paper should be an instrument in encouraging new money crops in Otoe County by promoting irrigation techniques along the lines of those he had observed in Europe, telling his father, "Sugar culture in Otoe Co is all right if properly done. I should not think of going at it without ditching the land so it could be irrigated from a tank if necessary." He had seen this sort of ditching in Switzerland and northern Italy, and he believed it could be done as economically in Nebraska for a fraction of what it would cost in a more arid state such as California. "The arid countries," he observed, "have no patent on irrigation."[29]

He also urged his father to become a strong advocate of increased crop diversification, explaining that such practices would eventually make Nebraska City a major agricultural center in southwestern Nebraska: "I believe that the more our people can produce the better; one can see, in the poverty of the south, the effect of a country depending on one crop. *The Dynamo* should advocate raising wheat corn oats beets potatoes vegetables cattle hogs chickens etc and so far as possible the preparation of all of these foods, for consumption, in Nebraska City." He estimated that if such a policy were followed, Nebraska City could have a population of 100,000 people within thirty years.[30]

As the paper was getting underway, the country was approaching an international crisis. Joy believed that his father should take a strong stand in his newspaper against the looming conflict with Spain. The sinking of the battleship *Maine* in Cuban waters on February 15, 1898, and the attempts by Cubans to break with Spain had been used by the press, namely William Randolph Hearst's newspapers, to goad the public and the McKinley administration into conflict. When Joy and Carrie were in Florida in March, the dispute with Spain in the Caribbean was escalating to the point at which a diplomatic solution seemed unlikely. Like his father, Joy was a fierce anti-war isolationist. He refused to think that war was an option for the United States at any time and for any cause. He had written to J. Sterling, "Note what you say about War and must agree that the outlook is bad and that our statesmen are worse. What a shame it will be if this country becomes involved in a war with Spain or any other country. I wish all the warships had sunk and we could never replace them."[31] But later, back in Chicago with the war well underway, Joy remarked to his father that his wartime business was "very good," noting the irony: "Have netted enough extra to pay war taxes for quite a spell. Still I am not in favor of war any more than for silver. . . ."[32] The Mortons were fearful that a silver standard would lessen the value of the American dollar.

Shortly before publication, J. Sterling decided to change the paper's name, calling it *The Conservative*. Joy approved wholeheartedly. Yet when the first issue of *The Conservative* appeared in July 1898, Joy offered strong constructive criticism to his editor father. As the principal investor, Joy wanted his father to edit a paper to which the public would subscribe. The first issue, Joy said, was "better mechanically than editorially." He asked his father to write "in a lighter vein," thinking it would "facilitate digestion." Joy thought the articles were "good and sound" but could not "yet be taken raw by the 400 'paid-u-for-one-year subscribers.'" Joy delighted in giving the old newspaper hand his advice. "You must be gentle with these 400. . . . Give them some pen sketches. . . . som Sarpy romances and 'sich like' after each shot from the 13 inch guns. It will act as a sort of pousse café and perhaps help the advertising department which in this first issue seems to have depended entirely upon JM&Co and their underlying companies. . . ." It was a not-so-gentle reminder that Joy Morton & Co. was the publisher.[33]

Joy remained attentive to subsequent weekly issues of *The Conservative*, telling J. Sterling that the second was a great improvement. Pleased with the quality but still trying to think of ways to have the paper pay for itself, Joy asked his father, "Why would it not be a good plan to have an advertising column in *The Conservative*, covering all of the Manufacturers in Nebraska City . . . putting a footnote reading 'Parties interested in any of the above articles are requested to correspond with the Manufacturers direct. . . .'"[34]

*A*s 1898 ended, Carrie's health improved sufficiently for her to make trips to both Arbor Lodge and Omaha. In December, Joy told his father that he thought she was "completely well again."[35] Still, she had frequent lapses, and being "completely well" did not mean that she was consistently robust or over her nervousness around people, including her family. At Groveland Park she was unable to come downstairs for several days at a time. But on Christmas Eve, Joy expected that she would be able to join the family the next day for dinner. She did so in what seemed to be her old spirits. On January 1, 1899, Joy wrote with relief to his father, "This family of mine begins 1899 in excellent health and spirits and I sincerely hope we may be spared another such illness as Carrie's has been, over a year of it and a very tedious and painful one for her. But she seems now to be almost fully recovered."

Even so, the Chicago winter, ever relentless, once again took its toll on Carrie, who, Joy said, had to withstand "a little grippe and a good deal of ulcerated tooth." This time her quick recovery from both led Joy to hope that her resilience was evidence that she was regaining full health. At the same time, Mark's son, for whom Joy was namesake, was thought to have contracted an illness from which, according to his doctors, was "well nigh hopeless." But he, too, eventually returned to health. Joy entered the final year of the century thinking that the Morton family was once again on the way to becoming whole.

With Carrie gaining strength, Joy turned his full attention to consolidating his many business interests in order to give him more freedom to pursue his personal interests. He set out to do this with all the analytical skills and patience he had honed in developing Joy Morton & Co. His wide experience and investments in agriculture, sales, banking, and transportation—combined with his considerable talent for management and marketing—had prepared him well for the challenges of consolidation. Throughout the decade, Joy had gained control over a number of Midwestern companies and had made popular brands such as Quail rolled oats and Argo starch, names that had become synonymous with the products. In the final days of 1898, Joy oversaw the incorporation of the United States Sugar Refinery, located on 140 acres on the Belt Line Railroad and Lake Michigan at Waukegan, Illinois. He was the treasurer and principal investor in the plant, which was under capitalization of two million dollars and bonds of one million. This was but the start of a period in which he became recognized as a central figure in the movement that helped transform a nineteenth-century individualist economy into a corporate industrial economy.[36]

Up to the end of the century the salt industry had pretty well been regionally operated with independent production and distribution companies in economic competition. Advances in transportation, mining, and processing were having their effects, however, and the push to combine production, manufacturing, and distribution efforts was underway. Although the Sherman Anti-Trust Act had been passed in July 1890, making illegal "every contract, combination in the form of trust or otherwise, or conspiracy, in restraint of trade or commerce among the several States, or with foreign nations," the tendency for centralization of businesses continued almost unabated throughout the decade. Joy and other members of the Michigan Salt Association were very much interested in the benefits of centralization. And in March 1899, Joy went with Daniel Peterkin to New York City, where the offices of the Retsof Salt Mining Co., of which he was a member of the board, were located and where the leaders of the country's salt industry and related concerns were making plans for the future.

At first Carrie was well enough to accompany him and look in on fifteen-year-old Jean, who was at Miss Spence's School for Girls, and thirteen-year-old Sterling, who attended the Princeton-Yale Preparatory School. When Sterling came to New York City, Joy put Peterkin in charge of showing him around. Sterling wrote enthusiastically of Peterkin to his grandfather. Peterkin and Sterling took in the city's entertainments, seeing *Sporting Life* at the McVickers, *On and Off* at the Columbia, Ringling's Circus, and "a great torch light parade downtown. . . ."[37] Clearly, Joy had come to think of the young Peterkin as a trusted employee whom he could depend upon as a companion and mentor to his son.

*J*oy was in his element in New York City. One of his first accomplishments was the sale of the Argo Manufacturing Company and the United States Sugar Company to a newly formed combine called the United Starch Company, makers of starch and glucose. Joy remained a director of that company and its subsequent larger company, Corn Products and Refining. In September 1899, Carl was named second vice president of the United Starch Company with offices in Waukegan. Carl's appointment justified Joy's demand that he develop the discipline and responsibility that would help him in business. "The best thing about the new Starch deal," he wrote to their father, "is that it has given Carl a fine position; he steps from a local manufacturer to a general officer of a big Company, both in regard to its general policy and as to the manufacturing, not only at Nebraska City but at all the Factories. He will have a good salary and is highly delighted with the new deal."[38] A few months later, after keeping a close watch on Carl's administration, he wrote to his father that he thought Carl was "getting along nicely at Waukegan," adding, "I talk with him several times every day. There was a little friction up there at first but everything seems to be lovely at this writing."[39]

"Am getting along nicely here," Joy wrote to his father from New York City in December. "Think may bring about all that is desirable both as to Starch and Salt before I get through here in N. Y. If successful in so doing, it will pay pretty well."[40] Just before the new year, he let his father know that "change in methods both as to Starch and Salt" would occupy him even longer than he had expected. But he was confident that the result would justify the months of work in New York. "Ultimately," he said, "unless I am much mistaken I shall have more leisure and no less income."[41] Joy worked through the holidays, taking time off only for a short visit from Carrie and Jean.

As the new century began, Joy was unrelenting in his pursuit of the mergers, believing that they would bring efficiency to an industry fragmented in production techniques and hobbled by geographic distance. Of course, he knew his success would also mean that he would have more time for family, travel, and, eventually, the founding of the estate on which he could indulge his love for horticulture and farming. He wrote to Carrie from the Waldorf-Astoria Hotel, giving her a general idea of his daily activity: "First the Kansas crowd. . . . Next was starch and then again the Worcester Salt Co. In all, the deals in progress aggregate millions and they are all in connection with and closely related to the work I have been at during the past six months. So far all is *well very well indeed* and the ultimate outcome will be *less* work for your poor old man *sure*."[42]

It is probable that Joy could not have foreseen the extent to which industrial centralization would become a major topic of public discussion in 1900. Like many corporate mergers of the time, the starch and sugar industries were subject to the restrictions of the Sherman Anti-Trust Act. Joy understood the limitations the act imposed on trusts, and he also understood the sound money conservative suspicions that his father held of monopolies. In January 1900, J. Sterling published a contributor's anti-trust articles in *The Conservative*, causing Joy to respond pointedly: "I hope no more articles on Salt and Starch trusts will appear in the *Conservative*. I don't care much how you lambaste the trusts generally but I wouldn't do it unless pretty well convinced of the truth in the articles and Mr. Holt [the author] is not an authority."[43] In the course of his work, Joy had been studying the complicated matter of trusts and had come upon the recently published *The Trust Problem* by Jeremiah Whipple Jenks, an economist and agent of the United States Industrial Commission, which had just published a report on trusts. He believed Jenks' textbook to be balanced: it presented both the potential good and evil of trusts but generally saw monopoly as the evolutionary result of the industrial revolution. He sent Jenks' textbook to his father, thinking it might give J. Sterling a better understanding of the benefits of corporate mergers.

In no time, Nebraska City's Argo Manufacturing Company and its merger with the United States Starch Company became a factor in the presidential election of 1900 and embroiled J. Sterling in a heated national debate with his former protégé and now political nemesis William Jennings Bryan. The views of both sides were reported in *The New York Times*. Bryan had come to Nebraska City on September 26, 1900, bringing with him his Democratic ally and fellow trustbuster, Constantine J. Smyth, the Nebraska attorney general who had brought anti-trust charges against Argo. Bryan's purpose was to gain votes by warning that Nebraska City faced losing the Argo industrial plant, then under Mark's management and heavily invested in by Joy, unless its citizens elected him president on a platform of eliminating all trusts. At that moment, Joy and others were working on a final merger that would bring the United Starch Company—with which Argo had originally merged in 1899—under the ownership of the National Starch Company, whose home offices were based in New York City. *The New York Times* reporter summed up his article by saying that Bryan had equated trusts with Republican policies that supported "militarism, imperialism, high tariff, &c."[44]

J. Sterling was enraged by Bryan's politicization of trust charges against Argo, probably because Joy and Jenks had convinced him that combines were not altogether the evil that Bryan and Smyth said they were. But because Bryan had made his charges in Nebraska City and leveled them at a plant identified with the Mortons, J. Sterling lashed out in print at his Democratic rival. In a diatribe against Bryan in *The Conservative*, much of which was reprinted with the title "Bryan's Impeded Veracity" in *The New York Times* on October 8, 1900, J. Sterling wrote that no trust such as Bryan described existed "except in free-silver organizations which have combined in a trust of candidature to prevent competition for office." J. Sterling, called by *The Times'* reporter Bryan's "repentant patron," said Bryan was "a destroying cyclone, howling through the country, cursing the upbuilders as cumberers of the earth, and assuming to be the guardian of the rights of the poor and the plain people." He asked, "Can insolence, assumption, and supercilious conceit go further?"[45]

For his part, Joy had no doubts about the positive effects consolidation would bring. He was buoyed by his success in managing the merger of the starch and sugar industries. As early as February 1900, he shared his pleasure with his father: "My associates here, among whom are the biggest men in the Wall Street world, seem very much pleased over what I have done. In fact, they are too complimentary for me to repeat what they tell me. The experience has been, I think, of great value to me. The work has been at times most difficult but all seems to be coming out splendidly and today I am quite happy over it as may be the Argo stock holders who gain much by the new deal."[46]

Indeed, the stockholders were the beneficiaries. In 1902, the Argo Manufacturing Company, as Bryan predicted, closed its doors in Nebraska City. In that year, the National Starch Company was acquired by the Corn Products and Refining Company, of which Joy was a director. E.T. Bedford, a director of Standard Oil until 1911, became president of the combine. Bedford built a huge plant near the tiny community of Summit, Illinois, and named it after the Argo product. The plant was so dominant and brought in so many new residents to the town of Summit that it became known as Summit-Argo, a fact that Joy recalled with pleasure in his later years.[47]

*E*ncouraged by his successes in New York City and the financial well-being they guaranteed, Joy was enjoying the best year he had had since Carrie became chronically ill. His outlook for his family's fortunes was more optimistic than it had ever been. His father was effectively occupied with *The Conservative*, which Joy, in a moment of largesse, offered to underwrite so that it would "in time become a living memorial for yourself and the rest of us when we are dead."[48] Carl was exercising the management skills that Joy had trained him to employ. Mark had long proved to be a good businessman and in 1902–1903 served as mayor of Lake Forest, Illinois, where he built his family's estate. Paul was a national leader in railroading. And Carrie's health, though tenuous, seemed once again to be holding. Jean, now at the Master's School (known as Dobbs) at Dobbs Ferry, New York, and Sterling were doing well at their preparatory schools.

While he was still occupied in New York City, Joy remained on top of his philanthropic and business interests in Nebraska. After the first two years of operation, the Overland Opera House and the Morton Library were well established cultural assets for Nebraska City, which, due in large part to Morton industries, had grown to 15,000 residents. In March 1900, Joy sent a letter to grain dealers in Nebraska pledging to purchase Nebraska produce exclusively: "The United States Sugar Refinery at Waukegan, in which I am largely interested, proposes to buy Corn hereafter in the West instead of on track at Chicago as has been the practice. Being a native of your good State and feeling that there are no other cereal products like those raised in Nebraska, I want to draw on that State for as much grain as possible."[49]

But even though the 1900 presidential election went the way Joy hoped it would with McKinley's second defeat of Bryan, he was dismayed by the level of support given to Bryan by the citizens of Nebraska City. The majority had voted for McKinley, but Joy thought the margin to be much too small. Shortly after the election, Joy reminded his father that on a recent visit to Nebraska City, he had made clear to him and to Nebraska City's leading citizens that his "ability to do the city any good in the future, would be based entirely on the vote," and, he added, "the vote has now been cast and I do not see anything in it to work on."[50]

J. Sterling thought that Joy was too hard on the citizens of Nebraska City. But Joy was in no mood to forgive them: "My personal opinion is that Nebraska City had a splendid opportunity to make a grand stand play, but most of the influential people of the town remained inert on election day and failed to influence a lot of cheap voters. . . ." Still, he was not ready to "quit doing business there nor anything of that sort," even though he decided that he could no longer depend upon the citizens to make decisions that were best for their economy. "If ever again we want to accomplish anything through the vote of Nebraska City," he said, "we shall take steps to accomplish it along the same lines as we build up trade: in short, we shall hustle and hump ourselves in every way possible, instead of depending upon a lot of people who are about as active as the burghers of New Amsterdam in the year 1650."[51] As if to prove his point, in 1901 Joy invested further in Nebraska City, going into a packing plant business with W.L. Gregson to form the Morton-Gregson Company. Joy and his associates held three-fifths of the shares in what would become Nebraska City's largest employer.[52]

The first year of the new century had been a summing up of successes, and Joy continued to feel enthusiastic about his prospects. Then, on January 1, 1901, a troubling message came from Carl's wife, Boatie: Carl was confined to bed with pneumonia. Six days later, a month short of his thirty-sixth birthday, he died, leaving his wife and children, Wirt, nine, and Martha, almost two. Although he had been in business in Nebraska City and then headed up the United States Sugar Refinery for Joy and other investors, Carl left but a small estate. It would fall on Joy to help the family with expenses and to become the children's guardian.

Carl's initial success as leader of the United States Sugar Refinery, a subsidiary of the National Starch Manufacturing Co., had made Joy proud and had given Carl the confidence that he had lacked during his youth. But unlike his older brothers, Carl had never been in robust health. Carl's lament to his father years before that he would die before his brothers proved prophetic. Carl was the only Morton son to be buried in the family plot in the Wyuka Cemetery in Nebraska City. All of the Mortons but Carrie, who was too ill to take the trip, attended the funeral. After the burial, J. Sterling retreated into virtual seclusion.

As usual, when dealing with personal loss, Joy preoccupied himself with business. He had become the sole agent of the National Salt Co. as well as the Michigan Salt Association, thus giving him control of the market throughout the Midwest, and he was in the process of negotiating further leverage for his company. His investments in and management of enterprises such as starch, glucose, meatpacking, cereals, railroads, and banking gave him little time to mourn his brother's death. It was at this time that his confidence in Daniel Peterkin began to pay dividends. In September 1901, Joy turned over some of his duties as treasurer of the United States Sugar Refinery to Peterkin, giving him the authority to sign and countersign checks as Assistant Secretary of the company.

Throughout 1901, Joy sought a way to assure that his salt distribution firm remained highly competitive. In the end, he found that to do this, he needed to reorganize his company as a subsidiary of the International Salt Company of New Jersey. On March 1, 1902, he distributed an announcement that read, "It gives us pleasure to inform you that we have this day disposed of our Salt business, together with all our warehouses, docks and facilities of every kind for handling salt—the largest and most complete equipment of the kind in existence—to the International Salt Company of Illinois." Although it underwent organizational restructuring, the company remained under the management of Joy Morton & Co., retaining its plants in Michigan and Kansas and adding the Port Huron Salt Company in Port Huron, Michigan, and the Anchor Salt Company in Ludington, Michigan.

The pleasure of this accomplishment was short-lived, however. The family was just recovering from Carl's death when J. Sterling, physically and emotionally weakened by the loss of his youngest son, fell ill. He died at the age of seventy on April 27, 1902, at Mark's Lake Forest home where he had gone to convalesce. J. Sterling was mourned by friends and foes, presidents and common people for his political integrity, his championship of agriculture, and the founding of Arbor Day. Joy had lost not only a father but also a friend with whom he had corresponded for forty years.

Joy did not have long to mourn, however. He was the executor of J. Sterling's estate, even as he was fulfilling his obligations as administrator of Carl's estate. Joy, Paul, and Mark buried their father in Wyuka Cemetery, next to his wife and youngest son. The details of J. Sterling's will had long been known. Joy inherited Arbor Lodge, its contents, all farm equipment and animals, and one quarter of the estate's land. Paul, Mark, and Carl's children and wife inherited the other three-quarters of the estate, including parcels of land in Lancaster County, Nebraska. They also received equal shares of a cash balance of $26,962.46.[53]

Joy had to bear J. Sterling's death at a time when Carrie's emotional and physical health was once more desperate. Attended to by Rena Ross, her full-time companion, she was convalescing at the Sagamore Sanatorium in Lake George, New York. Joy kept in constant communication with Miss Ross and visited Carrie as often as he could. In an undated letter, Miss Ross described Carrie's behavior, a condition that would persist for over a dozen years in various degrees of intensity. Carrie had been extremely nervous the day before she wrote. Early the next day Carrie had come into the room "absolutely crazy." She was calling for her "Blue" and didn't know Miss Ross, thinking she was a stranger. "She screamed, hurled herself upon me," Miss Ross said. "I was simply nothing in her hands. Steadily she calmed down then became quite unconscious. I then sent for Mrs. Brown and we brought her to herself again. . . . Carrie is now crying more quietly but I think almost between every two words. I have to go and hold her hands and keep her in bed. I am so afraid of her becoming violent again."[54]

*J*oy had expected that the twentieth century would bring a realization of his goal of spending a productive future with his family and pursuing interests beyond business. Within less than three years of the new century, the plans for his family had been dashed. There was now no question in Joy's mind that Carrie would need to be cared for during the rest of her life and that he alone would have to see their children into adulthood. Carrie's chronic illness and the abrupt absence from his life of his father and brother were sobering realities.

CHAPTER 8

Civic Commitment—1903–1910

As the twentieth century edged ahead, neither the deaths of his brother and father nor Carrie's ongoing illness could still Joy's enthusiasm for the promise of Chicago. The city appeared well positioned for commercial success under a nation presided over by Theodore Roosevelt, who succeeded William McKinley following his assassination by an anarchist in September 1901. While Joy did not agree with all of Roosevelt's "square deal" initiatives on issues of management and labor relations, trusts, and trade and demurred on his "big stick" policy in the Western Hemisphere, he and his brothers admired the boldness and vigor Roosevelt brought to the presidency and applauded his policies for preserving the nation's western forests. The support of the Morton brothers led to Roosevelt's appointment in 1904 of Paul Morton to the position of Secretary of the Navy, the second Morton to serve in a president's cabinet.

The Roosevelt administration looked to the future, and Joy thought he could best participate in securing that future in the city in which he administered his businesses. The Chicago region became Joy's personal passion. He spent the remaining productive years of his life contributing to Chicago's business and environmental potential just as his father had done for the Nebraska Territory when he settled there in 1854. In spite of its international reputation as a center of commerce, industry, agriculture, and transportation, Chicago was still experiencing growing pains. Joy believed that Chicago could achieve its promise as a great world metropolis only by following an aesthetic and environmental course of development that would benefit all who worked and lived in and near the city.

*W*ith a renewed commitment to Chicago, Joy began to explore its greater region, aided by a new mechanical innovation. In 1902, he bought a motorcar, an acquisition that altered his life as it did the lives of millions of others when, six years later, Henry Ford made the Model-T affordable for the middle class. Joy's Toledo 1902 Petrol Touring Car, the first motorcar in Groveland Park, required a mechanic who doubled as a driver, a position Joy added to his household staff and maintained for the rest of his life. He kept the Toledo in the stable previously occupied by his horses, carriages, a cow, and Sterling's chickens and rabbits. Although he sometimes used the three-cylinder car for the four-and-a-half-mile trip to his office, if he wished to arrive with a degree of certainty, he took the Illinois Central Railroad. The motorcar served him best as a way of getting around the countryside and entertaining Jean and Sterling in the bargain.

Sterling recalled that though the motorcar was a "wonderful and fearsome thing," it was not particularly well suited for journeys on Chicago roads or in unpredictable weather.[1] Earthen byways strewn with sharp objects and rocks took their toll. Rain was certain to interrupt a trip or soak everyone since there was neither a windshield nor top. The "panting monster" frightened approaching horses. A hefty turn of a dangerously recalcitrant crank was required to start the engine. And it was not unusual for the mechanic to have to make four tire changes within a hundred miles.

Still, Joy was determined to be among the first to meet and master these challenges. The motorcar allowed him to become acquainted with Illinois towns and later motivated him to produce a history of how roadways affected the way the region was settled.[2] Sterling believed that "a good deal of the pioneer was present in Joy Morton in buying and being driven in such contraptions." For his part, however, Sterling regarded these early "trials and troubles of pioneer motoring" to be "nothing but a rather grotesque memory."

Even though, as Sterling remembered, Joy was not "at all mechanically inclined" and did not drive, he was fearless in cross-country trips. During the summer of 1902, Sterling and Jean rode in a detachable tonneau, entering through a rear door. Two seats were in each corner of the tonneau and a third was hinged to the door. Sterling described the latter "as a rather precarious perch, as the door lock was none too firm." In this car, Jean, Sterling, Joy, and the factory expert (who was both a mechanic and a driver) set out from Groveland Park shortly after noon on a sunny day on Labor Day weekend to drive to Wheaton, some thirty miles west, where Jarvis Hunt, Joy's friend and the architect for the addition to Arbor Lodge, summered. They planned then to drive into southeastern Wisconsin and return to Groveland Park the day after the holiday. Upon their arrival at nine o'clock in the evening, the car broke down on the outskirts of town. While Jean and Joy proceeded on to Hunt's home, Sterling and the mechanic driver repaired the car. The next morning they gave their hosts their first ride in the motorcar, which performed "beautifully."

But the next day, Sterling recalled, they were just out of sight of Hunt's house when they broke down again. The daylong trip continued to be "strenuous," for they managed only six more miles, arriving in West Chicago "in a seriously crippled condition." Joy had to send the factory mechanic by train to Chicago for spare parts. The next day they were able to make it as far as Fox Lake, Illinois, "where," Sterling wrote, "we got stuck in deep sand and had to spend the night at a very low class but extremely popular resort." On the following morning, Labor Day, they arrived at Lake Geneva, Wisconsin, where the police chief and other officials requested that they not enter the main street because the town was having a Labor Day parade and the car might disturb the farmers' teams.

They forged on toward Kenosha, but their brakes failed near Burlington, and the car "gracefully rolled backward down the hill and into a ditch, breaking a rather important part." While Joy and Jean rested, Sterling and the factory mechanic forced their way into a blacksmith's shop that was closed for the holiday and forged a new part that allowed them to continue. In Kenosha, a politician's audience deserted him to ogle the "strange contraption" parked at the hotel across the street. The next afternoon, five days (one day longer than they had intended) and 200 miles after leaving, they arrived safely back home in Groveland Park.

*J*oy's interest in mechanical and technological advances was not limited to such exploratory, if larky, adventures. In 1902 he backed an idea by a young Nebraskan by the name of Frank Pearne for development of a simple Teletype system that could become practical and economical.

Joy asked Charles L. Krum, the chief mechanical engineer and vice president of the Western Cold Storage Company, to oversee the project. When Pearne withdrew from the project after two years, Krum continued on under Joy's sponsorship. In 1906, Krum was joined in his efforts by his son, Howard, an electrical engineering graduate of the Armour Institute of Technology. The Krums and Joy formed the Morkrum Company, combining the names of both the financier and the inventors. The Krums set up a demonstration of an early model of their system between Chicago and Bloomington, Illinois, along the lines of the Chicago & Alton Railroad, of which Joy was a director. The experiment worked well enough to encourage them to continue perfecting the system. The father and son's combination of expertise began to generate results that in a few years led to one of the most important contributions to instant long-range communication in the first half of the twentieth century. In another ten years, the Morkrum Company came under Sterling's direction.[3]

At the end of 1902, Joy was more determined than ever to get the addition to Arbor Lodge underway. As usual in such an endeavor, he oversaw every detail of the work, meeting often with Hunt in Wheaton to go over architectural plans. Yet even as work at Arbor Lodge began, Joy invited a number of well-known American sculptors to submit ideas for a statue of J. Sterling. They displayed their maquettes in the Art Institute of Chicago, where Joy selected the work of the young Rudulph Evans, a sculptor J. Sterling had admired when he was secretary of agriculture. The sculpture was to be ready when Arbor Lodge was finished. It would be an integral part of the dedication of the family home and grounds. Joy also asked his Nebraska City attorney to get the treaty picture from the library and have it installed in Arbor Lodge because the decorator needed to have it hung "in order to govern him in his colors."[4] For just below his own bedroom, Joy commissioned an Italian terraced and bricked garden, likely influenced by the well-known landscape architect Warren H. Manning.[5] At the outset of 1904, Joy was preparing for a first summer visit to the completed Arbor Lodge. "Mark and I," he alerted Emma, "have today purchased a team for Arbor Lodge, a fine pair of six year old well bred horses. We expect they will make a fine pair of leaders for a four in hand. You can tell Gus [the stablehand] it is only a question of time before another and larger team will follow them."[6]

The final addition doubled the size of the mansion, bringing it to almost 17,000 square feet with fifty-two rooms.[7] Besides a reception room, a library, a sunroom, and a main hall on the first floor, the home contained five bedroom suites and three single bedrooms on the second and third floors. To entertain both children and adults, Joy built a bowling alley in the basement, complementing an existing billiard room on the first floor, and he built an observatory on the roof. In its previous phase Arbor Lodge sported elegantly columned double-deck porches. Hunt's neocolonial design gave it a more imposing stature. After its completion in 1904, when visitors approached the mansion from Nebraska City on the drive leading through the arboretum, they came upon a monumental two-story portico supported by Corinthian columns. Similar porticos also graced the south and north sides.

By March 1904, the mansion was finished to such a point that Carrie could be cared for there rather than in Chicago, where she had remained through the final months of 1903. With a new doctor and fresh air, she was sleeping better with less medicine and began to gain weight. Encouraged, Joy wrote to Emma that should the doctor "be successful, I think I would almost be willing to back him in a Sanitarium for nervous people."[8] Even so, Carrie could not bear to be in social situations. This posed a problem for Joy, for with its new addition, Arbor Lodge became a destination for Morton family celebrations. The housekeeper's records show that an average of thirty-three people per day were served meals at various events during the first two years following the completion of Arbor Lodge.[9]

Carrie could not attend a large party given in July 1904 for Paul who earlier in the year had been appointed to the post of secretary of the navy by President Theodore Roosevelt. But more troubling to Joy was that Jean, who at twenty-one was engaged to Joseph M. Cudahy, a scion of the Chicago meatpacking family, wished to be married in a large ceremony at Arbor Lodge on October 1, 1904. As this event approached, Joy had to make a difficult decision. He wrote to try to persuade Carrie that it would be better for her not to be present at her daughter's wedding. Joy's plan was for Carrie to go to Colorado with a companion until the wedding was over. Carrie tore up his letter in anger but, later, painfully aware of her condition, agreed: "The more I see people, the more acutely do I realize how dreadfully changed I am," she wrote to Joy.[10] Two weeks after Jean's wedding, Carrie returned to Arbor Lodge, growing more irritated with her circumstances by the day, including Joy's suggestions that she play croquet, billiards, and tenpins with her niece who was visiting.

Joy, too, was somewhat out of sorts, particularly with the cost of Jean and Joe's wedding. He complained to his aunt Emma, saying that had Jean followed his advice, he would not have been taken in by tradesmen, particularly the florist, whose bill came to $1,122. Like his father, Joy always fretted over what he believed to be exorbitant expenses. Nevertheless, he concurred with Jean that the "wedding was absolutely perfect."[11] No doubt he was feeling a little strapped: Sterling was in his second year at Princeton; Carrie's medical expenses were constant; and Joy had just paid Hunt $66,000 for the Arbor Lodge addition.[12]

*E*ven as Arbor Lodge was being reconstructed, Joy was undertaking other building projects in Chicago. In April 1903, a disastrous fire at the South Chicago warehouse and dock on the Calumet River destroyed frame warehouses that covered seventeen acres and held 200,000 tons of salt.[13] While the warehouses were quickly rebuilt, the fire signaled the susceptibility of the wooden warehouses where barrels were also made. The new warehouses remained in use until 1908, when once more they were destroyed by fire. Conscious of a need for more aesthetic and fire-resistant buildings, Joy had Jarvis Hunt design and build a fireproof warehouse for iron and steel near the mouth of the north fork of the Chicago River, between Lake and Randolph Streets. Later, Hunt designed a building near the mouth of the Chicago River to house the Western Cold Storage Company, of which Mark became president in 1905.

But Joy's most significant Chicago building project at this time was planned with Daniel H. Burnham. Ever since the construction of his Boston Town House office, which Joy Morton & Company's enterprises had quickly outgrown, Joy had been seeking more efficient office space. He listed his business addresses in 1902 as 77 Jackson Street, Chicago (where he had moved from the cramped quarters at Pier I), and 170 Broadway, New York. In that year, he joined with Burnham, the president of D.H. Burnham and Company, Architects; E.P. Ripley, by then president of the Atchison, Topeka & Santa Fe Railroad; and E.J. Earling, president of the Chicago, Milwaukee & St. Paul, to build what would become the Railway Exchange Building, a seventeen-story, 380,000 square-foot structure at the corner of Jackson and Michigan.[14] Joy was president of the Standard Office Company, the corporation that held the title to the building.

Locating the Railway Exchange Building at the corner of Michigan and Jackson was thought by many to be a poor business decision, because the area was considered to be squalid. Moreover, a building facing out on the vast emptiness to the east seemed to be turning its back on the Loop commercial district and La Salle Street financial centers. But Burnham convinced Joy and other investors that this site overlooking railroad tracks lapped by Lake Michigan beyond would be an advantageous investment, if not a symbolic statement, for anyone who was committed to the city's future. Burnham had already begun the design of the new Orchestra Hall to be built on the adjoining site to the north, then occupied by a livery and transfer business. Even as the Railway Exchange Building rose, Jackson Street, which then ended at Michigan Avenue, was designated a boulevard in response to the desires of bicyclists and pedestrians who wanted a route relatively safe from carriage and motor traffic.[15] Burnham's new buildings were located among architectural anchors such as Shepley, Rutan, and Coolidge's Chicago Public Library and the Art Institute to the north and east and Adler and Sullivan's Auditorium Building to the south. The lakefront remained a work in progress as recommendations of the *Plan of Chicago* were undertaken.

The Railway Exchange Building itself was forward-looking, the distinctive façade clothed in white glazed terra-cotta for ease of cleaning the eternal coal soot, a bane of city buildings that Joy had come to despise. The interior was light and airy, with a massive two-story rotunda greeting visitors and occupants. From the third to the seventeenth floor, a central court provided natural light for offices. A two-story basement housed a power station for Commonwealth Edison and an engine room. The building was set firmly upon columns of concrete and steel sunk to bedrock level at 150 feet. The four principal investors occupied eight floors, with Joy's salt company and the Great Western Cereal Company offices spreading throughout the seventh floor and Burnham's offices housed on the fourteenth. Other tenants included the Chicago & Alton and the Erie railroads, the Quaker Oats Company, and a variety of railway supply firms. The location proved to be inspired. Over a century later, the building (now named the Santa Fe Building) at 224 South Michigan Avenue defines the block on which it and Orchestra Hall sit side by side, essential components of Chicago's architectural and cultural iconography. There the *Plan of Chicago,* published in 1909, was to be completed in the penthouse from which Chicago's shoreline could be scanned for miles.

Joy became one of the principal contributors to the conception and realization of the *Plan of Chicago.* He had become directly involved when the Commercial Club of Chicago, an organization of powerful leaders of which he had long been a member, began in 1906 to provide funds for the design of a plan that would assure an orderly urban development while enhancing the natural features of the lakefront. A member of the Commercial Club's executive committee on the plan, Joy served as chairman of the plan commission's important committee on railway terminals. In 1909, when the city accepted the basic idea of the plan, Charles H. Wacker was appointed chair of the Chicago Plan Commission and Joy became a member of the executive committee. His involvement in the work of the Chicago Plan Commission continued for the remainder of his life.[16]

As soon as he had moved into his new offices, Joy left the country for a four-month visit to the Middle East and Europe, confident that his businesses were being well managed. Joy wrote to Mark from Egypt that he was staying at the Grand Hotel in Luxor on his way to Khartoum, Assouan, and the Fayoum Oasis on an extended hunting trip with his friend Walter S. Eddy, the president of the Michigan Salt Association.[17] He had purchased a "very handsome" twelve by fifteen foot Arabian tent that he sent back to be erected at Arbor Lodge.[18]

Throughout his trip, Joy received letters from Daniel Peterkin, detailing activity in the salt business ("we are drumming the trade constantly and hope to show an improvement from now on"[19]) such as decisions on the pricing of Wisconsin and Illinois medium and granulated salt and the transportation of salt by boat and railway lines. Peterkin also voluntarily stepped aside as a director of the Western Cold Storage Company in order to allow Howard Krum to take his place, a move, Peterkin said, that would leave "the Morton Cold Storage interests entirely on [Mark's] shoulders."[20] As usual, Peterkin gave Joy the final say, telling him that if he did not approve, the decision could be changed when he came home. Peterkin also kept Joy abreast of a gas and oil venture Joy had entered into near Hutchinson, Kansas. Peterkin had urged the contractors and engineers to sink a hole 400 feet deeper than the 770 feet they had gone in the past, a decision that he knew Joy would have made.

Peterkin was not only Joy's eyes and ears in the company, but also his trusted family confidant. He kept Joy informed about Carrie's condition, telling him in March, "Reports from Arbor Lodge state that Mrs. Morton is keeping fairly well, but there is not very much change in her condition."[21] More troubling news was of Paul. In his first year as Secretary of the Navy, Paul had come under fire for allegedly fixing prices on the Atchison, Topeka & Santa Fe while he was that line's second vice president. Although he was eventually cleared of the charges, he resigned from the cabinet on July 1, after serving for just one year. Roosevelt, who never doubted Paul's innocence, remained a friend and hunting companion and stood by him until his name was cleared.[22]

On his way home, Joy stopped in Paris, where he found Rudulph Evans' sculpture of J. Sterling almost completed. He was so pleased with it that he began to take people to Evans' salon almost daily. "The pose,"

he told Mark, is "quite natural and characteristic and the likeness . . .
good while there is a suggestion of vigor in the figure which is strong and
also pleasing."[23] About to depart for home in a few days, he assured Mark
that he had not been worried about business, knowing that things were
being handled well during his lengthy European sojourn.

Rested and determined to put his personal life in order as he approached
his fiftieth year, Joy returned to the Chicago apartment on Oak Street he
had taken when Carrie went to Arbor Lodge. As he explained to his aunt
Emma, "the monotony of keeping house alone was too much."[24] With
Carrie at Arbor Lodge, Jean and Joe living in Lake Forest, and Sterling
heading into his final year at Princeton, the Groveland Park house, lived
in by the family for nearly fifteen years, sat empty, and Joy decided to sell
it. He soon informed Carrie that he had found a buyer, with whom he had
carefully negotiated a contract that would assure him a good return on his
investment. The sale was to a builder indebted for a mortgage of $30,000
on a twenty-one flat building that he had erected. Joy took the flat clear
and loaned the purchaser $10,000 at $5\frac{1}{2}$ percent on the mortgage.[25]

As he was completing the sale, Joy was also preparing for the dedication
of J. Sterling's statue and the Arbor Lodge grounds, set for October 28,
1905. Paul confirmed that former President Grover Cleveland would
attend to dedicate the monument and would spend the weekend. Another
attending dignitary would be Adlai Stevenson of Illinois, Cleveland's vice
president during J. Sterling's term as secretary of agriculture.

Rudolph Evan's bronze sculpture, elevated on a massive pedestal, was
placed behind a smaller bronze of Daphne, the mythical girl who had
been turned into a laurel tree by her father to keep her safe from Apollo.
The pedestal of J. Sterling's statue was inscribed with these words:

J. STERLING MORTON

1832–1902

AUTHOR OF ARBOR DAY

The statue had been paid for in large part by donations of pennies and
nickels from children around the United States in honor of the founder
of Arbor Day. And, in honor of J. Sterling, both Grover Cleveland and
Joy planted trees in Monument Square, where the statue was placed.
After the weekend of ceremonies, the suite on the north side of the new
addition of Arbor Lodge became known as the Cleveland Room. Joy's
bedroom was on the south side. Both rooms have continued to remain
essentially as they were decorated and furnished in 1905.[26]

Joy returned to Arbor Lodge for Christmas of 1905 with Carrie, Judge Lake, and the judge's third wife, Abbie.[27] A day after the Lakes left, Joy was thrown from his horse and badly shaken up. Judge Lake, distressed by the news, wrote to Carrie from Omaha, "To be thrown in the manner in which Joy seems to have been is at any time, and to anyone, a very dangerous experience, but to one of his weight, and upon the hard frozen ground, it is doubly so."[28] Judge Lake might also have mentioned that Joy's survival of the fall was all the more remarkable for a person who had just turned fifty. As welcome as Joy's quick recovery was the news that Carrie had gained sufficient strength at Arbor Lodge to decide to attend the opera in Chicago in March. The good fortune of the Morton family maintained its momentum. Paul rebounded from his brief political setback when he was named president of the Equitable Life Assurance Society with offices in New York City. Sterling, having graduated from Princeton with honors in June 1906, returned to Chicago and began work for his father as a billing manager.[29]

$\mathcal{W}$ith Daniel Peterkin, Sterling, and Mark available to help him run the extensive operations of the International Salt Company of Illinois, Joy turned to new business ventures and to relaxing in his characteristically active style. He wrote to C.M. Aldrich, his agent at the Morton-Gregson Company, that he was reorganizing Joy Morton & Co. as "a co-partnership, not a corporation" that would "take over, under a lease, all of the real property of the Morton-Gregson Co., consisting of lands, packing houses, cars and stock yards."[30]

Joy's interest in Nebraska and in agriculture led him to a different sort of enterprise in Scotts Bluff County in the North Platte River Valley. Since the 1880s, the region along the old Oregon Trail had had a strong agricultural base made possible by an extensive irrigation system. After 1900, one of the oldest irrigation projects, known as the "farmer's ditch," needed rebuilding and enlarging. Joy's interest was piqued. The area was becoming known for beets, a crop that Joy had urged his father to promote in Otoe County in 1898. As Sterling related later, "there were 50,000 acres of land lying there as smooth as Chicago and all susceptible of irrigation."[31] After a personal inspection of the land, Joy paid $4.00 an acre for 50,000 acres and deeded the land to his brother-in-law Charles Deuel of Omaha (the husband of Mary Lake, Carrie's half sister), one of the trustees of the project while the canal was being rebuilt. Within two years, the land and water rights were sold at $5.00 an acre.

"It was only natural," Sterling later wrote, that, having made a success of the North Platte River Valley enterprise, his father "should feel, as he says, that he was an irrigation expert."[32] Coincidentally, Joy turned his attention to a project in the Wind River Valley on the Wyoming Shoshone Indian Reservation where irrigation rights were promised to the surveyor. Joy and a group of investors—some from the North Platte River project—paid $20,000 for an independent survey that revealed preliminary estimates of the cost of irrigating the nearly 500,000 acres were extraordinarily low, mainly because porous soil required that the ditches be lined with concrete. Joy had an experimental irrigation system built some fifteen miles around Riverton, Wyoming, but though he said it "carried water well enough," it was not commercially successful because, as he put it, "of the character of the settlers" who were more interested in speculating than they were in the "hard work in the fields." Joy and his syndicate finally sold the rights to the landowners for 65 percent of cost.[33]

Eventually the reclamation service took up the project along the Wind River, building a supply canal to fill reservoirs. But Joy's independent survey proved correct. The volcanic ash would not hold water, and the appropriated money was insufficient to complete the system. Still Joy and his syndicate were defendants in a number of lawsuits related to this project, which had not been completed by 1933, when Sterling summed up Joy's Wind River irrigation venture, saying, "The experience on the whole was a most unsatisfactory one."[34]

From 1906 through 1910, Joy also found himself heavily engaged in banking activities that, for the most part, were positive, even though 1906 started with a troubling event. Tenants of the Railway Exchange Building felt the need for a readily accessible banking facility. In 1906, the Jackson Trust and Savings Bank, founded in 1903, became a tenant of the Railway Exchange Building after Joy and others had purchased a portion of its stock. The economy was uncertain at the time, and when a rumor circulated that the Jackson Trust and Savings held paper in the troubled Bank of America and a failed lumber company, Joy, by then a director, received word of a run on the bank. He responded from Nebraska City, where he was doing business, that he personally would make a large deposit, declaring that no bank of which he was director would forego its responsibilities to its depositors. He lost considerably more than his shares were worth, but the depositors were paid off and the run on the bank was stopped.[35]

This experience did not deter Joy and others from organizing the Railway Exchange Bank. Joy served as vice president, which listed him,

Sterling, Daniel Peterkin, and Daniel Burnham as four of the nine directors. Unlike the Jackson Bank, the Railway Exchange Bank had a single focus of serving the building's tenants. But it also contributed to liquidating the assets and assuming payment to depositors of the Jackson Bank.

Thinking that smaller, non-specialized banks could not function effectively in a large metropolitan business and industrial economy, Joy began negotiating in 1906 with John C. Black, president of Continental Illinois Bank, a possible merger with the American Trust and Savings Bank of Chicago, which he served as director and vice president. In 1909, American Trust and Savings merged with Continental Illinois, with George M. Reynolds, then president of Continental, and E.A. Potter retaining the presidencies of their respective banks and becoming the first vice presidents of the other banks. One year later, Joy was instrumental in helping create an even larger merger of the Commercial National Bank, American Trust and Savings Bank, the Hibernian Bank (a savings institution), and Continental and American Trust Savings. The new bank was called the Continental and Commercial National Bank; its savings group was known as the Continental and Commercial Trust and Savings Bank. Upon completion of the merger, E.A. Potter, Joy's friend, decided to retire, but Joy remained with the new bank as a director, having had a hand in creating what at that time was the largest financial institution in the country outside of New York.

$\mathcal{T}$aking a few days away from work in the summer of 1908, Joy and Sterling motored in a new Premier car to Nebraska City to visit Carrie. Joy, Sterling, and the mechanic driver left Chicago in good weather but encountered heavy rain when they crossed the Mississippi. "The roads of Iowa were bottomless," Sterling wrote. The trip was reminiscent of the trip taken in the Toledo, except more difficult. At times through Iowa they went cross-country, not attempting treacherous roads. When they were about fifty miles from Nebraska City, the Premier hit a stone that rendered it inoperable. They finished their trip to Arbor Lodge "ingloriously," Sterling remembered, towed behind a farm wagon powered by four mules.

Sterling did not say how Joy reacted to his car being towed ignominiously into Nebraska City, but one can imagine that he confronted the situation with a degree of humor and stamina. His hunting license of 1908 described an imposing figure at six feet of height weighing 197 pounds. He had a piercing brown-eyed gaze and grey hair. Although a city man for many years, he had kept relatively fit by hunting, fishing, and horseback riding. Mules were nothing new to him. That they were still necessary in an age of motorcar travel would have struck him as a pleasant irony. Having seen as a youngster the breakdown and junking of the experimental steam wagon that had been heralded as a replacement for oxen-powered transportation between Nebraska City and the Rockies, Joy would find the inconveniences that Sterling described merely temporary distractions.[36]

Undaunted by frequent encounters with road hazards, Joy continued to take motoring trips around Chicago in 1909, particularly around the western communities, often with the purpose of finding a good piece of land he might buy. There were a number of advantages to moving to the west of the city where Joy's brother, Mark, had already purchased farmland just south of Wheaton, Illinois. The coal dust that begrimed the city was far less prevalent there, and Joy was thinking that he might build a home where Carrie could be cared for and they could once more live together.

Motoring about twenty-five miles west of the Loop on a summer day in 1909 with Edwin A. Potter, Joy came upon a site that interested him. Over two decades later, he reminded Potter—by then long retired from banking and living in Florida—of how they had discovered the property near Lisle, Illinois, that, by 1932, Joy had lived on for twenty-two years. "You were one of the discoverers of the Thornhill property, if not THE original discoverer. I well remember the day when I first visited it with you and went up on the hill where the house is now to put out a prairie fire. I wish you could see it in its new dress. . . ."[37] The east branch of the DuPage River ran from the north below the hillside along what was then Joliet Road.[38] A brook bisected the property and flowed into the river valley below. Stands of native woods were still in abundance beyond productive farmland. Joy soon arranged to purchase the hillside and the woods and farmland below.

Buying property in the country did not signal that Joy was preparing to retire. He continued to prove himself a formidable competitor. At the turn of the century, Joy had sold his shares in the National Salt Company, the predecessor of the International Salt Company, just as other vendors were investing heavily. Joy purchased the National Salt Company's salt and stored it in new warehouses built for that purpose on the south side of Chicago. When the combine collapsed as he expected it would, the salt was his while the other vendors held only worthless paper. When the International Salt Company was organized, Joy and his associates had cornered the salt market in the Midwest. In 1902, the disgruntled vendors brought suit against the defunct National Salt Company, Joy Morton and Associates (as the company was named in the suit), and the International Salt Company of Illinois of which Joy was then president. Eventually, the case was heard by the Supreme Court of New York in 1908 and 1909. Joy and his fellow defendants engaged Elihu Root, Theodore Roosevelt's former secretary of state, as their attorney.

During a business trip to New York, Joy asked Root if he could look in on the proceedings. At first, Root thought it unwise, knowing that Joy would be called to the stand if he came into court. Finally, however, he agreed. Upon entering the courtroom, Joy was immediately subpoenaed by the attorney for the plaintiffs and was questioned for a day and a half. Following Joy's testimony, Root rested his case, saying he had nothing further to add. The judge, after a brief recess, found in favor of the defendants and required the plaintiffs to meet court costs. Joy later told Sterling, "They didn't know the business as well as I did and any man has an advantage as a witness if he knows his business better than the average lawyer who talks to him."[39]

The court victory came while Joy's International Salt Company of Illinois was in the process of purchasing the western holdings of its parent company, the International Salt Company of New Jersey, which had itself experienced financial problems. The new company was renamed Morton Salt Company on March 1, 1910, partly to identify it as an individual company not having connections with increasingly unpopular trusts. Joy, as president, owned 70 percent of the stock; Mark (who was vice president but not active in the business) 10 percent; Peterkin, treasurer, one-tenth; and Sterling, secretary, one-tenth. Later Joy allowed key employees to purchase stock as a means of rewarding them for their service.[40]

The statement of incorporation was issued publicly by Morton Salt Company on March 19, 1910:

> We announce that we have purchased all the real and personal property and business owned or controlled by the International Salt Company of New Jersey in the west, including the warehouses, offices, docks and manufactories in Chicago, Minneapolis, Toledo, Detroit, New Orleans, Sheboygan, Milwaukee, St. Louis and Manistee; and have also purchased properties of various companies, having an aggregate producing capacity of more than 10,000 barrels of salt per day, located at Port Huron, Michigan; Wyandotte, Michigan; St. Clair, Michigan; Ludington, Michigan; and Hutchinson, Kansas.

We are the exclusive western sales agents for the salt produced by: Retsof Rock Salt Mining Company of New York; Avery Rock Salt Mining Company of Louisiana; Crystal Salt Company of Kansas; Pennsylvania Salt Manufacturing Company of Wyandotte, Michigan; R. G. Peters Salt and Lumber Company of Manistee, Michigan; Louis Sands Salt and Lumber Co. of Manistee, Michigan; and State Lumber Company of Manistee, Michigan.

The officers of this company have had long experience in the salt business, our president having, in 1880, become a partner in the firm established by Richmond & Comstock in 1848; a business which has been continued uninterruptedly, under the name of their several successors, for sixty-two years. Confident that our facilities for doing a salt business are unequaled, we respectfully solicit your patronage.[41]

With this announcement, Joy declared to one and all that during the years in which the salt company was under title of the International Salt Company of Illinois, Joy Morton & Co. had expanded its salt operations significantly. Early on, Joy had recognized that the lumber industry in Michigan was quickly losing its advantage of having a natural resource for distilling salt and that coal was becoming a preferred fuel for separating salt from brine. He had set up vacuum pan plants that dried salt quickly in Michigan and Kansas and was preparing to close less efficient production plants in both states.

*E*ven while Joy was reestablishing his own name among consumers and purveyors of salt, Nebraska City interests required his attention. As hog prices fell, Joy employed a strategy for his Morton-Gregson stockyards that had worked in the salt industry. He gave orders to C.M. Aldrich that the company should not butcher hogs when the price was low. Joy also expressed to Aldrich his annoyance at Nebraska City for wanting to tax his property that lay just outside the city. Saying that he supported a "first class High School, one that will be a credit to the Town," he was willing to be taxed for it on land he owned within the city limits. But once again he was impatient with Nebraska City's citizens' reluctance to pledge their fair share. "If the people of Nebraska City would more willingly pay for the things they ought to pay for, instead of trying to work it out of somebody else, I think the Town would grow faster." He authorized Aldrich to make his statement public.[42]

With waning interest in Nebraska City since purchasing his land in Illinois, Joy once again began to divest himself of property there. In the spring of 1910, he sold the printing office building, one of the last vestiges of his father's newspaper career. Later in the year, he wrote to Aldrich that because he had purchased the farm near Chicago, he wanted to sell off 365 acres in Nebraska, including farm buildings that he had bought several years earlier north of the Steam Wagon Road.[43]

Still, Joy wanted to help his hometown out if he thought his efforts would be productive. After Aldrich wrote to him that the Nebraska City Commercial Club wanted "to put the hospital on its feet and put it in good working condition,"[44] Joy responded by saying that when the administration promised that it could assure the future of the hospital, "I shall be glad to furnish a room, as a memorial to my brother Carl—provided it meets with the approval of Mrs. Carl Morton. . . ."[45] Later, Joy encouraged the Nebraska City Commercial Club to join the national organization. Knowing what the Commercial Club of Chicago had achieved with the Chicago Plan, Joy advised Aldrich, "There is no question in my mind but what the Commercial Club can do Nebraska City a lot of good by working vigorously along this line and keeping yourselves before the public in that way, and I think it would be well to have an account of the meeting of the Commercial Club published in the local papers. . . ."[46]

Since the reorganization of the Morton Salt Company a year earlier, the growth and development of salt products had only increased. Now Joy was in the process of shedding some of his other holdings so that he could concentrate on the major task at hand. One of his first moves was to help his fellow directors dissolve the Railway Exchange Bank after a successful operation of five years, selling the assets to the nearby Peoples Trust and Savings Bank. He wrote to his aunt Emma that he was "now a Director only in the Continental & Commercial and shall not again become a director in a small bank, notwithstanding that the Railway Exchange Bank has been a success and everything is wound up in a satisfactory manner."[47] A few weeks later he sent a letter to C.M. Aldrich, asking his advice on getting out of the packing business in Nebraska City. He also negotiated the sale of the Great Western Cereal Company, the makers of "Mother's Oats," to the Quaker Oats Company, thus ending his two-decade interest in the cereal business in which he had first invested in Nebraska City.[48]

As president and chairman of the board, Joy was determined that the Morton Salt Company, now a year old under its current organization, would be the most recognized name in the salt industry, not just because of its centrality to the many phases of salt production and distribution, but also because of the quality of its product. Without salt, the country's western exploration and development would have been impossible. But salt was difficult to store and transport because of its tendency to become bulky from moisture. Joy relied upon product quality and new techniques in marketing to advance the name of Morton Salt above its competitors. In 1911, researchers for Morton Salt perfected a free-flowing salt by adding magnesium carbonate. The product allowed for the first practical home use of a two-pound round package designed in 1900. It was constructed of three-ply paperboard, with an asphalt-treated, waterproof barrier. Later the package would have a metal spout. A blue label contained the words "Morton Salt" and, in a diamond-shaped frame, the slogan, "It Runs." As explained in a company publication in 1973, "The color blue was selected for two reasons . . . contrast of color with the product would make the salt appear whiter, and dark blue would tend to soften the appearance of dust and fly-specks on the package. These were the days before air-conditioning and insecticides."[49]

Also in 1911, the Morton Salt marketing group, led by Sterling, contracted with N.W. Ayer advertising to develop a trademarked brand, one that might prove as effective as Argo Starch had been. Ayer submitted a picture of a smiling little girl in a knee-length dress awkwardly holding the shaft of an open umbrella in the crook of her right arm and a two-pound box of salt tucked under her left arm. Trying to stay dry in pelting rain under an umbrella clearly too big for her to handle, she was oblivious to the fact that salt from the container was trailing in her wake. The slogan accompanying the picture read, "Even in rainy weather it flows freely." Sterling liked the idea of the little girl, mainly because his own daughter seemed to be about the same age. But he argued that the slogan had to be shorter, saying, "We need a slogan like 'Ivory Soap—It Floats.'" Someone then suggested, "It pours," and another recalled the English proverb, "It never rains but it pours." The latter statement, thought to be too negative for the product, finally became, "When it rains it pours,"[50] a slogan so popular since its release in 1914 in twelve monthly *Good Housekeeping* issues that it has essentially replaced the original proverb in common usage. The Morton Salt Company, having borne the Morton name for just one year, had enlivened the salt industry with the basics of twentieth-century corporate success: research, development, and marketing.

CHAPTER *9*

The House on the Hill—1905–1915

By the late summer of 1910, Joy's house, designed by his old friend Jarvis Hunt, was underway. Like Arbor Lodge, the estate would become a center for the Mortons, a fulfillment of Joy's sense of patriarchal obligation, heightened since his father's death. His family had grown with Sterling's marriage on November 2, 1910, to Preston Owsley, the daughter of Heaton and Carolyn Dudley Harrison Owsley and the granddaughter of Chicago's Mayor Carter Harrison, Sr. Like Jean and Joe Cudahy, Sterling and Preston would live within an easy drive. Joy's estate was also to be a sanctuary from the city. He looked forward to walking the fields and woods, gardening, raising cattle and sheep, farming a soil he thought equal in quality to that he had planted along the banks of the Missouri River, and doing a little hunting. To Emma he marveled that he had "paid only $100" an acre for the one thousand acres. The twenty-five mile commute to his office in the city by train from Wheaton would take but fifty minutes; by car over newly macadamized roads, only an hour and a quarter.[1]

Still, Joy's primary concern had to be Carrie. Her father had died on August 3, 1910, and for over a month, she had been in mourning at Arbor Lodge, cared for by Miss Margaret Gray, a companion since 1905.

Thinking that a change of scenery and climate would be helpful, Joy rented a spacious house for her in Pasadena, California, and, needing a second companion for her, he rehired Rena Ross who had been with her at the Sagamore hotel in Lake George, New York, in 1902. He continued to rely on information from Miss Gray about Carrie's condition, which, once they arrived in California, she found to be "neither better nor worse, apparently for the change of climate."[2]

At the outset of 1911, however, Joy's focus on Carrie and his new home was stunningly diverted. On January 19, Paul was found in a New York hotel hallway near death. Ironically, three days before he had written a positive letter to Emma, telling her that the fortunes of his family and company were at an all time high and that he was planning a vacation in southern France in late February.[3] On the day of his death, Paul, Joy, and a friend had a congenial lunch together. A couple of hours later, Joy and Paul's wife, Charlotte, were called to the Hotel Seymour where Paul had collapsed; they arrived only minutes after he died of—as the coroner determined—natural causes. Because of the suddenness of the death of his well-known brother, Joy issued a public statement, saying that in early December 1910, the chief examiner of the Equitable Life Assurance Society, of which Paul was president, had turned Paul down for the company's first "Christmas policy" because of fragile health. Joy had been concerned and had urged Paul to take a vacation "as a theoretical invalid," thinking it would help him bring down his blood pressure.[4]

With Emma, Joy took a stolid approach to Paul's death, saying, "There is nothing to say except that we must go on and make the best of it."[5] But he was more forthcoming with Abbie Lake, Carrie's stepmother. They had begun to correspond frequently when she turned to him to advise her as administratrix of her husband's estate. Addressing her affectionately as "Grandma," Joy wrote introspectively, "Yesterday I was so depressed that I took my open car and went out to the Farm and spent most of the day and was very much refreshed by being out of doors."[6]

Joy's melancholy deepened after he read a sympathy note from Carrie in which she implied that she still harbored ill feelings toward both Paul and J. Sterling. Joy sent her letter on to Abbie, saying, "Am more sorry for this than I can tell you as, to me, it means that she is no better and probably never will be."[7] From the time that she balked at living close to Paul and Charlotte just before she and Joy were married, Carrie had been distant from Joy's family, especially the Morton men. With his ingrained belief in family loyalty, Joy found Carrie's lasting dislike for his brother and father impossible to comprehend other than as a function of her mental illness.

But Joy had little time to dwell on Carrie's note. Once again while mourning the loss of a brother, he was called upon to assume the emotional and complicated task of settling the estate. He had to return to New York City where Charlotte lived. From there he wrote to Abbie of an additional family concern. Mark's wife and their son, whom Mark had named Joy II, were at Hot Springs, Arkansas "on account of Joy's muscular rheumatism."[8]

$\mathscr{I}$n the spring of 1911, Joy decided that Carrie should return to Arbor Lodge to "make that her permanent home."[9] The fact was that Joy's separation from Carrie troubled him more than most of the family members knew. In describing to Abbie the design of his new house, which he said was at Wheaton,[10] Joy revealed his loneliness. The house, roofed and plastered, had eight rooms: on the first floor, a kitchen, dining room, and living room; upstairs, three large bedrooms and two smaller ones for servants. "It is all I expect to build at present," he said, "and is enough for a man more lonesome, probably, than either a bachelor or a widower could possibly be."[11] Joy advised Abbie to send his letter and one from herself to Carrie asking Carrie to give her required approval for renewing her administration of Judge Lake's estate. Carrie responded to Abbie on July 23, giving her consent, but she closed the letter lamenting, "My life is worth absolutely nothing to me—each day grows more hopeless and more discouraged. My fond love for you all." She signed the letter, "Carrie Lake Morton," adding this postscript: "This will probably reach you on one of the saddest days of the year for me, and I shall be thinking of you."[12] It finally fell to Joy, who had Carrie's power of attorney, to sign the formal approval for Abbie to continue to act as agent for the Lake estate.

The final months of 1911 were mixed with a litany of despairing news from California balanced with satisfying Chicago family events and solid progress on the farmhouse. By July the house was well enough along that Joy planned a picnic there with Jean and Joe, Sterling and Preston, but rain forced the two couples who were motoring out to the farm to turn back home to Lake Forest. In good spirits, Joy wrote to Emma, "I ate all I could of the chicken dinner I had had prepared for them, and then returned to Town and went to Lake Forest and spent the night there. . . ."[13] Joy sent a photograph to both Abbie and Emma of the grounds, telling Abbie that "the view down the valley . . . is very beautiful."[14] To Emma he pointed out that the little lake in the picture was populated with ducks from Arbor Lodge and, later, having moved in, he pronounced the house to be "very comfortable indeed." Three servants shared the quarters: Alexander ("boss inside the house"), Alexander's wife (who helped out by mending), and a cook.[15]

On August 24, 1911, Joy celebrated the birth to Sterling and Preston of his first grandchild, Suzette Preston Morton. A month later, he wrote to Abbie, saying, "It is surprising what an important figure she is in that household—it seems to me I never knew anything just like it before, but, perhaps, my point of view in this case is different from any other I ever had." He wished Carrie could see their grandchild.[16] Suzette was, he proudly wrote to Abbie, "gaining in weight each week as regularly and rapidly as a milk-fed chicken."[17]

Joy also had come to regard his nephew Wirt, Carl's son, as an intimate family member. In the early 1890s, Joy had little tolerance for any employee who could not be completely devoted to his developing business. Carl's health problems and his youth seemed to perplex Joy, and he had been impatient with Carl throughout his apprenticeship, recognizing his younger brother's potential as a competent business leader only shortly before he died in 1902. He would not make the same errors with Wirt. He gave him the same advantages that he gave his own son. He had put Wirt through college and, at age twenty-one, Wirt was Joy's choice for an administrative position at the Hutchinson plant. By November 1911, Joy was happy to report to Emma that Wirt was doing well and was in the process of becoming a man and earning a man's wages.[18]

Through the winter of 1911–1912, Joy welcomed distractions, knowing that he must make difficult decisions about Carrie in the coming spring. He celebrated his first Christmas on the farm with Sterling, Preston, and Suzette. In January he attended the Republican Presidential Convention where he was seated next to former Vice President Levi Morton. They watched as Theodore Roosevelt, defeated by William Howard Taft for the nomination, led his supporters out of the hall to start the Progressive ("Bull Moose") party that would eventually split the Republican Party and lead to the election of Woodrow Wilson, the first Democrat to be elected president since Grover Cleveland. Later, in February, Joy spent two weeks hunting near New Orleans.

Only upon his return from the south on February 19, 1912, did he learn that Carrie had had an operation, although he was assured by Miss Gray that she was recuperating and not in any grave danger. But on the 28th, he received a telegram from Miss Gray that read, "Mrs. Morton is very ill. Had complete collapse beginning Sunday. . . . Doctor assures us she will pull through."[19] With that, Joy and Jean left Chicago for San Diego, even though Carrie protested their coming. Once there, they found her improved physically but more determined than ever to remain in California, where the salutary weather and relative peace and quiet appealed to her.

Exasperated by Carrie's seeming indifference toward him and her children, Joy acted decisively on Carrie's request. He and Jean went up to Pasadena where in two days he bought a new 11-room house for Carrie at No. 34 Congress Place, only two blocks away from where a Cudahy relative was living. "I bought it," Joy informed Abbie, "and will have it furnished and ready for her by the 15th of April. She approved of the plan before the purchase was made and is counting the days until she can get well enough to move into it."[20]

Having settled where Carrie would live, Joy returned home only to find that on a trip to the West Indies, Sterling had contracted typhoid fever. Then in April, as Sterling's health deteriorated, Joy received word that his aunt Emma, who was seventy-four, had died after undergoing an unexpected operation. No sooner had Emma been buried in Wyuka Cemetery, next to J. Sterling, Caroline, and Carl, than Joy began to learn of even more troubling behavior from Carrie, causing him to pen an unusually morose letter to Abbie. After Carrie had moved into the Pasadena house, she wrote to Daniel Peterkin to send her money from Joy Morton & Co. to purchase the lot next door. This was too much for Joy, who revealed to Abbie that he had been under "a constant strain since the 9th of April . . . and the result is I am about used up."[21] Even so, Joy believed that Carrie would not have persisted in trying to purchase the lot next door had she understood what he had been going through with Sterling's illness and Emma's death.

However, it soon became clear to Joy that Carrie's obsession with the lot next door to the Pasadena house was not an isolated extravagance. She began to owe a number of retail creditors in Pasadena, and finally, Joy had to employ a manager to handle her household accounts. Most troubling of all to Joy was that Carrie had become dependent upon a doctor whom Joy thought was after money and whom he lumped with "dead beat doctors and other grafters." He was angered when he learned that Carrie showed the doctor his and others' letters, complaining to Abbie, "I think she has treated me outrageously, not only in regard to the beautiful house I have furnished for her but in submitting my letters to that infernal doctor for advice." More troubling to Joy was that Carrie seemed completely indifferent to Sterling's worsening condition. On May 6, the sixty-fifth day of his illness, Sterling was given a fifty-fifty chance of living. He had recognized neither Preston nor Joy for three weeks.[22]

At a loss concerning what to do about Carrie, Joy wrote to Abbie in May that he was once again considering putting Carrie into a sanitarium, saying, "my patience has been taxed beyond endurance, and nothing but an absolute apology and promise of different treatment in the future will even make me feel toward her as I should like to on her account and on account of our children."[23] But after Carrie had implied to Preston that, as Joy said, she was "passably interested in Sterling's terrible illness," Joy expressed hope to Abbie that he might "avoid taking the drastic action that must surely be taken if Carrie gets on the rampage again."[24] Still, throughout the summer, Carrie continued to exhibit erratic behavior, threatening Joy in one letter, then following it by others that Joy termed "pleasant" and "sweet." Joy concluded, "I do not think she remembers what she writes to me from one day to another."[25]

By late summer, Joy could take a measure of comfort in Sterling's progress. Sterling, Joy told Abbie, was "tickled to death that he is still on earth."[26] After five months, Sterling could sit up for a few hours at a time, although he was still unable to walk. In November, Sterling, Preston, and Suzette moved in with Joy, where Preston took to her bed from exhaustion. Joy told Abbie, "The place is a regular hospital, and the patients all seem to be doing well." But Suzette, he happily reported, had learned to walk "all over the house," adding, "the Farm seems to agree with her immensely."[27]

In early fall, Joy informed Abbie that Miss Gray reported that Carrie was having "'terrific headaches' and is generally pretty miserable."[28] Carrie had also engaged a lawyer to bring suit against him. A few days later he wrote, "The latest reports from California are that Carrie has improved in strength and in her determination to secede from this Branch of the Morton family—but nothing definite has been done yet."[29] Finally, Carrie agreed to assign to Sterling her personal property and "in the future to be governed by my wishes."[30] She had consented to remain in California for the winter and return to Arbor Lodge in the spring. But two days later, she had no memory of their agreement. Carrie's unpredictable behavior frustrated Joy even more because doctors were unable to give a definitive diagnosis of or effectively treat her recurring emotional problems.

In December, Sterling had casts placed on his legs, but circulation problems required their removal just before Christmas. In spite of this, Joy hosted a gala party for the family and a few neighbors. Preston "invited a lot of little children from the neighborhood," Joy told Abbie. "Suzette was hostess and seemed delighted to meet the youngsters, with each of whom she solemnly shook hands. Sterling took a flashlight picture of the tree with some of the children sitting around it eating ice cream. . . ."[31]

As 1913 began, Joy was encouraged by his farm and by signs that both Carrie's condition and Sterling's health were improving. Carrie's bouts of animosity to those close to her, including her nurses, had diminished. Joy told Abbie that he thought Carrie to be "very much more friendly to her Chicago relatives than last year. It looks like 1913 [is] going to bring us some good luck from California."[32] Sterling's health improved to the extent that he was now able to walk with a cane and could go to his office three or four days a week.

The period of optimism was once again disappointingly short-lived. In March, Sterling was still experiencing great difficulty walking, and Carrie was balking at returning to Arbor Lodge. And Joy, in his late fifties, had just learned from his own doctor that he had overextended himself. He was suffering from shortness of breath caused by "slow heart action." Though the doctor did not think it to be serious, he told Joy that he should stay at the farm as much as possible. Given his condition, Joy said to Abbie, "I am more than ever anxious to have Carrie there with me and have the children there, too, as much as possible."[33]

He knew the difficulty of trying to convince Carrie to make the move. In a letter to his uncle Will's daughter, Joy wrote that he planned to go out to Hutchinson to attend the wedding of Wirt and Ada Whiteside on April 12, then travel on to California and stay for a couple of weeks. At that time, he was determined that Carrie would return with him or make the journey soon after to spend the summer at "Thorn Hill Farm," the name Joy had given his estate.[34]

Abbie advised Joy to reconsider, thinking Carrie might be too disruptive to the life Joy had made at Thorn Hill. Joy responded that it was the right thing to do, putting the reasonableness of his view into the context of his conviction that Carrie should be reunited with the family. "If she comes," he said, "I will have some member of the family with us whenever she wants to have them, and it will make life worth living." Joy was tired of the long separations. "This having one's family scattered all over the country and being left entirely alone, is not right, and I am mighty tired of it." Joy had had too much of living alone, and, though he was feeling better physically, he still had shortness of breath, saying, "I have been careful and think I must be just a little more careful than I used to be, particularly with regard to running or any exercise of that sort."[35] He still enjoyed a good cigar and an occasional whiskey.

On May 10, 1913, Carrie, her nurses, and Joy were met by Sterling and Preston at the station in Wheaton. The next day, Joy told Catherine, the wife of his brother-in-law, Fred Lake, that Carrie "bore the trip well indeed and seems very much pleased with Thorn Hill Farm."[36] She already loved motoring in the countryside where she was driven by Sterling the day they arrived and then was accompanied by Joy the next day before he went to his office. But once again, Carrie's happiness was short-lived. When Abbie sent her a check to purchase a piano, Joy wrote that not only should she not have sent it, but also that Carrie said she did not want to hear from her stepmother again. Predictably, though, Carrie soon began to speak of Abbie, who had raised her from childhood, in the highest terms. In spite of these moments of irrationality, Carrie appeared fond of Thorn Hill, although she continued to voice her dislike for "every 'born Morton,'" as Joy said she termed his family.[37]

Joy hit upon the idea of motorcar trips as a means of getting Carrie "away from herself." For several weeks, they explored roads in northern Illinois. In June and July they took short trips to Elgin, St. Charles, Aurora, Geneva, Batavia and Joliet, traveling over 300 miles all told and taking in "a moving picture show . . . wherever such a show is in operation." Surprisingly, since Carrie either picked at her food or overate when at home, wherever they stopped for lunch along the way, she ate what everyone else ate. "I think it is doing her no end of good," he told Abbie, "and that she is beginning to be more self-reliant and stronger physically, but I don't see any improvement otherwise."[38] In late summer they drove seventy-five miles southwest to Starved Rock State Park then on to LaSalle, where they spent the night. A week later they motored west to Rockford, staying overnight before returning to Lisle. Carrie, Joy said, "enjoys the trips very much and eats at the hotels and restaurants about twice as much as she does at home."[39]

These trips not only served to strengthen Carrie physically, but they deepened Joy's interest in Illinois history and roadways. "There is so much to see motoring in Illinois," he exclaimed to Abbie. "It will surprise you. It has me. I had no idea that the country was so interesting. Up to date we have been in the car in more than fifty towns of Illinois, and all within 75 miles of Thorn Hill Farm. The roads are fine. . . ."[40]

But even as Joy described the trips across Illinois, he had no illusions that Carrie was improving to the point of emotional stability. His skepticism was reinforced by a doctor's diagnosis of her mental condition that was echoed in Dr. Stewart Paton's 1905 *Psychiatry: A Textbook for Students and Physicians*. Chapter 14, "The Dementia Praecox Group," convinced Joy that Carrie's symptoms were as those described and that he was doing the right thing for her. Carrie's headaches and fainting spells in Europe, her operations (apparently gynecological following two miscarriages), and her years of alternating periods of good nature and lucidity followed by violence, hallucination, apathy, paranoia, acquisitiveness, forgetfulness, drug dependency, deceitfulness, depression, antagonism, passivity, and indifference certainly would provide mental health practitioners today with a rich number of symptoms to diagnose her disease. Paton gave this diagnosis in his book: "The symptoms should be studied with a view to determining the degree of liberty that may with safety be given to the sufferer. In the milder forms of the disease there is sufficient intellectuality left to render it possible for him to be employed, preferably out-of-doors in work about a farm or garden. . . ."[41] Carrie's moments of lucidity and calm, Joy reasoned, were lengthened by her being in the country. That was all he knew to do for her.

Over the next two years Joy made even more frustratingly ineffectual attempts to help Carrie through her illness. To Abbie, he recorded a downward spiral that had few plateaus and, finally, overwhelmed him. He knew Carrie liked Thorn Hill but sulked, saying that she was "careful" not to let him know it. Although Carrie's nurses were in constant attendance, Joy felt that he had been left alone, complaining, ". . . I think the experiment might have been more successful if I had had any cooperation from either of my children, but, as usual, they left the 'old man' to carry the burden."[42] Of course, helping out was difficult for Sterling, who had been recuperating in Europe with his family in the summer of 1913 and returned in September with noticeable difficulty in walking, even eighteen months after his illness. By November, Sterling had to return for a month to St. Luke's Hospital where his legs were put back into casts and stretched. Why Jean was not helpful with her mother remains a mystery, since she is not included in the Morton correspondence, either by design or because she did not take up the family habit of writing letters.

Carrie suffered a hard fall in September 1913. Then in November she began to demand excessive doses of her headache medicine, often raiding the medicine cabinet when she was not watched. When told that she would not be allowed to abuse her medicine, Joy reported to Abbie that she "raked up no end of old grievances, and has gotten herself to a point where she cannot see me nor anybody else. I hope it will pass . . . but in the meantime it is a most disastrous situation."[43] His options were now limited to keeping Carrie "at Thorn Hill Farm as long as possible, and do all I can to avoid putting her in a sanitarium." He added, "Miss Gray is pretty well worn out lately. Carrie has her up every hour and she is making herself very hard to take care of."[44]

In mid-November, Joy hoped Blanche Deuel, Abbie's granddaughter, would return to the farm. She had spent a part of the summer there and had endeared herself to Joy. Blanche wrote to her uncle, "It is certainly too bad that Aunt Carrie is acting up so, and I wish I might see you and we could then take a walk, either to the pigs or down by the sheep and have a nice talk like we used to. . . ."[45] But though he wished for Blanche to come, the atmosphere at Thorn Hill was too "hostile, both out and in."[46]

Within weeks, however, Carrie's behavior improved, and Joy wrote to Abbie that he and Carrie were "very comfortable at Thorn Hill Farm." Carrie urged Joy to take a trip to South America, but he did not know whether she wanted him to go for himself or to be rid of him. "I think," he said, "probably the latter." [47] Still, the tension eased sufficiently that Joy rented a furnished apartment at 999 Lake Shore Drive for the winter. With some difficulty, he convinced Carrie to join him. At the same time, after another stint in the hospital, Sterling was "really improving."[48]

At first the move to Chicago proved salutary. Surprisingly, Carrie enjoyed seeing the family on a daily basis. But her abuse of her medicine increased. In early January 1914, she overdosed and was in a "comatose state," Joy told Abbie. But in a few days she and Joy attended a picture show and she had a good time.[49] Then, on the third anniversary of Paul's death, Carrie requested that she be allowed to return to Pasadena. In no mood to honor her request, Joy lamented to Abbie, "It was three years ago today that Paul died, and I certainly have had a strenuous time since then as regards illness and death. I hope the next three years will be more peaceful."[50]

By late February 1914, Joy was anxious to return to the farm, telling Abbie, "The place is going to be much more attractive this Summer, I think, than heretofore, as I have done an immense amount of planting and we should have an even better display of flowers of various kinds than at Arbor Lodge."[51] A few days later, he reported, "Even Carrie, of late, is talking about going to the farm—not with any great pleasure (she says she hates it), but just the same she is looking forward to it, and I think it is the best place for her; so do the children and Miss Gray."[52] But at the apartment, Carrie continued falling when she insisted on getting herself out of bed. Her injuries prompted Joy to tell Abbie that "she looks as though she had been in a train wreck."[53] A few days later, he wrote again, saying, "She is in worse mental condition than I have ever known. . . . Miss Gray and Celia [another companion] are devoted to her and one of them is with her all the time. She is most obstinate and insists on getting out of bed whenever she thinks she isn't watched."[54]

The move back to the farm brought no improvement in Carrie's condition, convincing Joy that her disease had entered a final phase. Carrie, he told Boatie, "is in a state of torpor a good part of the time. Miss Gray seems to think she will pull out of it. . . ."[55] As her birthday approached and she did improve somewhat, she asked for something of her own for the house. Joy bought her a Circassian walnut chiffonier "to match the set of furniture in her room," he told Abbie. "I was glad to have her feel that she wanted something for the place. It seems like a slight sign of contentment."[56]

It was, however, another difficult summer as Joy tried to unite the family. Not only was Carrie's condition worsening, but Helen Morton, Mark's daughter, had created a public scandal by running away with a dashing Virginian named Roger Bayly. For Joy, who was taught by his father to eschew scandal at all costs, the journalistic heyday that followed was a disaster. Joy tried to explain to others in the family what he considered to be an aberration, believing Helen's behavior could not be traced to Mark. To Abbie he explained, "[Helen] is a good girl—very bright but is a little inclined to advanced notions, somewhat due, I think, to the influence of that finishing school in New York, the head of which is tinctured with socialism."[57] In June, he wrote to Wirt, "Uncle Mark's troubles are just sapping the life out of him. He is all shaken to pieces by it. It is too bad that a man like him should have to be all upset on account of the action of stupid, foolish people. Your Aunt Martha is responsible for the whole trouble. Her refusal to permit the children to be disciplined when young is bringing its reward."[58]

At last, a marriage was arranged in Geneva, Illinois, in a private home, with only Jean, Joy, Mark, and Martha present. Afterward, Joy hosted the couple at Thornhill while Boatie prepared Arbor Lodge for their honeymoon. "Everything is done in order," Joy concluded.[59] Later he wrote to Boatie about Helen and Joy II, who also had had an argument with his father and was managing a farm in Pennsylvania: "My private opinion is that both he and his sister will, in time, realize the advantages that they have lately spurned and be very glad to line up with Mark, who is and always will be their best friend."[60]

Although Mark and Martha separated with finality in 1915 at the height of Helen's public escapade, they never divorced. Helen and Roger remained in a tumultuous marriage for only a brief time, when they separated and Helen reconciled with her father at Wheaton, where Mark built a $20,000 art studio for her. Helen and Roger divorced two years later, during which time Mark and Joy were constantly besieged by the press. Helen's involvement with Roger Bayly and a temporary estrangement from her father dominated Chicago society news from May 1914 until her divorce in October 1916. Over the two years, reporters from Chicago's *American, Journal, Examiner, Record-Herald,* and *Tribune,* and from papers throughout the region descended on Mark's home in Wheaton and on Thorn Hill and followed the movements of both Helen and Roger Bayly until the story played itself out. But the damage was done. The Morton family name, so precious to J. Sterling, had become a part of one of the most sensational scandals of the time.

Joy, however, never wavered in his support for his brother and Helen, even though Carrie's condition during this time was at a nadir. "We feel that she is failing gradually but surely," he told Boatie. "It is only occasionally that she knows any of us; doesn't know when she eats or drinks; everything is done automatically."[61] A few weeks later, Joy informed Boatie that Carrie seemed to have lost her ability to communicate. "While her condition is about what the doctors predicted," he wrote, "it seems awful to have her so ill."[62] She began to hallucinate frequently about having a baby and seeing strange men. One day, Joy carried her downstairs for lunch, but she refused to eat, thinking there was a strange man under the table. Once back in her bedroom, she became violent toward Miss Gray, then immediately apologized.[63]

As often as possible during these trying days, Joy distracted himself by overseeing farm work. A new barn was almost finished and five miles of drain tile installed. He expected to have 500 acres of land under cultivation in 1915. Once again, though, in late September Carrie became well enough to motor to Lake Forest with her favorite chauffeur, Miss Gray. When she returned to the house, Joy wrote Abbie, "she didn't know whether she had been horseback riding or motoring," but her temporary recovery surprised Joy, who wrote to Abbie: "We hardly know what to think of it."[64] He was so buoyed that he had thoughts of taking her to Pasadena during the winter and occupying the house he had purchased and furnished for her.

In October, at the end of a two-week visit by Sterling and his family, Joy felt positive enough about Carrie's condition that he hired a five-piece band and hosted a picnic for about 150 office workers, salesmen, plant superintendents, and their families who were transported from downtown Chicago by the CB&Q. He arranged for Carrie to look on at the festivities from the parlor, if she wanted, although she declined. His employees and family chose up sides for competitions on the ample lawn, including a baseball game between the "sacks" and "barrels." Finding the day successful, Joy decided to make it an annual event each September near his birthday.[65]

Carrie's attitude toward Sterling's family seemed to have eased a bit during their stay at Arbor Lodge. She "enjoyed Sterling and is beginning to like Preston better, but she hasn't any use for the 'Little Highwayman' as she calls Suzette," Joy told Abbie.[66] Carrie remained jealous of her privacy. People—particularly lively children—made her nervous. Carrie's improving condition was accompanied by an equally marked improvement in Sterling's illness. Joy was pleased that Sterling had gained sufficient strength to cut stumps while on the farm. By December, he had improved enough that Joy sent him to Kansas City where, he told Abbie, "He is to have charge of the western business of the Salt Company, a very responsible position; will live in Kansas City. . . ."[67] A bonus of this move for Sterling and Wirt was that they would be working within proximity of one another and would further strengthen the family bonds.

$\mathcal{T}$he year 1915 began positively. After spending three months in Pasadena, Joy and Carrie returned to Thorn Hill where Joy was planning an addition to make Carrie more comfortable. "Carrie," Joy told Abbie, "seems to be improving right along. She told me yesterday that she thought she liked Thorn Hill better than any place in the world; believed it agreed with her better. . . ."[68] The additions to Thorn Hill that Joy had in mind included an ell of rooms to the north, an archway to a drive and a new garage; to the west, he wanted to add a conservatory. "I am making these improvements," he wrote to Abbie, "on the theory that Carrie would be better off to remain at the Farm next winter than to leave home as we did last winter."[69]

Construction progressed steadily throughout the summer. But in September, Joy was impatient for the work to be completed sufficiently to begin landscaping and have the estate ready for a second picnic for his Chicago employees. He wrote excitedly to Abbie not only of Carrie reaching 102 pounds in weight and improving in appearance, but also of his satisfaction with the addition. It was, he said, "going to be very fine, better than I had expected and it greatly improves the place." He had decided to remove hawthorns from the east of the house, "leaving a wide vista which will be in blue grass." As visitors turned into the gate below, they would be greeted by "a fine view of the house. . . ."[70] No doubt, Joy was thinking of the approach to Arbor Lodge.

The company picnic was held on September 30 for 180 employees and their families. Joy later described his satisfaction with the day to Abbie: "Sterling was major-domo and everything went off beautifully. Refreshments were served in a big tent, which was located east of the house in the little bay in the woods, directly between the house driveway and the front gate." He was also pleased by Carrie's increased interest in the house, which he was now calling Thornhill.[71] Joy was now satisfied that his estate would become the center of the Morton family during his lifetime, as Arbor Lodge had been for his father. As if to strengthen that symbolic link, he decided to furnish the addition as much as possible with items from Arbor Lodge. He, Jean, and Miss Gray made a trip there to select furniture that would best fit into the new rooms at Thornhill.

The early fall's events had inspired Joy. He informed Abbie that Carrie continued "to do splendidly" and was up walking about her room. But in the same letter, Joy was moved to reveal to Abbie an insight into himself that in recent years he had let few people understand. In her role as agent for Judge Lake's estate, Abbie had taken out a bank loan, and Joy had written to her in a purely business-like tone admonishing her for having done so. When Abbie replied, saying that she was sorry if she had angered Joy, he answered, assuring her that such was not the case: "I am surprised that you got the idea that I felt hurt. . . . I must have put my business face on when you talked to me about that business matter. I didn't in the least disapprove. . . ."[72] It was a rare revelation of character, but a moment that indicated that Joy was aware of how his behavior affected others. In a moment of distraction, he had forgotten which countenance he was wearing.

Joy knew Carrie's apparent recovery was but an interlude. And in November, her condition descended rapidly from promising to precarious. Joy soon wrote to tell Abbie, ". . . Carrie is down again."[73] This time, there was no recovery. On December 9, 1915, Carrie died at Thornhill. For nearly twenty years, Joy had done everything to provide Carrie with the best care even as she grew ever more intractable. At the end, he was more contented when Carrie lived with him than when they lived apart. Her death created a palpable vacancy in his life. Within days, he wrote again to Abbie, "This house seems strange and lonely without Carrie. It did not seem possible that her passing could make such a difference, but we have got to get used to it and will try to be philosophical."[74]

Carrie had been the dominant person in Joy's life for three and a half decades. Now, upon her death, he arranged for her burial in her beloved father's plot in Omaha and for the perpetual care of the graves. In Carrie's memory, he made a memorial gift of $25,000 to Brownell Hall, the Episcopalian girl's school in Omaha founded in 1863 from which Carrie had graduated in 1875.[75]

The acts of remembrance completed, Joy fell into a blue mood that was compounded by his own health problems and by yet another death in the family. He had had the grippe throughout the winter. Early in 1916, a baby boy born to Wirt and Ada died of a defective heart. Joy's principal comfort during this time was that Margaret Gray remained on at Thornhill in the role of manager of the house. When Abbie's granddaughter, his niece Blanche Deuel, visited, Joy persuaded her to extend her stay. He was getting a new car, and he expected Margaret would drive Blanche and him to visit Jean in her new Lake Forest home.[76] Now in her capacity as governess of Thornhill, Margaret had become more a member of his family than an employee.

In late February, Joy decided to go to Pasadena to ready for sale the house that he had purchased for Carrie. He stayed through March, time enough for the worst of the Chicago winter to abate and for most of the Thornhill new construction he had begun for Carrie to be completed. Upon his return in early April, he told Abbie, "We are well at the farm and are beginning to use the new part of the house. The new drawing room from over the driveway is delightful and I think it is going to be a very popular room. The two new bedrooms are likewise exceedingly attractive."[77]

Nearing his sixtieth birthday, Joy could, after fifteen years of constant familial uncertainty, take pleasure in the present and look forward to the future. He had his "badly diseased" teeth pulled, and he wanted to assure Abbie, "After two weeks of misery, I have a new set of teeth that are just beginning to work."[78] He had also sold the house in Pasadena for $19,000, which he gave to Sterling and Preston with "some additional" money added in, to be used for construction of a new house for them and their two daughters. (Sterling's family had grown to four on March 27, 1915, when Preston gave birth to Carolyn Owsley.[79]) In June 1916, Joy invited Boatie, Martha, and Wirt and Ada (called "Lady" by the family) for a ten-day visit to celebrate the addition to Thornhill. Sterling, Preston, Suzette, and Carolyn joined them for almost a week. Joy wrote to Abbie, "The house is now in fine order and we have enjoyed the visit very much. . . ." The "we" included Margaret Gray, who, Joy said, "is well and handling the house very efficiently. I know if she knew I was writing, she would send her love."[80] Joy could now turn his mind to business and family with a degree of equanimity.

Part

THREE

1916～1934

C H A P T E R *10*

War—Home and Abroad—1916–1919

Joy could look back on the last several years with the satisfaction that in spite of almost constant adversity Thornhill had become the estate he had long wanted to build. Although Paul's sudden death, Carrie's erratic but ineluctable mental and physical disintegration, Sterling's prolonged and nearly fatal illness, and public scandal in Mark's family had brought Joy, at the age of sixty, to near exhaustion, he did not turn in on himself as his father had done in less trying situations. Fortitude—the trait he associated with his mother—had gotten him through. And now, as he seemed always to do when the blue mood of the Mortons descended on him, he took a fresh perspective on life.

The world of 1916 differed drastically from the one Joy had known at the turn of the century, but he was well prepared for its challenges. He had embraced technological innovation, wrestled with ideological and economic policy changes, and become an active participant in civic affairs. Now, with the completion of Thornhill, he was poised to explore both the natural and human history as well as the potential of the region of Illinois in which he lived. He was also seeking to plan an appropriate legacy for future generations.

The unknown was the war in Europe. No one in the United States—still neutral in 1916—understood what turn this upheaval would take, although it seemed probable to many that German aggression against noncombatants on the high seas would cause the United States to throw its lot with the Entente against the Central Powers. President Woodrow Wilson had managed to keep the United States out of the war during his first term but was now readying the country for its eventuality. A year earlier, his first secretary of state, William Jennings Bryan (J. Sterling's old nemesis), had resigned during the crisis brought on by the German U-2's sinking of the *Lusitania* on May 17, 1915, taking 128 American lives. For the next two years, the country, with its shipping increasingly threatened by German submarines, remained in a perpetual state of uncertainty until war was declared on the Central Powers on April 6, 1917. All the while, Joy was preparing Morton Salt Company and other companies under the management of Joy Morton & Co. to meet the obligations the times imposed upon them.

*A*lthough he had been occupied with Carrie and Thornhill over the last years, Joy had stayed on top of changes in business culture. The country's suspicion of trusts had intensified during Roosevelt's progressive Republican administration, and prosecutions and legislation continued through the presidencies of Taft and Wilson. Contributing to anti-consolidation sentiment were the muckraking investigations of well-known journalist-photographers, such as Jacob Riis, and novelists, such as Upton Sinclair, whose messages were so powerful that many industrialists were led to distance themselves from combines, at least in the public mind. While Joy understood the value of consolidation and had been involved in developing combines when he thought it good business, he had assiduously maintained oversight of his own companies and staffed them with managers he had personally trained. In 1910, the creation of the Morton Salt Company out of the corporate-sounding International Salt Company of Illinois had been a decided declaration of business independence. It paid off. In a short time, the new brand, packaging, and marketing of Morton Salt made Morton a synonym for the household staple.

An instance of Joy's refusal to go along with the tactics of trusts in the new business culture was his sharp reaction to an apparent threat issued to C.M. Aldrich, his agent at the Morton-Gregson Company in Nebraska City, from an Omaha agent of Swift and Company. Aldrich reported to Joy that Swift's Omaha office had suggested Morton-Gregson should sell only to them. Joy told Aldrich that "it is so much more fun to peddle [meat] than it is to sell to any members of the 'trust'" and followed with the corollary that "it is quite contrary to the spirit of the times to give away stuff with a view to crushing a competitor and thereby creating a monopoly. I have had a little experience in this—in fact, am having some now in the Oatmeal trade, and I think I know what I am talking about."[1]

Joy was, of course, determined that his companies, while maintaining independence, would remain competitive. As Morton Salt sought to expand its production opportunities, Germany shut off exports of potash. The Morton Salt Company contracted with the Salt Lake Chemical Company, a subsidiary of the Diamond Match Company, to process common salt that resulted from the manufacture of potash at a newly constructed plant in Burmester, Utah, thirty miles from Salt Lake City. The move was an early step toward Morton Salt's dominance in the west as a producer of salt made in the solar evaporation process.[2] By August 1918, the company had expanded to become the exclusive sales agent for all salt made by the Salt Lake Chemical Company of Burmester, Utah, its first major venture beyond the Rockies. It was also supplied by the Retsof Mining Company in New York, Detroit Rock Salt Company, Avery Rock Salt Company at Avery Island, Louisiana, and the Crystal Salt Company at Kanopolis, Kansas. With works at Port Huron, Ludington, and Hutchinson, sales offices in Chicago, Detroit, Milwaukee, New Orleans, Superior, St. Louis, Kansas City, and Salt Lake City, and docks and warehouses at Chicago, Superior, Milwaukee, and St. Louis, the Morton Salt Company was now the largest in the country. The operation was complex, but Joy had carefully prepared for such an expansion, having personally trained many of the key personnel in the intricacies of the industry.

*N*o matter how large his companies grew, though, Joy's management style remained focused on personnel. From the start he had kept a close watch on the young people in his employ, looking for those he could groom for administrative positions. Wirt Morton represented a new generation entering the business, and Joy took special care to clarify his expectations of him, particularly since he was a Morton. In February 1914, Wirt, who had been at the Hutchinson plant for three years, asked Joy whether he could buy shares of the Morton stock that only Joy, Peterkin, Sterling, and Mark then owned. It was an opportunity for Joy to explain to Wirt some facts about what he expected of potential stockholders, particularly those who belonged to the family. The stock was not now for sale, he said, but in any case, Wirt's chances of purchasing stock depended not on money but on his showing a consistent quality of work over several years. "I think," Joy assured Wirt, "you are doing pretty well, but it takes time to create a first-class salt maker and some considerable time, even if that individual salt-maker digs in hard every day of the three hundred and sixty-five and uses his brains as well as his hands in an effort to create net results for the Company."[3]

Joy was thinking of a recent lapse in management Wirt had had as head of carton production at Hutchinson. After a recent fire in Texas, Wirt had acted too slowly, Joy thought, to supply needed cartons. A few weeks later, however, Joy assured Wirt's mother that Wirt was "doing splendidly in Hutchinson, better . . . than ever before. . . . We are counting on him to make one of the most valuable men of the Morton Salt Company administraton."[4] In October 1914, Joy made Wirt the superintendent of the Hutchinson plant.

Joy had less patience with another close relative whom he thought should be experienced enough to avoid problems within the company. His uncle Will, J. Sterling's brother, for whom Joy had worked briefly as a teenager, had joined the Detroit office of Morton Salt Company after retiring from banking. In September 1915, Will had written to Joy that he was disappointed in the way Joy had handled telling him about a falling out with Otto Huette, the office manager. Joy was clearly annoyed at what he considered to be his uncle's lack of professionalism: "I think you have acted in a petty and childlike manner about it, and if you wish to retain your position in the office, you must cut out that kind of thing in the future and work harmoniously with Mr. Huette, whose conduct meets with my entire approval, and who is now conducting the office in a manner that is entirely satisfactory to me."[5] Joy sent a copy of his letter to Huette, ending the matter.

It was perhaps a consequence of Joy's fascination with the region in which he had settled, his forty years in an industry that depended heavily upon transportation, and his propensity to build the future on the past— as he had done symbolically by housing his offices in the replica of the Boston Town House—that in 1912 he championed an experiment in Illinois inland waterway transportation carried out solely by the Morton Salt Company. Joy's predecessors in the salt business had come to Chicago the year the Illinois and Michigan Canal opened, because it was the best means of distributing salt from Chicago to LaSalle, down the Illinois River, and onto the Mississippi and western markets. Within six years of the canal's opening, however, the Rock Island Railroad began operating along a parallel route, eventually threatening the economic logic of shipping on the I&M Canal.[6] While the canal continued to be useful for shipments of some bulk products, in the 1880s it suffered another threat from strategies used to manage the pollution of the Chicago River from untreated waste of its population and industries. In 1884, pumps reversed the flow of the river, sending waste into the I&M's upper reaches from Lemont to Lockport. Then in 1900, with the opening of the Chicago Sanitary and Ship Canal, the Des Plaines and Illinois Rivers were gorged with untreated industrial and human waste. By 1912, the I&M, the only viable inland waterway from Chicago to the Illinois at LaSalle, had fallen into disrepair and, in some portions, was nearly filled with sediment.

Ironically, as the end of the I&M Canal seemed eminent, a more efficient, wider, and deeper seventy-five-mile long Illinois and Mississippi Canal (known as the Hennepin) was completed in 1907 between the Illinois River at Hennepin and Bureau to just below Rock Island on the Mississippi, with a feeder canal from the Rock River close to Rock Falls, Illinois, twenty-four miles to the north. While the Hennepin was hailed as an engineering marvel and shortened the distance from the Great Lakes to the Upper Mississippi Valley by a distance of 419 miles, it seemed an anachronism before it was finished. Without a viable I&M Canal or a dependable barge channel on the upper Illinois, the Hennepin could never attract the commercial transportation business that politicians and locals had hoped for.[7]

In spite of the condition of the I&M and the lack of commercial traffic and suitable port facilities along the upper Mississippi at Davenport and Rock Island, Joy believed that if Morton Salt proved that the canals could be navigated and the company could come close to breaking even, government and private investment interest in inexpensive and dependable inland waterway traffic would be reinvigorated. In June 1912, the Morton Salt Company began to ship salt from Chicago to the Mississippi River via the I&M Canal, a short stretch of the Illinois River, and the five-year-old commercially unused Hennepin Canal. The experiment, continued until 1914, was far from being quixotic, for its lessons helped refocus the attention of government, business, and the public on the usefulness of inland waterways.

In 1916, Joy described that first voyage to members of the National Rivers and Harbors Association in Washington, D.C. Morton Salt had resurrected a "decrepit and leaky" forty-year-old steam-propelled canal boat. Less than a week later it had carried, Joy related proudly, "the first load of through freight that was ever shipped from Chicago to the

Mississippi River via the United States Government's Hennepin Canal, which had then been completed for more than five years, fully manned and watchfully waiting but without a single through shipment." Along the sixty-mile Illinois and Michigan Canal, the barge, drawing only four feet, "was snaked through mud by teams on shore for a good part of the way." It then went down the Illinois for eighteen miles and entered the Hennepin Canal at Hennepin and Bureau for the final ninety miles. The trip took almost a week. Upon its return, Morton Salt raised two more canal boats from the Illinois River's bottom where they had been sunk "for preservation of what little remained of them." In all, six Morton Salt barges plied the canals until 1914, taking salt west and returning with grain, lumber, and other bulk goods. Even though it was obvious that these dilapidated, relatively small vessels would not be suitable in the long run because they could not carry sufficient freight in the inadequate I&M Canal to make a profit, Joy concluded that the venture "confirmed us in our original belief in the practicability of water transportation."[8] Joy knew, though, that the canal systems would have to be reconstructed to a uniform width of two hundred feet and a depth of eight feet and that if this were done, private companies like Morton Salt would build barges that could carry loads large enough to turn a profit.

Joy could champion barge transportation of bulk goods with the authority of having had long experience in lake and canal traffic. Since 1899, Morton Salt had owned a fleet of Great Lakes carriers crossing Lake Michigan from Port Huron, Manistee, and Ludington to Chicago. His argument was made even stronger since he did not promote inland waterways over railways as the answer to the country's transportation needs. On the contrary, the role that Joy and Paul had played in the railroad industry was well known. As Joy told the National Rivers and Harbors Association, "I regard canals as supplemental to and co-operative with the railroads, not as competitive."[9] Barges were less expensive to operate than railroads for some bulk commodities, and they could reduce the overload on railcars during the peak of the harvest season.

During the war, Joy was on the Water Transportation Division of the Council of National Defense and the State Board of Water Resources and continued to be an advocate of canal use. In 1917, he joined Governor Frank Lowden and others on an inspection trip of the canal system from Joliet on up the Hennepin Canal to Sterling, reigniting local interest. As a *Sheffield Times* reporter wrote, "We are told that the purpose of the inspection trip is to ascertain the condition of the canal and whether it will be possible to open up the waterway to Chicago."[10] After the war,

Joy continued to argue for a waterway from LaSalle to Chicago with even greater urgency. Upon returning from Europe, he addressed members from the Illinois Chamber of Commerce who were taking a waterway trip from Chicago to Peoria. He told his companions how impressed he was that even before the French began to cultivate their fields or rebuild their villages following the war, they reconstructed their canals between the Meuse and the Marne. "It was," he said, "the most convincing proof I have ever seen of the practical utility of inland waterways."[11] As late as 1923, Joy appeared before the Waterways Committee of the United States Senate, making the case for the economic practicality of waterway transportation, including by canal: "I believe that Chicago exists today," he said, "as a result of the construction of the Illinois & Michigan Canal, which made it a shipping point and afterwards attracted the railroads."[12]

Even though the I&M Canal received an infusion of funds as a part of the war effort, and Davenpot, Iowa, and other cities improved their port facilities to receive barge traffic from Chicago through the I&M and Hennepin, a major reconstruction of the waterways was not to be.[13] The government's long-range plans focused on bringing traffic to the upper Illinois River through construction of a barge channel and an adequate lock and dam system from Utica to Lockport and the Des Plaines River. It was a plan that Joy could support, although he continued to maintain that reengineering the existing I&M Canal would be less expensive. The upper Illinois River channel was completed in 1933, allowing barges larger than the Hennepin could accommodate. It was a final irony; the question of barge traffic from the Great Lakes to the upper Mississippi became moot. Eventually, the I&M and Hennepin canals became public parkways, a result that Joy would have accepted if his vision for the waterway was not to be realized.

*O*n September 27, 1916, Joy celebrated his sixty-first year with improved health and a burst of activity. There was the annual picnic outing for the office workers of Morton Salt at the newly enlarged Thornhill. Then in October, Joy and Mark (who had recently separated from his wife), joined Sterling in Kansas City for a brief duck hunting trip and an inspection of Morton Salt's Kansas facilities. In early December, the Michigan newspapers carried stories of the decision by the Morton Salt Company to purchase the 230-acre site and inventory of the long-abandoned R.G. Peters Salt & Lumber Company of Manistee, Michigan. Robert K. Warren had arrived to oversee the refurbishing of the plant, and the town of Manistee expressed great hopes for a return to a healthy economy.[14]

During a quiet period at home in the late fall, Joy began research on settlements on and around his Thornhill property. He conducted personal interviews with neighbors whose European ancestors were early landowners in the area, and he engaged the help of the Chicago Historical Society (of which he had been a board member since 1910) to locate an ancient Indian trail running through his property and leading from the Des Plaines River to the east branch of the DuPage River. In December, after finding a number of Indian artifacts, he wrote to the Chief Clerk of the Smithsonian Institute to ask for help in identifying them. His purpose in studying these items, he said, was in anticipation "of preparing a collection which I believe will be of special interest to archaeologists."[15]

Salt, too, had become a natural focus of Joy's interest in history. Morton Salt had become a household name, but the history of salt itself and of the Morton Salt Company was largely a mystery to the general public and even to some in the industry. In January 1915, the company began publication of a series of booklets entitled *Salt Talks*. Two years later, Morton Salt had published seven booklets that provided a history unrivaled at the time and not equaled for many years. Beginning with a description of Morton Salt plants, the booklets included the history, geography and geology, and manufacture of salt; the history and process of deriving quality salt from brine; the history of curing and packing salt; the history and process of purifying salt; and the history, mining, and processing of rock salt in mines that supplied the Morton Salt Company: the Retsof in New York, the Avery on Avery Island in Louisiana, the Detroit Rock Salt Company, and the Crystal Rock Salt Company in Kanopolis, Kansas.

Even with all of this activity, Joy felt the need of a companion with whom to share his life. Two years after Carrie's death he asked Margaret Gray to marry him, which surprised no one who knew him well. Margaret had been a faithful companion to Carrie, and she had remained on as manager of Thornhill when Joy most needed her. Twenty years younger than Joy, Margaret had been born in Newburgh, a tiny southern Indiana town near Evansville on the Ohio River. Intelligent and caring, Margaret, like Joy, was from a pioneering family. Her grandfather had owned one of the first Ohio River ferryboats in Newburgh, and her father, James, had farmed there.[16] She and Joy decided to marry in the new year.

Joy immediately considered a grand trip to launch the marriage. Because of the war, Europe was out of the question. Then in December 1916, at a luncheon meeting at which the directors of the Continental and Commercial National Bank of Chicago were hosting a Chinese diplomat, Joy mentioned that he might like to go to China, a country hospitable to American tourists and host to a substantial community of American businessmen, missionaries, and educators. The diplomat quickly offered to make contacts for him. Joy later wrote to Sterling that his fellow directors hailed him as "Envoy Extraordinary," likely giving the diplomat the impression that he was "'some dog.'"[17] Within a week, Joy invited Sterling and Preston to accompany him and Margaret and purchased tickets to China on the *Empress of Russia,* a Canadian ship sailing from Vancouver on January 25. Joy and Margaret married on January 16, 1917.

The decision to make a journey of four and a half months to China via the Philippines, Japan, and Korea was not as precipitous as Joy's letter to Sterling made it seem. George M. Reynolds, the president of the Continental and Commercial National Bank had arranged for a five-million-dollar loan to China. Joy was curious about the financial negotiation, which was to be paid off by taxes on wine and tobacco in several Chinese provinces. As usual, Joy wanted to see for himself, thinking that it would be best if someone could, as Sterling later wrote, "learn something of the country, its resources, manners and customs."[18]

During several weeks in Peking, Joy and his party visited with members of the American community, and he and Sterling were granted a meeting with President Li Yuanhong and other administration officials. The minister of finance was, however, imprisoned during their visit. This was but one disconcerting circumstance in Joy's attempt to learn of the soundness of the Continental and Commercial National's loan. He soon began to understand just how complicated Chinese financial methods were. "He came to the conclusion," Sterling wrote, "that Bret Harte was right in his famous poem—'The Heathen Chinee'—as the revenues on which the loan was based had previously been hypothecated several times; in fact, bonds with approximately the same security could be bought for less than half price in the open market." When Joy pointed these things out, the Chinese officials simply smiled, Sterling said, with "equanimity" confirming Joy's "ideas that the loan had perhaps been made without proper investigation and information."[19]

Although Joy and his traveling companions had had a relaxing and informative journey and he and Margaret would return to China several years later on an around-the-world trip, Joy came home to Chicago in early June 1918 determined to get out of banking, particularly speculative international banking. Joy soon resigned as director of the Continental and Commercial National Bank and began to dispose of his stock. Since beginning his career in banking at James Sweet & Co. in Nebraska City at the age of fifteen, Joy had been wary of speculation. Later, from the perspective of the Great Depression, he would maintain, as Sterling recorded, "The industrial development of the past thirty years [had] found the banking system unprepared and unfitted to serve it."[20] Joy believed bankers had forgotten the purpose of banking, which "was the handling of money for the depositors and the maintenance of the ability at all times to pay that money upon reasonable demand."[21]

What Joy learned of Chinese financial methods confirmed for him once again that his habit of carefully investigating an enterprise before entering into it was the only way to conduct business. Later Sterling was certain that the Chinese venture proved Joy's business perspicacity: "That his judgment of the situation was correct is shown by the fact that, according to the best records available, not a cent of principal or interest has ever been paid by the Chinese government on this loan."[22]

In June, less than three weeks after the trip to China, Joy accepted an invitation to speak at a Nebraska City homecoming in August, saying that unlike his father he was not an orator, but he felt "a great interest in Nebraska City" and "heartily" approved "of the home-comings and other celebrations which our people occasionally indulge in. . . ."[23] But his real reason for going to Nebraska City was that it gave him an opportunity to put into context his recent trip to China. His subject would be a comparison of agricultural practice and production in China and the United States.

Six days before the speech was to be delivered on August 16, 1917, Joy told C.M. Aldrich that he and Margaret (whom he always referred to as Mrs. Morton when speaking to subordinates) would arrive in Nebraska City by train and would bring some servants along. He would want a "good car and a driver," he said, adding, "Would prefer to have something better than a Ford, if it is obtainable. If you can't get it locally, you can, perhaps, arrange to get a high-class car from some of the wealthy farmers in the neighborhood who have been selling us some of these 17 cent hogs. . . ."[24]

He followed this letter to Aldrich on the same day with one much less cordial. Aldrich had written to Joy that instead of making a profit, Morton-Gregson had suffered a $17,000 loss in July 1917, mainly due to an accounting error. Joy, for whom accurate accounting was an absolute, upbraided Aldrich, saying, "It knocks a fellow's confidence to have that sort of thing happen and I hope it won't occur again. . . . And please don't ever send me another statement showing a big loss without any comments. The first impression one gets is that nobody cares a damn whether we win or lose, and that isn't cheerful to contemplate."[25] His tone might have been more severe than usual, because Joy had just had a firsthand look at China's agricultural economy that, in spite of ample workforce and resources, remained, he believed, relatively impoverished because of centuries of cultural indifference and managerial ineptitude. Joy was bent on bringing to the agricultural community of Nebraska City a reminder of the benefits of what good business practices had accomplished in America in but a few decades.

The speech was straightforward, with none of the florid rhetoric that characterized his father's political talks. Joy told his audience that "there are no better agriculturists than the Chinese" and that Chinese farmers worked harder and longer than American farmers. (Workers in the United States had only recently achieved a forty-eight-hour workweek.) There were also large expanses of well-watered ground and climatic conditions resembling those of the Mississippi Valley in China. Thus, he concluded, "There seems to be no reason why, if we admit, as we must, that agriculture is the basis of all wealth, the per capita wealth of the Chinese should not be as great as that of the people of the Mississippi Valley."

His answer to the conundrum was simple economics. Asking, "What is it that Nebraska has and China lacks?" he answered, "It seems to me that the missing essentials are transportation, credit, and a sound monetary system." Of the three, Joy told his audience, "transportation is undoubtedly the greatest of all, and when China equips herself with enough railroads to transport her freight at less than a cent a ton per mile, America will have competitors for her products of agriculture that will make her producers sit up and take notice."[26]

Joy knew that his speech at Nebraska City would not be complete without at least one mention of the planting of trees, for which his father was revered. In this field, too, Joy said, China had not realized the potential of its neighbors, including Japan (which had just planted 80 million trees over a three-year period), Korea (which had planted 110 million trees in three years), and a portion of Japanese-occupied Eastern Manchuria.

Joy was so enthusiastic about the Japanese expertise of planting arborvitae, cedar, spruce, and fir that one day he helped workmen plant well-rooted three-year-old trees that had been started on mountain terraces. He admired the manner in which the Japanese were succeeding in forestation: "Scientific forestry in Japan is not a new thing," he said.

Although the Chinese were taking notice, he said, they "are a good deal like Americans in procrastinating and I am afraid they will put off their planting until it is a very long time before China has much timber."

It had been forty-one years since Joy had helped celebrate a Nebraska City homecoming. In closing, he recalled that though his name had not appeared in the July 4, 1876, program, he had been an assistant marshall and rode a "fine black horse, over 16 hands" and "constituted a very large part of the procession that day." It was not the image of the horse or himself in the procession that he wanted to leave his audience with, however. In a rhetorical turn that would have made J. Sterling proud, he said it had been "a great day" because "it will always be a great day for Nebraska City when the people cooperate to do things worth while." It was a message that Joy had repeated to the citizens of Nebraska City during many years of philanthropic and business activity there.

Whether he was frustrated by a lack of civic cooperation among the leaders of Nebraska City, preoccupied with his work in Illinois, or exasperated by ongoing problems at Morton-Gregson, Joy was preparing, even as he was helping the city celebrate, to divest himself of his largest holding there. In October, he and Mark sold the packing operation to Wilson & Co. Inc., a New York corporation, for $250,000. The name Morton-Gregson remained, but Joy was no longer a major employer in his native city. He continued to own Arbor Lodge and property in the city, however, and in the fall he hired M.M. Vaughn to manage four cottages on 7th Street, one cottage on 1st Avenue & 18th, one cottage on 22nd & 1st Ave., the Club House, Overland Theatre, Arbor Lodge, and the Cereal Mill accounts.[27]

*J*oy had returned to the United States at a time when industry was trying to keep up with wartime demands as able-bodied men from the ages of eighteen to forty-five were being conscripted. Wirt wrote to Joy and "Aunt Margaret" after a visit he and Lady had made to Thornhill in June saying the Hutchinson plant was "Losing lots of men for the army and harvest."[28] In July, the loss of workers was compounded at the Morton Salt Company by a brief strike, which Sterling and Wirt helped settle. When Sterling returned to Chicago, he wrote to Wirt of the "war spirit": "There are flags everywhere [in Chicago] and almost all the young men are in training or have already joined some Militia or Hospital Unit. . . . I know it will be a source of everlasting regret to me that my infirmities prevent my taking an active part in this trouble."[29]

In the spring of 1918, Wirt enlisted in the army as a private in the

Quartermaster's Mechanized Repair Shop, where he rose to sergeant after one month. Thinking Wirt's age, education, and management experience made him officer material, Joy chided Wirt on the style of a letter Wirt had sent him from Camp Jessup in Georgia: "You better be more careful about spelling 'barracks' right—not 'barricks'; you have spelled the word twice in your letter that way. You are having experience enough with them to notice how the word is spelled. . . . It isn't impossible that such a careless spelling as this might be prejudicial in the manner of your getting a promotion."[30]

Wirt understood the meaning of his uncle's reprimands, intoned in a style J. Sterling had used when writing to Joy. They revealed a sincere interest in his welfare. Wanting Wirt, now twenty-eight and the father of Carl, his newborn son, to become an officer, Joy petitioned his nephew's superiors, emphasizing that Wirt had successfully managed large numbers of men in business, had graduated from the Lawrenceville School, and had taken courses at the Rensselaer Polytechnic Institute. In August 1918, Wirt was made a first lieutenant. In addition, Joy II, Mark's son, had followed his older cousin into the army.

Morton Salt followed the fortunes of each of its employees who had enlisted or were preparing to enter the service by forming the Morton Salt Company Patriotic Association, which sent clothing, food, and reading material to employees who had enlisted or were drafted. In September 1918, the Association published the *Morton Salt Bulletin,* an eight page, three-column paper filled with information for the 148 employees who were now scattered throughout the United States and Europe. Dedicated to Joy on his sixty-third birthday, the issue featured a short biography of him, the names of employees recently conscripted, and ten letters from troops at home and abroad. One letter written by Wirt to Dan Peterkin told of the few left at Camp Jessup, where Lady and their baby, Carl, had joined him. In October, Wirt, too, shipped out to France.

The *Bulletin* featured lively stories about what was happening with employees at home and in the service. Accounts of competitive baseball games at Port Huron, Chicago, and France provided a motif that ran throughout. One writer with the pen name "Gris" in a wryly titled story, "News from the Front," reported on the "ticker" next to Joy's office that was being watched attentively for the 1918 Cubs and Red Sox World Series scores (in the only season to be completed in September) and on the mock battles in Grant Park and above Lake Michigan that could be seen from the "front," the windows of the Railway Exchange building. Sterling, now a lieutenant in the Home Guard Volunteer Training Corps, wrote of Chicago's efforts to be certain that no one was illegally escaping military service.

The *Bulletin* also offered to help inform its workers on the draft. The salt industry had been designated essential, which gave the company's employees the same draft classification as workers in shipbuilding, railways, fuel, and munitions. The Patriotic Association explained, "We will, perhaps, claim deferred classification on industrial grounds for some of our employees, but each case will be handled individually." The second issue of the *Bulletin* was promised for October 31. There was no need. The Armistice was signed on November 11, 1918.

The war's conclusion led to a downturn in the economy that Joy had predicted, and, like most of his fellow industrialists, he did not believe the government should be asked to interfere. He wrote to Wirt, who was still in the service, "Until labor and commodities have been some deflated, I don't look for much activity. A general reaction seems to me to be but natural and the future business health of the country will be more benefited by an immediate and severe slump all along the line, it seems to me, rather than to let things down easy through governmental aid directed by Utopian dreamers."[31] As a producer and distributor of an essential commodity, Morton Salt had made money during the conflict. Joy understood that an adjustment for all industry was forthcoming, and he preferred to let supply and demand determine the direction it would take.

The end of the war gave Joy a chance to direct his undivided attention to his family. Mark's son, Joy II, had, since his release from the army, been working for the salt company in Chicago and had been promoted to assistant superintendent. Joy was also anxious for Wirt to return to work. As he and Margaret were preparing for their winter trip to warmer climes—this time to Florida—Joy wrote to the chief of the Motor Transport Corps in an effort to get Wirt discharged early.

Joy and Margaret intended to remain on vacation for a month, but as they often did, they extended their visit. Sterling—deeply involved in his position as head of the Morkrum Company—took time to send Wirt a letter about Joy's trip that was written in the familiar and good-natured style that always marked the cousins' exchanges: "I do not see what Father figures on doing down there as he doesn't play golf, is not a good fisherman, doesn't believe in playing the wheel, is too heavy to dance and Florida is a dry state. It looks to me as though he were going to have a rather dull time of it."[32] A few weeks later, Sterling reported to Wirt, "J. M. has been joy riding in airplanes and, for all I know, has been dancing and frequenting the gambling houses at Palm Beach (but

I much doubt it). . . . They will . . . get home about the first of April."³³ In March, Joy and Margaret wended their way home with stops in New Orleans, Dallas, and Hutchinson.

The salt business had regained its momentum during Joy's absence, and in the spring Joy was able to turn his full attention to Thornhill and the Lisle Farms operations once again. From his Railway Exchange office, while looking out of the window at a mock air battle on the lakefront between the Americans and Germans, he wrote to Wirt, enthusiastically describing what was happening at Thornhill. He was having excellent success with his hogs, which at eight months averaged 246 pounds each when readied for market. He had recently sold a carload for a net yield of $50.80 per hog, which, he said, "is more than we used to pay for a horse in Nebraska when I was a boy, but it did not cost nearly as much to raise the horse in those days as it cost [sic] to feed the pig now." He was equally proud of his herd of Holsteins, writing, "We had four cows in March that each, on official test, gave over 700 lbs of milk in seven days, and we have one cow on a year's test who has given 24,000 lbs of milk in 10 months, an average of 80-lbs per day for 300 days. Some cow, I think, for a city farmer!" Joy also marveled at the spring improvements at Thornhill, saying, "Have planted thousands of young evergreen trees, besides many shrubs and deciduous trees. The place is looking better than it ever has."³⁴

By the summer of 1919, Illinois was beginning to put into perspective the months during which over 300,000 of its citizens had been in the war; leaders were also starting to calculate the recent ravages Illinois' citizens had suffered from the world-wide influenza epidemic of 1918. But the state of Illinois had also celebrated its first centennial in 1918 and was preparing to begin construction on its first state-wide system of hard roads. World War I had helped Illinois solidify its position as a principal industrial and agricultural power, and Joy was keenly aware of the place that Illinois held in the nation's affairs and felt that its young citizens should be prepared to take up their responsibilities. With that thought in mind, he composed a commencement speech for the students of Blackburn College who would graduate on June 4, 1919.³⁵

The speech lasted only ten minutes, but it revealed Joy's deeply held beliefs about education, government, individual responsibility, democracy, the economy, and the exemplary role of the Illinois farmer. His forum was tailor-made. Blackburn College, located in the farming community of Carlinville, Illinois, opened its doors in 1859 as a "self-help" institution that Joy believed to be an ideal preparation for the individualism that he prized. Saying that "our domestic affections are the proper fundamental basis" of good government, Joy insisted that such a government could not succeed without citizens who had the "courage of their convictions" and thought independently. "Individualism," he said, "must be maintained." As to the fear of Bolshevism, which had emerged in Russia and had created the "Red Scare" in the United States after World War I, Joy told the graduates that he did not have "the slightest fear" of its gaining a stronghold in the United States, because "the American people have altogether too much sense to indulge in that sort of foolishness." What concerned him was the American misuse of the word *equality*, particularly when it meant the "*equality of mediocrity*," that is, "leveling *downwards* instead of *upwards*." He did not object to organized labor, so long as collective bargaining was "based on merit" in which unions would "establish a high plane for their members—not . . . drag the good ones down to the level of the poor ones. . . ."

As to the recent war from which industry had benefited, Joy wanted his young audience to know that he believed "Uncle Sam" should never again be in the market "under the stimulus of war." The laws of supply and demand, which he termed "immutable," must return, he said, if the country were to escape "the influence of artificial prices and give economic laws a chance to work." In conclusion, Joy addressed what he believed to be the ethos of most graduates of this small college in southwest-central Illinois, an agricultural area similar to that in which he had spent his own youth and manhood. As he had in his Nebraska speech, he described the agrarian culture in Jeffersonian terms:

> Agriculture is not only a basis of all wealth, but our very life depends upon it and nothing that I know of will respond more favorably to fair treatment than the soil of Illinois; no worker on earth gets more for *overtime* than the farmer of this great State who gives a few extra hours of his brain and muscle, in the proper season, to the preparation of his seed beds and the tillage of his crops. The difference between poor crops and good crops is more often due to the difference in the farmer than to weather conditions. Any Illinois farmer with intelligence, industry, and judgment is bound to succeed. He is a post-graduate of Blackburn College in spirit, if not one of the alumni, because Blackburn is a 'self-help' college, and unless a man has that spirit, he cannot succeed in college or out of it.

Since building Thornhill, Joy had become more convinced than ever that the country was the best place for young people to raise a family. Following Wirt's discharge, Joy asked him to come to Chicago to take the position of assistant purchasing agent for the company, while at the same time cautioning him against moving his family into the city proper:

> I will be frank to say that I should not like to see you come here to live with Lady, unless you were prepared to live quietly in a suburb and forego the pleasures of any of the swift, expensive, and foolish society doings of the city. For the first ten years I was in the salt business, it was necessary for me to live quietly and there were just as many opportunities to spend money and waste time as there are now, even if some of the young people of the present generation seem to think that, in those old times, nothing of that sort existed. . . . The only legitimate way for a young man to build up a fortune is by thrift and painstaking application to business. . . .
>
> According to my view, the young people's idea of a good time nowadays is a perfectly rotten idea, and unless young people can find pleasure in a right sort of domestic life and the bringing up of their children, it would be far better for them not to come anywhere near a great city like Chicago.[36]

Joy's letter to Wirt was not just an avuncular admonition. It was a confirmation of a way of life. Joy had lived for nearly ten years far west of the city's center and had little interest in or appreciation for the social life of post–World War I Chicago. This did not mean that he had isolated himself from the world at large. In fewer than five years Joy witnessed the greatest upheaval of western culture and certainties his generation had known; he personally investigated banking and agriculture practices in the Far East while war was being waged in Europe; and when the United States finally entered the war, he committed himself to helping end the conflict as quickly as possible. All the while, the natural surroundings of Thornhill had provided periods of respite from the dissonance of the marketplace and noise of the city. He could nurture his thoughts there without distraction. And now, with the world at last at peace, Joy's thoughts turned to his long-held wish to develop the grounds of his estate in such a way as to share with others the natural world he cherished.

CHAPTER *11*

The Morton Arboretum—1920–1925

In late 1920, Joy asked the manager of the St. Louis branch of Morton Salt to visit Shaw's Garden, the noted botanical garden founded in St. Louis, Missouri, in 1859. He wanted him to "make inquiries as to how the thing is working now from a practical point of view. . . ." Because Joy and Margaret were to leave in a few days for several months in Europe, he directed that the materials be sent to Wirt at the Chicago office. "The chief object of my trip," Joy explained, "is to study the working of botanical gardens in various countries of Europe, hoping, next year, to begin the carrying out of my own plan."[1]

A few days later, on Joy's behalf Sterling contacted Professor Charles Sprague Sargent, the founder and director of Harvard's Arnold Arboretum, which Joy and his father had visited in 1873. He wanted to know about "the organization and provision for the maintenance of the gardens and their administration—in other words, the business end of it." He also explained that Arbor Lodge was not suited for his father's purpose because its distance from a major urban center "precludes its being of great value and the proposition is under consideration for the establishment of something of the sort near Chicago." For Sterling, even Thornhill was too far removed from Chicago: "There is *doubt* in my mind," he told Sargent, "as to the usefulness of an Arboretum so far removed from the center of the city, that is, would it be sufficiently accessible to give enough pleasure and benefit to enough people to make it worth while?"[2]

Responding to Sterling, Sargent argued that twenty-five miles from Chicago was not too distant, for by the time new plantings reached their full growth, the arboretum would be surrounded by suburbs. He pointed out that the arboretum trees would also benefit from not being near the city's lake winds and air pollution. Sargent knew the region well. He liked the fact that Joy's farm and estate at Thornhill already encompassed 1,250 acres, a much larger area than the confined Arnold Arboretum.[3] It was also bordered on the west by a 650-acre farm that Mark owned, suggesting that there would be room for expansion in that direction.[4]

Joy and Margaret began their trip tentatively in the art galleries of Paris and Nice, knowing that Sterling's daughter Carolyn, who had been diagnosed with ovarian cancer, was to have an operation in late January. But when Sterling wired them that all had gone well, they pursued their main purpose, which was to visit as many European gardens as possible. In February, they began a motor trip through southern Spain, visiting gardens with Charles Deering, the chairman of the board of International Harvester. Deering shared Joy's interest in horticulture and was an informed guide to Spain, having purchased a home there after being appointed a naval attaché by Paul in 1904. He and Joy had much to share. Deering had begun building his own estate near Miami in 1913, surrounding it with 435-acres of botanical gardens.

As they toured, Joy was thinking of Thornhill's potential as an arboretum site. From Barcelona, he proclaimed, "The more I have thought of the Arboretum idea the better I like it." This comment, which was often repeated during the development of his arboretum, preceded the first detailed directions for Sterling to begin overseeing a large nursery planting. Joy was meticulous. In the spring he wanted to plant trees, "placed in clumps for specimen trees. . . . not very large trees as they don't grow well. The evergreens should be about 4 or 5 feet high but *good* ones." Telling Sterling of local and area vendors who had good stock and prices, Joy emphasized that he wanted to proceed "on a *plan*." Sterling "would have some idea from the Arnold Arboretum," Joy knew, but he insisted that he wanted to "confine" the "efforts to *trees* not flowers nor many shrubs, only enough for effects."[5]

A week later, Joy told Sterling that he had asked Wirt to procure "15 to 20 thousand" small evergreens for a nursery planting in rows spaced close enough for hand hoeing. He included a diagram of just how the nursery surrounded by a fence should be placed near a Japanese garden he had put in at Thornhill, and he urged Sterling to have Fred Berg, a trusted foreman at Lisle Farms, prepare the ground as soon as possible.[6]

It was as if Joy were on site, rather than in Europe. When Sterling replied that Berg believed a wider spacing of the evergreens would make it possible to use a farm cultivator between rows of white pine, Scotch pine, jack pine, white cedar, and larch and added that he was also trying to find spruce to plant, Joy agreed. But he continued to elaborate on what he wanted for the initial nursery plantings, not wishing cost to be a factor. The stock should be no smaller than 10" and some 15" or more and should come from local nurseries whenever possible. As for the species preference, he observed that white pines "do not grow well," Scotch and Austrian pines were "ok" (though he did not want over 2,500 of each), and "all the spruces are good." He also requested that deciduous trees should be obtained from DuPage County nurseries because they would weather better: "I want to put in quite a lot of Poplars—Carolina and also Lombardy—some Maples of various kinds—some ash if can get good ones. May find some of these in the woods that will do."[7] Later from Tours, after having driven out twice in a single day, Joy told Sterling that "*all* of the attractive places are embellished *chiefly* with conifers." He urged Sterling to "Put all the steam you can on this tree planting. If you can find one or more *good* nursery foremen who have had experience, you can hire them at once."[8]

Touring gardens in Europe also convinced Joy that his arboretum should contain water features. From Biarritz he wrote, "I have seen so many fountains in these European gardens I am stuck on them. A little flowing water makes all the difference in the world in gardens, and I mean to have plenty of it. . . ."[9] He thought the fountains should also serve a useful purpose, the water from two fountains near the mansion "utilized" for irrigation purposes, getting their water from two lakes he was planning to the west and south of Thornhill.

With things moving rapidly ahead, Sterling believed it was time to let his father know what he and others at home were thinking: Thornhill, he maintained, was too far from the city; the arboretum "should be administered by a self-perpetuated board of the right sort of people, rather than by a family affair"; and affiliations should be made with educational institutions. After a visit to the Arnold, Jean reinforced her brother's views. Also while she was there, Sargent stressed that an arboretum must have an herbarium and a library, estimating that to get the arboretum underway, an initial investment of a million dollars would be necessary. The most pressing matter for Sterling, however, remained accessibility. Most prospective visitors, he believed, would not own automobiles and would not take the trouble of getting to Thornhill from the nearest train stations at Glen Ellyn or Lisle.[10]

Joy responded conclusively to Sterling's arguments, declaring that Thornhill "is the *only* place for it and there it must be." He went on to clarify his personal motive for his decision: "I want something to develop during the balance of my life on ground for which I have a personal affection, and I hope the work may prolong my life. So you see that I have a selfish motive as well as an altruistic one." He reasoned that if the arboretum were any good, people would come, "even if they have to walk from the railroads." He was not interested in pleasing "rubber neckers," he said and closed by saying, "The thing to do *now* is to plant all the trees we can get in."[11]

In spite of his reservations about the location of the arboretum, Sterling remained an assiduous overseer of the work at Thornhill. In early April, the first pond was excavated, and some 23,750 pine trees costing $1,500 dollars were planted. Sterling hoped he was not proceeding too fast for Joy, saying, "It seems to me that if you are going to have a pine plantation you might as well have a good one." Governor Lowden, Sterling said, had placed a million pines around his Oregon, Illinois, estate, making it "a high executive example to follow."[12] Later in the month, Sterling ordered a thousand each of balsam and Douglas fir from a Wisconsin nursery and, "from various sources," hard maple, American elm, Carolina poplar, black walnut, red oak, weeping willow, and Russian golden weeping willow, vowing, "I shall be only too glad to do what I can to keep the planting moving along."[13]

Within days, however, Sterling's oversight of the arboretum work and Joy and Margaret's European trip were sadly interrupted. In early May, Joy and Margaret were at Kew Gardens when they received news that their granddaughter Carolyn's condition had unexpectedly worsened and that she was hospitalized in serious condition. They immediately left for home, but Carolyn died while they were at sea. Although Joy had been planning to visit Sargent at the Arnold, he and Margaret continued on to Thornhill to be with Sterling, Preston, and Suzette before they, too, left on an extended European trip in June to recover from their loss.

Soon the long distance discussion about the arboretum resumed with Joy now at Thornhill and Sterling in Europe. Back home, Joy began to search for personnel to fill key positions at the arboretum. But one of the first letters he received from Sterling—who had visited the Arnold and Professor Sargent on his way to Europe—did not sit well with him. Sterling maintained the view that he believed Sargent also held: the "personal and family aspect" of the arboretum "must be minimized" and "the arboretum must be impersonal, otherwise it becomes nothing but an exceptional country estate."[14]

Joy responded as emphatically as he had done on his position concerning the arboretum's location. He explained his arboretum was to be "very personal" and "agreeable" to him, and he would look for personnel who agreed with that view. He wanted paths laid out for his comfort. Most important of all, he wanted the arboretum to be a "monument" to him and his family. Whether or not the arboretum became a public or private park, Joy wanted it to be "a meritorious thing in itself." He would not, he assured Sterling, "make any white elephants out of Thornhill under the delusion of public benefaction or any other delusion."[15]

Late in the spring of 1921, Joy invited Ossian Cole Simonds, who had been recommended by Sargent, to advise him on the arboretum. Simonds had been the principal architect of Chicago's Graceland Cemetery, consulting designer of Lincoln Park, and in 1920 had published *Landscape Gardening*, a book that extolled the virtues of naturalistic gardens that use native plantings and water schemes. He had also studied civil engineering at the University of Michigan and had been a partner in the noted Chicago architectural firm of Holabird, Simonds, and Roche. Following a luncheon meeting on June 15, 1921, with Joy and Jean, Simonds accepted Joy's invitation. Within a week he completed a topographical survey and told Joy that his proposed arboretum would "preserve forever some native forest without molestation."[16]

Joy soon let Sterling know that he was "quite pleased" with the work of Simonds, whose ideas coincided with his.[17] Joy had Simonds' support for his intention to maintain personal oversight of the arboretum before dedicating it to future generations. "It is better," Joy explained to Sterling, "to deed something tangible and existent rather than an idea, and inasmuch as I greatly enjoy the development of it and am liable to change my mind from time to time, I don't want to be hampered by other people. I am going to develop it just the way I am now, and am having a lot of fun doing it." He and Simonds were getting "on together beautifully," he told Sterling, who, he said, would be surprised by the work being done when he returned home.[18]

$\mathcal{W}$herever Sterling went in Europe, he was careful to observe how the botanical gardens he visited matched his father's ideas for his arboretum. In late August, with Professor Charles Bommer, the director, he toured the approximately 240-acre arboretum at Tervurnen, near Brussels. It was very much what Joy and Simonds had in mind. Grass and underbrush grew naturally on a rolling topography of valleys and ridges. Grass paths "with open swales and frequent intervals" led the visitor through groups of botanical specimens. "It is all very pleasing and makes a fine show," Sterling concluded. But from his point of view, Thornhill had greater potential than did Tervurnen: "You have a much better place to start with than he had and can make, in a few years . . . a very attractive showing. Above all, do not make it too tame. The wildness of this one was one of its main attractions."[19]

Joy was impressed by Sterling's description of Tervuren, saying, "Shall be governed very largely by Professor Bommer's plan in making our own plans."[20] He sent Sterling's letter on to Simonds. Later, on a visit to Kew Gardens, Sterling wrote that he thought his father's arboretum had "a good deal of advantage over Kew in natural beauty of land and . . . water." Kew, Sterling said, lacked the hills and natural forests that graced Joy's estate and farm, and it was "too much of a garden to suit" him. "I like [an arboretum] more like Boston or Brussels."[21]

Commitment to the development and preservation of natural areas around Thornhill required patience. Joy was continuing to reroute roadways and acquire adjacent real estate, expanding his holdings to the east beyond Old Joliet Road.[22] Work on the large lake at Thornhill, which Joy decided to call Marmo after Margaret, took longer than expected because additional excavations had to be made in an effort to save as many mature trees as possible. Twenty-five men and twenty mules employed by Simonds' landscape company worked throughout August. Joy told Sterling, "When the lake is filled, it will be a beautiful body of water."[23]

With Lake Marmo nearing completion, Joy and Margaret decided to motor the 550 miles to Nebraska City where he would celebrate his sixty-sixth birthday. Planning on doing a lot of entertaining, they sent servants ahead to prepare for their arrival. The evenings at Arbor Lodge were filled with dinner parties for friends, business acquaintances, and politicians. On the final Saturday night, they gave a dance for thirty "young people" from Omaha and Nebraska City. The visit was a pleasant close to a productive summer.[24]

On September 27, the day Joy was celebrating his birthday, Simonds hired Clarence Godshalk to work at Thornhill. A recent graduate of the University of Michigan with a Bachelor of Science and Master's in landscape design, Godshalk was immediately put to work on a grounds crew. Within days, however, with the resignation of a foreman, he was moved into a supervisory role. Godshalk soon impressed Joy with his effective use of dynamite to remove stumps around the lake excavation and his success at clearing large areas of woodland with a small crew, few tools, and a team that Godshalk later remembered as "a sore-footed stallion and a discarded black horse from Lisle Farms Company."[25] Godshalk was obviously a good hire, but Joy was not convinced that he had the experience necessary to supervise older men.

In October, Joy and Margaret visited the Arnold Arboretum, and Professor Sargent accompanied them back to Illinois. Sargent, Joy told Sterling, was so enthusiastic about the work at the arboretum that he expressed regret that he was not younger so that he could come to Lisle to be a part of it. Nevertheless, Sargent pledged his "very earnest cooperation" and that of the Arnold. Grateful for the guidance that Sargent had given him throughout 1921, Joy continued to find ways to repay him and the Arnold. He put Sargent in touch with a Chicago brass company that could make tree markers that were lighter and longer lasting than the cast-iron markers being used by the Arnold. And during Sargent's visit, Joy asked him to select a site on the grounds that would be named in his honor and would be planted with trees brought to America by the Arnold's overseas expeditions and chosen for the arboretum by Sargent himself. Following Sargent's departure from Thornhill, Joy made a $2,500 contribution to the Arnold. It was the first of many gifts given to support the work of the Arnold, particularly its botanical expeditions, from which, in turn, Joy's arboretum would benefit greatly.[26]

In anticipation of incorporation of Joy's arboretum, correspondence between the two men touched on details that assured that Joy's institution would be of the highest professional caliber. Joy wrote that he was working with his attorney on incorporation documents and told him that the propagating house, a reconstructed pig barn, was being completed. He assured Sargent that he would heed his advice on "what a scientific arboretum should be" and that he would "incorporate the objects in the charter and by-laws in accordance" with his suggestions. In addition, he had located the "Sargent Plot" to honor his mentor in "a protected glade between the two lakes." Joy believed that the entire arboretum would eventually comprise 400 acres.[27] Meanwhile, Sargent sent Joy catalogues of books, marking the titles the believed to be essential for a well-stocked research library. And in December, Sargent recommended an experienced propagator to Joy, a "young Austrian" by the name of John van Gemert, who had trained at the Arnold. Joy hired him on January 3, 1922.

Before the end of the year, Joy and Sterling visited Shaw's Garden in St. Louis, accepting an invitation to a dinner from George T. Moore, the director. There Joy became even more convinced that he had, indeed, made the right decision to place what he was now calling The Morton Arboretum far from the heart of Chicago. "[Shaw's] Garden, so far as outside planting is concerned, was a disappointment to me," Joy told Sargent of his visit. "The smoke of bituminous coal, used almost exclusively in St. Louis, has ruined most the trees: there are hardly any conifers left; nothing in the Garden looks good to me except the plants under glass and they are very well kept and look fine."[28] Two days later, on New Year's Eve, Joy received assurances from Sargent that he was doing all the right things as his arboretum took shape: "You are founding a great institution which is going to have an immense influence on the knowledge of trees and their planting in your part of the country."[29]

In early January 1922, Joy and Margaret were preparing for an extended vacation in Hawaii, not to return until April. But the impending incorporation of what Joy was now calling The Morton Arboretum was uppermost in his thoughts. As usual, he left nothing to chance. He sent Sargent the details of his progress on incorporation, which he hoped to accomplish without a special act of the Illinois legislature, and he made a will providing for 400 acres and an "ample endowment." Both Jean and Sterling, he said, were "just about as enthusiastic about the Arboretum" as he and would carry out his plans, should anything happen to him.[30]

On his way to Hawaii, Joy wrote to Sterling that he was pleased to learn that through Sargent the arboretum had secured the services of Henry Teuscher, a German botanist. Still living in Germany, Teuscher, like van Gemert, received several months' training at the Arnold before coming to Lisle. Teuscher's appointment as botanist settled two of the three principal positions Joy thought necessary for the Arboretum's administration. John van Gemert was to arrive at Thornhill in April after completing his training at the Arnold. Joy was still seeking a superintendent, although he had noticed that the young Clarence Godshalk was performing his duties well.

In Joy's absence, Sterling was again in charge of moving the Arboretum ahead. Late in January, he informed his father that he had engaged John Root of the firm Holabird & Roche (of which Simonds had at one time been a partner) to design a gatehouse and the houses for the propagator, botanist, and the prospective superintendent. Root also began drawing up a plan for the library to be located at Thornhill. Sterling thought that to be a good idea, he told his father, for someday the combined structures would make an excellent education center.[31] The library was scheduled to be finished in May 1923. Construction proceeded on a road and a bridge from Joliet Road (Route 53) westward over the channeled East Branch of the DuPage River. The road would take visitors around Lake Marmo and provide access to the smaller lake named Jopamaca after the ill-fated lake built by J. Sterling at Arbor Lodge. Although the arboretum would be separate from the estate, Joy would have a vista from Thornhill over the entire acreage.

Back at Thornhill, Joy began final preparations for the Arboretum's opening in the spring of 1923. He had given two men trial appointments as superintendent, but neither had proved satisfactory. On June 1, 1922, after Clarence Godshalk had overseen the planting of some 138,000 trees and shrubs and had successfully supervised relocation of a large elm on the Thornhill side of the excavation for the new lake, Joy gave him the job.[32] John van Gemert, the propagator, arrived in early April to join Godshalk. Cottages for Godshalk, van Gemert, and Henry Teuscher—who was still training at the Arnold and would not arrive until January 1923—were under construction.

*J*ust before leaving for another extended winter vacation, Joy sat down with six members of his family and two officers of the Morton Salt Company to sign the indenture. Dated December 14, 1922, the document dedicated The Morton Arboretum to

> scientific research work in horticulture and agriculture, particularly in the growth and culture of trees, shrubs, vines and grasses by means of a great outdoor museum arranged for convenient study of every species, variety, and hybrid of the woody plants of the world, able to support the climate of Illinois, such museum to be equipped with an herbarium, a reference library, and laboratories by the officials and students of the arboretum, in order to increase and improve in their growth and culture.

The signatories were Joy, Margaret, Sterling, Jean and Joseph Cudahy, Mark, Wirt, Daniel Peterkin, and Edward Stearns, the salt company attorney. These close family members and trusted associates comprised the first self-perpetuating board of trustees. Joy's relationship to the signatories and his position as chairman of the board and director meant that The Morton Arboretum would be under his personal supervision for the rest of his life.

The wording of the indenture—emphasizing that the Arboretum would be equipped with a library, herbarium, and research facilities—clearly reflected the influence of Professor Sargent. Joy wrote to Sargent that the arboretum's growth would be an incremental process, primarily because of tax restrictions. Section A, the first parcel to be transferred to the arboretum in 1922, was 175 acres. "The other sections," Joy explained, "will be deeded as we reach them with the development work, and I should not be surprised if the total area were considerably greater than I had originally expected to make it. The trust will be perpetual."[33]

In January 1923, Joy and Margaret left on a trip to South America where they soon received word from Sterling that things were running smoothly in their absence. Godshalk and van Gemert had been joined by Teuscher, whom Joy had not had time to meet. Teuscher impressed Sterling sufficiently that he wrote his father about him in detail. Sterling described Teuscher—who had been a German artillery officer and airman in World War I and had been educated in Berlin—as fitting a Prussian stereotype: "He was attired in a beautiful corduroy suit and shiny high shoes," Sterling wrote. "I don't know whether you have seen him or not, but he could go into a movie as a German officer, with no change in his make-up. He clicks his heels and bows in the most Teutonic fashion imaginable. I don't think he is particularly popular with the rest of the gang, but seems to know what he is doing."[34] Although Sterling was somewhat uneasy about Teuscher's superior demeanor, he assured Joy that all was well.

As usual on their vacation, Joy and Margaret made a number of visits to gardens and arboreta. He told Sargent that they had visited the Rio de Janeiro Botanical Garden "several times." They were "charmed" by the forests, but Joy did not think the trees would grow in the temperate zone in which his arboretum specialized. He considered the Argentine "good farming country" and thought Buenos Aires was a "well-built city" with quite beautiful parks, although the eucalyptus, willow, and other softwood trees that dominated them did not "suggest permanency." Hard wood and conifers were in short supply, and these were the woods in which he was most interested.[35]

$\mathcal{B}$ack home, Joy assumed for the first time the responsibilities he had taken upon himself as the person solely in charge of The Morton Arboretum's operations. On the occasion of sending yet another donation of $2,500 to the Arnold Arboretum, he wrote to Sargent, "I am beginning to learn something about arboretum economics myself and find it somewhat different from some of my business experience. At the same time, I don't feel discouraged at all—quite the contrary. I am gradually becoming the Director and I find it necessary to assume that role purely as a business proposition."[36]

The following months at Thornhill were pleasantly busy and restful for Joy. For the library, which would be a part of his residence and would have restricted access, Joy purchased 2,150 duplicates of photographs of Chinese and Japanese trees taken by the Arnold's well-known botanist, E.H. Wilson. During Sargent's second visit to Thornhill, Joy asked him to begin purchasing books. In the fall he told Sargent, "The reading room of the library is a gem. . . . Everything, both library and the planting, is most encouraging," adding his litany, "The further on I get with the development of the Arboretum, the better I like it."[37] He was particularly proud of the initial selection of books Sargent had suggested for the library. "Several botanists who have examined my collection," he said, "have spoken in most complimentary terms as to the quality of the books, for the selection of which I am, of course, wholly indebted to you."[38] Content to remain at Thornhill through the early part of the winter, Joy walked along the paths leading to the initial plantings of the various botanical groups that had been selected by Teuscher and placed in locations decided upon by himself, Godshalk, van Gemert, and Teuscher. Throughout 1923, almost 64,000 plantings and transplantings had been added to the 138,000 of the year before.

In February, just before he, Margaret, Sterling, and Preston left for a Mediterranean cruise, Joy told Sargent that long-awaited "quite extensive plans" had finally been made for the Arboretum. These included a grouping of European trees and a small, man-made island planted with Japanese trees and shrubs. Another major planting was already under way along what had been designated "Joy Path," leading from Thornhill to near Lake Marmo. "This follows the ravine," he wrote. "Sargent Glade will be on the west of it and a form garden to the east. We are going to have fine specimen trees and shrubs all along the path; shall make a particular effort to grow the broad-leafed maples along the path, which is well protected on all sides and I think will ultimately become one of the prettiest parts of the Arboretum. We have put in a lot of time on these plans and our planting this Spring ought to count tremendously."[39] While they were away, Teuscher documented 3,500 varieties of trees, shrubs, and vines on the grounds of The Morton Arboretum that in the spring had been visited, Joy said, by "hundreds of visitors" who "seem to be really interested in our work, which is a great encouragement."[40]

Joy returned refreshed from the ten-week Mediterranean trip. They had sailed on the S.S. *Lapland*, visiting Athens, Haifa, the Holy Land (by automobile), Palestine, Egypt, Naples, Rome, Florence, Venice, and Milan. On the way home, the party stopped at Kew and Tervurnen. But, as an observer of national behavior, Joy seemed most interested in the rejuvenation of the Italian people after the Great War. "They are animated by a different spirit than ever before," he wrote to Sargent. He found it "hard to realize" that he was in the same country he had visited many times. Like many American political leaders, businessmen, and tourists, Joy attributed this spirit to Benito Mussolini, whom he called "the greatest individual who was evolved from the Great War."[41]

*G*rateful for Sargent's help, Joy continued donating to the work of the Arnold, and for his part, Sargent was not timid in his requests. At a time of nationwide recession, Sargent confided in Joy, "We are terribly hard up this year, many contributors having fallen off while costs are increasing."[42] Joy replied immediately that he had not been home long enough to understand how his own interests were affected by the economic downturn. Still, he sent another check for $2,500 "with full confidence that nobody can spend that amount of money to better advantage than you can in the splendid, living, and I hope, everlasting monument you have created in the Arnold Arboretum."[43]

The relationship between the Arnold and The Morton Arboretum would remain mutually beneficial for the rest of Sargent's life. With Sargent's advice, Joy purchased books for his new library from various publishers and duplicates from the Arnold. He also bought plants from the Arnold and paid for half the traveling expenses for an expedition in Mississippi and for 510 photographs taken by E.H. Wilson, who had led expeditions in Australasia, India, and South Africa. In 1924, Joy and Godshalk visited the Arnold where they met Wilson and discussed a proposed expedition to China.

On his arrival home in the spring, Joy wrote enthusiastically to Sargent about the work that had been done during his three-month absence: "Enjoyed the day immensely and was so well satisfied with the great interest that has been taken in the work not only by Godshalk, Teuscher, and van Gemert, but by all of our foremen who are in immediate charge of the gangs. Every man seems to be as interested in getting his trees in right and in the general upkeep of the Arboretum as though he owned the entire property. It takes time to get an organization like this and I feel so appreciative of it that I am telling you about it."[44]

Joy was convinced that The Morton Arboretum had matured to the point at which it should begin publishing a bulletin of its research, collections, and other activities. He used as his model the Arnold's publication, although Joy felt it could be written by several hands. Teuscher was the sole author of the first issue of the *Bulletin of Popular Information,* and Godshalk wrote the second. Joy sent both issues to Sargent who found a few botanical errors in Godshalk's that led him to suggest that subsequent issues be written by a single hand, namely Teuscher. But the decision had already been made for the third issue, which concentrated on landscape design, to be written by O.C. Simonds. After that, Teuscher had primary responsibility for the *Bulletin* until he left The Morton Arboretum three years later. It remained the principal publication of The Morton Arboretum for the next forty years.[45]

In less than three years, The Morton Arboretum had gained prominence as an outdoor museum and research center of woody plants. In 1925, Teuscher's plant list for the arboretum was published with the title *List of plants—trees, shrubs, perennials, annuals, and ferns—recognized as growing naturally in the territory of the Morton Arboretum.*[46] This was the first comprehensive record of the indigenous plant life that Simonds and Joy had vowed to preserve. In the fall of 1923, Professor Sargent told Joy, "If the Morton Arboretum grows in the next seventy-five years as Chicago has in the last seventy-five years it will be the wonder of the world. I believe there is no reason why it should not for it has the two great essentials for an Arboretum, soil and money."[47] Two years later, in a letter wishing Joy a prosperous New Year, he commented, "You realize, I hope, that you will be remembered for the Arboretum long after the salt business is forgotten."[48]

Not fully appreciating the indelibility of branding, Professor Sargent was only half right. Both The Morton Arboretum and Morton Salt have carried the name of their founder into the twenty-first century. But the founding of the Arboretum, the monument by which Joy wished most to be remembered, was a remarkable feat, made more so considering the fact that he began to develop it in earnest in his sixty-fifth year. Although such an institution was the culmination of an interest that had been engendered in him since his childhood at Arbor Lodge, the creation of an arboretum that had the resources to be continued and developed into the future required skills and decision making that today could keep planning committees working for years before anything was done. In four short years, Joy, in complete charge of the project from start to finish, was able to see his vision come to fruition. And he accomplished this while simultaneously running his businesses, traveling, and managing several other projects.

Investing in Illinois—1920–1925

At a time when most men his age were retired, Joy was president and chairman of the board of Morton Salt and chairman of the board and director of The Morton Arboretum. He also was preparing to turn over Arbor Lodge and its surrounding arboretum to the state of Nebraska, start an apple orchard on land he owned in Nebraska City, publish a historical account of the Chicago region, construct a twenty-two-story office building in Chicago, and, quite literally, create a 6,000-acre farm in central Illinois. How he was able to do this was no secret. During his forty-six years in the salt business, Joy had found a way to manage far-flung, time-consuming, and complex projects and get them done to his personal satisfaction. He had hired young managers who shared his work ethic and who could make decisions independently within a context of a mission they fully understood. He had brought into his company the Warren boys, Carrington, Dan Peterkin, Sterling, Mark, Wirt, Carl, and many others—all of whom he supervised until they worked independently of his immediate oversight. The Arboretum, too, was succeeding to a large degree because of the work of the young Clarence Godshalk.

A few months after reaching his seventieth year, Joy composed an essay in which he explained his method of management. On his birthday, he had been given a plaque with the names of thirty-five men associated with him at Morton Salt for fifteen to forty years. He mentioned this because of his abhorrence of adhering mindlessly to rules of business that stated that tasks could be done by freshly hired officers. While Joy kept on top of everything, he did not want to keep his "nose to the grindstone." Early on, he had made certain this would not happen, writing, ". . . because in many cases I have known and trained officers from boyhood on; because I know their strong points and their weaknesses, and they know mine, I am taking no chances when I delegate important decisions to them. . . . Of course, I keep my hand on the throttle, but I back the decisions of my men so consistently that they are made to feel the weight of their responsibility, and thus they exercise more than ordinary caution." [1]

This philosophy served him well when he decided what he wanted to do with Arbor Lodge. In Joy's mind, The Morton Arboretum and Arbor Lodge were capstones to his and his parents' lives respectively, and their legacy had to be prepared for with care. In early 1920, he had sought a manager for the homestead who could also develop an orchard for him on an acreage he still owned just across the road from Arbor Lodge. As a stockholder in a Shubert, Nebraska, apple orchard, he learned of the horticultural skills of a young employee by the name of Grosvenor (Grove) Porter, a 1916 graduate of the University of Nebraska College of Agriculture and a veteran of World War I. Unlike the men who filled the Arboretum's positions, Joy's Nebraska City manager could not be under his daily supervision. He needed to be certain that Grove had the maturity and knowledge to act on his own, so he invited him to Thornhill to spend the night and discuss the position, "without any commitment."[2]

The visit proved productive for both. Porter immediately drew up a prospectus for orchards and vineyards to the south and west of the Arbor Lodge estate and negotiated an arrangement that would make him a partner in the corporation that would be known as Joy Morton Orchards Company. It was the sort of business acumen that Joy respected. When Joy later purchased 160 nearby acres from Mark in 1924, the venture became "the largest contiguous apple orchard between the Missouri River and the West Coast (not including Washington State)."[3] Grove became not only an enterprising young partner but also a trusted manager and, as often happened with Joy's employees, a friend. When Joy and Margaret visited Arbor Lodge for his sixty-sixth birthday in 1921, Joy found it in the best condition he had seen it in for a long time.[4] As he had with Peterkin, Joy counted on Grove in his absence.

In June 1922, Joy asked Grove to ready the estate for a meeting with Nebraska Governor Samuel R. McKelvie to discuss transferring Arbor Lodge to the State. Following the meeting, *The Nebraska City Weekly News* announced that Joy proposed donating not only the house and grounds but also, "if agreeable to the people of Nebraska City," the adjacent Morton Park. Joy wanted "the residence to be used as a museum of natural history and the grounds to be a State botanical garden, the name of Morton, Arbor Day and Arbor Lodge to be thus perpetuated."[5] When he returned to Thornhill, Joy informed Sargent that he was in the process of donating Arbor Lodge, the 43 acres surrounding the mansion, and the park. Even so, he knew that since this would be the first park for the state of Nebraska and would entail a perpetual maintenance obligation, the acceptance of the gift was at the mercy of the state's politicians.[6]

During the rest of the year, Joy oversaw final preparations for the opening of his arboretum, attended to business, and participated in civic duties. In the fall of 1922, the international competition for the design of the Tribune Tower to be built on North Michigan was in its final phase. Because of Joy's prominence on the Chicago Plan Commission and his demonstrated interest in architecture, he was asked to serve on a six-member advisory committee to recommend three final designs to the award committee that included Alfred Granger, president of the Illinois chapter of the Institute, and Col. Robert McCormick and Joseph Patterson, co-editors of the Chicago Tribune.[7] The winners of the competition, receiving $50,000, were New York architects John Mead Howells and Raymond Hood. Construction was begun on this iconic Chicago structure in 1925.

Early in 1923, Joy and Margaret left for South America. But as Joy anticipated, during their absence his gift of Arbor Lodge hit a political snag. It was only after a heavy lobbying effort organized by Grove that the Nebraska house accepted the gift and sent the bill on to the senate in February 1923. Just before Joy's return, he learned that the bill was still in the senate, prompting him to write to Grove, "I can say to you, privately, that if the gift is refused, I shall shed no tears, though I think it would be just as well for me and for Nebraska City and the State that it should be accepted and made a permanent shrine for tree lovers, maintained as it should be maintained, because if that were done, its value as an object lesson would increase tremendously as the timber supply of the United States disappears, as I think it certainly will disappear in spite of all efforts of this kind to encourage forestry."[8] Joy had carefully chosen the phrase *object lesson*. In the seminal letter his father had written to him twenty-five years earlier from Biltmore, J. Sterling had used the phrase to urge Joy to think of developing his own arboretum in either Nebraska or Illinois.

Within weeks, after the full Nebraska legislature accepted Arbor Lodge, Mrs. N.A. Ryan, Joy's secretary, wrote on Joy's behalf praising Grove for his efforts, saying, "I certainly want to congratulate you on the outcome of the Arbor Lodge bill. I don't believe it would ever have been accomplished without your zeal and persistence...."[9] Shortly, Joy asked Grove to ready the grounds and the mansion for the transference to take place on his sixty-eighth birthday, September 27. Joy also sent Henry Teuscher out to Arbor Lodge to put zinc labels on trees, bearing their botanical and common name. Teuscher would, Joy said, "keep a record of all the species, so that I will have it in the Arboretum library."[10] Teuscher's visit seemed to confirm Joy's intention to make certain that Arbor Lodge would be used for the purposes he had designated.

*O*n Transfer Day, an estimated 25,000 people attended events in Nebraska City, then a town of 8,000.[11] Another 15,000 were unable to get to Nebraska City because of torrential rains the day before. In the afternoon, following a lengthy morning parade that was carefully organized to display the history of Nebraska City, Joy made his transference speech through an electrical amplifying system—one of the first to be used in Nebraska—and turned over the property to Governor Charles A. Bryan who, at the time, was also head of the Nebraska State Park Board.

The half-hour speech, which Joy distributed to acquaintances around the country, was almost entirely about his father's political involvements, his prominence as an agriculturist and horticulturist, his adherence to sound money, and his lifelong antagonism to "special interests." As to the latter, Joy saw fit to quote at length from a letter written on November 25, 1858 by his northern Democrat father to his Republican and "fervent Methodist" grandfather, J.D., in which J. Sterling spoke of his pride in helping kill a territorial bill that would have given a state charter to a combined biblical institute, banking house, and manufactory at Plattsmouth. J. Sterling wrote, "I think States and Territories should never foster, by special legislation, any denominational religion." That Joy should quote this letter at such a time and to such a crowd as that in Nebraska City was a none-too-subtle lesson in civil liberties to those who were to receive Arbor Lodge and its grounds. In closing, Joy directed his audience's attention to their obligations as recipients of the property. The grounds were to be used as a botanical garden and the house "to be used solely as a Museum of Natural History and for the custody of such historical property as may be given or loaned by citizens or by the Nebraska State Historical Society."

The importance of Arbor Lodge to the history of the state and nation, was, Joy made clear, symbolized in the portraits within the mansion's library: "First, the Buffalo; next, the Indian; then Napoleon stands for the claims of France—he sold an empire destined to be greater and richer than France, to Uncle Sam, the fourth owner; Father's portrait completed the group. Now, it passes to the State of Nebraska forever, with the earnest hope that the work begun may be continued, that new varieties of trees and plants adapted to this climate may be studied and developed here and that its greatest usefulness has but just commenced." Leaving no doubt in the minds of his audience as to their responsibility for Arbor Lodge, he told them what it had meant to his family: "The spirit of Arbor Lodge is Faith, and Work, and Self-Reliance. Faith without Work is a dead thing. . . . The solution of most of the world's troubles can be found only in self-reliance and hard work."[12]

Transfer Day brought to an end the nearly seven decades the Mortons owned Arbor Lodge, a period paralleling Joy's age. With the transference, Joy placed the fate of his family's homestead in the hands of the citizens of Nebraska. Joy must have thought of that fact during his and Margaret's long journey home in the Pierce in driving rain and washed-out roads through Iowa.

The day Joy gave Arbor Lodge to Nebraska by no means marked the end of Joy's interest in Nebraska City. As he had promised Grove, he maintained his investment in the Joy Morton Orchard Co., which, long after the apple orchard was no longer productive, became the site of the Arbor Day Foundation and Lied Conference Center. Joy also retained the right to stay at Arbor Lodge when he visited Nebraska City, although at least on one occasion, he and Margaret stayed with the Porters who lived in a modest house the Mortons had built on a lot adjacent to the Arbor Lodge grounds, which included the one-room schoolhouse Joy had attended.[13] In 1926, Grove honored Joy by naming his newborn son Joy Morton Porter.

*W*hen Joy was solicited late in 1917 to support publication of a history of Nebraska, he responded, "Publishing histories is not my line, and I do not care to engage in a new business at my time of life."[14] Two years later, he changed his mind, but it was to Illinois that he turned. Since 1905 he had been an inveterate explorer of the northern half of Illinois by automobile, and since 1910 he had been a board member of the Chicago Historical Society, serving on the committee investigating historical sites and roads to and from Chicago. It was time, he believed, to share with the public his fascination with Chicago roads.

In December 1919, Joy wrote to Dr. Milo M. Quaife, the superintendent of the State Historical Society of Wisconsin and the author and editor of numerous books on Illinois and the Midwest, to ask him if he knew of someone who would conduct research at the Chicago Historical Society, Springfield, Madison, Wisconsin, and Galena for "an interesting and artistic book with maps showing all of the old roads in use between 1825 and 1850, together with a story of the life of each road. . . ." Joy assumed the research, some of which he had already undertaken himself, would take a competent researcher only a few months. "My idea," he explained, "is to prepare a work that will be valuable to historic societies and at the same time be interesting to motorists and to the State Highway Commission, which is just starting to spend a lot of money on Illinois hard-surfaced roads." Joy was "willing to go to considerable expense" to pay for the research himself.[15]

Rethinking the scope of the book a few days later, he said it should focus on the years 1837–1857: "The growth of the city during this period will be the subject of the study. This period, begun and ended with a panic, shows a remarkable growth, as evidenced by the exports and imports by Lake. . . ."[16] Quaife (who had edited a collection of essays entitled *The Development of Chicago 1674–1914: Shown in a Series of Contemporary Narratives* for the Caxton Club, of which Joy was a member) responded that he would be interested in taking on the job himself. But the project was delayed, initially because Joy had fractured a rib and could not meet with Quaife. It was not until 1922 that Joy commissioned Quaife to begin the research and writing, promising that he would finance the book's publication upon completion of the manuscript.[17]

Once he had completed the first three chapters, Quaife spent a weekend with Joy at Thornhill, during which time they visited a DuPage County collection of antique vehicles that had been used on the Chicago area roads of the mid-nineteenth century. Joy wrote to Sterling that he was pleased with Quaife's work and had helped him outline the remaining chapters, "according to my original plan to discover and record the early traffic before the days of the railroads." Joy wanted the book on historic roads to be as much his as it was Quaife's.[18] By July 1923, Quaife, having quit his position in Wisconsin to devote his full time to the book, finished a draft, and Joy became personally involved in its editing and production. He chose the Chicago publishing firm of D.F. Keller over R.R. Donnelly Lakeside Press, which had expressed an interest in it, because, as he explained to Thomas E. Donnelly, "we have rather close relations with Keller & Co. and I gave them the order without asking for competitive bids."[19] As the book was readied for publication, Joy searched for a title that would appeal to the general public, declaring to Quaife, "The selling of the book depends so much upon the title, we must be very careful."[20] They finally settled on *Chicago's Highways, Old and New: from Indian Trail to Motor Road* as a means of attracting the attention of motorists to the book. Joy assumed the task of writing the introduction.

The completed book defines highways and byways in a broad sense, detailing the means by which the earliest travelers from the east got to Chicago (by river and stagecoach or over the Great Lakes) to the building of the Erie and later Illinois and Michigan Canals and, finally, the coming of the railroad in 1852. Chapters explore the history of the earliest roads to Chicago from Detroit, the Vincennes Trace (which brought settlers from the south and east), the roads to Ottawa and further west, the road to Galena and the surrounding lead mines, and the road to Wisconsin, as well as the various improvements, such as plank roads, used to lessen the difficulty of traveling during adverse weather conditions or through marshland. These roads determined population growth and the commercial and communal life of Chicago and towns within its radius. An appendix, comprising almost a quarter of the book, describes for the motorist points of interest in Wisconsin, Illinois, Indiana, and Michigan that could be made in a day's journey in 1923. They are places Joy had visited, such as Green Bay, Lake Geneva, Beloit, Madison, Galena, Dixon, Bishop Hill, Peoria, and Springfield. Altogether, Quaife described nearly seventy sites, including thirteen of historical interest within Chicago.

Joy was delighted with the initial acceptance of *Chicago's Highways, Od and New*, which was released in November. In early December, he told Quaife that of nearly 5,000 in print, several hundred had been sold. He had initiated a marketing plan: "My chief dependence for customers," he wrote to Quaife, "is upon the motorists and if we can dispose of a substantial amount of the first printing to the holiday trade, it will give the book a great start for a vigorous campaign among the motorists in the early Spring."[21] A week later, he wrote again to Quaife to tell him how he intended to make those sales. He had entered into a contract with Marshall Field's and with McClurg's bookstore on Wabash to sell the book wholesale.[22]

Three months after the book's release, Joy made a detailed account of its total cost, down to the dollars and cents of "miscellaneous supplies." From research to production, Joy figured he had spent $9,674.67.[23] When Joy sent Quaife the figures, he replied that he was most satisfied to have cost Joy only 60 percent of the original $5,000 promised for his year's work. (With Joy's help in the research, Quaife had taken only seven months to write the book.) Quaife's remarks were somewhat tongue-in-cheek, however, for he added that he would be even more pleased when Joy recovered his initial outlay and his share of royalties began. By mid 1924, Joy was less sanguine about sales figures. While he found the book had done fairly well in spring sales, he wrote to Quaife that he thought he would contact the editor of *Publisher's Weekly*, hoping, he said, "to saponify" him and "to make 'book sales' bubble."

With the book completed, Quaife was in need of a job. Earlier, he had petitioned Joy to suggest him as a historian for the Chicago Historical Society. Although Joy and others were willing to pledge the initial $10,000 cost of the position, the Society decided, Joy told Quaife, that it could not afford such an appointment in the long term.[24] Quaife eventually secured a job as managing editor of the *Mississippi Valley Historical Review*, of which Joy was one of the "guarantors." He was pleased that Quaife, who had given up his job in Wisconsin to complete the road book, was now settled.[25]

The road book continued to occupy Joy's thoughts during the summer of 1925. He had come to speak of it as his book, asking one correspondent in May, "Have you read my book, 'Chicago Highways, Old and New'? I collected the material and Dr. M. M. Quaife wrote it. All the bookstores keep it and you will find in it a lot of interesting data concerning Chicago."[26] Later, an admirer of Quaife's recorded a conversation he had with Joy on a Chicago street after he had read the book: "He was very shy about taking credit but said nice things about you and I am indebted to him for your address."[27]

Joy's assertion of ownership of the book did not seem to bother Quaife. He even wrote to Joy, albeit enigmatically, to say that "if your share of credit . . . does not equal my own it at least equals mine and I hope you will not fail to see it in this light, and accept for yourself any bouquets that may be tendered you."[28] Joy responded to Quaife that he was discouraged that the book had not sold as well as he thought it might. "It is my first venture in the book business and I have been somewhat disappointed in its sale," he said. "Despite our efforts, it does pretty slowly. . . . It is a good book. Unlike ourselves, it will not grow old and again, unlike ourselves, it will, perhaps, be more interesting as time goes on."[29]

*J*oy's involvement in the Chicago Historical Society prompted him to invest in another historical project as the Chicago book was being marketed. Late in 1924, he wrote to an acquaintance, Mrs. Guy (Jean) Howard of Wilton, Connecticut, with a question concerning his intention to purchase from her a death masque of Napoleon, purported by *Putnam's Magazine* to be one of only two in existence. Wanting to give the masque to the Chicago Historical Society, Joy asked her about its authenticity. "I don't want to make any statements that would destroy my reputation as a future vendor of Napoleonic relics," Joy said. He closed his letter by telling Mrs. Howard of his pleasure in his new library at The Morton Arboretum, proclaiming, "I feel quite proud of my collection and the manner in which it is housed." In a few days, convinced by Mrs. Howard of the rarity of the Napoleon masque, Joy decided to purchase it for the Chicago Historical Society.[30]

On February 18, 1924, just before leaving on his Mediterranean cruise, Joy presented Napoleon's death masque to the Chicago Historical Society. In his dedicatory address, he outlined the circuitous route by which the masque had come into his possession, telling his audience that it had been made and carried to South America by the doctor who attended Napoleon at St. Helena. Joy said that he wanted to present the masque to the Society because it was "the owner of valuable documents relating to the transfer of Louisiana to the United States by the man whose portrait it is." Joy was also personally interested in the masque. As he had pointed out in his Transfer Day speech a few months before, he was very much aware that the French had possessed the land that his father and mother had pioneered only a generation after Napoleon sold it. Joy had always marveled at what France had lost in the Louisiana Purchase, and he offered a concise history of the transaction tying it in with the personality of Napoleon.[31]

*F*or several years, Joy had been a member of Thompson's Lake Rod and Gun Club in Fulton County, Illinois, just across the Illinois River from Havana, Illinois. The club, in existence since the latter part of the nineteenth century, was also known as the Indianapolis Rod and Gun Club, named for the city in which Major Hervey Bates, the founder of the club and the owner of the American Hominy Company, lived. He and his son, Hervey, Jr., had been Joy's hunting companions at the club since he had been involved in cereal milling. Together, Thompson's Lake and a smaller body of water called Flagg Lake, both backwaters of the Illinois, were about three thousand acres in size. The club owned the lakes and the three-thousand-acre surrounding floodplain, which could be farmed in the summer but in the fall and spring was submerged. The hunting and fishing were excellent, and local citizens asserted their right to share the bounty.

In the early 1900s, following the construction of the Sanitary and Ship Canal that reversed the flow of the Chicago River from Lake Michigan down the Des Plaines and Illinois rivers, the water level in the marshy floodplain areas of the Illinois River began to rise. The resultant pollution from Chicago sewage flowing downstream had an incrementally catastrophic effect on the natural ecology that had made waterfowl, fish, and mussels plentiful in the Thompson Lake area of the Illinois River just north of Havana, Illinois. By the late teens, the commercial fishing industry and sports hunting that had thrived there began to diminish perceptibly. When pollution that had already lowered the oxygen levels in the upper Illinois reached below Peoria, interest in the club waned, and Joy started buying up the fourteen memberships with the purpose of turning the fertile floodplain into farmland.[32] He was following the lead of many floodplain landowners along the Illinois who, by 1929, drained over 200,000 acres for farming.[33]

Begun in 1920, Joy's multi-year project to develop what became known during his ownership as Thompson Farms was at first marginally successful. Sterling commented wryly in his unpublished biography on Joy's motivation: "We have already spoken of Mr. Morton's ventures in irrigation, which, on the whole, were not entirely successful. Feeling that perhaps he was approaching the problem of land and water from the wrong angle and that if he could not successfully put water on the land he might achieve a measure of success in taking water off the land, he became interested in a drainage district in Fulton County in central Illinois."[34] What Joy actually intended to do was establish a livestock ranch where feeder cattle would be fed from crops grown on-site. One Illinois River historian, while by no means condoning the draining of floodplain on the lower Illinois, later called Joy's livestock ranch a "model operation."[35] After numerous surveys, a lengthy study of farming potential, legal disputes over rights of access, and Illinois legislative and water and sewage district decisions, Joy initiated the building of a twenty-five-foot high levee. By 1921 he had acquired the remaining memberships of the Thompson Lake project and began installing pumps. He told Sterling that he hoped some acreage there would be ready for cultivation in the fall of 1922.[36] Four years later, the levee was fourteen miles long with a bottom width of 120 to 150 feet. During the building of the levee, crews dredged canals in the lake bed and erected a pumping station. Almost 1,300 acres had been pumped free of water at Thompson and Flagg lakes, and the foreman, John McDorman, expected to plant 1,000 acres in the spring. But it was not until the spring of 1925 after crews laid down a huge amount of silt in a weakened part of the levee that the area was deemed arable. The soil had dried to the extent that Joy was optimistic about its ability to produce a crop by fall.

Joy wrote to Sargent that of some 5,000 drained acres, he had planted 3,500, mostly in corn, and he thought the yield "prospect exceedingly pleasing." An old growth of trees also existed on the land just above the floodplain; Joy described the stand of trees for Sargent: "On my Fulton County farm are many chestnut leaved oak and pecans, also Kentucky coffee trees—all of enormous size. Teuscher has just been there and I am going to have him write you about them." Joy had come to depend heavily upon Teuscher's expertise in botanical matters, even though he found Teuscher a somewhat difficult personality because of his superior demeanor. Joy was too astute a judge of character not to notice that Teuscher's disdainful attitude toward others was beginning to evince itself even toward him. Years later, Teuscher revealed just how he felt about Joy when he wrote in his autobiography of Joy's efforts to develop the Thompson Lake site for farming: "That is how millionaires play to be agronomes."[37] He obviously was not aware that Joy had been a successful farmer for many years before leaving Nebraska City.

It was only after a flood in 1926 destroyed twenty-one of twenty-eight drainage districts on the lower Illinois River that farming of the full 6,000 acres became possible. Joy remained personally involved in the project and in the hunting lodge he established on a ridge overlooking his land. He called it Hilltop. His presence on that ridge eventually proved fruitful in ways that went far beyond farming.

*A*s if there were no limit to the ventures he could handle at one time, two weeks before his seventieth birthday Joy received authorization from the State of Illinois to build an office building at Washington and Wells in Chicago. It was to be financed by the Morton Building Corporation, comprised of Joy, Dan Peterkin, Sterling, Wirt, and Edward Stearns (with capital stock of $1,500,000).[38] In November, Joy wrote to Sargent, "It may interest you to know that I am now building a new office building, which is going to cost me as much as several Arboretums. I am enclosing [for] you a picture of it herewith. I expect that my own Company and other companies in which I am interested, will occupy the upper floors of the building, which is to be completed the latter part of 1926."[39] He put the building in perspective for Sargent again in December, linking it to

The Morton Arboretum: "I quite agree with you that I am expecting to get more fun out of the Arboretum than out of the building, but arboretums require income and the Morton Building will assist The Morton Arboretum permanently and very materially in that regard."[40]

The Morton Building, designed by the prominent Chicago architect Ernest R. Graham,[41] successor to Daniel Burnham, who died in 1912, was planned in such a way that the sixth through the seventeenth floors would be on an exact level with those of the Illinois Bell Telephone Company office building just to the west. Joy knew that the Morkrum-Kleinschmidt Teletype Company, among other communication companies in his building, would complement the services of the communication giant.[42] Although the construction of his building had been delayed by problems in sinking caissons, by mid-March 1926 that work was within days of completion, and derricks were being placed for erecting the steel framework.

Joy thought of the Morton Building as a capstone to his entrepreneurial presence in Chicago, but the address at 208 West Washington also held sentimental and historical value for him as this was the site where Wilbur F. Storey had published the *Chicago Times*, the paper whose accounts of Civil War battles Joy began to read to his younger brothers when he was seven. Storey's paper, located in a building that had been erected after the Chicago fire in 1871, had also been a consistent outlet for J. Sterling's conservative northern Democrat positions, and he had been offered the job of publisher when Storey died.

When Joy and Margaret returned from vacation in California in 1926, Joy confirmed the importance of the site to his family history by dedicating the cornerstone for the Morton Building on May 14, 1926, Carrie's birthday. In the stone, he placed a succinct, handwritten, biographical note, summing up the family's history:

> This building was built by Joy Morton who was born in Detroit, Mich., Sep 27, 1855, and taken to Nebraska in infancy and lived there until 1879 when he came to Chicago and on May 1st, 1880, entered the salt business as a member of E. I. Wheeler & Co, Agents, Michigan Salt Association. They were succeeded in Dec. 1885 by Joy Morton & Co, and in 1910 the business was incorporated as Morton Salt Co.
>
> This corner stone was laid May 14th, 1926, the birthday of Carrie Lake, mother of my daughter Jean Morton Cudahy and Sterling Morton—my only children—she died in 1915 and would have been 69 years old had she lived until this day.
>
> On Jan 16, 1917, I married my second wife, Margaret Gray.[43]

Characteristically, Joy was precise about what was to be placed in the stone. Jean and Joseph Cudahy provided handwritten notes as well, although Sterling, who was in Europe with his family, could not participate. Other items included a letter from Judge W.A. Day written just before Joy's seventieth birthday, a brochure of Joy's birthday celebration, Joy's address given at the transfer of Arbor Lodge to the state of Nebraska, a documentation of the trees and other plants at Arbor Lodge in place when it was donated, and a pamphlet describing Arbor Lodge State Park.

Also included in the package were several items representing Joy's connections with the Chicago area: *Seventy-Five Years in Chicago*, a thirty-six-page history of the Morton Salt Co. and its predecessors, published by Morton Salt in 1923; *Chicago's Highways, Old and New*, which Joy identified as being by M.M. Quaife with "material collected by Joy Morton and publication financed by him"; a "Pamphlet of General Information on The Morton Arboretum at Lisle, Illinois"; "*Morton Arboretum Bulletins*, 1 to 6 inclusive"; Teuscher's "list of trees, plants, shrubs, etc., growing naturally in vicinity of the Morton Arboretum"; the May 14, 1926, issues of the *Chicago Tribune* and the *Herald-Examiner*; and specifications for the Morton Building. Joy included a note that the box was "tightly soldered" in his office, Room 711, of the Railway Exchange Building, with ten employees of the Salt Company and his family in attendance. From there it was carried to Wells and Washington where they witnessed it being "completely enclosed by the masons."

*J*oy assured Sterling that the Morton Building was not going to put him in a weakened economic condition. On the contrary, in renting up to eight floors to American Telephone and Telegraph's Illinois Bell Telephone, he estimated that the Morton Building Corporation would realize a million and a half dollars in ten years. Sterling suggested that the Morton Building might gain other tenants who supplied electrical services and equipment and that the building would become "identified" with the booming electrical communication industry.[44] Sterling, who was combining his family's vacation in Europe with marketing the teletype company of which he was president, eventually negotiated a $30,000,000 sale of Morkrum-Kleinschmidt to AT&T in 1930, as the Depression descended.[45]

On the occasion of his granddaughter Suzette's fifteenth birthday, Joy wrote to Sterling that it was "a memorable one on her account, and also because it is the day that the telephone company lease is effectuated." The Western Cold Storage Company, in which Joy and Mark continued to hold the major interest, also moved into the building. As the building neared completion, Joy said, they would "work harder on prospective tenants."[46] One tenant, however, was housed at little cost. Joy invited the Chicago Plan Commission to move its operations there.

Construction was ahead of schedule. Brick was being laid at the 16th floor, and elevators were ready to be installed. Joy ventured up to the unfinished 23rd floor, where he would have his office, and told Sterling that the noise he feared from the elevated was not nearly as bad as it was at the Railway Exchange Building where he could hear switch engines from across Michigan Avenue. Joy was also "surprised and delighted at the view." He could see Lake Michigan, he said, better than he had from his seventh floor office in the Railway Exchange Building. To the north, before taller buildings like the Merchandise Mart intervened, Joy had a view of Lincoln Park and the north branch of the Chicago River where he was building a new salt warehouse on Elston, between Division Street and North Avenue. The new warehouse was needed because Illinois Central Pier I was being torn down to make way for the extension of Lake Shore Drive and the bridge over the Chicago River, as suggested by the Chicago Plan. It also meant that the replica of the Boston Town House, which had been used for Morton Salt printing machines since Joy had moved his offices in 1905 to the Railway Exchange Building, had to be razed.

Joy and Sterling's correspondence about the Morton Building was interspersed with another thought. Joy was interested in exploring options for land he had purchased to the east of his original Thornhill property and the arboretum. Sterling had rented a house in France for approximately $387.00 a month, a relatively high rent, leading Joy to think of developing houses on a private park on what had been known as the Puffer property. Joy asked Sterling to "make a careful investigation" of country houses and villas in southern France so that he could know what was attractive to potential renters. His purpose was twofold: he would make more money by building permanent or rental houses than he could by farming at Lisle, and, as he expected of the Morton Building, the income would benefit "the Estate or the Arboretum."[47]

Noting that because of the warm summers, the county of DuPage did not offer the allure to people who could "afford to go to a cooler spot," Sterling suggested that five-acre, well-developed home sites assuring the utmost in privacy for those who wanted weekend and seasonal get-aways would be best. Indicating the economic level of the residents he envisioned, he thought each house should contain "three to five master bedrooms, with a minimum of one bath for each two rooms, and at least two maid rooms, with bath." The vacation houses, he thought, might be built for twelve to eighteen thousand dollars each. For recreation, he thought there should be a golf course, tennis courts, putting greens, a swimming pool, stables, a polo field, traps for shooting, and paths for walking and riding.[48]

But Joy soon gave up on the idea of building on the Puffer property, even though the cities of Downers Grove, on which the Puffer farm bordered, and Lisle were growing rapidly. Thanking Sterling for his visionary suggestions, he said only, "Some day something may be developed on that land."[49] It eventually became an extension of The Morton Arboretum, although a small portion was, much later, taken by the government to build Interstate 88.

The signal event of the fall of 1925, even though it seemed in danger of being overshadowed by his many activities, remained Joy's seventieth birthday party, attended by an estimated two thousand employees and their families on September 25, two days before his actual birthday. Sterling and others had arranged chartered buses to ferry office and warehouse workers from Grant Park at the foot of Monroe to Thornhill, twenty-five miles away. Following a picnic lunch were races, ball games, and dancing to a local orchestra.[50] Of the names of the thirty-five employees engraved on the plaque Joy received, twenty-seven of them had begun service from 1886 to 1910. The original board of the Morton Salt Company, which included Peterkin, Mark, Wirt, and Sterling, was still intact fifteen years later. The occasion confirmed that loyalty and longevity, important ingredients of Joy's method of management, were a tradition at Morton Salt.

Joy ended 1925 with a respite at a hunting club on Avery Island in Louisiana, the site of yet another project he had undertaken. The club had been proposed by Edward Avery McIlhenny, a naturalist, conservationist, and president of the family-owned company that created Tabasco Sauce, an invention of his father. He also owned the Avery salt mine, whose product was sold by Joy's company. Joy and other investors purchased approximately 125,000 acres when McIlhenny did not follow up. They used much of the acreage for an organization called Louisiana Furs, Inc., which allowed investors to market animal products trappers "farmed" from the rich resources, such as muskrat, raccoon, alligator, and, ironically, the fur from the invasive beaverlike rodent nutria that had been introduced to the island by McIlhenny. The site was a few miles away from the Paul Rainey preserve, the Audubon Society's wildlife refuge founded in 1924.[51] The day before Joy left on December 11 to hunt, he told Sargent, "I have shot ducks there, more or less, for many years. I do not hit as many as I used to, but I still enjoy the sport."[52]

Rather than a lamentation, Joy's comment seems a metaphor for the way he chose to live the final years of what had already been a long and productive life. With his management methods providing him with more leisure than he had had in half a century, he seemed content that the principal goals of his life had been achieved. But he was far from ready to retire from a world that brimmed with potential. The United States had emerged from World War I, the influenza epidemic of 1919, and the Red Scare into Prohibition and the Jazz Age. The young, whom he knew primarily through his teenage granddaughter Suzette, seemed to have inherited the earth. New ideas were in the air, and the economy appeared to grow relentlessly. Joy had the time and the resources to explore this new world, and he set out to do it with the same enthusiasm he had shown when he began to distribute salt and plant his Arboretum.

CHAPTER *13*

Embracing the Future—1926–1934

In his seventies, Joy was confident that understanding the past was the best preparation for the future. But he also knew that he had to look for clues to the future through the eyes of those who would inherit it—the young born into the twentieth century. Thornhill summers were filled with visits from Margaret's niece and nephew from Evansville, Indiana, and Carl, Wirt's teenaged son who came out from Chicago. Young people from throughout the region joined them during their lengthy visits, riding horses and swimming in the pool Joy built for them. But it was Suzette, who was often far away at school, in whose opinion Joy was most interested. In 1926, she spent part of her summer studying art at Julian's Academy in Paris, where her family was residing. While there, she began an intimate correspondence with her grandfather, one marked at first by his references to the past and her espousal of the present and future. Over the next few years, the exchange evolved into a give and take between equals. In the fall of 1926, Suzette, whom Joy addressed as Sue, enrolled in the college preparatory Master's School at Dobbs Ferry, New York, which her Aunt Jean had also attended. Joy told Sue that her description of the schoolwork she was doing at fifteen reminded him of Talbot Hall, which he believed to be "just as strenuous," adding, "I cannot find I was in any way injured by that strenuous effort to acquire an education. On the contrary, I have always thought they were among the best years of my life."[1]

Joy continued in a grandfatherly way to compare his pioneer post–Civil War childhood with his granddaughter's 1920s Jazz Age culture:

> We did not play hockey, nor basket ball—I do not know that those games had been invented at that time, at least not in Nebraska; but we did have a little archery, as the Otoe Indians came in from their reservation every spring to receive their annuity from the Government; they camped, always, near Talbot Hall School, and we had many contests in archery, running, and jumping with the Indian boys. As I remember it, they could beat us with the bow and arrow, but we generally beat them in running and jumping.
>
> We began to play baseball in 1866, had a very good ball team, one that beat the Nebraska City town team several times. Baseball was new in those days. I remember how excited I used to get when there was a match. I played on the scrub team and was not old enough to play on the regular team, but I was just as much interested in it as any of the players.
>
> We had just as much church as you have—perhaps a little more, as we were obliged to memorize all of the Collects and the Gospel for the day. While I have gotten somewhat out of practice now, I guess this infusion of Episcopalianism never did me any harm in after life.
>
> Time flies when one is busy; you do not have time to be homesick, nor discontented in a school like you are now in, and a man or woman in business with lots to do, is always happy. I have always told my employees that the first thing for them to do was to fall in love with their work, and I say the same thing to you as regards your school. . . .[2]

Joy was more forthcoming about his personal feelings with Sue and less critical of his young correspondent than he had been with his son and other young men in his family. When she attended a Princeton football game, he told her that he had always liked the school from which Sterling had graduated because of its spirit "that one does not find anywhere else."[3] In early 1927, when Sue told him that she was proud of her father, Joy said she should be, saying, "He is a good trader and altogether a very competent business man, as well as [a] mighty nice father and son."[4]

*𝒰*sually Joy and Margaret traveled after the first of the year, but in the winter of 1927 they remained at Thornhill. The Morton Building was being prepared for occupancy, and, as a member of the Chicago Plan Commission and the Wells Street District Owners' Association, which he served as vice president, Joy was speaking publicly on issues that he had been working on since the release of the *Plan of Chicago*.

In January 1927, the *Chicago Daily Tribune* published his opinions on two highly debated topics: the straightening of the Chicago River as it flowed southward from its north branch and its link with Lake Michigan; and the replacement of the elevated trains that had given the central city its "Loop" appellation.[5] Joy called the river project, which would allow traffic to flow freely south of Wacker Drive on Wells, Franklin, and Market Streets, "one of the most important improvements in the entire history of Chicago." He advocated an extension of Wacker Drive south along what would be the straightened east side of the Chicago River. It would connect, he argued, all of the city's passenger railway terminals and provide access to the western suburbs via Congress Street, which had recently been enlarged. Bringing his interest in European inner-city design to bear, he said, "Such an arrangement of streets would give Chicago an avenue comparable to the Ringstrasse in Vienna and at the same time serve to relieve the congestion in the present Loop." His argument effectively described what has become the street layout in the western portion of the business district of the city.

On the issue of the Loop, Joy wrote from within the context of the *Plan of Chicago*. As chairman of the plan's railway terminal committee that provided direction for the crucial chapter on transportation, Joy endorsed its call for an efficient system that was conducive to the health and well-being of its citizens. This passage from the plan expressed his views perfectly:

> Again, the noises of surface and elevated road cars is often excruciating. It is not denied that this evil can be largely mitigated. These conditions actually cause misery to a large majority of people who are subjected to the constant strain, and in addition they undoubtedly cause a heavy aggregate loss of money to the business community. For the sake of the state, the citizen should be at his best, and it is the business of the state to maintain conditions conducive to his bodily welfare. Noises, ugly sights, ill smells, as well as dirty streets and workshops or offices, tend to lower average efficiency. It does not pay the state to allow them to continue. Moreover, citizens have pride in and loyalty to a city that is quiet, clean,

and generally beautiful. It is not believed that 'business' demands that our present annoying conditions be continued. In a state of good order all business must be done better and more profitably. With things as they should be, every business man in Chicago would make more money than he does now.[6]

Joy was painfully familiar with the clatter of the elevated on the Wells Street side of his new Morton Building, and he expressed his frustration in no uncertain terms:

Any plan for subways must take into consideration the removal of the elevated loop. It should be entirely removed without delay. In fact, it never should have been built in the first place. I do not favor elevated extensions in the downtown district under any pretense. Complete demolition of the elevated loop is the only thing which will satisfy the public.

Remove the elevated loop and Chicago will make its own business district. It will spread west beyond the river and south beyond Polk Street. The idea that Chicago should be penned up by any artificial boundary such as the elevated loop is intolerable. It has the psychological effect of a stone wall.

Joy's argument did not prevail, but he articulated a sentiment that has lingered throughout the existence of elevated transit in downtown Chicago.

Several months later, Joy was quoted at length in the *Chicago Daily Tribune* as one of only two members of the executive committee of the Chicago Plan Commission to urge no further delay by the Illinois Commerce Commission in granting air rights to two major projects. He argued that the granting of air rights to the *Chicago Daily News* to begin building its offices over Union Station property and to the Marshall Field family to construct the Merchandise Mart (destined to become the world's largest commercial building) over North Western railway property should begin immediately. Joy argued, "The use of air rights should be of immense interest to the city itself. It would be a public benefit. Every one abhors waste, and the failure to utilize air rights is in effect promoting waste." Joy pointed to New York City's development from 42nd Street to 59th Street as a model of what granting air rights over rail lines could do for Chicago's commercial center. When air rights were finally granted and the buildings were finished in 1929 and 1930 respectively, they became the first major buildings to front onto the Chicago River, giving the river a distinct position within the commercial life of the city it had not previously enjoyed.[7]

$\mathcal{I}$n late January, Joy and Margaret finally began their vacation to the south, motoring to Biloxi, Mississippi, and Hot Springs, Arkansas, where Joy went to ease his recurring bouts of gout and rheumatism. During their travel, he received word that his good friend and mentor, Charles Sprague Sargent, had died on March 22, 1927, at the age of eighty-six of influenza. Sargent had been growing less physically active for a couple of years, but he had conducted office work almost until the end.[8]

Through the summer of 1927, Joy concentrated on further development of the Arboretum and on leasing the remainder of the Morton Building. Then, in the fall, he and Margaret went east where they visited Sue at Dobbs Ferry. On their return, he commented proudly on the large number of autumn visitors: "The Arboretum is very beautiful now, more color in the leaves than I have ever seen, and having so many varieties of trees, our color scheme is very unusual. There was a line of cars all day yesterday driving through. All the roads were filled; by night they were pretty dusty."[9] Sue responded to her grandfather's descriptions of the arboretum in kind, obviously practicing her prose style on him: "The Hudson, which I see through a giant cob-web of tree skeletons, is imperturbed [sic] as it moves slowly, lost perhaps in the apathy of its Quakerlike grey."[10] Joy was delighted with her writing.

$\mathcal{B}$y 1927 The Morton Arboretum had become known around the country and was becoming a model for others to follow. Joy had been advising Beman Gates Dawes and his wife, Bertie, on the development of their proposed arboretum in Newark, Ohio. As a way of letting people know about the arboretum that he was designing, Dawes began a program of dedicating tree plantings to well-known people, organizations, or events in 1927. He invited Joy to plant a tree in honor of J. Sterling Morton as founder of Arbor Day.[11] Accompanied by Wirt and Carl, Joy traveled to Ohio in November to speak at the ceremony and plant two American elms,[12] saplings from trees first planted by J. Sterling at Arbor Lodge in 1871. Concluding his remarks, he reflected on the idea of an arboretum from the perspective of having directed The Morton Arboretum for four years:

> An arboretum is not a plaything. It can be of great benefit in demonstrating what varieties of trees to plant and where to plant them. It is necessary that we restore as much of our original forests as possible. They improve the climate and help to retain the fertility of the soil, fertility that absolutely must be retained if this country is to continue to grow. History shows us that countries which have lost their soil fertility and become unable to produce

food crops have also lost their people; as, for instance, Babylonia—most fertile of the ancient countries; Northern Africa, or Mauretania, which, for hundreds of years, was the bread basket of Rome and is now sandy deserts except where reclaimed by the skill and industry of the French, but to compare their feeble efforts with ancient Mauretania is like comparing a kitchen garden with a bonanza farm.

Upon his return to Thornhill, Joy experienced such a severe attack of rheumatism that he and Margaret decided to leave before winter to spend the season in Palm Beach. But before he left, Joy wrote to Sue that he had sent Teuscher to Europe to "make a careful survey of all the arboretums and botanical gardens" and to report back to him as he made each visit. Teuscher, he said, would also be bringing his wife and children back to Thornhill. Knowing that Sue, like everyone, was aware of Teuscher's condescending attitude toward the rest of the staff, Joy told her that he thought that Teuscher was making progress in his relationships with people, saying, "Notwithstanding he was about as bullheaded a German as I have ever undertaken to handle, his five years in the Morton Arboretum have improved him very much—looking at it from my point of view. I think he feels that way himself."[13]

On their return to the Arboretum in May, Joy wrote, "The place looked exceedingly well this morning and will have on its very best garb by next Sunday, when we shall open the gates to the public." In a plaintive tone meant to reveal how much he missed Sue, he added that the saddle horses at Thornhill were "in fine fettle," although there was no one around to ride them but Wirt's son Carl.[14]

In the presidential election year of 1928, the exchange between Joy and Sue took a different turn. Sue informed her grandfather that she was studying "the subject of light" in physics and Shakespeare in English, but she was most interested in current politics, treating the subject with an irony that she knew would engage her conservative grandfather. In American history she was studying the World War I presidency of Woodrow Wilson. Aware that her great-grandfather J. Sterling had been a close friend and a cabinet appointee of another Democrat, Grover Cleveland, she wrote to Joy, "What I don't understand is that if great-grandfather was a Democrat, that we are Republicans. On the other hand, grandmother Owsley is strongly Democratic while her ancestor President Harrison was a Republican. Well, politics are funny! Anyhow I'm glad of the results of the Chicago primary—even if you and Pop were for that Small-Thompson faction!"[15] Although during the Al Capone years, the administrations of William Hale "Big Bill" Thompson, mayor of Chicago, and Lennington "Len" Small, governor of Illinois, were marked by accusations of corruption, neither was convicted of ties to organized crime, and they were actively supported by the business community.

Joy, who always gave the impression that he eschewed politics, although his acquaintances knew of his strong opinions about presidential candidates and policies, responded by saying that he was not surprised by her questions concerning "the politics of the family," and he assured Sue that as she got older, she would find "that politics are very hard to understand. . . ." The summer would allow plenty of time for them to talk about how politics affected the Morton family, he said. "I sincerely want you to come out and you will have plenty of time for horsebacking when you are not discussing politics." Proud of Sue's intelligence, Joy declared, "It is certainly a pleasure to have a granddaughter who is such a capable correspondent."[16]

The conversation about politics waned during the long summer as the presidential nominating conventions were prepared to convene to nominate their candidates, while in Sterling's family concern was building over the health of Sue's baby sister, Millicent Joy, who had been born in 1925 and was experiencing chronic stomach pains. Later in the summer, after Sue returned to Dobbs, Joy and Margaret looked after Millicent Joy at Thornhill, and Joy assured Sue, "Your sister is doing well and you would think I was bragging about the benefits of life on the Farm if I told you how much she has improved."[17] Still, remembering the early death of his granddaughter Carolyn, he had cause to worry.

Soon the presidential campaign of 1928 between Democratic nominee Al Smith and Republican nominee Herbert Hoover gave both Sue and Joy a reason to renew their conversation about politics. Sue announced to Joy, "I have become a Smith-ite. Am I not a disgrace to a Republican family!"[18] In a wide-ranging letter, Joy answered in kind, saying wryly, "I do not think it a disgrace at all, but rather an aberration of the mind which I think you will get over before you are able to vote." Millicent, Joy reported, was "fine," and he and Margaret were looking forward to taking an apartment in November in Chicago at 257 East Delaware Place, to be close to Sterling's and Wirt's families. They would spend Christmas with everyone at Thornhill before leaving on their winter vacation planned for Arizona and southern California.[19]

In November, after Al Smith was soundly defeated by Herbert Hoover, Joy sat down to compose a letter of grandfatherly condolence to Sue. "Now that the election returns are in," he said, "I suppose you feel as regards to your favorite candidate, as I often have felt after the votes were counted. Politics is a mighty uncertain business. It is not a good thing for one to be too sanguine during the campaign. I say this because your father and mother told me that you were just as rabid for Smith when they saw you in New York recently, as you were when you delivered a political lecture to your poor, old grandfather during the summer. . . ." Joy ended by telling Sue, who was approaching eighteen and preparing to enter Chicago society in her debutante year, "It takes a girl of mature judgment to become a debutante in this town without becoming demoralized."[20]

In response to Joy, Sue kept to political issues. She explained that one reason she thought a Democratic administration was necessary was that the Volstead Act had given the country eight years "void of any degree of moderation. . . ." She believed the law enforcing Prohibition had been badly enforced in the country under the Republican administrations of Harding and Coolidge: "To me," she told her grandfather, "Prohibition is a great moral issue upon which hinges much of the welfare of this generation and those of the future. Perhaps I am more of an idealist than a materialist. If so I guess I am a bit out of place in the modern property-greedy era."[21] But beyond the Prohibition issue, Sue also had hoped that Smith would win because she believed in the position "of non-interference in Latin American affairs except to uphold the Monroe Doctrine," referring specifically to United States' interference in Nicaraguan politics under Calvin Coolidge and saying, "I think any case where lives, American or otherwise, are at stake that the uttermost attempts at pacification should be made."[22]

Joy understood her sentiments. He drank in moderation and, like his father, was adamantly against any attempt by the government to legislate morality. He also had had reservations about the Spanish-American War and World War I. His answer to Sue was reassuring. "I don't think you are any more of an idealist than you should be. It is a good thing to have ideals. We find enough of the material as we go through life without looking for it very much." Looking back at his father's long connection with the Democratic Party, he remarked, "The Democratic platform has always been more or less of an ideal; they never have lived up to it very closely during the democratic administrations we have had in the last seventy years, although I think Cleveland came the nearest."[23] The exchange with Sue had rekindled Joy's interest in politics. He recognized in his eighteen-year-old granddaughter's attitude toward the election of 1928 a perspective on politics that he himself shared. It caused him to reflect on his family's past ties with both the Democratic and Republican parties. When pressed, he had always declared himself an independent, but, like Sue, he took strong positions on candidates and issues during times of major elections.[24]

*J*oy and Margaret returned to Arizona and California in February 1929. The trip to the southwest had become a favorite winter sojourn. Again Joy relied on Wirt to keep him abreast of the business of the salt company and other projects in Illinois, including that of Wirt's wife. Joy was intrigued that Lady had opened a shop on Walton Street specializing in upscale interior decoration. She was the first Morton woman of her generation to enter into business for herself.

Joy also realized that a major change in arboretum personnel awaited him upon his return. On March 1, Henry Teuscher left the Arboretum to take an administrative position at the Boyce Thompson Institute for Plant Research in Yonkers, New York. Joy's satisfaction with Teuscher as a botanist had been increasingly challenged by Teuscher's difficulty in working with fellow staff members. Clearly Teuscher needed to be in a position where he could manage things himself. In 1936, Teuscher became superintendent and chief horticulturist of the 185-acre Montreal Botanical Garden, where he had a distinguished career as a designer, planner, and administrator. Before Teuscher left, Joy had hired E.L. Kammerer, a graduate of the landscape architecture department of the University of Illinois, who was working as Teuscher's botanical assistant. Kammerer proved to be an excellent replacement for Teuscher, and Joy gave him the title of arboriculturist within a few months.[25]

The winter months were not without apprehension. Four-year-old Millicent's health deteriorated rapidly, and in spite of the best of care she died in the early spring. Margaret and Joy returned to Thornhill in time to help Sterling and Preston through their grief. Sue, still in school in the East, was particularly grateful for the solace Margaret, who had become Sue's confidante, gave her mother. Sue herself was so moved by her sister's death, that, as she wrote to Margaret on June 1, 1929, she had been confirmed in the Episcopal Church, saying "religion is a great comfort to us sometimes, I think." She added, "We all count you as a true member of our family more than ever, and more than you know. I surely am a lucky girl to have so many sweet grandparents and relatives as well as friends."[26]

Once again, as they did following Carolyn's death, Sterling, Preston, and Sue left for Europe in the summer to recover from their grief. Joy and

Margaret spent their usual summer at Thornhill, from which Joy went into his office almost daily, coming home to take stock of the considerable progress that was being made in the Arboretum under Godshalk's supervision. They also entertained many summer visitors, in particular Margaret Gray (or "little" Margaret as Joy called her), Margaret's teenaged niece, who, with her brother Marion, had spent several summers with them. In July they were visited by Margaret's brother and his wife, who were on their way to see Marion, whom Joy had recommended for a job at the Morton Salt Co. plant in Ludington, Michigan. Joy wrote to his nephew, Carl, that Marion was "doing well in the salt business."[27]

But the summer and fall also found several members of the Morton family confronting further health difficulties. Sue wrote from Europe that Sterling was suffering from gallstones, and in a letter that crossed Sue's, Joy said that he was combating a weight problem: "I am still on my diet. This morning I weighed 194 pounds, which is just 24 pounds less than when I returned from California, but I feel much better than during the past year."[28] Within a week, Joy was able to return to work. Sue, usually in the best of health, wrote from Dobbs Ferry in October that she was recovering from a broken leg.

The health of the nation's economy was also uncertain in the fall of 1929. Most citizens had come to believe that historically prolonged successes in speculation in the stock market and real estate would continue indefinitely—certainly far into the presidency of the "Great Engineer" Herbert Hoover who succeeded Warren G. Harding in January 1929 and promised everyone pots of chicken and garages filled with automobiles. Joy, always cautious about speculation and a veteran of economic turmoil, was not sanguine about the economy, although he continued calmly on in his business and personal affairs. The salt business had always come through panics and depressions relatively unscathed. Joy felt confident that it would do so again. During the subsequent years of the Great Depression, neither Morton Salt nor The Morton Arboretum suffered layoffs. The Arboretum, in fact, became a destination for men looking for work on the streets of Chicago.[29]

The day before Thursday, October 24, 1929, which the economist John Kenneth Galbraith called "the first of the days which history . . . identifies with the panic of 1929,"[30] Joy wrote matter-of-factly to Sue, "Granny left at noon today for New York with little Margaret, who sails on the SS Augustus of the Navigazione Generale Italiana line at midnight Friday. Granny will return the next day. . . ."[31] The day Margaret and her niece arrived in New York saw, in Galbraith's words, "disorder, fright, and confusion" among thousands of investors across the country. The panic lasted only until shortly after noon of that day, but it reemerged as the economic disaster now known as the "Great Crash" of "Black Monday," October 29, 1929.

$\mathcal{N}$ot naïve to the possibility that the next day or the next could be the one that would confirm the fact that something was terribly wrong with the economy, Joy informed Sue that he and Margaret had decided to set out on an ocean voyage of their own: "We have decided to go around the world," he said simply. "We have two large rooms. Mrs. Barnet [a companion] is going with us, and part of one room will be divided for a library. I think we are going to be very comfortable and will have a chance to see a lot of the world that we have not visited."[32] Like the decision to go to China in 1917 with Margaret, settling on the trip around the world might have seemed impromptu. As Margaret later described it, she had been sitting with Joy during the long autumn evenings of 1929, thinking of a place where they could "escape from four months of severe cold." She later wrote that they both were bored with the repetitious trips they had taken in recent years. "Of late, we had alternated between Florida and California, and had traveled abroad until we could think of no interesting resorts here we might enjoy the coming months. Then, one evening, out of a clear sky, my husband invited me to go "around the world."[33]

As usual, however, Joy's suggestion was not an idle thought. His recent gout attacks had been severe, and his weight loss, now at twenty-eight pounds, made him susceptible to winter colds. He told Sue that an almost five-month trip that would take them away for a prolonged sojourn into the tropics made sense. He had also just turned seventy-four, and while he was in relatively good health but for recurring painful attacks of gout and rheumatism—which he hoped the warm sea air would assuage—he knew that he would not have many more opportunities to travel to places of cultural and botanical significance.

Margaret wrote in *Around the World*—her journal, which Joy published in book form upon their return—that the trip was even better than they had expected. In deft and often whimsical accounts, Margaret told of life on sea and land at the thirty ports of call the ship made. The seven-deck *The Empress of Australia* sailed with a passenger list of 369, "reduced in number, it was said," Margaret wrote, "on account of the crash in the stock market." There were also 500 "service passengers" who made certain that everything from entertainment to exercise would be readily available for the guests, who paid up to $25,000 per person for the cruise and an itinerary that allowed the 369 passengers to travel comfortably inland. At one stop the passengers were picked up in Haifa at the foot of Mount Carmel in 125 new 1930 Buicks "just out of paper," to tour the Holy Land during the Christmas holidays.[34]

But Margaret did not dwell on the amenities of the well-off passengers. From previous visits and reading she made historical associations, often bringing to bear insights into poverty, class divisions, and the condition of women that make a contemporary audience think of her as a social analyst or at least an insightful travel guide. On one occasion in Tiberias on December 24, she and two other women went out alone and were asked by an Arabic boy to visit his home, which consisted of one room shared by a sick father, mother, and eight children. "It was a subtle way of asking alms," she said. "We returned to a cozy hotel room, bright with a grate fire, and found our friends writing their notes of the day. We have seen the cradle of Christianity—Nazareth, Tiberias, Capernaum, where Jesus labored that we might learn how to live."[35] Margaret, of course, implied in this story that the way people act toward one another should not depend upon their economic well-being. She closed the journal with this observation: "I have always been keenly interested in the human element in life, and, therefore, on this trip around the world, I intensely enjoyed observing the multitudes of the earth's people in their strange and contrasting ways of living. To see the greatest names down through the ages, as well as to witness the smaller things they have done, those accomplishments of daily life that bring love and peace to the world,—to do this is in truth inspiring."[36] It was a remarkable statement during a remarkable journey in 1930, just a few years before the Mediterranean, the Middle East, the Indian Ocean, the Sea of Japan, and the Pacific Ocean and all their ports of call would be fraught with dangers that would make a journey such as theirs foolhardy.

Joy and Margaret had been able to wander freely in the countries they visited, observing the horticultural and architectural creations of their cultures. While in Peking, Joy was encouraged by his friend Dr. John C. Ferguson, an archaeologist and educator he and Margaret had visited in 1917, to contribute funds sufficient to complete the reconstruction of the temple Ching Jen Kung in the Forbidden City, which had been heavily damaged during the 1900 Boxer Rebellion. The temple was a museum of Chinese Jade and bronzes, first built during the reign of the Dowager Empress Hu, about the time that Columbus sailed across the Atlantic—a fact that further encouraged Joy to make his contribution.[37]

Around the World was Margaret's book, but Joy appeared as a significant figure in the narrative, always standing within arm's reach, even though she might be off on a lark of her own with other passengers. At fifty-five, she could ramble up hillsides and into city streets with much more agility than he. Often she was amused by the way he chose to entertain himself when she was not nearby. On the way to Algiers on the ship, she wrote, "Mr. Morton has allowed a bachelor girl of his own vintage to engage him in long morning talks. His first choice, a dashing western widow, caused him to break his diet the day we sailed by inviting him to tea and serving cake." When they had six new friends into their suite for tea, she remarked that the conversation was all about "His Seventieth Birthday."[38] On a visit in March to the volcanic crater of Kilauea, she recalled their first time there a few years before. It had been night, and she with several of the party had crawled close to the crater's edge. "My philosopher," Margaret remembered, "who is ever by my side on these sight-seeing expeditions, had refused to join this peeping party, but stood back at a distance of twenty-five feet to get his impressions in his own way. However, he was not able to endure for long the sight of his wife leaning out over the rim of that fiery cauldron, and soon came stealthily up behind me, seized my feet, and dragged me back to a safer place. This gave me as great a thrill as though I had felt the earth moving away from under me."[39]

Joy, too, was enjoying the trip immensely. As late as January, however, he was still looking for weather warm enough to ease the pain of rheumatism in his right shoulder and his gout. It had, he complained from Bombay, gotten "no better."[40] But upon their arrival home four months later, Joy told Sue, "Had a wonderful trip around the world. . . . It was by all odds the most satisfactory trip that we have ever had."[41]

*J*oy had little time to get settled at the Arboretum and at work before he found himself involved in another project that turned out to be among the most interesting of his long and productive life. Fay-Cooper Cole, the chairman of the Division of Anthropology and Psychology at the University of Chicago, and Thorne Deuel, Cole's research associate and a doctoral student, were determined to focus their attention on a three-year anthropological excavation, primarily in the region of Joy's Thompson Lake farm across from Havana on the Illinois River. It was a study driven by three factors: a chance to conduct the first major investigation of what Cole and Deuel termed "two very rich cultures— one of the Mississippi type, the other closely resembling the Hopewellian of Ohio"; another was the opportunity to exhibit the results of their investigations at the upcoming 1933 Century of Progress Exposition in Chicago; and a third was the stark economic fact that, although this was a significant archaeological site, the Depression and the consequent lack of money helped focus such activities inside the United States.

Anxious to begin digging in the summer of 1930, Cole sought access to Joy through a mutual acquaintance, Joy's friend Rufus C. Dawes, the oil magnate who had been named to chair the Century of Progress Exposition. He wrote to Dawes thanking him for agreeing to see Joy, telling him, "The three types of cultures represented in the Lewiston region should go far toward solving the riddle of Mound-builder occupation of the Illinois Valley."[42] Joy was still nearly three weeks away from returning home from his trip, but Dawes told Cole that he was certain he would have his cooperation.

Joy was, indeed, more than happy to cooperate, for he believed that the project had the potential to advance American anthropology. Two weeks after Joy's return, Cole wrote to Dr. Don Dickson, who, although an amateur, had made expert excavations of mounds on his own land next to Joy's property. Cole reported, "Mr. Morton is opening his property and his lodge to us."[43] The lodge, which Joy had named Hilltop, was used for hunting by Joy, Mark, Wirt, and their close friends. It looked out from a low bluff onto the nearly 7,000 acres of land and lake Joy owned, and it sat almost on the site next to where Cole and Deuel wanted to conduct their Morton excavations. Joy also contributed other housing for students who worked under Cole and Deuel's supervision, and he helped support the digs for the next two summers while also urging others whose land contained archaeological sites to give Cole's team access.[44] In July 1930, Cole reported to Joy, "Everything is going along nicely and we are beginning to find some burials and materials. Your people have been exceedingly kind and we are enjoying ourselves very much."[45] Approaching the age of seventy-five, Joy found himself in a position to support work that proved central to the way American anthropology would be conducted in the future.[46]

The summer of 1930 also brought major changes in the Morton family businesses. As head of the teletype company in which his father had been the principal investor since 1902, Sterling had led it to prominence after becoming president in 1917. Since then, it had become the Morkrum-Kleinshmidt Teletype Company in 1925 and in 1929, as a marketing move, the Teletype Corporation. By late 1928, the Teletype company had become the sole supplier of ticker machines to Western

Union and to the New York Stock Exchange. Although the economic boom of 1928 and early 1929 had come to a catastrophic conclusion, Sterling believed 1930 was a propitious time to sell the company to larger corporate interests. This was accomplished by September 1930 when the Teletype Corporation became the property of the American Telephone and Telegraph Company.[47]

Joy was extremely pleased by Sterling's deft engineering of the sale, which involved international negotiations and netted the stockholders, particularly Sterling, significant profits. On September 25, Joy told Sue, who was studying at Vassar, "Everything is settled, now, except the final delivery of the stock and cash, which will be made in New York on Tuesday. . . . He is entitled to the credit for having conducted a very large operation most successfully and I hope you are as proud of him as I am—no doubt you are." With the sale, Sterling no longer needed to guide the company, which he had done assiduously for a dozen years.

The salt company, too, was undertaking a major venture in the summer of 1930. It had not been in the business of mining rock salt in the past. But rock salt mined in three mines in Louisiana was too competitive in that part of the country for the Morton Salt Company to ignore. Joy's company began sinking a shaft in Grand Saline, Texas, to be operated by a Morton Salt Company subsidiary known as Kleer Salt Company. The company became competitive almost immediately after it became operational in 1931.[48]

*M*uch had happened in the brief time that Margaret and Joy had returned from their trip around the world and renewed their activities at Thornhill and Chicago. But knowing that the Midwest winter would soon be upon them, they booked passage to South Africa for the winter months, a warm destination they knew would be good for Joy's rheumatism. When that cruise was canceled, they decided to sail in late January on the S.S. *Hamburg* with the intention of again touring the Mediterranean and then traveling through Europe in the spring.

Joy had a number of commitments before they could leave, however. In October, he and Margaret traveled once again to Nebraska where Joy spoke at the dedication of the Waubonsie Bridge. The bridge had been built near where Joy and his mother first entered Nebraska from Iowa in 1855. Since then, there had been a ferry, a railroad bridge, and a pontoon bridge. But there had not been efficient access for motor traffic. Joy told the citizens of his native town that this was the time for them to make their city grow, now that they had become a "great motor crossroads city," and he urged them to build an "up-to-date hotel, one that is distinctive and creditable to the town." As he had over the years, he wanted Nebraska City to take advantage of its location and to grow into a major center of commerce.[49]

The trip to gardens and other favorite sites in Europe proved unremarkable but restful. Joy was prepared on their return to Thornhill to turn his attention to the economic condition of the country and his businesses. Toward the end of May, Joy penned a lengthy letter to Carl, now a student at Lawrenceville Academy. Joy told Carl that both his aunt Margaret and a favorite riding horse named "Big Boy" were well, saying he hoped Carl would ride Big Boy during the summer "and not give all your time to driving Flivvers. . . ."[50] But Joy's letter to Carl contained an avuncular message as well. Knowing that Carl was destined to enter the Morton Salt Company, Joy gave his teenaged grandnephew a reason for concentrating on his studies: "The Morton Salt business is not very good. Like all lines of business, it is not making as much money as it should. I realize that is what is keeping you in school and while I hope business will pick up, I think you better study hard and take full advantage of the opportunity you now have, because should the salt business peter out, you might have to go to work before you are fifteen, so you want to make hay while the opportunity is yours."[51]

Joy also told Carl of his pleasure in the Arboretum. "Trees in the Arboretum and also shrubs are doing well. We have lots of flowers. I think you will notice that there is a distinct improvement in the entire place when you see it."[52] Under the supervision of E.L. Kammerer, the Arboretum had begun it first trial hedges in expectation of establishing a hedge garden as a feature of the 260 acres that, in Joy's scheme of incremental accession, would be turned over to the Arboretum in 1932, bringing the total acreage in that year to 435. By 1934, the plantings had been tested and the hedge garden installed. It was destined to become the oldest such garden in the United States.

$\mathcal{J}$oy's general concern about business had little or nothing to do with his decision in 1931 at the Morton Salt Company's annual board meeting to step down from the presidency. He had, of course, been the owner and chief officer of Joy Morton & Co. since 1885 and president of Morton Salt since 1910. But he now thought it time to acknowledge formally that Daniel Peterkin was in charge of day-to-day operations of Morton Salt. Joy arranged to have the board's charter changed so that he could remain chairman of the board. The move assured stability in the transition. The chief administrators of the company did not change, other than in their titles, as Sterling recorded in January 1934: "Mark Morton became First Vice President, B. W. Carrington, Preston McGrain, Wirt Morton and A. G. Warren Vice Presidents. R. K. Warren was elected Treasurer, while Sterling Morton retained his old position as Secretary. Messr. Carrington and Wirt Morton were also elected to the Board of Directors." It was, Sterling said, "indicative of the conservatism and permanence of the company to record the fact that this was the first change in either officers or directors that had occurred since the formation of the company in March 1910."[53]

As the transition at the Morton Salt Company was taking place, Joy attended to the progress of the dig at the Morton site. Fay-Cooper Cole and his associates hoped to complete a full report by the winter of 1932, well ahead of the opening of the Century of Progress Exposition. Joy visited Thompson Lake and came away thinking that Sue might like the work. On the 14th of July he wrote to his granddaughter that Cole's "big party of archaeologists" included a recent graduate of Vassar, and he wished that she could also engage in archaeology. He gently chided Sue, who was spending her summer on the Atlantic Coast, by adding, "It is just as interesting and exciting to look for skeletons and trinkets of the old Indians as it is to be digging crabs in your front yard."[54]

While Joy was pleased with the successes of the excavations on his property in central Illinois, the most personally satisfying event of 1931 for him was that Margaret was offered an honorary degree in October by Blackburn College following the publication of *Around the World*. "Your grandmother," he wrote proudly to Sue, "is to receive a degree on account of her book. By the time you get this, or very soon afterwards, she will be an LLD or something of that sort."[55]

*O*n April 22, 1932, the anniversary of J. Sterling's one hundredth birthday and the sixtieth celebration of Arbor Day, Joy and Sterling gave joint speeches to a large crowd at Nebraska City. Joy's brief contribution dwelt on his father's life and love of trees. He concluded the speech by quoting the inscription on the nearby monument to J. Sterling at Arbor Lodge State Park: "Other holidays repose upon the past; Arbor Day proposes for the future." Pointing out the signal difference between the words "repose" and "propose," Joy urged his Nebraska City audience to plan for the future by substituting trees for grain farming along the rough lands of the bluffs extending at points twenty-five miles inland from the Missouri River. Not only would they be able to halt erosion by doing so, he said, but they would eventually realize profits from the hardwood the land yielded. It was an idea, of course, before its time. He also urged farmers to plant orchards, citing his own success in Nebraska City in doing so. His definition of the word "propose" was synonymous with vision that looked far into the future. He and his father had tried it, and he could point to the grounds of Arbor Lodge for the results.[56]

$\mathscr{B}$ack at Thornhill, Joy penned a chatty letter to Sue, telling her that Margaret had furthered her career interest in the health professions by becoming the president of the Edward Sanatorium in Naperville. After spending much of her career as Carrie's private nurse, Margaret had now become a respected advisor to a major community health care institution. She had helped reorganize the institution dedicated to the care of tubercular patients, and Joy thought that it was "doing quite well." But his main subject in the letter was that he had started a book on his life with the help of Frank Dalton O'Sullivan, a professional biographer. With several of his staff, O'Sullivan spent weeks interviewing Joy at Thornhill. Amused by the activity, Joy wrote to his granddaughter that O'Sullivan was the leader of a "literary band." O'Sullivan likely had come to Joy's attention because his "studio" and "literary workshop" were located in the Railway Exchange Building. His stationery read "Biographer."[57]

Joy assumed from the first that the finished book would be more of an autobiography than a biography and referred to O'Sullivan as his "editor."[58] When O'Sullivan attempted to rush to print with a manuscript that he titled "Seventy-Five Years in the Midwest," Jean, Sterling, and Joy did not think it was ready for publication. Moreover, having chosen the publisher himself, O'Sullivan told Sterling that the book should not be printed "by the outstanding character in the book, as a private edition." Joy still thought of the book as his autobiography and intended to publish it himself. At the bottom of six pages of notes responding to Jean and Joseph Cudahys's editorial suggestions, O'Sullivan wrote, "If too many cooks spoil the broth, it is just possible that too many editors may also spoil a book."[59] Like the Cudahys, Sterling, a practiced writer and editor himself—he had been the editor of the *Nassau Lit.* at Princeton—was not amused. The "literary band" led by O'Sullivan had produced a manuscript that hid Joy's "in person" account. Sterling decided to attempt a complete rewriting but abandoned the task for want of time.

$\mathscr{W}$hile Joy and Margaret were at Thornhill in 1932, the presidential contest between Herbert Hoover and Franklin Delano Roosevelt was concluding amid acrimony generated primarily by conflicting views as to what should be done about the Depression. In late August, Joy wrote to Sue, who was now at the Sorbonne, "Tomorrow you will be old enough to vote. I suppose you would vote the Democratic ticket if here; therefore, from a political viewpoint only, I am glad you will not be here to vote in November, although I think your vote and many thousands of others will be needed to put the presidential candidate on the Democratic ticket in office. . . ."[60]

Joy clearly missed his granddaughter, and his letters began to take on a pensive if not wistful tone. Writing to her again in October after he and Margaret had taken an off-season motor trip to the warm southeast, stopping at Hot Springs and White Sulphur Springs for his gout, Joy said that he thought it strange that she should have gone so far away as France, only to be studying art from a lady from Wheaton, Illinois. He reminded her that she could be happy in the Midwest, saying, "it only goes to show, since you like her so well, that we have some pretty nice people in [DuPage] County and I hope you will get acquainted with more of them when you come home."[61]

From the province of Touraine where she was studying, Sue described the landscape and its chateaux in some detail, prompting Joy, who had visited there several times himself, to suggest that she "explore the Province on cobblestone roads," adding with an obvious reference to himself, "It may have a tendency to keep your weight down. I think it is something you will have to give attention to, sooner or later." Her description of Touraine led Joy to expand on his and Margaret's recent trip to the southeastern United States, possibly in an attempt to entice Sue to return home: "We had a very fine motor trip; traveled 2,300 miles; visited nine States in the Southeast. . . . Asheville is a beautiful place and nowhere else have I seen such a fine landscape effect from the planting of evergreen trees. I am so well pleased by it that I shall plant many more evergreens in the Arboretum this coming Spring—arrangements have already been made to that end."[62]

*F*ollowing Roosevelt's victory in 1932, and in spite of his admonishment to Sue several months before about casting her first vote for Roosevelt, Joy was intrigued by the forthright efforts of the administration to lessen the terrible effects of the Great Depression. In June 1933, with Roosevelt's administration barely in place, Congress established the National Recovery Administration. The NRA was widely criticized by corporate America for its potential to impose codes such as the right of workers to organize, a forty-hour week, and the abolition of child labor. But in October 1933, Joy wrote to Sue from the perspective of a corporate leader who did not have anything to fear from the codes. Even though his granddaughter was educated in the arts and not business, Joy wrote to her as an equal who represented a generation of young people who would be working within the culture of a new economy:

> Business, I know, is a matter of no particular interest to you, but we are all interested in the working out of the NRA. Most people seem to be against it. There are many critics, who, I am sure, do not know what they are talking about. The salt people are not ready to commit themselves, but, so far, the thing has worked fairly well. We feel it is only a question of patience and fair dealing for a few months until the benefits of the new deal will be apparent. It will be fortunate if it comes about as soon as a few months, as it will take a good many old merchandisers as long as that, or longer, to learn how to be honest and square in their dealings. We assume and believe that we are o.k. and are patiently waiting for angels' wings to sprout on some of the other fellows.[63]

At seventy-eight, Joy was still very much an astute observer of economy and politics. He had accepted the "new deal" as a policy that should be tried. These words in which Joy indicated his willingness to look at the larger picture are among the last he penned to his beloved young correspondent.[64]

During the next few months, Joy and Margaret stayed close to home, although they made one more trip to Hot Springs to try to ease his suffering from gout and rheumatism. But neither Joy's age nor his health deterred him from overseeing the development of the Arboretum that had been expanded to over 400 acres or from regularly going downtown to his office in the penthouse he had built atop the Morton Building. He kept busy at what he loved doing up until the evening of May 10, 1934, when quite suddenly he was felled by a heart attack.

Days later Sterling tried to put Joy's death into perspective in a long letter to Howard Krum, who had been his and his father's associate in the Morkrum-Kleinschmidt Teletype Company. In his last visit to Hot Springs, Joy had been examined by a physician and was told he was better than he had been two years earlier. But both Sterling and Preston believed that Joy "seemed smaller and less vigorous" than he had before he left on his final trip to Hot Springs. Sterling recalled that on the Sunday before he died, his father "was in a rather queer mood; in fact, talked as though he were rather summing things up—spoke of his age, the fact that he got very tired even on what he had formerly considered short walks."[65]

On the day he died, Joy drove into his office with Wirt in a new Ford Joy had given him and "seemed to be in the best of spirits." It was remarkably hot when Margaret picked him up in Chicago around three o'clock in the afternoon to come back to Thornhill for dinner with some of her family. The party left to see a movie, but Joy, complaining of the heat, read for a while in the library, then was helped into bed by the butler, who noticed that his hands were blue. When Margaret and her niece arrived home a half hour later, they rushed to Joy's room just as he was breathing his last. Sterling closed his letter to Krum, "As the days pass I realize my loss more and more. He was the greatest single factor in our lives and was like a great rock on which we could always lean."[66]

Walter Eickhorst, who had been hired at the Arboretum in 1931 and was employed there until 1977, described Joy's funeral as "very, very simple." While his body was being prepared at Thornhill for burial, Arboretum workers covered a two-wheeled garden cart, including the tires, with green paint. Around the skirt they arranged white pine boughs. Joy's body was placed on the cart at Thornhill; two workmen pulled it a short distance to the cemetery over a trail of lilacs. It was a funeral procession, Eickhorst thought, that Joy would have wanted.[67]

Epilogue—1934–2008

In a manner that befitted the way he lived his life, Joy's death received relatively subdued notice other than the customary obituaries. There is little in the written history of Chicago or the Midwest that recognizes his contributions, other than the occasional association of his name with Morton Salt or The Morton Arboretum. Like his peers who succeeded in business in Chicago following the Great Fire of 1871, Joy was intent upon capitalizing on the city's geographical advantage as the central hub of westward expansion. But also like many of his contemporaries, he was committed to the future of the city and the nation, and he knew that the resiliency of that future resided in generations yet to come. There is no question that he himself wanted to be remembered and that he wanted The Morton Arboretum to be his monument. One need only visit The Morton Arboretum to marvel at how a single, carefully orchestrated gesture could affect the lives of so many succeeding generations.

Joy's death did not restrain the robust growth of the Morton Salt Company. As usual, he risked nothing on chance. Daniel Peterkin, for four decades a key figure in Joy's administration, had succeeded him as president of the company. When Peterkin died in 1941, Daniel Peterkin,

Jr., who joined the company in 1928, became president, and B.W. Carrington, Sr., one of the original "Groveland Park boys," whom Joy had brought into the company forty years previously, became chairman of the board. Upon Carrington's death in 1948, Sterling was elected chairman. As uses for salt expanded exponentially and the specialty chemical arm of the company (known as Morton Chemical) developed bromide and magnesium carbonate products and provided magnesium oxide for the rubber and steel industry, Morton Salt assured itself of a central position as a national and international corporation.[1] Even after the company was acquired by the Philadelphia-based chemical giant Rohm & Haas in January 1999, Morton Salt International, Inc. remains the producer of the brand of salt that the nation has known for over a century.

Jean Cudahy, a member of the board of the Garden Clubs of America, followed her father as chairman of the board of trustees of The Morton Arboretum, and she immediately began strengthening the educational mission and to construct an administration building as a memorial to her father. When Jean died in 1953, she was succeeded by Sterling, who served as chairman until his death in 1961. Sue, Joy's only surviving grandchild, was the last of the Morton family to chair the Arboretum board of trustees, serving from 1961 until 1977.

The Arboretum's continuance as a privately owned institution open to the public had been assured through Joy's endowment, which was sufficient to maintain the grounds for a number of years and is now supplemented by private philanthropic support, a growing membership, and earned revenues. Clarence Godshalk, the youngest of Joy's hires, retained the title of superintendent until he became the director in 1939. After Joy's death, the Arboretum continued to expand according to the incremental plan he had devised, eventually becoming the 1,700-acre park and educational and research institution it is today. Among the many legacies within The Morton Arboretum is the hedge garden introduced on the 419-acre Arboretum in the year of Joy's death. It is now the oldest formal hedge garden in the United States.

*J*oy left his imprint on many institutions that influenced the development of Chicago in the twentieth century. One of his most significant contributions was to the Chicago Plan Commission, which was sponsored by the Commercial Club of Chicago after it merged with the Merchants' Club that had initiated the study that led to the *Plan of Chicago.* Joy served from 1909 until his death on the Executive Committee of the Chicago Plan Commission, which allowed him to speak with authority on issues raised by the *Plan of Chicago*. In a scriptorium issued in Joy's honor, the Chicago Plan Commission declared, "He was one of the first citizens to appreciate the importance of a definite scheme for the development of Chicago." The citation also linked The Morton Arboretum to the plan's emphasis on parks: "Joy Morton believed that the care and fostering of our forests were fundamentally important. This belief he inherited from his father. He was fortunate in being able to give expression to it in the establishment and endowment of The Morton Arboretum, which combines a beautiful park and botanical garden and fits in perfectly with the recommendation in the *Plan of Chicago* for preserving the forests of this region."[2]

Several other business and civic organizations benefited from Joy's counsel and philanthropy. For years he had been the director of the Equitable Life Assurance Society of America, the company that early in the century had been led by his brother Paul. At Joy's death, he was an active director of the Chicago and Alton Railroad. In 1931, he gave the Chicago Historical Society, of which he had been a trustee for twenty-two years, $35,000 toward its building fund. And in 1948, following the death of Margaret Gray, Northwestern University Hospital received $1,500,000 for the construction of the Morton Research Center. Edward Sanatorium in Naperville (later Edward Hospital), which Margaret had served as board president, was also the beneficiary of a major gift from the Morton estate.

Today the Arbor Day Foundation Lied Conference Center just to the southwest of Arbor Lodge sits on property in Nebraska City that Joy thought he might retire on before purchasing Thornhill. The Morton Apple Company, Inc., which had its orchards on the site, came under the ownership of Joy's partner Grove Porter, who eventually sold the property to the Foundation. And the Morton-James Library sits grandly on a prominent corner in Nebraska City, its expansion complementing the Richardsonian architecture of the original.

The Thompson Lake property that Joy once owned and farmed between Havana and Lewiston on the Illinois River was purchased in 2001 by The Nature Conservancy, and the land has been returned to a floodplain. In cooperation with the U.S. Fish and Wildlife Service and Dickson Mounds Museum of the Illinois State Museum, the 7,000 acre site, now renamed Emiquon, is destined to become one of the most important ecological sites in Illinois.

In 1937, three years after Joy's death, the University of Chicago Press published *Rediscovering Illinois*, the book written by Fay-Cooper Cole and

Thorne Deuel detailing their archaeological explorations in and around Fulton County. They dedicated it "To the late Joy Morton, in appreciation of his interest and his assistance in making much of this study possible." Since the establishment of Emiquon, the continuing relevance of the area as an archaeological site has been assured by interpretative exhibits at the Dickson Mounds Museum and by the renewed interest in the area's earliest inhabitants. After eighty years, the Hilltop site, now known as the Morton Village site, still yields important information on the Mississippian and Oneota habitations briefly established there between A.D. 1225–1275 and 1300–1325 respectively.[3]

*I*ncreasingly in his later years, Joy made an impact on the lives of many young people other than his close family members who were born in the second and third decades of the twentieth century. Katie van Gemert Eickhorst, the daughter of The Morton Arboretum's first plant propagator, recalled that when she was a little girl, Joy found her fishing from the bridge at Lake Marmo, something she had been forbidden to do. When she told him she was just feeding worms to the fish, he offered to pay her a penny for each worm she fed them. She never forgot that moment. Later, he offered to pay Katie's tuition for college.[4]

Joy's namesake, Joy Morton Porter, the son of Grove, was only six when Joy stayed with them in Nebraska City. The children were told to be on their best behavior before the visitor who often seemed formidable in countenance and demeanor. But at breakfast when the young Joy whispered into his mother's ear that Mr. Morton's toupee was askew, the elder Joy's countenance noticeably softened and a twinkle came into his eye. Forever after, Joy Morton Porter championed Joy Morton, thinking highly of the man who shared a work ethic and a passion for horses and arboriculture with his father and who passed that ethic and passion on to him.[5]

Joy also influenced the long life of Ted Vandenberg, who was a high school student in Naperville, Illinois, when he unexpectedly met Joy at the impressively well-appointed Thornhill library. Ted had tarried by himself in the library after being shown around by his friend, the houseboy, and he recalled being startled when Joy loomed in the doorway. When Vandenberg explained nervously that he was merely reading a book, Joy not only gave him permission to stay and read that day while he worked at his desk but ordered the servants that he should thereafter be allowed into the library anytime he wished. From then on, the local teenager and the septuagenarian of wealth and stature shared their reading of western history and biography.[6] Even into his nineties, Vandenberg, who spent much of his adult life as a delivery truck driver in Lisle, remained a lover of books and never tired of talking about his respect for "Mr. Morton."

Katie van Gemert Eichhorst, Joy Morton Porter, and Ted Vandenberg did not work for Joy in the salt company. Nor were they—like Mark, Paul, Carl, Jean, Sterling, Wirt, Suzette, Peterkin, Carrington, and the Warren brothers—of a generation that knew Joy on a daily basis. But their lives, they all agreed, were affected by the attention he paid to them when they were very young. He had the ability to inspire others, whether he first knew them as brothers, workers, neighborhood ruffians, aspiring immigrants, or legendary botanists. The Morton Arboretum, the monument by which Joy wanted most to be remembered, has continued to embody that spirit of inspiration for hundreds of thousands of people who visit this great outdoor museum of woody plants, study in its educational programs, and benefit from the research that is conducted there to assure that future generations will enjoy the beauty and bounty of trees.

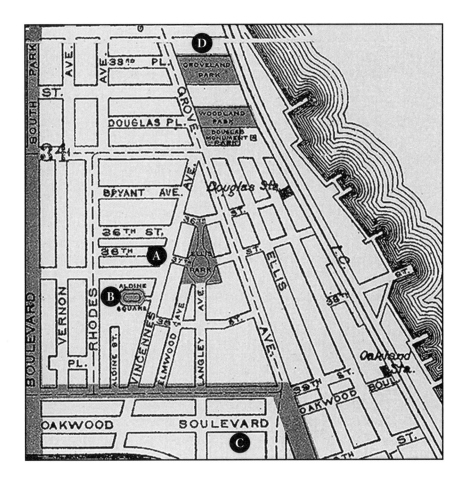

The Morton Family's Chicago—1880–1905

Addresses *(A, B)* on Aldine Square and Vincennes Avenue were Joy and Carrie Morton's first Chicago residences from 1880 to 1881. In 1882 they moved to a row house on East Oakwood Boulevard *(C)* where their children were born. In 1887 they rented a larger home on the south side of Groveland Park, an environmentally appealing wooded area near Lake Michigan that attracted upscale residents. Finding the area suitable for raising their children, they built a permanent residence in 1889 on the north side of Groveland Park *(D)*. Joy sold it in 1905.

The Mortons were close to the city limits on the far south side of the city, which, until the city extended southward in 1889, was bordered by 39th Street. These addresses were all changed by the city in the twentieth century, and the locations are now approximate. Aldine Square no longer exists. Neither does the house Joy built at Groveland Park.

Joy Morton's Immediate Family

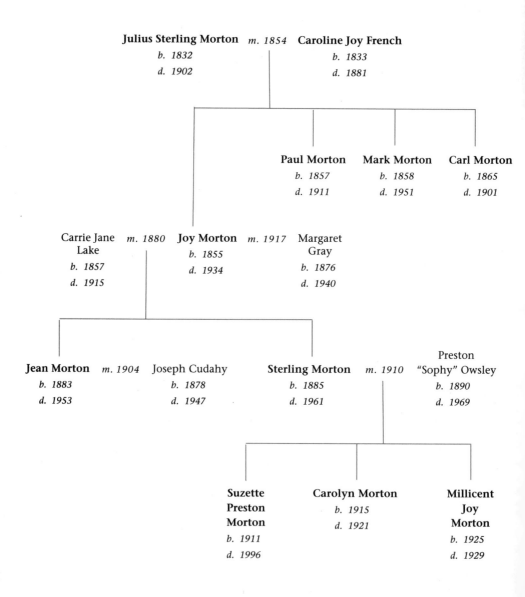

Julius Sterling Morton *m. 1854* **Caroline Joy French**
b. 1832 *b. 1833*
d. 1902 *d. 1881*

Paul Morton **Mark Morton** **Carl Morton**
b. 1857 *b. 1858* *b. 1865*
d. 1911 *d. 1951* *d. 1901*

Carrie Jane *m. 1880* **Joy Morton** *m. 1917* Margaret
Lake *b. 1855* Gray
b. 1857 *d. 1934* *b. 1876*
d. 1915 *d. 1940*

Jean Morton *m. 1904* Joseph Cudahy **Sterling Morton** *m. 1910* Preston
b. 1883 *b. 1878* *b. 1885* "Sophy" Owsley
d. 1953 *d. 1947* *d. 1961* *b. 1890*
d. 1969

Suzette **Carolyn Morton** **Millicent**
Preston *b. 1915* **Joy**
Morton *d. 1921* **Morton**
b. 1911 *b. 1925*
d. 1996 *d. 1929*

Joy Morton's Brothers' Families

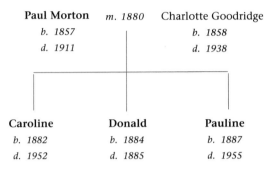

Paul Morton	m. 1880	Charlotte Goodridge
b. 1857		b. 1858
d. 1911		d. 1938

Caroline	Donald	Pauline
b. 1882	b. 1884	b. 1887
d. 1952	d. 1885	d. 1955

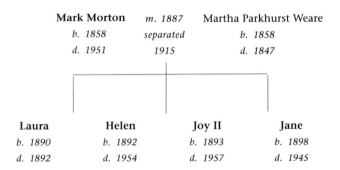

Mark Morton	m. 1887	Martha Parkhurst Weare
b. 1858	separated	b. 1858
d. 1951	1915	d. 1847

Laura	Helen	Joy II	Jane
b. 1890	b. 1892	b. 1893	b. 1898
d. 1892	d. 1954	d. 1957	d. 1945

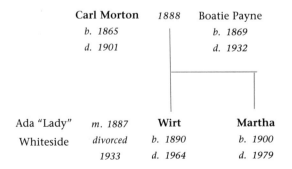

Carl Morton	1888	Boatie Payne
b. 1865		b. 1869
d. 1901		d. 1932

Ada "Lady"	m. 1887	Wirt	Martha
Whiteside	divorced	b. 1890	b. 1900
	1933	d. 1964	d. 1979

Notes

Abbreviations of Archives

CHM.   Chicago History Museum, Chicago, Illinois
        Unpublished biographies in CHM:
                SM. Sterling Morton
                FDO. Frank Dalton O'Sullivan
NSHS.   Nebraska State Historical Society, Lincoln, Nebraska
SML.   Sterling Morton Library, The Morton Arboretum, Lisle, Illinois.

Preface

1. Speech at dedication of The Morton Arboretum's Cudahy Auditorium, September 17, 1956.
2. CHM. August 11, 1932. (Hereafter all correspondence by or to Joy Morton unless otherwise noted.) The Henry B. Joy Research in Detroit was founded by Henry Bourne Joy, a president of Packard Motors, to conduct research on his father James F. Joy, a distant relative of Joy Morton, and railroad expansion in the nineteenth century. It later became Lincoln-Joy Research.

Prologue

1. CHM. Sterling Morton, unpublished biography (hereafter SM followed by chapter headings). "Prairie Boyhood," pp. 1–2.
2. NSHS. J. Sterling to Joy, November 28, 1886. I use J. Sterling's account of this journey. In his seventies, Joy gave a slightly different account during interviews with Frank Dalton O'Sullivan and Sterling Morton for their unpublished biographies.
3. CHM. SM. "Prairie Boyhood," pp. 1–2.
4. James C. Olson, *J. Sterling Morton* (Lincoln: University of Nebraska Press, 1942; Reprint: Nebraska State Historical Society Foundation, 1972), pp. 3–49.
5. *American Families* (New York: The American Historical Society, Inc. 1929), p. 145.
6. NSHS. J. Sterling to Joy, March 8, 1899.
7. NSHS. J. Sterling to his son Paul Morton, November 30, 1897, on the arrangement Caroline's foster parents made so that she could learn to manage a household: "During these months of experimental housekeeping she did the marketing and kept the accounts; and, in short, ran the entire establishment."
8. Olson, p. 15.
9. NSHS. J. Sterling to Joy, July 22, 1895. J. Sterling, then Secretary of Agriculture, was referring to Dr. Combe's *The Constitution of Man* (1828), a book that made Combe a leading phrenologist of his day. Later in his letter, J. Sterling combined Combe's ideas with his concept of Darwinian evolution, saying to Joy, "The time is not distant when a man will be as careful in the selection of a woman for his wife to become a mother of his children, as he is now in picking out a fine horse or other domestic animal."
10. Professor D.D. Whedon to J.D. Morton, July 3, 1854. Quoted in Olson, p. 23.
11. *The Detroit Free Press*, May 16, 1854. Quoted in Olson, p. 28.
12. See Olson, p. 29. With no apparent reason other than that he had been acting governor of the Nebraska Territory, J. Sterling was awarded a degree from Union College, Dr. Tappan's alma mater, in 1856. Michigan gave J. Sterling his degree in the fall of 1858, but only after Democratic President James Buchanan had named him Secretary of the Nebraska Territory.
13. Justin E. Walsh, *To Print the News and Raise Hell!: A Biography of Wilbur F. Storey*

(Chapel Hill: University of North Carolina Press, 1968). See also George B. Catlin, "Little Journeys in Journalism—Wilbur F. Storey," *Michigan History*, X (October 1926): pp. 515–533.

14. NSHS. November 18, 1854. Quoted in Olson, p. 36.

15. Olson, pp. 38–39.

16. NSHS. November 18, 1854. Quoted in Olson, p. 40.

17. *Nebraska Palladium*, December 6, 1854. Quoted in Olson, p. 40. The *Palladium* was a territorial newspaper that ceased publication in 1855.

18. CHM. To Emma, March 11, 1855. Also quoted in Olson, p. 40.

19. NSHS. November 25, 1886.

20. Ibid.

21. NSHS. February 21, 1855. Quoted in Olson, pp. 48–49.

22. NSHS. April 7, 1855. Quoted in Olson, p. 49.

23. Fort Kearney was the first settlement originally located on the site. In 1847, the War Department began the process of relocating the fort near what is now Grand Island. Nebraska City was incorporated around the old fort.

24. Citing Augustus F. Harvey, *Sketches of the Early Days of Nebraska City, Nebraska Territory, 1854–1860*, St. Louis: 1871, p. 11, Olson wrote that Nuckolls' slave, "probably was furnished the editor on printing days as an economy for both the town company and the editor. Shack was an enterprising Negro, but evidently he didn't absorb much of the Democratic doctrine preached by the *News*, for after the Civil War he is reported to have become a colored carpetbagger, and to have gone to Mississippi where he was last heard of as taking part in the deliberations of a Reconstruction Convention," p. 51.

25. See Gail DeBuse Potter, "The Evolution of Arbor Lodge, 1855–1904," *Nebraska History*, 73, no. 2 (Summer 1992): pp. 54–68.

26. NSHS. July 1855. Quoted in full in Margaret V. Ott, *Sterling's Carrie: Caroline Ann Joy French, Mrs. J. Sterling Morton,1833–1881* (Lincoln, Nebraska: 1989), pp. 43–45.

27. NSHA. Quoted in Ott, pp. 43–45.

28. CHS. SM, "Prairie Boyhood." Story as told by Joy to his son, pp. 1–2.

29. Olson, p. 58. This issue came back to haunt J. Sterling and, Olson contended, is probably a reason that no major city or site in Nebraska is named after J. Sterling, one of the state's most prominent settlers.

30. Olson, pp. 50–63. While J. Sterling acquitted himself as an articulate and passionate legislator in his first elected office, Olson concluded that he had a less comprehensive vision of the territory's needs than he did when he returned two years later.

31. Olson, p. 78. Olson suggested that J. Sterling had made Cuming something of a straw man for getting his own political agenda in place. After Cuming's death, J. Sterling praised him and, in 1866, spoke at a fund-raising event in Omaha to provide a memorial to Cuming.

32. Olson, pp. 89–92. Olson told of J. Sterling's sound advice on nonexistent Nebraska gold and decisiveness in the absence of the governor in putting down a brief Pawnee uprising on July 2, 1859.

33. Olson, pp. 95–115.

34. CHM. Hiram Joy to J. Sterling, August 22,1858.

35. CHM. November 25, 1858.

36. CHM. April 22, 1864.

37. Diary entry of April 15, 1865, quoted in Charles Olson, *J. Sterling Morton*, p. 133.

38. Following the Democratic Convention of 1864 nominating General George B. McClelland on an ambiguous platform, taking a stand against neither peace nor war, J. Sterling wrote, "I am for Peace, Peace Platform & Peace Man . . . and so we would deceive no one who is for war as the only means of restoring the Union. Peace *might*

restore it. War cannot & war makes disunion." Diary entry of August 23, 1864, quoted in Olson, p. 129.

39. NSHS. Quoted in Ott, pp. 97–98.

1—A Prairie Education

1. CHM. Joy to J.H. Sweet, Editor, *The Nebraska City News-Press*, October 23, 1929, published in the paper's Diamond Jubilee Edition.

2. CHM. SM, "Prairie Boyhood," p. 4.

3. Ibid., pp. 6–7.

4. Ibid., p. 6.

5. Ibid., p. 3.

6. The building still existed in March 2003, located behind the home of Joy Morton Porter, with whom I conducted an interview. The schoolhouse was used in the summers for tuberculosis patients until J. Sterling stopped the practice.

7. CHM. To J.H. Sweet, October 23, 1929.

8. CHM. SM, "Prairie Boyhood," pp. 4–5.

9. CHM. From typewritten notes of interviews by O'Sullivan and Sterling, unordered pages.

10. CHM. SM, p. 5.

11. Ibid.

12. CHM. SM, "Prairie Boyhood," p. 8.

13. Ibid., pp. 10–11.

14. Ibid.

15. Ibid., p. 12.

16. Ibid.

17. When Charles E. Perkins and Henry Strong of the Burlington and Missouri River Railroad came to Nebraska in December 1868, J. Sterling helped convince them of the wisdom of building a line that would afford transportation directly from Nebraska City. By 1869 he met with Lee Thielson, the chief engineer of the B&M, who carried word that the company would commit to the railroad. J. Sterling had already become involved in raising bond money to enable the enterprise. J. Sterling's acquaintance with Thielson helped him procure the job for Joy, who worked under the supervision of Thielson's son, Henry. See Olson, pp. 167–179, for J. Sterling's involvement in bringing rail transportation to Nebraska City.

18. CHM. SM, "Prairie Boyhood," pp. 13–17.

19. CHM. SM, "The Boy Freighters," pp. 1–7.

20. Ibid., pp. 7–8.

21. CHM. September 4, 1870.

22. CHM. October 13, 1870.

23. CHM. October 14, 1870.

24. CHM. October 28, 1870.

25. CHM. October 29, 1870.

26. CHM. November 7, 1870.

27. CHM. December 3, 1870.

28. CHM. November 20, 1870.

29. CHM. December 12, 1870.

30. CHM. December 24, 1870.

31. CHM. December [n.d.], 1870.

32. CHM. March 7, 1871.

33. CHM. April 6, 1871.

34. Ira Mayhew married Adelaide Sterling, Joy's grandmother's sister. (Information

gathered by Dan Muszynski, a genealogist of the Mayhew descendants living in Erie, Michigan, in 2007.) By the time Joy attended his great-uncle's college—the equivalent of a secondary school — Ira Mayhew had become a nationally recognized educator and advocate of universal education. Among his books were: *Popular Education: for the Use of Parents and Teachers, and for the Young Persons of Both Sexes*, N.Y.: Harper and Brothers, 1850; *The Means and Ends of Universal Education*, N.Y.: A.S. Barnes & Co., 1867; and *Mayhew's Practical Book-keeping Embracing Single and Double Entry, Commercial Calculations, and the Philosophy and Morals of Business*, Boston: S.F. Nichols, 1866. From 1853 to 1854, he was the principal of Wesleyan Seminary of Albion (which both J. Sterling and Caroline had attended); from 1854–1859, he served as Superintendent of Public Instruction for the State of Michigan; in 1860, he established the Albion Commercial College and, in 1869, moved it to Detroit where it became Mayhew's Business College. See Frank Passic, "Historical Albion Michigan," *Morning Star*, May 23, 2004, p. 20.

35. CHM. February 6, 1871.
36. CHM. February 11, 1871.
37. CHM. February 25, 1871.
38. CHM. April 2, 1871.
39. CHM. April 11, 1871.

2—A Prolonged Apprenticeship

1. CHM. SM, "The Boy Freighters," pp. 8–9.
2. CHM. December 29, 1871.
3. Olson, pp. 155–166. Two years later the State Board of Agriculture set the annual celebration on the second Wednesday in April. In 1885, Nebraskans voted to celebrate Arbor Day on April 22, J. Sterling's birthday.
4. CHM. Joy to Fisk and Hahn, Mutual Life Insurance Co. of New York, June 3, 1872.
5. CHM. November 20, 1872.
6. CHM. December 29, 1872.
7. Ibid.
8. CHM. January 9, 1873.
9. CHM. January 12, 1873.
10. CHM. January 16, 1873.
11. CHM. January 19, 1873.
12. CHM. February 28, 1873.
13. CHM. March 1, 1873.
14. CHM. March 5, 1873.
15. CHM. March 8, 1873.
16. CHM. March 14, 1873.
17. CHM. March 16, 1873.
18. CHM. July 24, 1873.
19. NSHS. J. Sterling's diary, September 7–18, 1873. Also see Olson, pp. 197–200.
20. In a speech delivered in 1956 at the dedication of the Rotunda and Cudahy Auditorium of the Administration Building of The Morton Arboretum, Sterling Morton wrote that his father and grandfather visited the Arnold Arboretum in 1876 for the centennial. There is no evidence that they were in the east together at that time. Joy visited Philadelphia by himself during the centennial celebration.
21. CHM. December 7, 1873. J. Sterling to Caroline, April 2, 1875, and Paul to Caroline, January 28, 1878.
22. CHM. A.B. Sharp to Sterling, May 6, 1875.
23. CHM. February 16, 1874.

24. NSHS. January 1, 1874.
25. NSHS. January 19, 1874.
26. NSHS. May 1, 1874.
27. NSHS. May 11 and 12, 1874.
28. CHM. SM, "Reminiscences of Early Manhood," p. 1. In the early 1930s, Joy recalled his treatment: "An interesting part of the treatment consisted in their method of keeping me warm. Nebraska in the summertime is hardly noted for its coolness, but the doctors felt that the warmer I was kept the better my chances of recovery would be. The method finally used was to take an ear of corn and boil it, then when very hot wrap it in towels and put it around me. You may well imagine that, from the standpoint of heat, this was a most efficacious treatment."
29. NSHS. July 18, 1874.
30. NSHS. July 13 and 15, 1874.
31. NSHS. September 7, 1874.
32. NSHS. September 25, 1874.
33. NSHS. Farm Journal. Passim, 1874.
34. CHM. December 28, 1874.
35. NSHS. December 28, 1874.
36. CHM. January 4, 1875.
37. CHM. January 20, 1875.
38. CHM. February 11, 1875.
39. CHM. February 27, 1875.
40. CHM. March 2, 1875.
41. CHM. March 4, 1875.
42. CHM. March 6, 1875.
43. CHM. March 29, 1875.
44. CHM. March 15, 1875.
45. CHM. May 22, 1875.
46. CHM. May 12, 1875.
47. CHM. May 23, 1875.
48. CHM. June 30, 1875.
49. CHM. July 4, 1871.
50. The school became Morgan Park Academy.
51. CHM. January 1, 1876.
52. CHM. J. Sterling to Joy, December 15, 1874. On March 12, 1877, Paul Morton gave his father stationery with an image of the 1876 renovation of Arbor Lodge. A few months prior to that, J. Sterling used a letterhead that read "Arbor Lodge near Nebraska City, Nebraska."
53. CHM. March 26, 28, and April 9, 1876.
54. NSHS. September 30, 1876.
55. NSHS. October 2, 1876.
56. CHM. Joy to J. Sterling and Caroline, October 30, 1876.
57. CHM. October 23, 1876.
58. CHM. February 15, 1877.
59. CHM. May 13, 1877.
60. CHM. May 19,1877.
61. CHM. July 2, 1877.
62. CHM. August 25, 1877.
63. CHM. October 1, 1877.
64. CHM. October 3, 1877.
65. CHM. November 24, 1877.
66. NSHS. January 1, 1878.

67. CHM. March 31, 1878.
68. CHM. April 3, 1878.
69. CHM. July 23, 1878.
70. CHM. September 19, 1878.
71. CHM. February 12, 1879.
72. CHM. May 16, 1879.
73. CHM. June 27, 1879.
74. CHM. July 23, 1879.
75. CHM. July 25, 1879.
76. CHM. August 1, 1879.
77. CHM. September 26, 1879.
78. CHM. September 28, 1875.
79. CHM. November 4, 1879.
80. CHM. November 10, 1879.
81. CHM. December 16, 1879.
82. CHM. December 2, 1879.
83. CHM. December 25, 1879.
84. CHM. January 5, 1879.
85. CHM. December 28, 1879.
86. CHM. December 30, 1879.

3—A Place in Chicago

1. Garnett Laidlaw Eskew, *Salt the Fifth Element: The Story of a Basic American Industry* (Chicago: J. Ferguson and Associates, 1948), pp. 130–133.
2. CHM. April 5, 1880.
3. CHM. May 22, 1880.
4. CHM. July 14, 1880.
5. CHM. August 24, 1880.
6. CHM. September 13, 1880.
7. CHM. September 17, 1880.
8. CHM. September 25, 1880.
9. CHM. November 9, 1890.
10. Ibid.
11. CHM. December 28, 1880.
12. CHM. January 1, 1881.
13. CHM. January 2, 1881.
14. CHM. January 4, 1881.
15. CHM. January 12, 1881.
16. CHM. January 14, 1881.
17. CHM. February 24, 1881.
18. CHM. February 25, 1881.
19. CHM. March 28, 1881.
20. CHM. April 22, 1881.
21. CHM. April 11, 1881.
22. CHM. May 8, 1881.
23. CHM. May 20, 1881.
24. CHM. June 20, 1881.
25. CHM. July 12, 1881.
26. CHM. July 18, 1881.
27. CHM. July 19, 1881.
28. CHM. July 20, 1881.

29. Ibid.
30. CHM. July 27 and August 24, 1881.
31. CHM. August 22, 1881.
32. CHM. August 30, 1881.
33. CHM. August 30, 1881.
34. CHM. September 19, 1881.
35. CHM. September 26, 1881.
36. CHM. November 30, 1881.
37. CHM. December 22, 1881.
38. NHS. December 29 and 31, 1881.
39. CHM. April 21, 1882.
40. CHM. April 24, 1882.

4—Joy Morton & Co.

1. CHM. May 21, 1882.
2. CHM. July 8, 1882.
3. CHM. August 9, 1882.
4. Ibid.
5. CHM. August 15, 1882.
6. CHM. September 15, 1882.
7. CHM. November 9, 1882.
8. CHM. September 22, 1882.
9. CHM. November 22, 1882.
10. CHM. Joy to J. Sterling, December 26, 1882.
11. CHM. March 22, 1882.
12. CHM. To J. Sterling, May 10, 1883.
13. CHM. August 3, 1883.
14. CHM. February 11, 1884.
15. CHM. February 13, 1882.
16. CHM. February 18, 1884.
17. CHM. March 8, 1884.
18. CHM. March 11, 1884.
19. CHM. April 3, 1884.
20. CHM. May 26, 1884.
21. Ibid.
22. CHM. SM. "Banking," p. 2.
23. CHM. May 10, 1885.
24. CHM. June 10, 1885.
25. CHM. September 4, 1885.
26. CHM. September 17, 1885.
27. CHM. September 18, 1885.
28. CHM. November 3, 1885.
29. CHM. November 4, 1885.
30. CHM. August 21, 1885.
31. CHM. November 21, 1885.
32. CHM. November 24, 1885.
33. CHM. December 17, 1885.
34. CHM. December 19, 1885.
35. CHM. December 31, 1885.
36. CHM. March 1 and May 25, 1886.
37. CHM. November 9, 1886.

38. CHM. January 19, 1887.
39. CHM. Joy to J. Sterling, January 8, 1887.
40. Walsh, *To Print the News and Raise Hell!*, pp. 277–278.
41. CHM. August n.d, 1887; September 3, 1887; September 27, 1887.
42. CHM. Mark to J. Sterling, September 22, 1887.
43. CHM. September 27, 1887.
44. CHM. November 10, 1887.
45. CHM. Sterling Morton sent this document to Paul M. Angle, then head of the Chicago Historical Society, saying that he considered it to be "very precious" and that it "should be kept by the Historical Society rather than the Company archives where it might get lost." Sterling told Angle that "the document leaves little doubt as to who was to be the 'Head Man.'"

5—Two Cities

1. When addresses were later renumbered, No. 32 became either 639 or 641.
2. CHM. J. Sterling to Joy, September 12, 1887.
3. *Guide to the Old University of Chicago Records 1856–1886* (The University of Chicago Library: 1856–1886, 2006). Also see Ron Chernow, *Titan: The Life of John D. Rockefeller, Sr.*, 1998, pp. 301–302 and 307.
4. CHM. March 2, 1889. Olmsted's South Park plan as well as his involvement with Daniel Burnham and the World's Columbian Exhibition is well documented, particularly in Elizabeth Stevenson's *Park Maker: A Life of Frederick Law Olmstead* (New York: Macmillan, 1977).
5. CHM. Sterling Morton manuscript, "Personal Traits."
6. John Drury, "Above the Elms of Groveland Park," *Old Chicago Houses* (Chicago: University of Chicago Press, 1941). In 1941, the house had been owned by another family for thirty-six years. Drury gives the address as No. 638, on the north side of the park, the city having changed the addresses. Today, those houses have all been torn down, and only the houses on the south side of the park remain.
7. CHM. SM. "Personal Traits."
8. CHM. Joy to J. Sterling, September 23, 1889.
9. CHM. Sterling Morton manuscript, "Banking."
10. "Men You Read About," *Chicago Daily Tribune*, February 23, 1890.
11. *The Morton Salt Tapestry, 1948–1973: A History of the People, Products and Facilities of the Morton Salt Company* (Chicago: Morton-Norwich Products, Inc., 1973) Compiled by the company on the 125th anniversary of the firm, pp. 5–6.
12. CHM. Joy to J. Sterling, January 19, 1890 and January 22, 1890.
13. Ibid., 6. Also Eskew, *Salt, the Fifth Element*, pp. 140–141.
14. CHM. March 24, 1888.
15. CHM. Joy to William Morton, April 6, 1888.
16. CHM. June 1, 1888.
17. CHM. July 19, 1888.
18. CHM. July 26, 1888.
19. CHM. July 19, 1888.
20. CHM. SM: "Other Business Ventures" and "Notes on Meat Packing Business."
21. CHM. Paul to J. Sterling, November 7, 1888. J. Sterling to Erskine M. Phelps, December 25, 1888.
22. CHM, January 3, 1889.
23. CHM. January 22, 1889; March 25, 1889; April 22, 1889
24. CHM. September 25, 1889; October 7, 1889.
25. CHM. January 21, 1890.

26. CHM. March 22, 1890; March 25, 1890.
27. CHM. May 5, 1890.
28. CHM. July, 14, 1890.
29. CHM. October 1, 1890.
30. CHM. November 1, 1890.
31. CHM. November 10, 1890 and December 8, 1890.
32. CHM. December 9, 1890.
33. CHM. January 16, 1891.
34. CHM. February 21, 1891.
35. CHM. July 6, 1891.
36. CHM. April 16, 1892.
37. CHM. August 8, 1892.
38. CHM. November 12, 1892.
39. CHM. December 20, 1892.
40. CHM. January 19, 1893.
41. CHM. March 17, 1893.
42. CHM. May 8, 1893; May 24, 1893.
43. CHM. May 23, 1893.
44. CHM. May 24, 1893.
45. CHM. June 26, 1893.
46. CHM. July 1, 1893.
47. CHM. Frank O'Sullivan manuscript, and Sterling Morton manuscript, "Personal Traits."
48. CHM. August 30, 1893 and September 4, 1893.
49. CHM. September 27, 1893.
50. CHM. Joy to J. Sterling, October 31, 1893 and November 7, 1893.
51. Erik Larson, *The Devil in the White City* (New York: Random House/Crown, 2003).
52. CHM. To J. Sterling, December 27, 1893.

6—Business and Politics

1. CHM. January 11, 1894.
2. CHM. February 26, 1894.
3. CHM. March 9, 1894.
4. CHM. February 26, 1894.
5. CHM. March 9, 1894.
6. CHM. March 18, 1894.
7. For an account of Joy's first Hutchinson plant, see Eskew, pp. 137–138; 146.
8. CHM. June 18, 1894.
9. CHM. August 21, 1894.
10. CHM. November 18, 1894.
11. CHM. November 19, 1894.
12. CHM. December 20, 1894.
13. CHM. Judge George Lake to Joy, August 22, 1881.
14. CHM. SM, "Other Business Ventures," pp. 10–12.
15. Ibid., pp. 13–14.
16. CHM. July 22, 1895.
17. CHM. SM, "Other Business Ventures," pp. 12–13.
18. CHM. March 16, 1895.
19. CHM. Joy to Paul, July 26, 1895.
20. CHM. March 14, 1895.

21. CHM. May 20, 1895.

22. CHM. July 5, 1895.

23. CHM. October 14, 1895.

24. CHM. October 23, 1895.

25. CHM. August 21, 1893.

26. CHM. December 5, 1893 and December 21, 1893.

27. CHM. May 18, 1894.

28. CHM. January 8, 1896.

29. CHM. March 11, 1896.

30. CHM. February 3, 1896.

31. CHM. February 25, 1896.

32. CHM. February 15, 1896.

33. CHM. February 20, 1896.

34. As Secretary of Agriculture, J. Sterling is quoted at length on the Vanderbilt estate in "Farm Fit for a King, Vanderbilt Has a Fine Place," *Chicago Record*, March 13, 1896. He had the Weather Bureau send recording instruments to Charles McNamee and offered cooperation "in every legitimate way possible." On June 17, 1898 J. Sterling wrote to the Vanderbilt estate that his visit convinced him that Vanderbilt's improvements "would result in a practical school of forestry for the United States." Information supplied by William Alexander, Landscape and Forest Historian, the Biltmore Company.

35. CHM. SM, Sterling wrote of Peterkin, "Of a pleasing personality, quick and able in negotiations and with almost uncanny ability to get at the essentials of a problem, he is today undoubtedly the active leader not only in the Morton Salt Company but in the salt industry of the country."

36. CHM. March 12, 1934.

37. CHM. SM. "Morton Salt Company," p. 7. At the turn of the century A.G. Warren headed up a company that "cooperated with Morton interests," distributing Texas salt from the Fiedler and Richardson companies until 1905. In 1907, B.W. Carrington & Company purchased the Fieldler Salt Company's plant and the Lone Star Salt Company in Texas, operating it until 1920 when it was acquired by the Morton Salt Company and Carrington became the western manager of Morton Salt and later the vice president.

38. Ibid.

7—Toward a New Century

1. CHM. September 8, 1896.

2. CHM. September 10, 1896.

3. CHM. September 8, 1896.

4. CHM. December 21, 1896.

5. CHM. January 3, 1897.

6. CHM. January 8, 1897.

7. Ibid.

8. CHM. February 9, 1897.

9. Ibid.

10. CHM. March 15, 1897.

11. CHM. April 13, 1897.

12. CHM. May 16, 1897.

13. CHM. September 30, 1897.

14. CHM. April 11, 1897.

15. CHM. April 25, 1897.

16. CHM. October 9, 1897.
17. CHM. June 18, 1896 and June 21, 1896.
18. CHM. To J. Sterling, November 13, 1896.
19. CHM. Joy to Morton Library board of trustees, October 15, 1897.
20. CHM. July 1, 1897.
21. CHM. January 3, 1897.
22. CHM. September 30, 1897.
23. CHM. October 6, 1897.
24. CHM. February 22, 1898.
25. CHM. March 13, 1898.
26. CHM. June 2, 7, and July 17, 1898.
27. CHM. May 13 and May 18, 1898.
28. CHM. August 9, 1899.
29. CHM. March 19, 1898.
30. Ibid.
31. CHM. March 13, 1898.
32. CHM. May 2, 1898.
33. CHM. July 17, 1898.
34. CHM. December 5, 1898.
35. CHM. December 19, 1899.
36. See James D. Norris and James Livingston, "Joy Morton and the Conduct of Modern Business Enterprise," *Chicago History: The Magazine of the Chicago Historical Society*, X, no. 1 (Spring 1981): 13–25. Norris and Livingston trace the extent and effect of Joy's entrepreneurial activities in American business history.
37. CHM. April 12, 1899.
38. CHM. September 5, 1899.
39. CHM. March 13, 1900.
40. CHM. December 20, 1899.
41. CHM. December 28, 1899.
42. CHM. January 13, 1900.
43. CHM. February 7, 1900.
44. "Bryan on Starch Trust," *The New York Times*, September 27, 1900.
45. "Bryan's Impeded Veracity," *The New York Times*, October 8, 1900.
46. CHM. February 24, 1900.
47. CHM. SM, "Other Business Ventures," p. 8.
48. CHM. March 16, 1900.
49. CHM. To Messrs. Nye, Scheider & Co., Fremont, Nebraska, March 6, 1900.
50. CHM. November 12, 1900.
51. CHM. November 15, 1900.
52. CHM. February 2, 1901.
53. CHM. From Report of the Executor, filed December 30, 1905.
54. CHM. Undated, 1902.

8—Civic Commitment

1. CHM. SM. "Personal Traits," pp. 4–7. Sterling gives an account of Joy's fascination with the motorcar.
2. Milo M. Quaife, with an introduction by Joy Morton, *Chicago's Highways Old and New: from Indian Trail to Motor Road* (Chicago: D. F. Keller & Company, 1923).
3. R.A. Nelson and K.M. Lovitt, "History of Teletypewriter Development," <http://www.vauxelectronics.com/gil/tty/docs/nelson&lovitt--tty-development.htm> (1963), 3 pages, and Howard L. Krum, "A Brief History of the Morkrum Company"

(circa 1925–1928), 7 pages, <http://www.rtty.com/history/krum.htm>. (The latter essay is edited by Jim Haynes of the University of California, Santa Cruz.) Also see Sterling Morton's "Teletype's Salty History," *The Spout*, Morton Salt publication, SML.

4. CHM. Joy to John Nordhouse, October 14, 1903.

5. The garden's design is often attributed to the noted landscape architect Warren H. Manning. Iowa State professor and landscape architect William J. Gundmann and his colleague Robert Harvey were asked to develop a plan for the garden's restoration in the early 1990s. They found no original plans for the garden. Grundmann conjectures that Manning, who, like Jarvis Hunt, had contributed to the 1893 Exposition, conversed informally with the architect on a design for the garden.

6. CHM. January 23, 1904.

7. Potter, p. 66, gives the count of principal rooms as forty-two. Generally, however, hallway sitting rooms and large closets are counted in the total by the current managers of Arbor Lodge.

8. CHM. Joy to Emma, August 29, 1904.

9. CHM. This included Jean Morton's wedding and a large and distinguished gathering for the dedication of J. Sterling Morton's statue on the grounds.

10. CHM. September 7, 1904.

11. CHM. Joy to Emma, October 15, 1904.

12. CHM. Jarvis Hunt's itemization, January 30, 1904.

13. For a detailed account of the immensity of the 1903 fire, see Eskew, pp. 145–151. Also see letter from Daniel Peterkin to Sterling Morton, CHM, June 30, 1933. Peterkin recalled that in 1906 a fire also destroyed a Kansas plant at Hutchinson built by Joy Morton & Co. in 1896. Later in 1914, the Hutchinson works suffered two cave-ins that took 2,500 carloads of sand to fill.

14. CHM. SM. "Buildings," pp. 3–9 and Frank Dalton O'Sullivan, "A Famous Office Building," pp. 1–21.

15. CHM. SM. Sterling Morton explained the boulevard system in 1933 in "Buildings": "All cross-traffic was forced to stop before entering onto a boulevard. Thus these streets became much safer thoroughfares for the cyclists and for private and public carriages than the other streets which were filled with slow-moving wagons. . . . Had these arteries not been in existence before the coming of the automobile, Chicago's traffic problem, great as it is, would have been almost impossible of [sic] solution," p. 5.

16. CHM. Frank Dalton O'Sullivan, "Civic Activities."

17. CHM. See Sterling to R.K. Warren, July 28, 1944, p. 2. Joy refers to Eddy and their involvement in the salt business in Sterling's interview notes, untitled, circa 1932, pp. 2–3.

18. CHM. February 11, 1905.

19. CHM. January 26, 1905.

20. CHM. March 21, 1905.

21. Ibid.

22. "Right on Paul Morton, Roosevelt to Moody: President Finally Declares no Prosecution Was Possible," *The New York Times*, December 18, 1905.

23. CHM. To Mark, April 29, 1905.

24. CHM. March 21, 1905.

25. CHM. October 14, 1905.

26. Information supplied in publications by Nebraska Game and Parks Commission and the Nebraska City Centennial Committee of Arbor Lodge, as well as via personal visits to the mansion and grounds.

27. Judge Lake's third wife, Abbie, was the first public schoolteacher in the state of Nebraska.

28. CHM. December 28, 1905. Also, "Joy Morton Is Better," *The New York Times*, December 29, 1905. Doctors had determined that Joy's skull was not fractured.

29. *The Morton Salt Tapestry*, p. 9.

30. CHM. April 28, 1908.

31. CHM. SM, "Other Business Ventures," p. 16.

32. Ibid., p. 17.

33. Ibid. A contemporary newspaper account reported that the Morton syndicate, headed by Joy and Paul, sold its rights to a syndicate headed by George N. Roberts, President of the First National Bank of Chicago and former director of the U.S. Mint. "Takes Over Morton Plan: Syndicate to Complete Irrigation Project in Wyoming Promoted by Brothers," *New York Times*, February 4, 1911.

34. CHM. SM. "Other Business Ventures," p. 18.

35. CHM. SM, "Banking," pp. 8–9 and FDO, "In the Banking Business," pp. 10–23.

36. CHM. SM, "Personal Traits."

37. SML. May 18, 1932.

38. Now Illinois Route 53.

39. CHM. Transcript of interviews with Joy at Thornhill, 1932–1934, pp. 6–7, and SM, "Genesis of Morton Salt Co.," pp. 11–12.

40. CHM. SM, "Morton Salt Company," p. 3.

41. *The Morton Salt Tapestry*, p. 9.

42. CHM. February 23, 1910.

43. CHM. November 11, 1910.

44. CHM. April 6, 1910.

45. CHM. April 7, 1910.

46. CHM. August 1, 1910.

47. CHM. March 29, 1911. Also see SM, "Banking," p. 11–12.

48. CHM. SM, "Other Business Ventures," pp. 9–10.

49. *The Morton Salt Tapestry*, p. 10.

50. CHM. SM, "Morton Salt Company," p. 4. Also *The Morton Salt Tapestry*, pp. 10–11.

9—The House on the Hill

1. CHM. Joy to Emma, September 9 and 13, 1910.

2. CHM. Joy to Emma, November 16, 1910.

3. CHM. January 16, 1911.

4. Joy's comments appeared in *The New York Daily News*, January 20, 1911 and *The Nebraska City News-Press*, January 21, 1911.

5. CHM. January 30, 1911.

6. CHM. January 31, 1911.

7. Ibid.

8. CHM. February 17, 1911.

9. CHM. To Abbie, April 18, 1911.

10. CHM. June 18, 1911.

11. CHM. July 18, 1911.

12. CHM. July 23, 1911.

13. CHM. July 25, 1911.

14. CHM. July 31, 1911.

15. CHM. August 3, 1911 and November 6, 1911.

16. CHM. September 23, 1911.

17. CHM. December 13, 1911.

18. CHM. November 6, 1911.

19. CHM. February 28, 1912.

20. CHM. March 18, 1912.

21. CHM. May 3, 1912.

22. CHM. To Abbie, May 13, 1912 and May 20, 1912.

23. CHM. To Abbie, May 31, 1912.

24. CHM. June 5, 1912.

25. CHM. To Abbie, September 3, 1912.

26. CHM. September 3, 1912.

27. CHM. To Abbie, November 9, 1912; November 12, 1912.

28. CHM. October 21, 1912.

29. CHM. November 12, 1912.

30. CHM. December 6, 1912.

31. CHM. December 27, 1912.

32. CHM. To Abbie, January 28, 1913.

33. CHM. March 23, 1913.

34. CHM. March 25, 1913.

35. CHM. April 1, 1913.

36. CHM. May 11, 1913.

37. CHM. June 16, 1913.

38. CHM. June 27, 1913.

39. CHM. August 8, 1913.

40. Ibid.

41. The diagnosis of dementia praecox would, of course, be questioned today.

42. CHM. August 26, 1913.

43. CHM. November 8, 1913.

44. CHM. November 14, 1913.

45. CHM. November 10, 1913.

46. CHM. To Abbie, November 17, 1913.

47. CHM. November 25, 1913.

48. CHM. December 13, 1913.

49. CHM. January 6, 1914.

50. CHM. January 14, 1914.

51. CHM. February 27, 1914.

52. CHM. March 4, 1914.

53. CHM. March 10, 1914.

54. CHM. March 13, 1914.

55. CHM. May 4, 1914.

56. CHM. May 14, 1914.

57. CHM. May 21, 1914.

58. CHM. June 15, 1915.

59. CHM. May 16, 1915.

60. CHM. July 20, 1914.

61. Ibid.

62. CHM. August 10, 1914.

63. CHM. To Abbie. September 8, 1914.

64. CHM. To Abbie. September 29, 1914.

65. CHM. October 21, 1914.

66. CHM. October 26, 1914.

67. CHM. December 8, 1914.

68. CHM. May 3, 1915.

69. CHM. May 20, 1915.

70. CHM. September 16, 1915.

71. CHM. October 11, 1915.

72. CHM. October 30, 1915.

73. CHM. November 23, 1915.

74. CHM. December 14, 1915.

75. *Chicago Daily Tribune*, December 16, 1915. Talbot, the boys' school Joy attended on the outskirts of Nebraska City, and Brownell had been founded by Bishop Joseph O. Talbot in 1860 and 1863 respectively. Bishop Talbot had been the Episcopal Bishop of the Northwest, which included the Nebraska Territory. Today, Brownell has become Brownell-Talbot, a co-educational college preparatory school still located in Omaha, Nebraska.

76. CHM. To Abbie. February 16, 1916.

77. CHM. April 6, 1916.

78. CHM. June 6, 1915.

79. Carolyn Owsley Morton was named after her grandmother.

80. CHM. June 13, 1916.

10—War: Home and Abroad

1. CHM. June 6, 1913.

2. CHM. SM, "Morton Salt Company," pp. 11–12.

3. CHM. February 23, 1914.

4. CHM. To Boatie, March 22, 1914.

5. CHM. September 16, 1915 and September 20, 1915.

6. William Cronon, *Nature's Metropolis: Chicago and the Great West* (New York: W.W. Norton & Company, 1991), details how the railroad doomed the Illinois and Michigan Canal almost from the start.

7. For a concise history of the Hennepin Canal, see Mary M. Yeater, "The Hennepin Canal." Reprint from *American Canals* (American Canal Society, November 1976–August 1978).

8. CHM. "The Potentiality of Waterways," pp. 4–6.

9. CHM. Ibid., p. 7.

10. *Sheffield Times*, October 5, 1917.

11. SML. Delivered on Illinois waterway trip that took place June 16–June 19, 1921, 12 pages.

12. SML. October 17, 1923.

13. In addition to his speech before the National Rivers and Harbors Association, Joy continued to urge reconstruction of the I&M whenever he could. See letter to Lieut. Co. W.V. Judson, Corps of Engineers, in James William Putnam, *The Illinois and Michigan Canal: A Study in Economic History* (Chicago: University of Chicago Press, 1918), Appendix IV, pp. 175–180, and speech delivered to members of the Illinois Chamber of Commerce on a waterway trip in 1919, SML.

14. *Ludington Daily News*, Wednesday, December 6, 1916.

15. SML. Caroline McIlvaine, CHS librarian, to Joy Morton, November 16, 1916 and letter from Joy to the chief clerk of the Smithsonian, dated December 11, 1916.

16. Kay E. Lant, president of the Newburgh Historical Society, supplied information on Margaret Gray's family.

17. CHM. To Sterling, December 19, 1916.

18. CHM. SM, "Banking," p. 5.

19. Ibid., p. 6.

20. Ibid., p. 3.

21. Ibid., p. 7.

22. Ibid.

23. CHM. June 19, 1917.

24. CHM. August 10, 1917.

25. Ibid.

26. SML. Homecoming speech.

27. CHM. To M.M. Vaughn, November 30, 1917.

28. CHM. June 28, 1917.

29. CHM. July 19, 1917.

30. CHM. July 18, 1918.

31. CHM. January 6, 1919.

32. CHM. February 6, 1919.

33. CHM. February 26, 1919. Joy went up in a Curtis hydroplane.

34. CHM. April 29, 1919.

35. The invitation to speak at the commencement was initiated by W.G. Bierd, a trustee of the college and chairman of the Chicago and Alton Railroad. When Paul was Secretary of the Navy, he had been responsible for Bierd receiving an appointment as general manager of the Panama Railroad from President Theodore Roosevelt.

36. CHM. July 31, 1919.

11—The Morton Arboretum

1. SML. To Arthur Sherwood, December 11, 1920.

2. SML. December 22, 1920.

3. SML. January 19, 1921 and January 3, 1921.

4. Mark's farm was later sold and did not become part of the Arboretum.

5. SML. February 1, 1921.

6. SML. February 7, 1921.

7. SML. From Biarritz, March 25, 1921.

8. SML. From Tours, March 25, 1921.

9. SML. From Biarritz, March 25, 1925.

10. SML. Sterling to Joy, March 29, 1921.

11. SML. To Sterling, from Paris, April 12, 1921.

12. SML. April 1, 1921.

13. SML. April 27, 1921.

14. SML. From Scotland, June 18, 1921.

15. SML. July 6, 1921.

16. SML. See Simonds' meticulous notes from mid-June 1921 to the end of 1922 on his conversations with Joy and observations of the progress of the work.

17. SML. August 1, 1921.

18. SML. August 9, 1921.

19. SML. August 24, 1921.

20. SML. September 7, 1921.

21. SML. October 6, 1921.

22. Now Illinois Route 53.

23. SML. August 29, 1921.

24. SML. September 29, 1921.

25. SML. Clarence Godshalk outlined the principal facts of personnel, development, and other matters related to development of the Arboretum. His first entry is for 1921.

26. SML. October 14, 1921.

27. SML. November 28, 1921.

28. SML. December 29, 1921.

29. SML. December 31, 1921.

30. SML. January 12, 1922.

31. SML. February 28, 1922.

32. SML. Clarence Godshalk, "Outline of Arboretum Development."

33. SML. December 15, 1922. Today The Morton Arboretum occupies 1,700 acres.

34. SML. January 24, 1923.

35. SML. April 18, 1923.

36. SML. May 11, 1923.

37. SML. November 20, 1923.

38. SML. November 28, 1923.

39. SML. February 28, 1924.

40. SML. May 26, 1924.

41. Ibid.

42. SML. June 5, 1924.

43. SML. June 9, 1924.

44. SML. April 17, 1925.

45. *The Bulletin* was replaced by *The Morton Arboretum Quarterly* in 1965.

46. SML. Teuscher insisted on using the Latin title: *Enumeratio plantarum—arborum, arbusculorum, herbarum et filicum—in ARBORETO MORTONIANO observatarium auctore H. Teuscher; seu.*

47. SML. September 21, 1923.

48. SML. December 15, 1925. Still active almost until his eighty-sixth birthday, Professor Sargent died in March 1927.

12—Investing in Illinois

1. "Men and Methods," *System: The Magazine of Business* (February 1926): pp. 230–231.

2. SML. January 16, 1920.

3. Joy Morton Porter's accounts of the Joy Morton Orchards Company and the relationship between Joy and Morton Porter's father, Grosvenor, are at the Lied Conference Center in Nebraska City. Part of this account is also written from interviews I have had with Joy Morton "Mort" Porter in 2003.

4. SML. Joy to Sterling, September 29, 1921.

5. Morton-James Library. June 29, 1922.

6. SML. July 3, 1922.

7. "Architects of World Compete for the *Tribune*," *Chicago Daily Tribune*, November 2, 1922.

8. CHM. April 5, 1923.

9. CHM. April 14, 1923.

10. CHM. August 28, 1923.

11. Morton-James Library. From a perspective of six years after the Transfer Day speech, the editor of *The Nebraska City News-Press* recounted the scene in an article titled "When Arbor Lodge Park Was Donated to Nebraska in 1923," November 14, 1929.

12. SML. Joy used the language of James 2:26, words his audience would have known. The crowd would also have understood the Emersonian emphasis upon self-reliance, which had dominated American business philosophy since the mid-nineteenth century.

13. The original Nebraska City schoolhouse is in the rear of the house, which was still standing in 2005. Joy Morton Porter lived there until 2005.

14. CHM. To Ida N. Clendenan, December 31, 1917.

15. CHM. December 29, 1919.

16. CHM. January 5, 1920.

17. CHM. January 9, 1922.

18. SML. July 2, 1922.

19. CHM. July 10, 1923.

20. CHM. July 12, 1923.

21. CHM. December 6, 1923.

22. CHM. December 12, 1923. McClurg's later became Krock's and Brentano's, a well-known bookstore on Wabash Avenue in Chicago.

23. CHM. February 15, 1924.

24. CHM. December 6, 1923 and February 20, 1924.

25. CHM. June 11, 1924.

26. CHM. To Eames MacVeagh, May 19, 1925.

27. CHM. Eugene Prussing to Quaife, August 25, 1925.

28. CHM. August 26, 1925.

29. CHM. September 11, 1925.

30. CHM. December 5 and 10, 1923. Jean Howard was the widow of Colonel Guy Howard, who owned the masque. Howard died in action in the Philippines in 1899.

31. CHM. Professor James Westfall Thompson of the University of Chicago helped Joy prepare his remarks, in particular a remarkably detailed and insightful account of Napoleon's part in the negotiations for the Louisiana Purchase. (See letter to Joy from the CHS librarian, Caroline McIlvaine, in CHM.) The masque has now been de-accessioned.

32. CHM. SM. "Farming Operations," revised on February 28, 1934, shortly before Joy's death. Also see Stephen P. Havera, Katie E. Roat, and Lynn L. Anderson, *The Thompson Lake/Emiquon Story: The Biology, Drainage, and Restoration of an Illinois River Bottomland Lake* (Champaign: Illinois Natural History Survey Special Publication, 25 October 2003), pp. 18–33.

33. In 2002, The Nature Conservancy purchased the land and began to return it to its original floodplain state. Now, in cooperation with the U.S. Fish and Wildlife Service and the Illinois State Museum, the area consists of a 7,000-acre natural wildlife area with public access. It is known as Emiquon. This has been the Conservancy's largest purchase to date in Illinois.

34. CHM. SM, "Farming Operations," p. 5.

35. John Thompson, *Wetlands Drainage, River Modification, and Sectoral Conflict in the Lower Illinois River Valley, 1890–1930* (Carbondale: Southern Illinois University Press, 2001), p. 147.

36. CHM. August 18, 1922.

37. SML. Teuscher's unpublished memoir, "Memories," pp. 43–46.

38. CHM. September 15, 1925.

39. SML. November 23, 1925.

40. SML. December 7, 1925.

41. As it started work on the Morton Building, the architectural firm of Graham, Anderson, Probst and White was just completing Chicago's neoclassical Union Station, designed by Daniel Burnham in 1911.

42. On September 25, 1926, the *Chicago Daily Tribune* published details of Joy's lease to Illinois Bell. Two doorways between the building were to be cut through on each of six stories between the tenth and fifteenth floors. Illinois Bell had an option to take over the sixth and nineteenth floors as well, giving the telephone company a space of 100,000 square feet.

43. Copy of list of cornerstone contents, dated May 14, 1926, in CHM.

44. SML. August 24, 1926.

45. "Teletype: $30,000,000 Worth of Teletype . . . How Salt Helped It Grow and How Salt Finally Sold It," *Fortune,* V, no. 3 (March 1932): 44.

46. SML. August 15, 1926.

47. SML. July 28, 1926.

48. SML. August 9, 1926.

49. SML. August 24, 1926.

50. SML. "His Seventieth Birthday," a booklet of photographs and descriptions of the festivities distributed to attendees.

51. CHM. SM. Sterling provided a lengthy account of this enterprise in "Farming Operations," pp. 12–18. He wanted to assure his readers that strong measures were taken to preserve wildlife as well as to hunt it and that trapping was a common practice even on philanthropic refuges.

52. SML. December 10, 1925.

13—Embracing the Future

1. CHM. October 13, 1926.

2. Ibid.

3. CHM. November 22, 1926.

4. CHM. February 14, 1927.

5. CHM. Joy Morton, "Morton Visions Vast Expansion for South Side: Sees River Unkinking as Aid to Traffic," *Chicago Daily Tribune*, Thursday, January 20, 1927.

6. Daniel H. Burnham and Edward H. Bennett, edited by Charles Moore, with a new introduction by Kristen Schaffer, *Plan of Chicago, 1909* (New York: Princeton Architectural Press, 1993) pp. 74–76.

7. Oscar Hewitt, "City Planners Urge Air Right Development: Joy Morton, W.H. Wilson Deplore Delay," *Chicago Daily Tribune*, October 29, 1927.

8. See E.B. Sutton, *Charles Sprague Sargent and the Arnold Arboretum* (Cambridge: Harvard University Press), 1970.

9. CHM. October 31, 1927.

10. CHM. November 20, 1927.

11. See www.dawesarb.org.

12. SML. The American elms (*Ulmus americana*), which Joy praised in his speech for being "the most beautiful species of the elm family that we now know," later died of Dutch elm disease and were replaced by an American smoke tree (*Cotinus obovatus*).

13. CHM. November 28, 1927.

14. CHM. May 7, 1928.

15. SML. May 13, 1928.

16. CHM. May 23, 1928.

17. CHM. September 28, 1928.

18. CHM. October 4, 1928.

19. CHM. October 9, 1928.

20. CHM. November 7, 1928.

21. Sue was not the only woman in the Morton family who felt this way. She no doubt was influenced by the work of Joy's niece, Pauline Morton Smith Sabin, the youngest daughter of Paul and Charlotte. Pauline, who had grown into womanhood in the social stratosphere of New York and had been the first woman representative to the Republican National Committee in the 1920s, became a nationally known opponent of Prohibition when she founded the Women's Organization for National Prohibition Reform in 1929 to fight the corruption in government that she thought the 18th Amendment had promulgated. For that and other accomplishments, Pauline would be featured on the cover of *Time*, July 18, 1932.

22. CHM. November 11, 1928.

23. HM. November 19, 1928.

24. CHM. SM, "Personal Traits," p. 12. Sterling said that Joy "has usually been a Democrat, due undoubtedly to his father's life-long association with that part. He is, however, entirely independent and has probably voted for as many Republican candidates as Democrats. During the 'Bull Moose' excitement he followed Theodore Roosevelt. He has taken no active part in politics but has contributed generously when he felt that certain reforms were needed."

25. On June 11, 1931, Kammerer was joined by Walter Eichhorst who served as labeler and stenographer. Godshalk, van Gemert, Kammerer, and Eichhorst spent their long professional lives at the arboretum. Eichhorst was still volunteering at the arboretum as the twenty-first century began.

26. CHM. June 1, 1929.

27. CHM. July 23, 1929.

28. CHM. August 4 and 6, 1929.

29. Interview with Fred Berg, who worked at The Morton Arboretum for 47 years and whose grandfather, also named Fred, and father worked for Joy. Interviewed on February 5, 2001.

30. John Kenneth Galbraith, *The Great Crash: 1929* (Boston: Houghton Mifflin Company, 1954), (Cambridge: Riverside Press, 1961), pp. 103–5.

31. CHM. October 23, 1929.

32. Ibid.

33. Margaret Gray Morton, *Around the World* (privately printed, 1931), p. 3.

34. Ibid., p. 51.

35. Ibid., p. 56.

36. Ibid., p. 234.

37. CHM. FOD. "An Extensive Traveler" and Carol Doty, "Joy Morton and the Forbidden City: A Mystery Solved?" *The Morton Arboretum Quarterly*, 25, no. 3 (Autumn 1989): 33–48.

38. *Around the World*, p. 26.

39. Ibid., p. 214.

40. SML. January 17, 1930.

41. CHM. May 2, 1930.

42. CHM. April 1, 1930.

43. CHM. May 3, 1930.

44. One letter went to H. Bates, Jr. at the Columbia Club in Indianapolis on July 25, 1930. Joy described the work being done on his land by the University of Chicago and the Smithsonian Institute.

45. CHM. July 21, 1930.

46. Gordon Wiley and Jeremy Sabloff wrote in *A History of American Archaeology* (San Francisco: W.H. Freeman and Company, 1974) that the archaeological investigations of Cole and Deuel offered, "The first systematic attempt to view American archaeological data from a functional point of view . . . ," that is, "listing all of the discovered archaeological traits of any site component . . . under functional categories, such as 'Architecture and House Life,' 'Agricultural and Food-getting,' or 'Military and Hunting Complex,'" p. 135.

47. CHM. FDO. "'Teletype' Promotion and Sale."

48. CHM. "Morton Salt Company," edited January 1934, pp. 14–15.

49. SML. "Old Roads to Nebraska City." Speech at the dedication of the Waubonsie Bridge, Nebraska City, October 17, 1930.

50. CHM. May 26, 1931.

51. Ibid.

52. Ibid.

53. CHM. SM, "Morton Salt Company."

54. CHM. July 14, 1931.

55. CHM. October 14, 1931.

56. SML. Speech at Nebraska City for centennial of J. Sterling's birth and sixtieth year celebration of Arbor Day, April 22, 1932.

57. CHM. June 1, 1932.

58. CHM. August 11 and 15, 1932.

59. CHM. Box 50, November 11, 1932.

60. CHM. August 23, 1932.

61. CHM. October 11, 1932.

62. Ibid.

63. CHM. November 14, 1932.

64. CHM. November 17, 1932.

65. CHM. May 19, 1934.

66. Ibid.

67. Interview with Walter Eickhorst, former curator of plant collections for The Morton Arboretum, February 19, 2002.

Epilogue

1. *The Morton Salt Tapestry: 1848–1997*, p. 18ff.

2. Scriptorium from the Chicago Plan Commission, signed by James Simpson, Chairman, and Albert A. Sprague, Vice Chairman. Simpson was head of Marshall Field's, and Col. Sprague was a businessman and later a Chicago commissioner.

3. In the summer of 2008, the Michigan State University Archaeological Field School, hosted by the Nature Conservancy and Dickson Mounds, renewed investigations at the Morton site.

4. Interview with Katherine van Gemert Eickhorst, February 19, 2002.

5. Interview with Joy Morton Porter in Nebraska City in 2002. Porter has written at length about the relationship between his father and Joy Morton. His unpublished essays and speeches are in bound format in the Lied Lodge Library Lounge.

6. Interview with Ted Vandenberg in 2002 at his home in Lisle, Illinois. Vandenberg remained appreciative of Joy's early interest in him and was an avid reader until his death in 2007.

Selected Bibliography

Primary Sources

MORTON ARCHIVES

Sterling Morton Library, The Morton Arboretum, Lisle, Illinois
> Correspondence and other papers related to The Morton Arboretum, Morton Salt, and Morton family, 1910–present.
> Kerr, Bernice. Untitled Morton Salt Company History from Morton Salt Company, 1963.
>> Public Addresses by Joy Morton:
>>> Commencement Address, June 4, 1919. Blackburn College, Carlinville, Illinois.
>>> Homecoming address comparing Chinese and American agriculture. Delivered in Nebraska City, August 16, 1917.
>>> Joy and Sterling Morton, "Addresses Delivered by Sterling Morton and Joy Morton at the 100th Aniversary of the Birth of J. Sterling Morton and the 60th Anniversary of the Founding of Arbor Day." Nebraska City, Nebraska, April 22, 1932.
>>> "Old Roads to Nebraska City." Dedication of Waubonsie Bridge, Nebraska City, Nebraska, October 17, 1930.
>>> On the occasion of the Illinois Chamber of Commerce waterway trip, June 16 or 17, 1917.
>>> "The Potentiality of Waterways." Address before the National Rivers and Harbors Association at Washington, D. C., December 7, 1916.
>>> "Presentation of the Death Masque of Napoleon Bonaparte to the Chicago Historical Society by Joy Morton," February 18, 1924.
>>> "Transfer Day." Presentation of Arbor Lodge to the State of Nebraska, Nebraska City, September 27, 1923.
>>> To "Waterways Committee of the United States Senate," October 17, 1923.
> Porter, Joy Morton. Essays in remembrance of Joy Morton, courtesy of Joy Morton Porter and The National Arbor Day Foundation. Manuscripts in bound volume at the Lied Conference Center, Nebraska City, Nebraska. Copies at Sterling Morton Library, The Morton Arboretum, Lisle, Illinois: "Apple Promotions and Sales at Arbor Day Farm," "Joy Morton Remembered," "The Gentle Apple Man," and "Joy Morton: Entrepreneur and Philanthropist." 2003.
> Sloan, Lynda Frank. "'When It Rains It Pours': The Story of Joy Morton." Manuscript copy in Sterling Morton Library, The Morton Arboretum, Lisle, Illinois.
> *The Spout*, Morton Salt publication.
> Teuscher, Henry. "Memories." Manuscript copy in Sterling Morton Library, The Morton Arboretum, Lisle, Illinois.

Chicago History Museum, Chicago, Illinois
> Correspondence and other papers related to Joy Morton and his family. 1855–1934. Provenance of Suzette Morton Davidson. Some copies in Joy Morton Archives, SML.
> Morton, Sterling. Untitled and unfinished biography, 1933–1935.
> O'Sullivan, Frank Dalton. "Seventy-Five Years in the Midwest, A story that deals with the early settlers of Plymouth and Boston, the pioneers of the

Western prairies, and the romance of business in a great American City, as exemplified by the life of Joy Morton, 1932–1933." Unfinished biography.

Nebraska State Historical Society, Lincoln, Nebraska.
  J. Sterling Morton Papers, 1849–1902. Farm journals and correspondence from 1849–1902. Provenance of Mark Morton to the University of Nebraska Library. Transferred to NSHS in 1954. Some copies in Morton-James Library, Nebraska City, Nebraska.

INTERVIEWS

Ballowe, James, recorded: with Walter Eichhorst, The Morton Arboretum Plant Clinic (November 14, 2000); with Katie Van Gemert Eickhorst and Walter Eickhorst, The Morton Arboretum Plant Clinic (February 29, 2002); with Fred Berg, The Morton Arboretum (September 5, 2001); with Joy Morton Porter, at home in Nebraska City, (March 24, 2003); and with Ted Vandenberg, at home in Lisle, Illinois (March 7, 2002). Recordings in Sterling Morton Library, The Morton Arboretum, Lisle, Illinois.

Rosenaw, John, president of the National Arbor Day Foundation: transcripts of recorded interviews with Grosvenor (Grove) M. Porter, Joy Morton's partner in the Joy Morton Orchard Company, 1981 and 1983. Courtesy of the National Arbor Day Foundation. In Lied Conference Center, Nebraska City, Nebraska. Copy in Sterling Morton Library, The Morton Arboretum, Lisle, Illinois.

NEWSPAPERS

Chicago Daily Tribune (later, *Chicago Tribune*)
The Nebraska City News-Press
The New York Times

Secondary Sources

American Families. New York: The American Historical Society, Inc. 1929.

Arbor Lodge: J. Sterling Morton and Family, Vol. I Nebraska City, NE: Arbor Day Centennial Committee, 1972.

Arbor Lodge: State Historical Park, Vol. II, Arbor Day Centennial Committee, 1972.

Ballowe, James. *A Great Outdoor Museum: The Story of The Morton Arboretum*. Lisle, IL: The Morton Arboretum, 2003.

Burnham, Daniel H. and Edward H. Bennett. *Plan of Chicago*, The Commercial Club of Chicago, July 4, 1909; facsimile edition, New York, Princeton Architectural Press, 1993.

Catlin, George B. "Little Journeys in Journalism—Wilbur F. Storey." *Michigan History*, X (October 1926): 515–533.

Chernow, Ron. *Titan: The Life of John D. Rockefeller, Sr.* New York: Random House, 1998.

Cole, Fay-Cooper, and Thorne Deuel. *Rediscovering Illinois: Archaeological Explorations in and Around Fulton County*. Chicago: The University of Chicago Press, 1937.

Cronon, William. *Nature's Metropolis: Chicago and the Great West*. New York: W.W. Norton & Company, 1991.

Cunningham, Don. "Villains, Miscreants, and the Salt of the Earth," *NEBRASKAland*, Nebraska Game and Parks Commission, 63, no. 6 (July 1985): 14–19; 45–47.

Doty, Carol. "Joy Morton and the Forbidden City: A Mystery Solved?" *The Morton Arboretum Quarterly*, 25, no. 3 (Autumn 1989): 33–48.

———. "The Arboretum's Architectural Heritage," *The Morton Arboretum Quarterly,* Part I, 26, no. 4 (Winter 1990): 49–60; Part II: 27, no. 1 (Spring 1991): 1–9; Part III: 27, no. 4 (Winter 1991): 58–64.

Drury, John. *Old Chicago Houses.* Chicago: University of Chicago Press, 1941.

Eskew, Garnett Laidlaw. *Salt, The Fifth Element: The Story of a Basic American Industry.* Chicago: J. Ferguson and Associates, 1948.

Galbraith, John Kenneth. *The Great Crash: 1929.* New York: Houghton Mifflin, 1954; Reprint: Cambridge: Riverside Press, 1961.

Gilbert, Paul, Charles Lee Bryson, and Caroline M. McIlvaine (historical adviser), with a chapter on Chicago hotels and restaurants by Wallace Rice. *Chicago and Its Makers: A Narrative of Events, 1833–1929.* Chicago: Felix Mendelshon, 1929.

Griffin, Donald W. "The Commercial Failure of the Hennepin Canal," *Western Illinois Regional Studies*, XIV, no. 1 (Spring 1991): 27–48.

Grossman, James R., Ann Durkin Keating, and Janice L. Reiff, eds. *The Encyclopedia of Chicago.* Developed by the Newberry Library with the cooperation of the Chicago Historical Society, Chicago: The University of Chicago Press, 2004.

Havera, Stephen P., Katie E. Roat, and Lynn L. Anderson. *The Thompson Lake/Emiquon Story: The Biology, Drainage, and Restoration of an Illinois River Bottomland Lake.* Champaign: Illinois Natural History Survey Special Publication 25, October 2003, pp. 18–33.

His Seventieth Birthday. Joy Morton's birthday, celebrated September 25, 1930, Thornhill, Lisle, IL, privately printed.

Howe, Walter A., compiler. *Documentary History of the Illinois and Michigan Canal: Legislation, Litigation and Titles.* Issued by Division of Waterways, State of Illinois, 1956.

Illinois Steward, The, Vol. 11, no. 3 (Fall 2002). Special issue on the history of the Illinois River and recent restoration efforts on land owned by Joy Morton. See especially. Susan Post, "Time Along the River" and Douglas Blodgett, "Emiquon—A Place of Hope on the Illinois River."

Joy, James Richard, compiler. *Thomas Joy and His Descendants: A Portfolio of Family Papers.* New York: privately printed, 1900. Reprinted: Kessinger Publishing Company, 2007.

Kazin, Michael. *A Godly Hero: The Life of William Jennings Bryan.* New York: Alfred Knopf, 2006. Anchor Books edition, 2007.

Krum, Howard L. "A Brief History of the Morkrum Company: Ancestor of Teletype Corporation." Abstract circa 1925–1928. <http://www.rtty.com/history/krum. htm> Via Jim Haynes at University of California, Santa Cruz.

Kurlansky, Mark. *Salt: A World History.* New York: Walker and Company, 2002.

Larson, Erik. *The Devil in the White City: Murder, Magic, and Madness at the Fair That Changed America.* Random House/Crown, 2003.

McCarthy, Kathleen D. *Noblesse Oblige: Charity & Cultural Philanthropy in Chicago, 1849–1929.* Chicago: University of Chicago Press, 1982.

Miller, Donald L. *City of the Century: The Epic of Chicago and the Making of America.* New York: Simon and Schuster, 1996–2003.

Morton, Joy. "Men and Methods." *System: The Magazine of Business* (February,1926): 230–231.

Morton, Margaret Gray. *Around the World.* Privately printed, 1931.

Morton Salt Bulletin, published by Morton Salt Company Patriotic Association, Chicago, September 27, 1918, vol. I, no. 1.

Morton Salt Tapestry, The: 1848–1973: A History of the People, Products and Facilities of the Morton Salt Company, Chicago: Morton-Norwich Products, Inc., 1973.

Nelson, R. A. and K. M. Lovitt, note by Jim Haynes, formatted by Gil Smith. "History of Teletypewriter Development." 1923. <http://www.vauxelectronics.com/gil/tty/ docs/nelson&lovitt--tty-development.htm>2004.

Noble, Glenn. *Frontier Steamboat Town: First Fort Kearny—Nebraska City—Westward Impact.* Lincoln, Nebraska: Midgard Press, 1989.

Norris, James D. and James Livingston, "Joy Morton and the Conduct of Modern Business Enterprise," *Chicago History: The Magazine of the Chicago Historical Society*, X, no. 1 (Spring 1981): 13–25.

Olson, James C. *J. Sterling Morton.* Lincoln: University of Nebraska Press, 1942; Reprint: Nebraska State Historical Society Foundation, 1972.

Ott, Margaret V. *Sterling's Carrie:Caroline Ann Joy French, Mrs. J. Sterling Morton,1833–1881.* Lincoln, Nebraska: 1989.

Paton, Stewart. "The Correlation of Structure and Function in the Development of the Nervous System." *Proceedings of the American Philosophical Society* 52, no. 24 (September.– October 1913): 488–494.

———. *Psychiatry: A Text-Book for Students and Physicians.* Philadephia: J. B. Lippincott Company, 1905.

Potter, Gail DeBuse, "The Evolution of Arbor Lodge, 1855–1904," *Nebraska History*, Nebraska State Historical Society, 73, no. 2 (Summer 1992): 54–68.

Putnam, James William. *The Illinois and Michigan Canal: A Study in Economic History.* Chicago: University of Chicago Press, 1918.

Quaife, Milo M., with an introduction by Joy Morton. *Chicago's Highways Old and New: from Indian Trail to Motor Road.* Chicago: D. F. Keller & Company, 1923.

Rybczynski, Witold. *A Clearing in the Distance: Frederick Law Olmstead and America in the 19th Century.* New York: Scribner, 1999.

Salt Talks, a series of monographs, nos. 1–6, published by Morton Salt Co. for dealers,1915–1916, discussing history, processing, and Morton Salt Co. quality. Other occasional company monographs include "The Prevention of Simple Goiter," 1924, intended for the general public.

Schlesinger, Arthur Meier. *The Rise of Modern America: 1865–1951.* New York: Macmillan Company, 4th ed., 1951.

Seventy-Five Years in Chicago. Chicago: Morton Salt Company, 1923.

Simonds, Ossian Cole. *Landscape Gardening.* New York: Macmillan Company, 1920; 2nd ed., intro. by Robert E. Gresse. Boston: University of Massachusetts Press, 2000.

Smith, Carl. *The Plan of Chicago: Daniel Burnham and the Remaking of the American City.* Chicago: University of Chicago Press, 2006.

Stevenson, Elizabeth. *Park Maker: A Life of Frederick Law Olmstead.* New York: Macmillan, 1977. Transaction edition, New Brunswick: Transaction Publishers, 2000.

Sutton, E.B. *Charles Sprague Sargent and the Arnold Arboretum.* Cambridge: Harvard University Press, 1970.

"Teletype: $30,000,000 Worth of Teletype . . . How salt helped it grow and how salt finally sold it," *Fortune*, V, no. 3 (March 1932): 44 ff.

Thompson, John. "Coping with the Elements and Chicago on the Illinos & Michigan Canal: 1848–1933." *Canal History and Technology Proceedings*, XXVI (March 17, 2007): 77–111. Canal History and Technology Press: National Canal Museum, Easton, PA.

———. *Wetlands Drainage, River Modification, and Sectoral Conflict in the Lower Illinois River Valley, 1890–1930.* Carbondale: Southern Illinois University Press, 2001.

Walsh, Justin E. *To Print the News and Raise Hell!: A Biography of Wilbur F. Storey.* Chapel Hill: University of North Carolina Press, 1968.

Wiley, Gordon R. and Jeremy A. Sabloff. *A History of American Archaeology.* San Francisco: W.H. Freeman and Company, 1974.

Yeater, Mary M. "The Hennepin Canal." Reprint from *American Canals*. American Canal Society, November 1976–August 1978.

Index

Mayhew, Ira, 32, 269n34
Mayhew Business College, 32, 45, 93, 269n34
McClelland, George, 23, 268n38
McCormick, Robert, 223
McDorman, John, 231
McIlhenney, Edward Avery, 235
McKelvie, Samuel R., 223
McKinley, William, 132, 142, 156
McNamee, Charles, 133
meat industry, xii, 24, 76, 92, 100, 127; inspections of, 129
Merchandise Mart, 240
Merchants National Bank, 97, 110
Michigan Central railroad, 44
Michigan Salt Association, 75, 76, 99, 109, 112, 123, 148, 153, 163
Midway Plaisance, 106
Miller, George, 35, 89
mining, 102; silver, 52, 55
Mississippi type culture, 249–50, 261
Mississippi Valley Historical Review, 228
Missouri Compromise of 1820, 10
Missouri River, 130; bridge, 114
Moffett, J.A., 107
Monadnock Building, 145
Monroe Advocate, 8
Monte Carlo, 139
Montreal Botanical Gardens, 245
Moore, George T., 215
Morkrum Company, 159, 204
Morkrum-Kleinschmidt Teletype Company, 232, 233, 250, 256
Morton, Abner, 7, 8–9
Morton, Ada Whiteside, 179, 187, 245; death of child, 187
Morton, Boatie Payne, 111, 114, 123, 153, 183, 184, 187
Morton, Carl, 24, 31, 44, 47, 49, *57, 58,* 91, 123, 141, 152; career in Nebraska City, 110–21 *passim,* 123; death of, 153; marriage, 111; in salt business, 93–94, 97–98, 101–4 *passim*
Morton, Carl II, 203, 237, 241, 242, 252
Morton, Caroline, *57;* birth of children, 5–6, 17, 18, 24; childhood of, 6; correspondence, 37–38, 44–45, 46; death, 83–84; education of, 8, 9; family mediator, 54; health, 52, 80–82, 83; housekeeping and, 15–16, 19–20, 32, 77–78; importance of family, 20; legal issues, 41; social life,

35; wedding anniversary, 54
Morton, Caroline II, 137
Morton, Carolyn Owsley, 187, 209, 211, 281n79
Morton, Carrie (Lake), *59,* 85–87, 98, 103, 173; attitude toward Mortons, 174, 185; automobile trips, 180; child births, 92, 97; courtship and marriage, 51–56 *passim;* death of, 186; European trip, 137–40; health, 107, 120–21, 125, 140–41, 143–44, 147, 154, 159–60, 163, 176–77, 179–86 *passim;* house in California, 177; memorial for, 186–87; mental diagnosis, 180–81
Morton, Charlotte (Goodrich), 54–55, 79, 86, 137–40, 174, 175
Morton, Edward G., 8–9
Morton, Emeline (Sterling), 7; death of, 115
Morton, Emma, 11, 12, *65,* 82, 115, 118, 159, 160, 171, 173, 174, 175; death of, 177
Morton, George, 7
Morton, Helen, 183
Morton, Jean. *See* Cudahy, Jean (Morton)
Morton, Joy, *59, 62, 63, 65, 68, 70–71, 72,* 132–33, 216
biographies, xiv, 254; resources, xiv–xv
botanical interests, 106, 107, 131–33, 139, 144, 201–2, 218, 231. *See also* Morton Arboretum, The
community life: Ching Jen Kung temple, 248; Commercial Club railway terminals committee, xiii, 162, 239–40; hospital in Nebraska City, 171; Illinois history, 180, 229–30; Illinois roads, 180, 226–29; Indian artifacts, 198, 249–50; interviews with Illinois residents, 198; investment in Illinois, 221–36 *passim;* library to Nebraska City, xv, 127–28, 141, 152, 260; Napoleon death masque, 229; opera house in Nebraska City, 142; progress in Nebraska City, 114; speeches, 200–201, 205–6, 224–25, 241–42, 253–54, 281n13, 282n35; Tribune Tower contest, 223; water transportation, 196–97, 281n13
correspondence, xv; with Abbie Lake, 174–87 *passim;* with Boatie Morton, 183, 184; with Carl Morton, 31; with